FIFTY KEY THINKERS ON LANGUAGE AND LINGUISTICS

'Thomas successfully introduces readers to the ideas that have shaped a field which can be considered both ancient and modern. It is not hard to imagine the chapters of this volume as the essential gateway into a fascinating historical journey across time and far-flung places.'

Larry LaFond, *Southern Illinois University*

'The entries are beautifully written and very informative. The key ideas of each thinker are presented concisely, clearly and rigorously, and the biographical information brings them to life.'

Raphael Salkie, *University of Brighton*

What was the first language, and where did it come from? Do all languages have properties in common? What is the relationship of language to thought? *Fifty Key Thinkers on Language and Linguistics* explores how fifty of the most influential figures in the field have asked, and have responded to, classic questions about language. Each entry includes a discussion of the person's life, work and ideas, as well as the historical context and an analysis of his or her lasting contributions. Thinkers include:

- Aristotle
- Samuel Johnson
- Friedrich Max Müller
- Ferdinand de Saussure
- Joseph H. Greenberg
- Noam Chomsky

Fully cross-referenced and with useful guides to further reading, this is an ideal introduction to the thinkers who have had a significant impact on the subject of language and linguistics.

Margaret Thomas is Professor of Linguistics in the Department of Slavic and Eastern Languages and Literatures at Boston College. She is past president of the North American Association for the History of the Language Sciences, and the author of *Universal Grammar in Second Language Acquisition: A History*.

ALSO AVAILABLE FROM ROUTLEDGE

FIFTY KEY THINKERS ON LANGUAGE AND LINGUISTICS

Margaret Thomas

Routledge
Taylor & Francis Group

LONDON AND NEW YORK

First published 2011
by Routledge
2 Park Square, Milton Park, Abingdon, Oxon, OX14 4RN

Simultaneously published in the USA and Canada
by Routledge
711 Third Avenue, New York, NY 10017

Routledge is an imprint of the Taylor & Francis Group, an informa business

British Library Cataloguing in Publication Data
A catalogue record for this book is available from the British Library

Library of Congress Cataloging in Publication Data
Thomas, Margaret (Margaret Ann), 1952-
    Fifty key thinkers on language and linguistics / by Margaret Thomas.
       p. cm.
    Includes bibliographical references and index.
    1. Historical linguistics. I. Title.
    P61.T56 2011
    417'.7 – dc22
           2010050352

ISBN13: 978-0-415-37302-9 (hbk)
ISBN13: 978-0-415-37303-6 (pbk)
ISBN13: 978-0-203-81448-2 (ebk)

Typeset in Bembo
by Taylor & Francis Books

MIX
Paper from
responsible sources
FSC
www.fsc.org FSC® C004839

Printed and bound in Great Britain by
CPI Antony Rowe, Chippenham, Wiltshire

CONTENTS

ALPHABETICAL LIST OF CONTENTS

CHRONOLOGICAL LIST OF
CONTENTS

ACKNOWLEDGEMENTS

My first thanks go to the memberships of the North American Association for the History of the Language Sciences, and the Henry Sweet Society for the History of Linguistic Ideas. Through their writings and their fellowship, these two groups of scholars have taught me a great deal about the history of linguistics, and demonstrated how much more there is to learn. I also appreciate the painstaking critique, advice and encouragement of anonymous readers for Routledge.

Writing this book has made me conscious of how much I have learned from teaching almost twenty years of remarkable students at Boston College. I owe them my thanks. I'm also grateful for the help of research assistants Amber Smith, Amy Cram Kuiken and Michelle Steingiser, and for the help of the staff of Boston College's O'Neill Library, especially the office of interlibrary loan.

Most of all, I am grateful for the support of my husband, Dayton Haskin, and our three children, Thomas, Peter and Helen – key thinkers all.

INTRODUCTION

Fifty Key Thinkers on Language and Linguistics introduces fifty of the most creative and talented people whose curiosity about language led them to think, and to write, about words, meanings, sounds, sentences, or about how language is used in speaking, thinking and writing. These fifty people have asked such questions as: 'What was the first language, and where did it come from?'; 'What are the constituent parts of a language?'; 'Which languages are related to each other?'; 'Do all languages have properties in common?'; 'How do children learn language?'; 'What is the relationship of language to thought?'; 'Why do some people have different accents from others?'; 'Is there an ideal way to write down language?' The answers they come up with are sometimes surprising. Moreover, because these fifty people lived in different cultures and centuries, to try to answer their questions about language they employed diverse sources of evidence and diverse styles of argumentation. But by asking those questions, and searching for answers in the best ways then available, they built up a vast, heterogeneous treasury of reflection on language.

Twenty-first-century thinkers continue to pose some of those same questions about language, and to answer them using appropriate modern evidence and argumentation. Modern scholars also frame new questions about language, such as 'Are principles that constrain the sound structure of words the same, or different, from principles that constrain the forms of words?' or 'What features of the human voice must speech recognition software attend to?' or 'How does the acquisition of literacy alter the brain?' Some of these questions couldn't have been anticipated a hundred years ago. Assuming that human curiosity about language will continue to produce novel, unpredictable questions alongside new versions of perennial questions, students of the language sciences need broad preparation to seek answers to those questions over a wide intellectual range. Knowledge of the surprising results and the diverse sources and arguments of language scholars from the past is a vital resource for modern linguistics and its related disciplines.

However, these fifty key thinkers in language and linguistics are worth attention for more than utilitarian reasons. They are part of a worldwide intellectual network of people for whom language has been an object of wonder and perplexity and delight. The discoveries they made, the data they gathered, the problems that vexed them, the arguments they had with each other; and their lives, jobs, failures, political and historical contexts – everything we can find out about them helps us understand what they achieved and the reasons why, in their own varied terms, they found language so captivating. It helps us recognize how we ourselves can participate in the multi-dimensional, trans-national, trans-temporal community of language scholarship, within which there is always room for a new generation's ideas. It also helps erode any sense a modern student might have of either heroic or lonely isolation.

This book is written for students of the language sciences: under-graduates or graduate students in linguistics, literary and cultural studies, foreign languages, anthropology, philosophy, intellectual history – and for anyone, at any stage of life, who is curious about language. It presupposes only some exposure to the vocabulary and conceptual tools of modern linguistics of the sort that a one-semester introduction to the study of language would supply, or which a resourceful reader can acquire independently by consulting resources such as R. L. Trask's *Key Concepts in Language and Linguistics* (Routledge, 1999), or David Crystal's *A Dictionary of Linguistics and Phonetics* (Blackwell, any edition). Readers can also refresh their knowledge of important technical terms employed in *Fifty Key Thinkers on Language and Linguistics* by consulting the glossary. The short definitions given in the glossary are tailored to the use of technical terms in the text.

The latent metaphor behind the composition of this book is that of hosting a party to which students of language are invited, where they will meet for the first time many famous and accomplished language scholars. In advance of attending a party, it steadies one's nerves and sharpens one's anticipation to know at least something about the other guests. But modern students rarely have opportunities to learn about the history of the language sciences, and so in general have only shallow or sketchy knowledge about most, perhaps almost all, of these fifty thinkers. To ease students' entry into the group, this book introduces the lives, intellectual orientations and achievements of each one of the distinguished guests. My hope is that, after profiting from these introductions, readers will find some of the fifty figures congenial, or puzzling, or intriguing enough to approach first hand by immersing themselves in the primary sources listed at the end of each chapter and by consulting the other resources listed under 'Further Reading'. If readers go on to strike up lasting relationships with at least a few of the figures whom this book introduces, or whom they encounter by following up any of the strands of the intellectual network described here, then the party, and this book, will count as a success.

If attending a party requires certain preparation, hosting a party presents its own challenges. Principal among them is the challenge of determining the guest list. Metaphorical parties, like actual ones, cannot accommodate everyone whom one might ideally want to include. There is a substantial subgroup of invitees without whom one cannot really imagine hosting a decent party for the purposes of introducing novices to established community members, on the grounds of the latter's unquestionable influence and importance. Invitations therefore go out first to key thinkers in language and linguistics, such as **Plato, Ferdinand de Saussure** and **Noam Chomsky**. Then comes the difficult job of discerning who else to invite, granted that a crowd of eligible potential guests competes for a fixed number of places at the table.

Faced with this dilemma, the conventional etiquette of entertaining may assist the stymied host of a metaphorical party. First, a guest list benefits from variety: that is, one should avoid including only individuals in long-established, mutually acknowledged relationships nurtured in the same cultural context. No doubt each brings his or her unique contribution, but the gaps between individuals can be so small that, paradoxically, adding many of them shrinks the apparent size of the overall group.

Second, a complementary principle is to avoid across-the-board isolation of guests by ensuring that at least some invitees are each other's colleagues, teachers, students, rivals, adversaries or intellectual descendents. That will ease the conversation.

Third, a guest list can profit from the unexpected, insofar as inviting worthy but lesser-known individuals, or those who join the group from what count as temporal or spatial outposts, can enlarge the sense of community. The point is not merely to add novelty. Rather, the point is to call attention to, and implicitly question, tacit group boundaries. It is important, however, to recognize that meeting this criterion risks enriching the group at the expense the individuals involved, insofar as their individuality is obscured by the unfamiliarity of their intellectual and cultural context. Of course, all invitees' individualities must be respected. The task is just harder when a person's specific contributions aren't offset against a familiar backdrop. Still, it is worth the risk of distorting or failing to distinguish what is individual from what is contextual, if the alternative is to ignore both individual and context alike.

Finally, the host must be prepared to face the inevitable criticism of his or her hard choices ('But where is X?' 'What's Y doing in this company?' 'Why on earth would one invite Z *and* A?').

A different challenge facing a host is to ensure that guests have a good time. In the case of an imagined party assembling language scholars across space and time, the task would be easy. The guests are spectacularly interesting and accomplished people who share many interests, even if they by no means agree with each other, or even have ready means for articulating their disagreement. If they can overcome very great differences of idiom and stance, they will have plenty to talk about. One can imagine **Joseph Greenberg** patiently sketching out his Eurasiatic language macro-family on a napkin, in pencil, for an astonished and sceptical **Franz Bopp**. In another corner, **King Sejong** is explaining the graphic design of the Korean *hangeul* alphabet to **John Wilkins**, while **Roman Jakobson** listens in, excitedly waiting for a chance to interject his thoughts on the likely psycholinguistic ramifications of a feature-based orthography. Noam Chomsky is asking **Wilhelm von Humboldt** a question about *Ergon* versus *Energeia* in terms that don't fully make sense to Humboldt, but Humboldt is trying not to show it while keeping up his side of the conversation. **Samuel Johnson** and **James Murray** are graciously complimenting each other on their lexicographic techniques and gingerly disagreeing on matters of theory. **Edward Sapir** is exchanging field notes on Uto-Aztecan with **Kenneth Hale** while **J. R. Austin** eavesdrops, making some mental notes about Sapir's versus Hale's diction. **Lev Vygotsky** is quizzing **Roger Brown** about his data on spontaneous speech between parents and preschool children. **Marcus Terentius Varro** joins a discussion between **Priscian of Caesarea** and **Aelius Donatus** about the classification of parts of speech in Latin; **Leonard Bloomfield** discreetly scans the crowd, hoping to spot **Pāṇini**; **William Dwight Whitney** and **Friedrich Max Müller** try hard to avoid each other. Wallflowers **Condillac** and **Jacob Grimm** are checking the clock, each hoping to make an early exit so he can get back to his books. Such is the company into which modern students of language and linguistics are invited, and where they can join in a toast to the huge range of ways in which language matters.

Setting aside the party metaphor, I have included in *Fifty Key Thinkers on Language and Linguistics* figures who have made substantial contributions to our understanding of language, whose names students are likely to come across, or should come across, in their education in the field. Not all of these figures would have identified themselves as language scholars: some were philosophers, teachers, literary critics or, in one case, a medical doctor. Many lived before a distinction existed between the study of language (a particular language, or language in general) and linguistics. I acknowledge those differences as grounds on which members of the group vary, not as grounds for exclusion, because I want to represent the breadth of ways in which people have explored the nature of language. I have opted to include fewer thinkers from the late twentieth century than some readers may expect, reasoning that information about contemporary scholars is fairly readily accessible elsewhere. With some regret, I have favoured figures whose works have influenced or interacted with Euro-American scholarship at the expense of those whose relevance is local to non-Euro-American scholarship. I have tried to balance the representation of scholars associated with the diverse national traditions within western language science, and the representation of scholars whose attention has been directed at different subfields, including phonology, semantics, morphosyntax, philosophy of language, orthography, historical linguistics, lexicography, psycholinguistics, sociolinguistics, typology, linguistic theory, etc. I am sure I will not satisfy all readers on all scores. I have also manifestly failed to represent the contributions of women to the history of linguistics, and probably failed in my representation of the complexity of both small facts and large themes. Just as coming to know a person well can lead to revising, even totally effacing, one's earlier impressions, future research will no doubt supersede much that is written here. But making someone's acquaintance starts with an introduction.

The fifty key thinkers appear in chronological order by year of birth, actual or presumed. The book can be read cover to cover as a record of some of the successive discoveries and initiatives of language scholars, keeping in mind that these scholars have not always built on each other's achievements, or even known of these achievements. The book can also be consulted as a reference text, from which readers extract information at will about specific figures and their contributions, independently of the surrounding chapters. In each chapter I have highlighted in bold type the names of figures who are the subjects of chapters elsewhere in the text, so that readers can also browse backward and forward through the book following a chain of references from chapter to chapter. The index provides more in-depth access to the relationships of the fifty key thinkers to other persons, terms and concepts that appear in the text.

FIFTY KEY THINKERS ON
LANGUAGE AND LINGUISTICS

PĀṆINI (FOURTH OR FIFTH CENTURY BCE)

We know very little about the Indian grammarian Pāṇini. He probably lived around 500 BCE, probably in the northwest of the subcontinent in what is now Pakistan. His name has traditionally been associated with a massive corpus known as the *Aṣṭādhyāyī* (lit. 'eight chapters'), the earliest extant grammar of Sanskrit. The stunning complexity and finesse of this work set a lasting high-water mark for Indian language scholarship. It has also had significant impact on the study of language in the west.

The *Aṣṭādhyāyī* describes, for native speakers, an elite version of Sanskrit spoken in Pāṇini's lifetime. We don't know for sure, but can only assume that Pāṇini was motivated to compose it as a means of defining and preserving the structure of the language because of its ritual significance in Indian culture, even though Vedic Sanskrit was not exactly the Sanskrit that Pāṇini described, and even though his observations about dialectal variation suggest that his goal was not narrowly prescriptive. We can also only assume that Pāṇini participated in the general cultural assumptions of his day, which made it a matter of spiritual merit to bring implicit knowledge to consciousness: in this case, implicit knowledge of linguistic structure (Emeneau 1955: 146).

But in another sense – because the *Aṣṭādhyāyī* is so ambitious, so intricate, and has been studied by so many, over such a long interval – we know a great deal about Pāṇini. The centrepiece of the *Aṣṭādhyāyī* is Pāṇini's corpus of almost 4000 compact rules, or *sūtras*, collectively referred to as the *sūtra-pāṭha*. The *Aṣṭādhyāyī* also subsumes three other texts, for which Pāṇini may or may not have been responsible: an inventory of sounds organized into classes (the *śiva-sūtras*); a catalogue of about 2000 verbal roots, subclassified by their morphosyntactic properties (the *dhātu-pāṭha*); and a list of nominal stems and other lexical items subject to idiosyncratic rules (the *gaṇa-pāṭha*).

We also know a lot about Pāṇini in the sense that a giant literature of exegesis and commentary has grown up around the *Aṣṭādhyāyī*, created over centuries by traditional Indian scholars, and more recently by Indologists and by westerners trained by Indian scholars. Moreover, we know that Pāṇini's work has profoundly influenced Euro-American language science in several waves, sometimes by infusing genuine novelty, and sometimes by seeming to validate developments that occurred independently in western study of language.

Many who have studied the *Aṣṭādhyāyī* depict it as a work of genius, or of extraordinary, possibly unique, linguistic insight. But no-one depicts it as easy to read. One can hardly 'read' it at all, in the normal sense. The *Aṣṭādhyāyī* is a collection of pithy statements about Sanskrit phonetics, phonology, morphology, syntax and (in passing) semantics, presented with extreme conciseness in a kind of algebraic metalanguage to facilitate memorization. (In fact, Pāṇini's rules seem to have remained remarkably stable over centuries of oral transmission.) The material is organized to reduce redundancy to the starkest minimum. For example, Pāṇini exploited the classes of sounds set out in the *śiva-sūtras*, defining specific sequences of sounds by referring to the first ordered member of the sequence plus a single, strategically chosen, additional sound that indicated the last ordered member to be included. Likewise, at other levels of grammatical organization, he defined an elaborate metalanguage. For example, *sūtra* 3.4.69 establishes 'l' as a cover term for tense and mood markers. One subclass, which combines 'l' with 'T', labels present indicative ('lAT'), perfect ('lIT'), imperative ('lOT'), etc.; another subclass, with 'Ṅ', labels imperfect ('lAṄ'), aorist ('lUṄ'), etc. (Katre 1987: 340). This metalanguage allows Pāṇini to manipulate classes and subclasses of forms in an efficient manner. His rules admit processes of affixation, doubling and substitution (of one element by another, or by a zero form). Multiple rules may apply in sequence in the derivation of any one form: **Max Müller** (cited by Staal 1972: 138–39) famously recounted Pāṇini's derivation of the aorist of the root *jāgṛ* 'to wake', in the course of which nine rules apply. Along the way, intermediate forms may be produced that modern linguists would describe as highly 'abstract', that is, which display features that do not appear in the forms' familiar, end-state, representations.

Pāṇini also dispensed with complete sentences in stating his rules, using instead bare-bone fragments from which all predictable content has been elided. He ordered the *sūtras* to maximize what is predictable and therefore can be deleted, not according to topic. This means that the meaning of any one *sūtra* might depend on the content of multiple preceding and following *sūtras*.

These characteristics of the *Aṣṭādhyāyī* render it essentially unreadable, and barely translatable. But recall that Pāṇini created it to be inscribed in memory, not on pages. For example, *sūtra* 2.1.11 appears in a discussion of compound words. It consists in its entirety of the word *vibhāṣā*, 'optionally' (but see below with respect to this translation). Its purport in this context is to signal that compounds defined in subsequent *sūtras* (up to *sūtra* 2.2.35, as traditionally inferred) all freely co-occur with uncompounded forms. By another inference, then, compounds defined by the *sūtras* immediately preceding 2.1.11

are not optional. Falling within the scope of optionality established by 2.1.11 is *sūtra* 2.2.6, consisting in its entirety of the word *náÑ*, 'not'. With this one word, in this context, Pāṇini communicated that the Sanskrit negative particle may optionally (as defined by 2.1.11) combine with a particular class of syntactically connected nominals (as defined by another earlier *sūtra*, 2.1.4), to form a particular resulting class of compounds (whose properties are defined in *sūtra* 2.1.22) (Katre 1987: 105–28; Cardona 1988: 243, 254).

At this very fine level of resolution, expressed in arch-economical manner, Pāṇini inched over the whole tissue of Sanskrit's complex morpho-phonetics and morpho-syntax. The interpretive challenges posed by the *Aṣṭādhyāyī* have inspired many to analyse, elucidate, exemplify or counter-exemplify its claims. Indian tradition highly values textual exegesis, so that such works have often been elevated to share the status of the text they address. The earliest well developed commentary on the *Aṣṭādhyāyī* to which we have access today is by Kātyāyana (third century BCE). The most famous is Patañjali's *Mahābhāṣya* (second century BCE), which also comments on Kātyāyana's work; the *Mahābhāṣya* has itself become the object of a large exegetical industry. Both Kātyāyana's and Patañjali's works discuss the validity, formal properties and inter-relationships of Pāṇini's *sūtras*. Both remain essential tools for understanding the *Aṣṭādhyāyī*.

Europeans' first experience of Pāṇini's work and its long-standing, self-referential, commentarial tradition was as language students. Although the *Aṣṭādhyāyī* was not designed for foreign language instruction, British colonial administrators and scholars employed it, and the literature to which it gave rise, in that capacity when they began to learn Sanskrit starting in the late 1700s (Staal 1972: 33–34). As westerners both in India and back in Europe became familiar with Sanskrit, a new understanding opened to them of the historical relationships among the languages that they then began to arrange on branches of a single Indo-European family tree. Their recognition of the unmistakable relatedness of Sanskrit to Latin, Greek and other European languages set in motion comparative-historical linguistics, a central intellectual and cultural achievement of the nineteenth century (see **Wilhelm** and **Friedrich von Schlegel; Franz Bopp**). This constitutes one of the most far-reaching effects of Pāṇini's grammar on linguistics and language study worldwide.

Another effect of Pāṇini's work occurred as western scholars came to appreciate its structure as a descriptive grammar. Several waves of such appreciation have propagated through western language science. Among admirers of Pāṇini have been the English linguist **J. R. Firth**, who studied Indian linguistic tradition first-hand in India, and the American structuralist **Leonard Bloomfield**. Bloomfield characterized Pāṇini's descriptive grammar of Sanskrit as 'one of the greatest monuments of human intelligence and ... an indispensable model for the description of languages' (Bloomfield 1929: 268). In his analyses of Algonquian languages, Bloomfield adopted Pāṇinian concepts and apparatus, including the notions of form classes, suppletion, exocentric versus endocentric compounds, and zero forms. Above all, Bloomfield's avoidance of redundancy and his commitment to rigour in the statement of linguistic principles reveal Pāṇini's influence (Rogers 1987). That influence flowed forward to the post-Boomfieldian scholars who followed his lead in trying to create a formal science of linguistics.

Other waves of Pāṇini's influence constitute not infusions of novel terms or ideas, as much as recognition that certain concepts favoured in modern linguistics have long existed outside Euro-American language science, in radically different contexts. Pāṇini's conception of a grammar as a system of intricate, interacting rules (stated with maximum simplicity) that operate on a body of lexical items is also foundational to early generative grammar. Generative grammar resembles Pāṇini's descriptive technique in its receptivity to abstractness, and in distinguishing underlying versus surface forms. In addition, modern computer science and research on artificial intelligence has found Pāṇini's work congenial, including its decomposition of a grammar into a web of rules that are ordered, recursive (can apply iteratively), and context-sensitive (Bhate and Kak 1993).

Finally, Kiparsky (1979) made a striking sociolinguistic discovery about the *Aṣṭādhyāyī* that has achieved acceptance by at least some Sanskritists. Kiparsky scrutinized the distribution of three conjunctions in Pāṇini's text that are all conventionally translated as 'or' (*vā; vibhāṣā; anyatarasyām*) to show that, far from being synonyms, each one actually posits a different logical relationship between the conjoined terms: *vā* means 'preferably'; *vibhāṣā* means 'preferably not'; *anyatarasyām* means 'optionally'. Re-reading the *sūtra-pāṭha* by the light of these distinctions shifts our understanding of many passages. It also led Kiparsky to argue that Pāṇini deserves more credit as a keen observer of linguistic variation.

It is worth noting that the admiration, even awe, with which Pāṇini has generally been received in the West has not been unanimous. Aside from those who have found the *Aṣṭādhyāyī* simply impenetrable, there have been some, such as the late-nineteenth-century American philologist **William Dwight Whitney**, who dismissed it on other grounds. Whitney denied that the object of Pāṇini's description could ever have been a natural human language, claiming it was instead only an artificial, 'special and peculiar', version of Sanskrit (Whitney 1884: 282). His evidence was that he could not locate in Sanskrit literature many of the roots recorded in the *dhātu-pāṭha* and that, in any case, the *Aṣṭādhyāyī* was an improbably convoluted, pedantic system that could not reflect any real language.

Whitney was mistaken, of course: the language Pāṇini described certainly existed, as a genuine product of human cognition and social life. But Whitney's scepticism testifies to how incredible (in the literal sense of the word) Pāṇini's work might seem outside the context of its own century and culture.

Bibliography

A respected modern translation is S. M. Katre's (1987) Aṣṭādhyāyī *of Pāṇini*. Katre writes for linguists, not Indologists, rendering the Sanskrit in roman transliteration. An accessible English translation of the first 75 *sūtras*, by H. T. Colebrooke, appears in Kielhorn (1891). Cardona (1988) provides background information and elucidates much of the content of the *sūtra-patha*, but does not offer a formally organized translation. Rocher (1975) surveys additional translations and editions of the *Aṣṭādhyāyī*, including the *dhātu-pāṭha* and *gaṇa-pāṭha*, and also the commentarial literature.

Further reading

Bhate, S. and Kak, S. (1993) 'Pāṇini's grammar and computer science', *Annals of the Bhandarkar Oriental Research Institute*, 72, 79–94.
Bloomfield, L. (1929) 'Review of *Konkordanz Pāṇini-Candra* by B. Liebich', *Language*, 5, 267–76.
Cardona, G. (1976) *Pāṇini: A Survey of Research*, The Hague: Mouton.
——(1988) *Pāṇini: His Work and its Tradition: Vol. 1. Background and Introduction*, New Delhi: Motilal Banarsidass.
Emeneau, M. B. (1955) 'India and linguistics', *Journal of the American Oriental Society*, 75, 145–53.
Katre, S. M. (1987) Aṣṭādhyāyī *of Pāṇini*, Austin, TX: University of Texas Press.
Kielhorn, F. (1891) 'Die Colebrooke'schen Pāṇini-Handschriften der Königlichen Bibliothek zu Göttingen', *Nachrichten von der Königlichen Gesellschaft der Wissenschaften und der Georg-Augusts-Universität zu Göttingen*, 3, 101–12.
Kiparsky, P. (1979) *Pāṇini as a Variationist*, Poona/Cambridge, MA: Poona University Press/MIT Press.

Rocher, R. (1975) 'India', in T. A. Sebeok (ed.), *Current Trends in Linguistics: Vol. 13. Historiography of Linguistics*, The Hague: Mouton.
Rogers, D. E. (1987) 'The influence of Pāṇini on Leonard Bloomfield', *Historiographia Linguistica*, 14, 89–138.
Staal, J. F. (1972) *A Reader on the Sanskrit Grammarians*, Cambridge, MA: MIT Press.
Whitney, W. D. (1884) 'The study of Hindu grammar and the study of Sanskrit', *The American Journal of Philology*, 5, 279–97.

PLATO (*c.* 428/7–*c.* 349/7 BCE)

The ancient Greek philosopher Plato was a key figure in intellectual history, whose ideas have contributed to the construction of major institutions in western culture. In this sense his influence pervades Euro-American social and political organization, intellectual life and education. Moreover, Plato recognized language as foundational to philosophy. This made it important to him to probe the nature of language, and has made his work enduringly relevant to both philosophy and linguistics. Plato wrote one of the first extended reflections on language, the dialogue *Cratylus*, which modern scholars still find provocative. Some of his other writings and ideas also continue to be referenced in western language science up to the present day.

Plato was born into a distinguished and well connected Athenian family. He met the philosopher Socrates (469–399 BCE) through family connections, and later became attached to him as a student. On some accounts (Taylor 1926/2001: 3–4), it was the persecution and eventual execution of Socrates that turned Plato away from a career in politics. But although he chose philosophy over public life, he maintained a conviction that philosophers should stay attuned to the political world, and that political figures need exposure to philosophy. Plato put his commitment to the education of philosopher-kings into action by travelling several times to Syracuse, in Sicily, to try to raise the political–philosophical horizons of Dionysius II, who had been thrust prematurely into a position of power. Plato's efforts were unsuccessful, as Dionysius developed into a notorious tyrant. But Plato's experience probably deepened his understanding of the role of philosophy in moral formation.

At around the age of forty, Plato founded the famous Academy, located in a grove of sacred olive trees just north of what were then the city limits of Athens. The Academy aimed to prepare future statesmen and legislators by training them in 'science'. Under Plato's direction, that principally meant mathematics and moral education through the technique of dialectics, in which students explored philosophical issues of the highest order by repeated questioning (Marrou 1956: 67–78). Dialectics embodied Plato's epistemological assumptions since he believed that teachers and students should engage in mutually challenging conversational give-and-take, designed to inspire students to awaken their minds from within.

In the decade before the founding of the Academy, but after Socrates' death, Plato apparently began to write down a series of dialogues that modelled how to explore bedrock philosophical, political and ethical questions, using dialectics as an instrument. Scholars have conventionally divided Plato's dialogues into early, middle and later works, largely on the basis of stylistic criteria. In the early dialogues, Socrates always plays a role. They are characterized by more open-endedness and (to some readers) a less confident authorial voice compared with the later dialogues, with works from the middle period lying in between. Dialogues from the middle period include *Cratylus* and, arguably Plato's most literary work, the *Symposium*, as well as his best known, the *Republic*. Plato's later works (in which Socrates does not always appear) were probably produced after a twenty-year gap, when Plato was in his sixties.

Depending on how one counts certain manuscripts, more than thirty of Plato's dialogues survive today – a substantial body of work, miraculously intact, the impact of which can hardly be overstated. In language and linguistics, that impact is varied. Aside from the diffuse influence of Plato on western epistemology and educational practice, three specific matters addressed by Plato have inspired scholars of language: the roles of nature versus convention in language; the status of universals; and the existence of innate ideas.

All three of these matters surface in Plato's dialogue *Cratylus* (trans. Reeve, in Cooper 1997: 101–56; '383–440e' in the conventional Stephanus pagination of Plato's works), although the text centres on the nature versus convention debate. *Cratylus* opens with two speakers, Hermogenes and Cratylus, deep in earnest dispute over the relationship of names to their referents. Hermogenes asserts that names (which, for ancient Greeks, would include adjectives as well as common and proper nouns) are merely conventional, not intrinsic to their referents. Cratylus holds the opposite conviction, that, 'objects came into being with their names clinging to them like a skin' (Demos 1964: 595). Hermogenes and Cratylus agree to consult Socrates for his opinion. Socrates first questions the conventionalist Hermogenes, gradually bringing him to acknowledge that appropriate and inappropriate names exist, and that behind names there must be a name-giver.

Different languages' names for the same things vary because they are the handiwork of different name-givers. Socrates then analyses at least a hundred words, one by one, in a series of speculative etymologies that seem to lead Hermogenes to concede that name-givers choose intrinsically apt names for things. For example, the sea-god Poseidon is so named, Socrates asserts, because the name-giver noticed the difficulty of walking in seawater, and in Greek, '*poseidon*' can be parsed as 'foot' + 'shackled' (trans. Reeve, in Cooper 1997: 121; 402e).

For the modern reader, etymologies like this may fail as evidence that words necessarily reflect their referents, but Cratylus, the supporter of linguistic naturalism, welcomes that conclusion. However, Socrates then directs toward Cratylus a line of questioning that seems to undermine the authority of name-givers, and to challenge Cratylus' assumption that names accurately and fully represent the nature of things. The dialogue ends with Socrates suggesting that it is 'better and clearer' to 'learn about [things] through themselves than to do so through their names' (trans. Reeve, in Cooper 1997: 154; 439a–b), especially if the things words refer to are always mutable and in flux.

Readers have interpreted *Cratylus* in many ways. Some perceive Plato, via Socrates, as endorsing Hermogenes' position; others, Cratylus'; others, neither position; still others mine the text for different purposes (Demos 1964; Clerico 1992; Gera 2003; Sedley 2003). The sketch given above summarizes one popular reading. But on any interpretation, the dialogue constitutes a classic wellspring of curiosity about the relationship between nature and convention in language. Joseph (2000) analysed how varied claims about what he called 'linguistic naturalism and its opposites' have engaged scholars in the centuries since *Cratylus*. In one strand of his analysis, Joseph examined the history of the notion that grammar (the patterns or rules that associate words with other words) is in some sense 'natural', whereas lexical items, and the linkage of words to meanings, are governed by convention. This is not exactly the position of any party to the dispute in *Cratylus*, but it traffics in the same nature/convention dichotomy. Joseph cites **Marcus Terentius Varro**'s distinction between *declinatio naturalis* (such as the law-like operation of Latin inflectional morphology) and *declinatio voluntaria* (subsuming derivational morphology and other unpredictable features of words) as a first-century Roman expression of the natural grammar/conventional lexicon contrast. Earlier, **Aristotle**, and later, **Priscian of Caesarea**, **Claude Lancelot**, **Antoine Arnauld**, **John Locke**, **Condillac**, **Wilhelm von Humboldt** and **Ferdinand de Saussure** (according to Joseph) all adopted diverse positions at least partially consistent with the assigning of naturalness to grammar and arbitrariness to words. Following the story up to modern discussion of innate universal grammar versus a language-particular lexicon, Joseph concludes that *Cratylus* stands at the head of 'a tradition so deeply entrenched in Western linguistic thought as to pass for common sense', namely, a tradition that associates 'the grammatical and functional with what is natural, and the lexical with what is arbitrary, conventional, or local' (Joseph 2000: 137).

Cratylus is Plato's only dialogue explicitly focused on language. In working through its central nature/convention theme, however, Plato adverts to matters he addresses elsewhere, which are also pertinent to language. One such matter is his theory that abstractions like 'virtue', as well as objects in the physical world, each variously and imperfectly reflects its own ideal Form. Platonic Forms are immaterial but accessible to human cognition. Plato elicits the concept of Forms from Hermogenes in a famous analogy between the work of repairing a broken weaver's shuttle and the work of a name-giver (here called 'rule-setter').

SOCRATES: Where does a carpenter look in making the shuttle? Isn't it to that sort of thing whose nature is to weave?
HERMOGENES: Certainly.
SOCRATES: Suppose the shuttle breaks while he's making it. Will he make another looking to the broken one? Or will he look to the very form to which he looked in making the one he broke?
HERMOGENES: In my view, he will look to the form.
SOCRATES: Then it would be absolutely right to call that what a shuttle itself is.
HERMOGENES: I suppose so.
[...]
SOCRATES: And a carpenter must embody in wood the type of shuttle naturally suited for each type of weaving.
HERMOGENES: That's right.
[...]
SOCRATES: So, musn't a rule-setter also know how to embody in sounds and syllables the name naturally suited to each thing?
                    (trans. Reeve, in Cooper 1997: 108; 389a–d)

Plato's theory of the existence of underlying ideal Forms has infused western study of language in various ways. Its terms sometimes surface in discussion of what is universal to all languages versus

11

particular to specific languages, a perennial topic that has been debated since at least the **Speculative Grammarians**. One modern reflex of that debate which explicitly references Platonic Forms is the position taken by the philosopher of language Jerrold Katz (1981; see also Allan 2003). Katz rejected **Noam Chomsky**'s (1986) assertion that language consists of grammatical knowledge residing in a native speaker's mind/brain. Katz labelled Chomsky's position 'conceptualist', in opposition to his own 'realist' view that sentences and words are abstract concepts existing outside physical or psychological experience, like Plato's representation of the abstract concept of a perfect circle, or an ideal weaver's shuttle. Katz insisted that linguistics is the study of languages conceived of as collections of abstract sentences, sounds and words, not the study of sentences, sounds and words as empirical items (a position he attributed to **Leonard Bloomfield**), nor the study of mental states (a position he attributed to Chomsky).

In this way, Katz's Platonism parts ways with Chomsky metatheoretically. Chomsky, however, identifies another facet of his own work with Plato in his appropriation of the term 'Plato's problem' (Chomsky 1986). By 'Plato's problem', Chomsky refers to a passage in the (probably middle-period) dialogue *Meno* in which Socrates successfully elicits from an uneducated slave boy the principles of geometry (trans. Grube, in Cooper 1997: 881–86; 82b–86b). Chomsky interprets this passage to demonstrate the longevity of inquiry into how it is that 'we know so much, given that the evidence available to us is so sparse' (Chomsky 1986: xxvii). Plato attributes the slave boy's surprising grasp of geometry to a human capacity to recollect knowledge derived from a previous existence. Chomsky attributes untutored children's surprising grasp of grammatical structure to an innate linguistic faculty. That is to say, Chomsky solves 'Plato's problem' with respect to language by asserting the existence of inborn, unconscious knowledge of language. Scholars such as Sampson (2005) have disputed Chomsky's solution to Plato's problem and even his manner of framing it. It seems fitting that a debate labelled with Plato's name should continue, granted that Plato posed questions designed to elicit still more questions.

Plato's major works

Among many editions of Plato's works, C. D. C. Reeve's translation of *Cratylus* in Cooper's (1997) edition is particularly useful for modern readers because the etymologies are transliterated from

Greek, making the relations of words to other words relatively transparent without knowledge of the Greek alphabet.

Further reading

Allan, K. (2003) 'Linguistic metatheory', *Language Sciences*, 25, 533–60.

Chomsky, N. (1986) *Knowledge of Language: Its Nature, Origin, and Use*, New
York: Praeger.

Clerico, G. (1992) 'Lecture du *Cratyle*, 1960–70', *Historiographia Linguistica*,
19, 333–59.

Cooper, J. M. (ed.) (1997) *Plato: Complete Works*, Indianapolis, IN: Hackett.

Demos, R. (1964) 'Symposium: Plato's theory of language and Plato's philosophy of language', *The Journal of Philosophy*, 61, 595–610.

Gera, D. L. (2003) *Ancient Greek Ideas on Speech, Language, and Civilization*,
Oxford: Oxford University Press.

Joseph, J. E. (2000) *Limiting the Arbitrary: Linguistic Naturalism and its Opposites
in Plato's* Cratylus *and Modern Theories of Language*, Philadelphia, PA: John
Benjamins.

Katz, J. J. (1981) *Language and Other Abstract Objects*, Totowa, NJ: Rowman
& Littlefield.

Marrou, H. I. (1956) *A History of Education in Antiquity* (G. Lamb, trans.),
New York: Sheed & Ward.

Sampson, G. (2005) *The 'Language Instinct' Debate* (rev. edn), London:
Continuum.

Sedley, D. (2003) *Plato's* Cratylus, Cambridge: Cambridge University Press.

Taylor, A. E. (2001) *Plato: The Man and His Work*, Mineola, NY: Dover
(original work published 1926).

ARISTOTLE (384–322 BCE)

The existing texts attributed to the ancient Greek philosopher Aristotle
do not address language in a sustained manner. Relatively few contemporary linguists directly cite his work. Nevertheless, Aristotle's
influence on modern language science is pervasive. One reason is that
many of the topics he did address in a sustained manner became
foundational to fields adjacent to linguistics, including philosophy,
biology, logic and psychology. Another reason is that scholars in the
Middle Ages invested Aristotle with great authority and applied his
ideas in their analyses of language. His work deeply shaped medieval
language scholarship, and through this left an imprint on the history
of the discipline. As a result, even though he did not write much
about language, Aristotle's broad and powerful influence over the
development of intellectual life throughout Europe and the Middle

East has extended to how western language scholars have conceived of, and carried out, the study of language, although that influence is now only occasionally directly acknowledged.

Aristotle was born in Macedonia, in what is now northern Greece, the son of a doctor to the king of Macedonia. He went to Athens at age 18, studied with **Plato**, and allied himself with the Academy for twenty years until Plato's death around 347 BCE. Aristotle then travelled across the Aegean Sea to what is now the west coast of Turkey, at least partially because deteriorating political relations had made Athens inhospitable to Macedonians. He apparently spent considerable time during the next few years exploring the marine biology of the Aegean coastline, an unusual preoccupation for a scholar in his day. By 343, Aristotle had returned to Macedonia. King Philip II recruited him as a tutor to his teenage son, who later become Alexander the Great. When Alexander grew into a young man of towering ambition – probably one with little time for philosophy or science – Aristotle returned to Athens. He founded his own school, the Lyceum, where he taught for the next 13 years. His followers came to be called the 'Peripatetics', purportedly because of Aristotle's habit of walking around the school's garden while he talked with them. Another round of political realignments made Aristotle again unwelcome in Athens. He moved north to the island of Euboea but died within a year, at age 62 (Grene 1963; Barnes 1995).

Aristotle left behind not only his students, but also a huge collection of writings covering virtually every field of inquiry in the ancient world, from metaphysics to natural history to ethics to politics. For about 200 years after his death, his work attracted little attention. Eventually it began to be read again, although what we have today is a fraction of what is reported to have been the total corpus. In the sixth century, the scholar and Christian philosopher Boethius translated some of Aristotle's works and commentaries on them into Latin. Then, in the late twelfth century, Aristotle's writings were reintroduced into Europe through translations that had passed from Greek to Syriac to Arabic to Latin. In many instances, the authenticity of the surviving texts, their coherence and their relationships to each other are problematic. Some resemble lecture notes, either prepared by Aristotle or recorded by his students. Some contain obvious interpolations inserted by later readers or editors; others, passages that seem scrambled out of order. Even without these textual difficulties, Aristotle's brusque style lacks the colourful human-interest appeal of Plato's dialogues: Barnes (1995: 12) cites a remark by the eighteenth-century British poet Thomas Gray that reading Aristotle 'is like eating dried hay'.

Aristotle differs from Plato in substance as well as style. Although some of the younger man's views harmonize with his teacher's, their orientations and approaches contrast sharply. Conventionally, Plato is characterized as an otherworldly idealist and Aristotle as an empiricist. To Plato, physical and mental phenomena reflected ideal Forms, which were incorporeal but accessible through the intellect and (in some sense) more real than physical reality. Aristotle questioned Platonic Forms, and instead valued observation of the world through the senses and deductive reasoning as prime sources of knowledge. In writing about language, Plato asked whether names are natural or conventional. Aristotle analysed the relationships of thought, speech, writing and things in the world, asserting straightaway that names are conventional:

> Now spoken sounds are symbols of affections in the soul, and written marks symbols of spoken sounds. And just as written marks are not the same for all men, neither are spoken sounds. But what these are in the first place signs of – affections of the soul – are the same for all; and what these affections are likenesses of – actual things – are also the same. […]
>
> Just as some thoughts in the soul are neither true nor false while some are necessarily one or the other, so also with spoken words. For falsity and truth have to do with combination and separation. Thus names and verbs by themselves – for instance 'man' or 'white' when nothing further is added – are like thoughts that are without combination and separation; for so far they are neither true nor false. A sign of this is that even 'goat-stag' signifies something but not, as yet, anything true or false – unless 'is' or 'is not' is added (either simply or with reference to time).
>
> A name is a spoken sound significant by convention, without time, none of whose parts is significant in separation. […] A verb is what additionally signifies time, no part of it being significant separately; and it is a sign of things said of something else. […] A sentence is a significant spoken sound some part of which is significant in separation – as an expression, not as an affirmation.
>
> (On Interpretation [De Interpretatione] 16a4–16b33; trans.
> J. L. Ackrill, in Barnes, ed., 1984)

Aristotle wrote On Interpretation as part of his exposition of logic, so he was less concerned with the grammatical features or roles of the parts of language, and more with their semantic and logical roles. His goal was to analyse how language serves as an instrument of logic. In this passage, he established that isolated words are neither true nor false (rather, propositions are), and then began to depict the meaning-bearing properties of individual words. *On Interpretation* continues with discussion of (*inter alia*) affirmation, negation, contradiction, predication, contingency and judgement. But when Aristotle's works were rediscovered in the early Middle Ages, it was the first paragraph quoted above that was perceived as the seed of an issue that took on extraordinary importance, namely the matter of what is universal in human language (Arens 1984). Aristotle's enigmatic discussion of sounds, written letters, 'affections of the soul', physical reality, and what counts as universal was crucial to the **Speculative Grammarians'** efforts to redefine grammar as – in terms also borrowed from Aristotle – a speculative or theoretical science.

An extensive critical industry of commentaries and exegeses arose around Aristotle's work, applying his ideas to the analysis of language. In the Middle Ages, much of this work assumed Aristotle's authority *a priori*, and sought to reconcile apparent contradictions or to compare his claims with those of other writers. Medieval scholars also scrutinized and debated Aristotle's technical vocabulary. Modern readers continue to do so, because Aristotle was writing about language while using, and sometimes creating, a metalanguage that lacks neat equivalences to the terms of contemporary linguistics. For instance, Arens (1984: 24) pointed out that Aristotle's '*onoma*', the word translated above as 'noun', also carries the meanings of 'name' and 'word' in this passage. Later in the same text, '*onoma*' takes the sense of 'subject'. '*Rhema*' or 'verb' ranges over 'everything spoken', 'expression' and 'predicate'. Even more challenging is '*logos*', rendered here as 'sentence', but which also extends to 'definition', 'statement', 'proposition', 'speech' or even 'reason, rationality' (Arens 1984; Modrak 2001).

Working through these complexities is important because Aristotle's transmission of a set of linguistic terms and categories constitutes another of his major contributions to the language sciences. Embedded in the text *Poetics*, Aristotle labels a heterogeneous collection of constituents of language, including the three major lexical classes of nouns, verbs and 'conjunctions' (essentially, whatever is neither noun nor verb); case markers and varieties of bound morphology. He also mentions syllables, vowels, semivowels (glides) and 'mutes' (consonants); gender marking on nouns and tense on verbs; and what we now call 'speech acts' (commands, prayers, statements, threats) (1456b20–1459a14; trans. I. Bywater, in Barnes, ed., 1984).

Textual corruption heavily masks the passage (Pinborg 1975), but at least some of these terms and distinctions were probably already conventional by Aristotle's day. The Stoic philosophers, active in Athens from the third to first centuries BCE, organized and elaborated them. From the Stoics, they entered into the western grammatical tradition, which gradually achieved independence from philosophy. Many of Aristotle's terms and his manner of identifying them reappear, for example, in the grammars of **Aelius Donatus** and **Priscian of Caesarea**, and continue up to the present day.

The classificatory spirit that Aristotle applied to the parts of language in *Poetics* dominates another text that had a profound effect, *Categories* (1a1–15b32; trans. J. L. Ackrill, in Barnes, ed., 1984). Using linguistic and logical criteria, Aristotle defined ten conceptual categories or 'modes of being' that exhaustively distinguish phenomena, namely: substance; quantity; quality; relation; place; time; position; state; action; and affectedness. Scholars in the Middle Ages applied the ten categories widely as a tool for classifying and organizing not only things in the world, but aspects of language as well. Grammarians asserted that any meaningful statement necessarily expressed one of the ten categories; they aligned the ten categories with components of language or of logic; or they employed the categories to account for word order facts, explain properties of individual words, or define grammatical terms.

Aristotle's popularity crested in the Middle Ages, then declined. Some critics denounced Aristotelian scholarship as tainted by paganism. Others associated it with medieval scholasticism, which faced attack on philosophical grounds by the 1300s. Seventeenth-century scholars discredited Aristotle's writings in general because some of his specific scientific claims in fields such as astronomy had, by then, been shown to be false. It is a tribute to the penetration of Aristotle's influence, however, that early modern critics such as **John Locke** could explicitly reject Aristotle's philosophical claims on scientific grounds, while at the same time following Aristotle's footsteps in insisting that knowledge be based on empirical observation. The converse legacy is also attested, for example, in the latter-day British general grammarian James Harris (1709–80). Harris was avidly and explicitly anti-empiricist and anti-Lockean, but he championed the existence of a universal grammar in Platonic terms, while self-consciously adopting Aristotle's vocabulary, categories, definitions and overall taxonomic spirit in his analysis of language. Even those who tried to distance themselves from Aristotelianism couldn't get outside it in every way.

Contemporary linguistics presupposes empiricism as basic to science, and occasionally recognizes in Aristotle's work a capacity to speak across the ages. Zirin (1980), for instance, compared Aristotle's discussion of animal communication with his analysis of human language, finding evidence that he anticipated a conclusion that modern language science is still trying to articulate. Compared with the ancient Greeks, we know far more about neurology and cognition, but we are still trying to balance our relatedness to other animals against our uniqueness. Aristotle had tried to define that balance, too.

Aristotle's major works

The Complete Works of Aristotle: Vols 1–2, edited by J. Barnes (Princeton University Press, Princeton, NJ, 1984) is available online through the Intelex 'Past Masters' series. As an aid to comparison of editions, I have cited Aristotle's works with their conventional 'Bekker numbers', named for early nineteenth-century German philologist A. I. Bekker.

Further reading

Arens, H. (1984) Aristotle's Theory of Language and its Tradition: Texts from 500 to 1750. Philadelphia, PA: John Benjamins.
Barnes, J. (1995) 'Life and work', in J. Barnes (ed.), The Cambridge Companion to Aristotle, Cambridge: Cambridge University Press.
Grene, M. (1963) A Portrait of Aristotle, Chicago: University of Chicago Press.
Harris, J. (1801) The Works of James Harris, Esq.: Vols 1–2, London: Wingrave (original works published 1744–81).
Modrak, D. K. W. (2001) Aristotle's Theory of Language and Meaning, Cambridge: Cambridge University Press.
Pinborg, J. (1975) 'Classical Antiquity: Greece', in T. A. Sebeok (ed.), Current Trends in Linguistics: Vol. 13. Historiography of Linguistics, The Hague: Mouton.
Zirin, R. A. (1980) 'Aristotle's biology of language', Transactions of the American Philological Association, 110, 325–47.

MARCUS TERENTIUS VARRO (116–27 BCE)

Marcus Terentius Varro plays a singular role in the history of language science. He achieved high renown as a scholar within the ancient Roman intellectual world. However, in language studies Varro's ideas were unconventional to the extent that his influence was relatively slight. Others drew freely from his grammatical works according to their own purposes (Collart 1954: 344), but eventually most of his writings were lost. A few were rediscovered almost 1400 years after his death, and since then have been read with increasing appreciation. Today we cannot fully understand Varro's contributions because we possess only fragments of his voluminous writings, many of which pose complex interpretive puzzles as they have been gleaned from quotations embedded in other writers' texts. It may be impossible to assess Varro's legacy satisfactorily unless we discover more of his lost work, or until modern language science travels farther down the path Varro blazed more than 2000 years ago.

Born into a wealthy Roman family, Varro led a long and adventurous life. After studying under the pre-eminent scholar Lucius Aelius Stilo (among whose other pupils was the future statesman and orator Marcus Tullius Cicero, 106–43 BCE), he travelled to Athens to study philosophy. Varro returned to fight on the losing side in one of the power struggles in which Caesar eventually triumphed; he was forgiven and rose to a position of prominence under Caesar's protection, then fell precipitously out of grace under Anthony in 43 BCE. Varro escaped death, but suffered the destruction of his private library. He retired to spend the latter half of his life reading and writing, dying at age 89 (Kent 1938: vii–ix; Hammond and Scullard 1970: 1107–8). Estimates vary, but on some accounts he produced 620 books – granted that most Roman books are the length of modern chapters. Varro wrote on virtually every topic: astronomy, geography, agriculture, ocean tides, mathematics, law, history, philosophy, theatre, education, literature, rhetoric and language. He also left behind poetry, speeches and letters. Four hundred years after his death, Augustine of Hippo (354–430 CE), himself a prolific author, questioned (in *City of God* 6.2) whether anyone had the time to read everything that Varro wrote. Moreover, Augustine marvelled that Varro had had time to write, considering the vast number of books he read. Unfortunately only two texts attributed to Varro survive today. Among those two are six volumes of what was originally a 25-volume work, *De Lingua Latina* (*On the Latin language*, Taylor 1996: 1–6).

De Lingua Latina is the earliest, and most original, Roman treatise on language. In this, as in other fields, Romans were deeply influenced by the accomplishments and preoccupations of the Greeks, whom they had politically subjugated. From Greeks, the Romans inherited the logical and linguistic doctrines of the Stoic philosophers and a grammatical metalanguage. They also inherited a framework for classifying sentence constituents, or 'parts of speech' (Latin *partes orationis*), as in the Greek grammar controversially attributed to Dionysius Thrax (*c.* 170–90 BCE), but which actually may be of a much later date. Romans, however, moved away from the philosophical orientation of **Plato** and **Aristotle** to focus on more immediate educational goals. The Roman grammarians' greatest accomplishments extended the Greek grammatical tradition in analysing their own language, and applied that analysis in the linguistic and literary training of future orators.

This general tenor of Roman language studies, as indebted to the Greeks but redirected away from the speculative toward the practical, highlights the novelty of Varro's work. *De Lingua Latina* is not a pedagogical text, like most other Roman grammatical writings, but a descriptive grammar characterized by a number of innovations. Its central concerns are Latin etymology, syntax and morphology.

Of the six books of *De Lingua Latina* accessible today, three address etymology. Books V–VII discuss the origins of individual words, a long-standing fascination in the ancient world. Taylor (1991: 336) depicted Varro as 'arguably the most scientific of the ancient etymologists', citing his references to diachronically earlier word forms, and the fact that Varro reconstructed unattested forms to account for apparent irregularities in contemporary Latin. Quite a number of Varro's claims about the origins of specific Latin words have turned out to be accurate, although of course he had no access to the methods of historical reconstruction that raised scientific standards for etymology in the nineteenth century. Others of Varro's etymologies, such as the examples below, are flatly wrong, but still inform us about Roman culture:

An *agnus* 'lamb' is so named because it is *agnatus* 'born as an addition' to the flock of sheep. A *catulus* 'puppy' is named from its quick and keen [*catus* 'sharp, shrewd'] scent ... and from this, *canis* 'dog': unless, just as the trumpet and horn are said to *canare* 'sing' when they give some signal, so the *canis* is named because it likewise, both when guarding the house day or night, and when engaged in hunting, gives the signal with its voice.

(*De Lingua Latina* V.99; trans. Kent 1938: 95)

Assessment of Varro's syntax is more difficult in the absence of the books of *De Lingua Latina* devoted to that topic. But passages cited from them in later Roman literature led Taylor (1986: 180) to remark that if Varro's writings on syntax were to be found, we would see in them the influence of Stoic logic. The fact that the rest of Roman language science did not take up syntax until **Priscian of Caesarea**'s sixth-century *Institutiones Grammaticales* underscores Varro's originality. The highlight of the extant *De Lingua Latina* is Varro's innovative treatment of morphology in Books VIII–X. Varro declared the word to be the minimal linguistic unit, then set out to explore the properties of the Latin word stock. Along with other ancient grammarians, he viewed words not as assemblies of roots, stems and affixes, but as units reducible only to ordered letters or sounds. Words could be clustered together into paradigms, some 'derived' from others, like people in a family. But he did not decompose them into subparts representing individual versus shared features. The Greco-Roman grammatical tradition developed semantic or functional definitions of word types – *partes orationis* – typically numbering eight, sometimes five or nine. For example, 'nouns' were words that signify names (**Plato**), bodies or acts (Thrax), or objects or notions (**Aelius Donatus**). Sometimes the phenomenon of case was incorporated in the definition of nouns, but meaning was still the key criterion.

Varro's system of *partes orationis*, however, was discontinuous with the grammatical tradition of his day (Taylor 1996: 14). He worked out a complex tripartite system for classifying words entirely on the basis of form. Varro first divided words into those he called 'fruitful', the class 'which by inflection produces from itself many different forms, as for example *lego* "I gather," *legi* "I have gathered"', as opposed to the class of 'barren' words 'which produce nothing from itself, as for example *et* "and," *iam* "now," *vix* "hardly"' (VIII.9; trans. Kent 1938: 377–79). Varro added two more levels:

> The second division is that, of the words which can be changed by derivation and inflection, some are changed in accordance with will, and others in accordance with nature. I call it will, when from a name a person sets a name on something else, as *Romulus* gave a name to *Roma*; I call it nature, when we all accept a name but do not ask of the one who set it how he wishes it to be inflected, but ourselves inflect it, as genitive *Romae*, accusative *Romam*, ablative *Roma*.
>
> (X.15; trans. Kent 1938: 545)

> There is a third division, the words which are by their nature inflected. These are divided into four subdivisions: one which has cases but not tenses, like *docilis* 'docile' and *facilis* 'easy'; a second which has tenses but not cases, like *docet* 'teaches,' and *facit*

'makes'; a third which has both, like *docens* 'teaching,' and *faciens* 'making'; a fourth which has neither, like *docte* 'learnedly' and *facete* 'wittily'.

(X.17; trans. Kent 1938: 547)

Varro's third division establishes four word classes, roughly, nouns (and Latin adjectives); verbs; participles; adverbs. The purely formal basis of these distinctions, created by the interaction of two binary features, was wholly novel. Varro's second division was likewise ahead of his time in that it distinguished derivational from inflectional morphology, contrasting the arbitrariness of derivation ('*declinatio voluntaria*') with the regular, law-like, operation of inflection ('*declinatio naturalis*'). He elaborated in a memorable passage:

[W]hen three men have bought a slave apiece at Ephesus, sometimes one derives his slave's name from that of the seller Artemidorus and calls him *Artemas*; another names his slave *Ion*, from Ionia the district, because he has bought him there; the third calls his slave *Ephesius*, because he has bought him at Ephesus. In this way, each derives the name from a different source, as he preferred.

On the other hand ... when the names have been fixed, [people] derive the case forms of [the names] in like fashion, and in one and the same way they all say in the genitive case *Artemidori*, *Ionis*, *Ephesi*; and so on in the other cases.

(VIII.21–22; trans. Kent 1938: 389)

The issue is also at the centre of another of Varro's accomplishments, namely that he proposed what may constitute the first specific language universal, in stating that *declinatio* 'has been introduced not only into Latin speech, but into the speech of all men' (VIII.3; trans. Kent 1938: 373; see also IX.35; trans. Kent 1938: 465). Commentary on this passage has often interpreted it to indicate linguistic parochialism on Varro's part, under an assumption that his term *declinatio* refers narrowly to morphological inflection, which in fact is not present in all human languages. However, Varro acknowledged that Phoenicians and Egyptians do not inflect nouns for case (VIII.65; trans. Kent 1938: 423).

Rather, the universality of Varro's *declinatio* rests on the fact that it subsumes both *declinatio voluntaria* and *declinatio naturalis*. *Declinatio voluntaria* refers to derivation, which to Varro included word formation and, more generally, 'the designation of referents by linguistic symbols' (Taylor 1974: 117). He recognized many kinds of word formation as *declinatio voluntaria*: *scriptor* 'writer' from *scribere* 'to write' (VIII.57; trans. Kent 1938: 415); *equiso* 'stable-boy' from *equus* 'horse' (VIII.14; trans. Kent 1938: 381); *argentifodinae* 'silver-mines' from *argentum* 'silver' and *foditur* 'is mined' (VIII.62; trans. Kent 1938: 421). In contrast, *declinatio naturalis* is what we would call inflection, 'based not on the volition of the individuals acting singly, but on general agreement' (VIII.22; trans. Kent 1938: 389). It is regular and pre-dictable: alongside *dico* 'I say' there is imperfect *dicebam* and pluperfect *dixeram*, as 'lentils grow from planted lentils, and ... lupine from lupine' (IX.34; trans. Kent 1938: 463). Whereas *declinatio voluntaria* exhibits gaps and irregularities, emerging unpredictably from the accidents of language history, *declinatio naturalis* follows established, law-like generalities. Both are species of *declinatio*: 'the one is as it were the spring, the other the brook' (VIII.5; trans. Kent 1938: 375).

Varro's claim that all languages exhibit *declinatio* encompassed the notions of a 'spring' from which words unaccountably appear, as well as a 'brook', a path along which words pass in a predictable manner. It is by these lights that he declared the cross-linguistic universality of *declinatio*: all languages exhibit *declinatio* in the broad sense that includes, but is not exhausted by, inflection.

Distinguishing inflection and derivation was only one of Varro's initiatives. He also was first to establish five declensions and three conjugations for Latin; first to identify the Latin future perfective indicative; and first to employ an abstract mathematical model in characterizing Latin morphology as when he analogized '1:2 : 10:20' to '*rex:regi* : *lex:legi*' (X.43–47; trans. Kent 1938: 567–71). There was probably much more that would startle us in the full text of *De Lingua Latina*. Varro's independence and sophistication make our lack of access to his work even more regrettable.

Varro's major works

On the Latin Language: Vols 1–2, Books V–VII and VIII–X, 1938 (R. G. Kent, ed. and trans.), Harvard University Press, Cambridge, MA (original work *c.* 43 BCE).
De Lingua Latina X: A New Critical Text and English Translation with Prolegomena and Commentary (D. J. Taylor, ed. and trans.), Philadelphia, PA: John Benjamins, 1996 (original work *c.* 43 BCE).

Further reading

Collart, J. (1954) *Varron grammairien latin*, Publications de la Faculté des Lettres de l'Université de Strasbourg.

Hammond, N. G. L. and Scullard, H. H. (eds) (1970) *The Oxford Classical Dictionary*, Oxford: Oxford University Press.
Taylor, D. J. (1974) *Declinatio: A Study of the Linguistic Theory of Marcus Terentius Varro*, Philadelphia, PA: John Benjamins.
——(1986) 'Rethinking the history of language science in classical antiquity', *Historiographia Linguistica*, 13, 175–90.
——(1991) 'Roman language science', in P. Schmitter (ed.), *Sprachtheorien der abendländischen Antike*, Tübingen: Gunter Narr.

LANGUAGE IN THE BIBLE

The varied texts known collectively as the Bible were written down by many authors, over many years, for diverse purposes, using several languages. Each of the three major monotheistic traditions with origins in the Middle East – Judaism, Christianity, Islam – recognizes as its own some of these texts, although each differently interprets (and sometimes differently names) even those portions of the Bible it values in common with the other two traditions. Due to the profound, widespread and diversified influence of the Bible over a long interval, its impact on cultural phenomena is immense. This holds for the study of language, despite the fact that the Bible only sparsely addresses language and linguistic issues. Therefore even those few biblical passages relevant to linguistic matters have stimulated generations of 'key thoughts' about language and linguistics, collaboratively propagated and rarely attributable to specific 'key thinkers'. In this sense, it is not the Bible itself that this chapter addresses, but rather that portion of biblical hermeneutics dedicated to language.

Among biblical passages that have played important roles in the study of language is Genesis 2: 19–20, which tells how the newly created first man Adam named the animals:

> And out of the ground the Lord God formed every beast of the field, and every fowl of the air; and brought them unto Adam to see what he would call them: and whatsoever Adam called every living creature, that was the name thereof. And Adam gave names to all cattle, and to the fowl of the air, and to every beast of the field […]

As an account of the origin of language, this passage is much less developed than **Plato**'s reflections on nature versus convention in *Cratylus*. It does not indicate the basis on which Adam selected or constructed names for the animals, nor does it provide insight into the origin of any parts of language other than names. It only declares that whatever labels Adam assigned, those were adopted. Nevertheless, in the biblical narrative, language soon burst forth in all its complexity: by Genesis 2: 23 Adam provides an etymology for the name he applies to his newly created partner, 'woman'; and in chapter 3, Eve converses with the serpent, as do Adam and Eve with God during their expulsion from Eden. Another facet of Genesis 2: 19–20 that many readers (such as von Rad 1972: 82–83) have noted is that the naming of the animals was not a communicative task. Rather, Adam's initial linguistic act imposed order on his environment through language. Thus Genesis 2: 19–20 acknowledges from the start that language has a cognitive dimension, and is not purely a social phenomenon.

Despite its sparseness of detail, the Bible's cultural authority is such that for many readers Genesis 2: 19–20 has served as a touchstone for exploring aspects of the nature of language. The passage is also foundational to a topic of long-standing fascination – identification of the original language of humankind. From the ancient world through to the end of the eighteenth century, readers scrutinized Genesis as a literal account of the beginning of the world and hence of the historical priority of peoples and their languages. Putting aside the question of whether God used perceptible speech in the creation of the world in Genesis 1: 1–31 (one of many topics on which biblical interpretation varies), Adam's naming of the animals was assumed to have employed – or perhaps initiated – an original, 'perfect' language to which he had access before the expulsion from Eden, and in which words were intrinsically appropriate to their referents. Most early Jewish and Christian commentary on Genesis 2: 19–20 identifies Adam's language as Hebrew, while Muslim tradition sometimes identifies it as Syriac (Rubin 1988). Seventeenth-century Europeans found varied and ingenious grounds to pre-empt these traditional claims and to assert instead that Adam spoke Flemish, German, French or Swedish (Almond 1999: 126–36). As late as the early 1800s, the question of the origin of language was still famously debated by philosophers and philologists (including **Johann Herder** and **Condillac**; see Stam 1976), some of whom granted a prestigious role in the debate to biblical evidence.

Many readers for whom the Bible was authoritative, including Augustine of Hippo (354–430 CE; see *City of God* 16.11) and Dante Alighieri (1265–1321; see *De Vulgari Eloquentia* 1.vi), claimed that the original human language survived Adam and Eve's expulsion from Eden. The unified language of Adam's descendents was shattered, however, in the famous destruction of the Tower of Babel narrated in Genesis 11: 1–9. This narrative tells how survivors of the Flood settled in a spot now presumed to be in southern Mesopotamia. They decided to build a city and a tower 'whose top may reach unto heaven' by way of aggrandizing themselves and consolidating their power: 'let us make us a name, lest we be scattered abroad upon the face of the whole earth'. But their plans went awry:

> And the Lord came down to see the city and the tower, which the children of men builded. And the Lord said, Behold, the people is one, and they have all one language; and this they begin to do: and now nothing will be restrained from them, which they have imagined to do. Go to, let us go down, and there confound their language, that they may not understand one another's speech. So the Lord scattered them abroad from thence upon the face of all the earth; and they left off to build the city.
>
> (Genesis 11: 5–8)

The story of the Tower of Babel has been mined for centuries for its theological, historical and philological content. In the study of language, it has probably had even more impact than Adam's naming of the animals. Among its roles has been an explanation for how the unified language of Adam's descendents was replaced by the attested range of mutually unintelligible human languages (numbering seventy in some exegetical traditions, seventy-two in others; Eco 1995: 9). Another of its roles has been to cultivate a specific psycho-social stance in the face of linguistic diversity: people speak different languages because at Babel, God wilfully imposed cross-linguistic unintelligibility.

Genesis 11: 1–9 is intriguingly reticent on the matter of exactly in what way humankind went wrong at Babel, since the building of cities or towers is not in itself illegitimate in the Bible. But the story has traditionally been interpreted to mean that God took offence at the spirit of self-sufficiency and hubris behind the project. It is significant that the multiplication of languages at Babel has not conventionally been viewed as an expansion of human potentiality, but rather as a penalty for human transgression. Martin Luther (1483–1546), for example, depicted the events at Babel as a 'great punishment' superseding even that of Flood in Genesis 6–8. The Flood had spared Noah and his family, and it was never to be repeated, whereas the confusion of tongues necessarily affects all humans and 'continues till the end of the world' (Luther 1958: 195). The 'confusion of tongues' more effectively cuts humans down to size than the levelling of the city and tower, since it goes a long way towards preventing another outbreak of collaborative presumption.

In the seventeenth century, Babel was routinely referred to as 'the Curse'. Scholars such as Francis Bacon (1561–1626) in England, René Descartes (1596–1650) in France, and Gottfried Leibniz (1646–1716) in Germany tried to redress the Curse by developing 'universal languages', and in doing so stimulated novel kinds of linguistic engineering. Many universal language schemes were essentially techniques of writing that transcended linguistic differences, thereby permitting speakers of different languages to communicate. Among the most famous was British clergyman and scholar **John Wilkins**' 'Real Character', an invented script based on an original taxonomy of concepts and objects. In principle, Wilkins' Real Characters could be interpreted without reference to any spoken language. He designed his invention with the explicit goal of remedying the biblical 'Curse of the Confusion' (Wilkins 1668: 'Epistle'). Wilkins' solution displays the ingenuity and mechanical industry that characterized seventeenth-century scholars' fascination with the material world and their efforts to reconcile science and religion.

In the light of the long-sustained cultural power of the story of the Tower of Babel, it is noteworthy that Genesis 11: 1–9 follows a lengthy genealogical passage that gives an alternative account of ethnic dispersal and linguistic differentiation. Genesis 10: 5 declares outright that the sons of Noah split up and populated the land 'every one after his tongue, after their families, in their nations', apparently naturalizing linguistic differences as a matter of course. The sobriety of Genesis 10: 5 has long co-existed alongside the theatrical glamour of Genesis 11: 1–9. Only the latter has captured readers' imaginations.

A third passage has specifically influenced the language experiences and attitudes of Christian readers of the Bible. In the story of Pentecost in Acts 2: 1–12, Jesus' apostles miraculously gain the ability to speak in foreign languages, such that listeners of different ethnicities all understood as if they were being addressed in their own native language. This narrative is fundamental to Christianity's self-defined mission to address all people, on the grounds that the events in the story of Pentecost explicitly sanction the apostles and their successors to spread their message worldwide. Christian exegeses conventionally offset Genesis 11 with Acts 2: 1–12, viewing Pentecost as a remedy to the spiritual damage inflicted at Babel, albeit without actually restoring a unified Adamic language. Pentecost both copies and inverts Babel, since in both instances a miraculous multiplication of languages occurred as an impetus to people to disperse. However, at Pentecost the disciples did so with a single goal in mind, to spread a single message, while at Babel the city-dwellers dispersed because they could no longer participate in building a unified (and unifying) project.

Pentecost also implicitly sanctioned the importance of foreign language knowledge. As such its effects extend up to the present day, in the work of what is probably the world's single largest institutional support for study of minority languages, the controversial Christian evangelical organization SIL International (www.sil.org; see **Kenneth Pike**).

These three passages stand out as examples of the influence of the Bible on the study of language. The Bible also invites readers to reflect on language issues through its widespread use of linguistic terms and metaphors: 'Day unto day uttereth speech' (Psalms 19: 2); 'In the beginning was the Word' (John 1: 1); and pervasive references to 'the word of God' (see Augustine's *The Trinity* 15.20–39). There are additional outcroppings of linguistic interest, such as the famous '*shibboleth*' passage in Judges 12: 5–6, in which Gileadites use a linguistic test to identify disguised Ephraimites; taboos associated with names for God; and, especially for Jews and Muslims, the religious significance of a specific language as an instrument for recording divine revelation: for Jews, Hebrew and for Muslims, Arabic. Moreover, the centrality of scripture to the 'people of the book' – a term Muslims have used to refer to Jews and Christians, which implicitly recognizes all three groups' shared, if divergent, investments in the Bible – has entailed an enduring commitment to literacy and literary education. That commitment has inculcated linguistic self-consciousness in societies where the Bible holds high cultural value.

Further reading

Almond, P. C. (1999) *Adam and Eve in Seventeenth-Century Thought*, Cambridge: Cambridge University Press.

Borst, A. (1957–63) *Der Turmbau von Babel: Geschichte der Meinungen über Ursprung und Vielfalt der Sprachen und Völker: Vols. 1–6*, reprinted by Deutscher Taschenbuch, München, 1995.

Eco, U. (1995) *The Search for the Perfect Language* (J. Fentress, trans.), Oxford: Blackwell.

Fyler, J. M. (2007) 'The biblical history of language', in *Language and the Declining World in Chaucer, Dante, and Jean de Meun*, Cambridge: Cambridge University Press.

Luther, M. (1958) *Luther's Commentary on Genesis* (J. T. Mueller, trans.), Grand Rapids, MI: Zondervan (original work *c.* 1522–46).

von Rad, G. (1972) *Genesis, A Commentary* (revised edn, J. H. Marks, trans.), Philadelphia, PA: Westminster Press.

Rubin, M. (1988) 'The language of creation or the primordial language: a case of cultural polemics in Antiquity', *Journal of Jewish Studies*, 49, 306–33.

Stam, J. H. (1976) *Inquiries into the Origin of Language*, New York: Harper & Row.

Wilkins, J. (1668) *Essay Towards a Real Character and a Philosophical Language*, London: Gellibrand and Martyn.

AELIUS DONATUS (FOURTH CENTURY CE) AND PRISCIAN OF CAESAREA (SIXTH CENTURY CE)

The fourth-century grammarian Donatus lived in Rome, and taught Latin-speaking children at the beginning of their training in oratory. Among his students was Jerome (*c.* 347–420), future translator of the Bible into Latin. Aside from Donatus' grammar of Latin, the *Ars Grammatica*, he produced commentaries on the works of the dramatist Terence and the poet Virgil.

Two hundred years later, Priscian, who was probably of Greek descent, grew up in Caesarea, on the coast of what is now Algeria but what was then the capital of a Roman province. Priscian taught Latin to Greek speakers in sixth-century Constantinople (modern Istanbul). He left behind three important grammatical texts, among other writings.

These scant facts are essentially all that we know about the lives of Donatus and Priscian. What they have in common is that they both produced grammars of Latin that profoundly influenced western study of language. However, the two hundred years that separate their lives and their social and intellectual circumstances led them to create texts with different complexions and purposes: Donatus lived at the centre of Roman culture, and taught young native speakers of Latin about their own language; Priscian lived on the geographical and temporal edge of the Roman world, and taught adult non-native learners. Donatus' grammar is, above all, succinct, designed as it was to be memorized by beginners. Priscian's most important work addresses students with advanced skills in Latin. In a modern edition it fills almost 1000 pages with examples, commentary, theoretical asides, quotations from the classic literature, comparison of Latin with Greek, encyclopedic coverage of Latin word formation processes, and lists of special cases.

Donatus' *Ars Grammatica* is conventionally divided into two parts, *Ars Minor* (Shorter Grammar) and *Ars Maior* (Longer Grammar). The purpose of the *Ars Minor* is to define each of the parts of speech, enumerate and label their subclasses, and provide examples of how to identify the features of individual words within the inflectional system of the language. For ease of memorization, Donatus presented the text as a series of questions and answers, hierarchically organized with each level iteratively dividing into sublevels. It begins:

> How many parts of speech are there? Eight. What? Noun, pronoun, verb, adverb, participle, conjunction, preposition, interjection.
>
> CONCERNING THE NOUN
>
> What is a noun? A part of speech which signifies with the case a person or a thing specifically or generally. How many attributes has a noun? Six. What? Quality, comparison, gender, number, form, case. In what does the quality of nouns consist? It is two-fold, for either it is the name of one and is called proper, or it is the name of many and is called common.
>
> How many degrees of comparison are there? Three. What? Positive, as *learned*; comparative, as *more learned*; superlative, as *most learned*.
>
> (trans. Chase 1926: 29)

After moving in this way through the six attributes of nouns, Donatus illustrated how these features play out across individual words of various gender:

> *Magister* is a common noun of masculine gender, singular number, simple form, nominative and vocative case, which will be declined thus: in the nominative, *hic magister*; in the genitive, *huius magistri*; in the dative, *huic magistro*; in the accusative, *hunc magistrum*; in the ablative, *ab hoc magistro*; and in the plural in the nominative, *hi magistri*; in the genitive, *horum magistrorum*; in the dative, *his magistris*; in the accusative, *hos magistros*; in the vocative, *O magistri*; in the ablative, *ab his magistris*.
>
> (trans. Chase 1926: 31)

With almost uninterrupted symmetry, the *Ars Minor* thus inches over the eight parts of speech. The more elaborated, but still succinct *Ars Maior* comprises three books, ascending in structural complexity. Book I provides a terse introduction to Latin *littera* (a concept subsuming both sounds and letters); syllables; metrical feet, accents and punctuation. Book II returns to the eight parts of speech, subclassifying nouns (for example) more fully than in the *Ars Minor*. Book III addresses sentence-level features of Latin, with discussion of 'barbarisms' (word-choice errors), 'solecisms' (syntactic errors) and other irregularities; and also literary figures and tropes.

Much of the content and organization of the *Ars Grammatica* is continuous with the Greek grammatical tradition that stood behind Donatus. However, three traits of his work are important with respect to how the *Ars Grammatica* came to be used. First, because Donatus wrote for native speakers of Latin, his examples illustrated the language, rather than taught readers how Latin inflectional categories interact. Second, his approach subordinated formal relations to semantic ones, in that most of the categories into which he organized words are defined not by their shapes, but by their meanings (for example, words indicating quantity; words indicating nationality). Third, Donatus provided little coverage of Latin syntax, or of verbal mood, tense or aspect.

As Law (2003: 65–80) emphasized, these features of Donatus' work make sense in that, in his day, he addressed native speakers who did not need to learn Latin; they needed to learn categories for analysing the parts of Latin texts. However, Donatus' work ended up being employed for centuries in teaching second-language learners, which became necessary once Latin ceased to be anyone's native language due to natural diachronic change and to the extension of the Roman (and Christian) cultural and political world to speakers of Germanic, Celtic and other languages. The authority of the *Ars Grammatica* became such that by the 1400s 'Donat(us)' came to mean 'elementary foreign-language manual' as in '*Donat Proensal*' or '*Donatus Grecus*' (Bischoff 1961). And since education in the ancient world and Middle Ages began with grammar, for almost a thousand years the *Ars Minor* in particular played a key role in European education, despite its unsuitability for second-language instruction.

Starting in Donatus' own century, scholars and teachers tried to correct that unsuitability by adapting the text for non-native speakers of Latin. They supplemented the *Ars Grammatica* with commentaries, or brought forward material that Donatus presupposed. The record of this conceptually challenging work shows that, in trying to specify what it is that learners need to know about Latin as a foreign language, western language science achieved greater linguistic self-awareness. Wrestling with this task also drove Europeans to probe differences between languages, and the range of cross-linguistic variability. Thus Donatus' influence extended over centuries, reaching virtually anyone who was exposed to formal education, indirectly affecting the whole development of western culture.

Two hundred years later, Priscian's influence likewise spread far beyond his own time. The longest of his three grammatical works, the *Institutiones Grammaticae* (*Grammatical Doctrine*), is the most important. Its eighteen books are conventionally divided into two unequal parts. The first sixteen, together called '*Priscian Maior*', address many of the same topics, in much the same order, as Donatus' grammar. But Priscian provided far more detail and exhibited theoretical insight far beyond that of Donatus. He listed exhaustively the range of forms; compared Greek with Latin extensively; tried to explain why the facts of grammar are what they are; and cited many examples from classical authors. Priscian also proposed rules governing Latin accidence of the sort that would be a godsend to second-language learners, as when he wrote 'Latin nouns ending in -*or* which are either masculine or feminine or common gender, form the genitive by adding *is* and lengthening the *o*' (trans. Hovdhaugen 1982: 103).

The last two books of the *Institutiones Grammaticae*, '*Priscian Minor*', address Latin syntax. To pay attention to syntax in any sustained way was unusual in Priscian's day, but *Priscian Minor* extended the existing Greek grammatical tradition (here as elsewhere) by identifying complex syntactic constructions as built up from simpler ones, and identifying elliptic constructions as shortened versions of regular full constructions (Hovdhaugen 1982: 104–5).

Priscian also produced two shorter texts. The *Partitiones* (*Divisions*) is an example of what became known as a 'parsing grammar'. It is based on the first twelve lines of Virgil's (70–19 BCE) classic epic, the *Aeneid*. Priscian commented first on the prosody of each line of the poem, and then focused on each of the words in succession, analysing its features and its roles within the complex web of Latin word classes. Priscian's other text, the short *Institutio de Nomine et Pronomine et Verbo* (*Instruction on the Noun, Pronoun, and Verb*) summarizes in a systematic manner the formal, productive rules of Latin's inflected word classes, including participles along with nouns, pronouns and verbs. It begins: 'All the nouns which Latin speech employs are inflected according to the five declensions, which got their order from the sequence of the vowels forming the genitive case' (trans. Law 2003: 87), directly presenting to readers a key to the organization of the grammar of Latin nouns. Law (*ibid.*) remarked that the *Institutio* as 'what was lacking in Donatus' day – a systematic form-based description of Latin', supplemented by examples of actual words formed by the rules provided in the *Institutiones Grammaticae*, went a long way toward meeting the needs of second-language learners.

Like Donatus' *Ars Grammatica*, Priscian's grammatical writings had a lasting impact on the western study of language. Priscian's influence, however, travelled a different course. The *Institutiones Grammaticae* dropped out of sight while Germanic and Celtic speakers, and speakers of the Romance languages that descended from Latin, struggled to acquire the basics of Latin as a foreign language. They used Donatus' text, commentaries on Donatus, and works modelled on Donatus. But when Priscian's major work was rediscovered and became accessible again, starting in the ninth century, its theoretical orientation opened the possibility of developing an approach to grammar that would meet **Aristotle**'s definition of a speculative science. From the mid 1200s, the **Speculative Grammarians**, centred at the University of Paris, seized upon this opening, often framing their treatises as commentaries on the *Institutiones Grammaticae*. They picked up on Priscian's comparisons of Greek versus Latin, and expanded his speculations about the reasons why the facts of Latin are what they are. With the development of speculative grammar, language science moved from being focused on analysis or acquisition of a specific language into the examination of language as a general phenomenon.

Thus Donatus' terse questions and answers in the *Ars Minor* kept alive the means by which beginners could acquire Latin, the language of education and high culture, which had ceased to be spoken natively by the latter days of classical Greco-Roman civilization. Later, the vast detail of Priscian's texts provided a basis on which grammarians could redefine the nature of their work, turning away from the purely practical task of language learning and toward the task of building a theory of language. In the *Institutiones Grammaticae*, 'ancient language science utters its swan song' (Taylor 1996: 348), and with that, one might say that study of language moved out of the ancient world and into the Middle Ages.

Major works of Donatus and Priscian

Donatus

The Ars Minor *of Donatus, for One Thousand Years the Leading Textbook of Grammar*, 1926 (W. J. Chase, ed. and trans.), University of Wisconsin Press, Madison, WI.

Ars Grammatica, 1961, in *Grammatici Latini*, Vol. IV, 355–402 (H. Keil, ed.), Georg Olms, Hildesheim.

Holtz, L., *Donat et la tradition de l'enseignment grammatical*, 1981, Centre National de la Recherche Scientifique (CNRS), Paris (critical edition of the *Ars Grammatica*).

Priscian

Institutiones Grammaticae, in *Grammatici Latini*, Vol. 2, 1–597, continuing to Vol. 3, 1–384 (H. Keil, ed.), Hildesheim: Georg Olms, 1961.
Institutio de Nomine et Pronomine et Verbo (M. Passalacqua, ed.), Urbino: Quattro Venti, 1992 (also in *Grammatici Latini*, Vol. 3, 441–56 (H. Keil, ed.), Hildesheim: Georg Olms, 1961).
Partitiones, in *Grammatici Latini*, Vol. 3, 457–515 (H. Keil, ed.), Hildesheim: Georg Olms, 1961.

Further reading

Bischoff, B. (1961) 'The study of foreign languages in the Middle Ages', *Speculum*, 36, 209–24.
Hovdhaugen, E. (1982) *Foundations of Western Linguistics*, Oslo: Universitetsforlaget.
Law, V. (2003) *The History of Linguistics in Europe from Plato to 1600*, Cambridge: Cambridge University Press.
Robins, R. H. (1988) 'Priscian and the context of his age', in I. Rosier (ed.), *L'heritage des grammairiens latins de l'Antiquité aux Lumières*, Paris: Société pour l'Information Grammaticale.
Percival, W. K. (1987) 'On Priscian's syntactic theory: the medieval perspective', in H. Aarsleff, L. G. Kelly and H.-J.Niederehe (eds), *Papers in the History of Linguistics: Proceedings of the Third International Conference on the History of the Language Sciences (ICHoLS III)*, Princeton, 19–23 August 1984, Philadelphia, PA: John Benjamins.
Taylor, D. J. (1996) 'Roman language science', in P. Schmitter (ed.), *Sprachtheorien der abendländischen Antike*, Tübingen: Gunter Narr.

SĪBAWAYHI (d. *c.* 796)

Like **Pāṇini**, Sībawayhi is recognized as the author of a single, extraordinary text that stands at the head of a major grammatical tradition. Sībawayhi was Persian, a second-language learner of Arabic, and the son of a convert to Islam, who lived in what is now Iraq. He wrote a grammar of Arabic that goes by the name of *al-Kitāb* (*The Book*) and that has stood since the eighth century as the foundation of Arabic language studies. The *Kitāb* presents a comprehensive description of the classical language, as attested in the Qur'ān and in pre-Islamic poetry, and most importantly as attested in the speech of Bedouin desert nomads, whose language was considered uncontaminated by urban multilingualism.

Carter (2004: 7) emphasized the importance of attending to medieval Islamic grammarians' biographical details, sketchy and questionable as they may be, on the grounds that, in this tradition, scholarship 'is strongly linked to the personality and ethics of the individual, for knowledge is more than the property of the immediate community— it belongs to all subsequent generations'. About the life and character of Sībawayhi, a mass of variously credible lore exists. Some say that in Persian, the pseudonym 'Sībawayhi' means 'smell of apples', on account of his sweet breath (Versteegh 1997: 39). Most sources report that as a young man he travelled from the countryside to the city of Basra to study Islamic law, but abandoned law for grammar after being publicly humiliated for his non-native-speaker's errors in Arabic. Sībawayhi probably then became a student of the prominent scholar al-Khalīl ibn 'Aḥmad al-Farāhīdī (d. 791), whose contributions to lexicography and metrics arguably place him second only to Sībawayhi among Arabic grammarians. Eventually, Sībawayhi conceived and wrote the Kitāb, on which his reputation rests, while teaching a few students and participating in lively give-and-take with other grammarians in Basra and the capital Baghdad. Sībawayhi is conventionally portrayed as something of an inept genius – an ethnic outsider, ill at ease in the spotlight, possibly a stutterer – but gifted with superb linguistic insight. That gift may have aroused antagonism among his peers, because his career famously closed as it began: with public humiliation when he failed a test, apparently rigged, of his judgement of grammatical minutiae (Blau 1963: 48). Sībawayhi withdrew to his rural homeland in shame, and died soon afterwards (Carter 2004: 10–16).

Although the Kitāb was written in a cultural context that highly valued the study of grammar, it has no real precedent. Sībawayhi's object was to describe the syntax, morphology and phonology of a variety of Arabic for the benefit of second-language or second-dialect learners. Even though the prestige of Bedouin Arabic derived from its association with the language of the Qur'ān, and even though Sībawayhi also relied on the Qur'ān and on traditional poetry for data, he prioritized natural speech over the conventions of written texts. It is noteworthy, for example, that he accepted as legitimate a range of dialectal differences among Bedouin Arabic speakers (Levin 1994).

The Kitāb is very long and detailed, 571 chapters comprising more than 900 pages in Derenbourg's (1881–98/1970) edition. It opens and closes abruptly, without introductory or concluding fanfare. However, Sībawayhi's numerous cross-references make it clear that he was self-consciously creating a book rather than amassing a collection of notes. The first section, separable from the rest of the text as the Risāla (Epistle), is divided into seven chapters on various topics. This material is unusual in the context of the book in that Sībawayhi cites no other grammarians, suggesting that the *Risāla* may present what he considered his own contributions.

A first chapter distinguishes three basic parts of speech: nouns; verbs (sometimes translated as 'operations'), which indicate what is past, future or ongoing; and 'particles', which are neither nouns nor verbs, including (as later becomes clear) both individual uninflected forms and whole phrases. Sībawayhi then introduces a distinction between vowels that are intrinsic to words, and vowels inserted into words, for example by declensional marking. In Arabic, many words can be analysed into abstract, meaning-bearing roots, usually consisting of sequences of three radical consonants. Roots are inflected variously by infixation of particular vowels in particular patterns. The classic example is the root 'k–t–b', the basis for many words related to writing. Infixation of specific sequences of vowels (sometimes along with auxiliary consonants marking the application of other morphological processes) generates a family of words: *kitāb* 'book', *kataba* 'he wrote', *yaktubu* 'he writes', *yuktibu* 'to dictate', *maktaba* 'library', *kutayyib* 'booklet', etc. These features of Arabic had already been recognized in Sībawayhi's day. For example, al-Khalīl's lexicography organized words first by root, and second by the place of articulation of the initial radical from back to front, so that words generated from the root 'k–t–b' (where the first radical is velar *k*) precede words generated from the root 'b–t–k' (where the first radical is labial *b*), etc. What Sībawayhi added was the observation that vowels inserted into a root have a different linguistic status from vowels that are inherently part of indeclinable lexical items: the final *u* in *yaktubu* 'he writes' marks nominative case, whereas the *u* in *qablu* 'before' is simply intrinsic to the word. Versteegh (1997: 45) called this insight Sībawayhi's 'most essential innovation'.

Another distinctive contribution of the *Risāla* appears in a chapter 'On rightness and wrongness of speech', which introduces two independent axes of correctness, semantic and structural. For Sībawayhi, utterances are not only semantically 'right', or 'not right' (meaningful, but not in accord with the speaker's intent), or 'wrong' (nonsensical); but are also more or less structurally 'good' (well formed), or 'bad' (ill formed). Carter (2004: 61–65) considered these 'ethical criteria' for evaluating the correctness of speech to be a residue of Sībawayhi's early training in law. Moreover, because the rightness of speech reflects in part a speaker's capacity for meaningful exchange with a listener, this passage indicates that Sībawayhi was concerned with communication, not simply with whether an utterance obeyed a static set of prescribed rules.

In this way, the *Kitāb* opens with a number of claims, both theoretical and language-specific, that display some of Sībawayhi's
assumptions. Three major sections follow the *Risāla*. Their order –
syntax; morphology; phonetics/phonology – inverted the traditional
organization of western grammars, projecting as it did from a belief
that one can understand smaller units of language only after having
analysed larger units.

In Sībawayhi's exposition of Arabic syntax, two important notions
are ''amal* and *'qiyās'*. *'Amal* is sometimes translated as 'operation', or
perhaps less accurately 'government', as it names the action of one
word affecting the form of another, passive word. In the classic case,
'amal is responsible for nouns assuming a variety of cases in different
environments, and for imperfect verbs taking various endings for
mood. Carter (1973) emphasized the binary relationships that *'amal*
sets up, joining together pairs of affecting and affected elements in
such operations as negation, conjunction or substitution. Moreover,
in addition to words operating on other words, the relationship of
'amal can be abstract in the sense that an utterance can exhibit its
effect in the absence of any phonetically present operating ('governing'?)
element. The abstractness of *'amal* is one of various points developed
by Arabic grammarians who followed Sībawayhi (Bohas *et al.* 1990:
57–63).

The notion of *qiyās*, roughly 'analogy', likewise surfaces in the
Kitāb and in much subsequent Arabic grammatical literature. For
Sībawayhi, *qiyās* was a method for locating generalizations about
language. That is to say, starting with patterns and analogies he
observed in language data – and working through the difficulties of
defining what constitutes an adequate analogy – he aimed to identify
principles that account for the structure of Arabic. Sībawayhi rejected
another potential application of *qiyās*, the deductive creation of novel
utterances on the basis of their presumed analogy to attested data.
Instead, he deferred to the judgement of his sources, particularly
Bedouin Arabic speakers.

In addition to the role of *qiyās* in Sībawayhi's exposition of syntax,
it was naturally an important tool in his work on morphology, granted that the rich sublexical stratum of Arabic provides many opportunities for the exercise of analogy as a discovery procedure. The
Kitāb investigates many morphological and morphophonemic processes and principles that bear on the complex patterning of Arabic
roots and affixes, including for example the famous matters of 'hollow
verbs' (wherein the middle radical of a triliteral root is deleted) and
'broken plurals' (which involve ablaut).

In a final, thirty-page section on the sound system, Sībawayhi addressed the phonetic properties of Arabic, giving careful descriptions of sixteen places of articulation. Features that are subsumed by western linguistics under manner of articulation and voicing, he represented through a system of contrasts using terms such as 'sonorous' versus 'muffled', 'tight' versus 'slack', and 'covered with a lid' (presumably 'velarized'; Carter 2004: 127). The *Kitāb* ends with Sībawayhi's observations about the phonology of Arabic, including context-specific lowering of vowels, elision of consonants, and assimilation of adjacent sounds that share articulatory features.

Whether or not the story of Sībawayhi's final public humiliation is true, it sets a context for the reception of the *Kitāb*. The scene of the notorious test was Baghdad, but the grammarians who opposed Sībawayhi were from Kufa, a city to the south on the Euphrates, northwest of Basra. In some accounts of the history of Arabic language studies, a rivalry broke out between Kufan and Basran schools of grammar in the ninth century (Owens 1990: 203–19). (Some add a third, Baghdadian school.) At first, Kufa seemed ascendant, spreading a somewhat different grammatical vocabulary and a more liberal invocation of *qiyās* to generate possible, if unattested, linguistic examples. But eventually the Basran school triumphed, insisting that grammar be built on actual observed data. Taking the *Kitāb* as their masterpiece, generations of Basran grammarians created commentaries on Sībawayhi's work, developing, augmenting, illustrating, and sometimes criticizing his terms and concepts. Eventually, this work became the touchstone of Arabic linguistics in general.

Notwithstanding Sībawayhi's personal fate, the *Kitāb* is honoured to this day for its subtlety and comprehensiveness as 'the Qur'ān of grammar'. Evidence for the finesse of Sībawayhi's ear and the accuracy of his analysis is still being amassed. Levin (1994: 218–20) noted that exceptions to a process of conditioned fronting and raising of medial *ā*, exceptions first recorded in the *Kitāb* twelve centuries ago for a subset of speakers, can be heard today in certain Iraqi, Anatolian and Syrian dialects of Arabic.

Bibliography

The most readily available edition of the *Kitāb* is that of Derenbourg (1881–98/1970). No complete English translation exists, although Versteegh (1997: 36–38) rendered the first two chapters into English, and Troupeau (1973–74) all of the *Risāla* into French. De Sacy (1829: 361–407) published some excerpts in French, alongside samples of commentaries on Sībawayhi's text. Jahn (1895–1900/1969) provided a complete translation into German, the accuracy of which has been criticized.

Further reading

Blau, J. (1963) 'The role of the Bedouins as arbiters in linguistic questions and the *mas'ala az-zunburiyya*', *Journal of Semitic Studies*, 8, 42–51.
Bohas, G., Guillaume, J.-P. and Kouloughli, D. E. (1990) *The Arabic Linguistic Tradition*, London and New York: Routledge.
Carter, M. G. (1973) 'An Arab grammarian of the eighth century A.D.: a contribution to the history of linguistics', *Journal of the American Oriental Society*, 93, 146–57.
——(2004) *Sībawayhi*, London and New York: I.B. Tauris.
Derenbourg, H. (1881–98) *Le livre de Sībawaihi. Traité de grammaire arabe: Vols 1–2*, Paris: Imprimerie Nationale (repr. 1970, Hildesheim: Georg Olms).
Jahn, G. (1895–1900) *Sībawaihis Buch über die Grammatik übersetzt und erklärt: Bd. 1–3*, Berlin: Reuther & Reichard (repr. 1969, Hildesheim: Georg Olms).
Levin, A. (1994) 'Sībawayhi's attitude to the spoken language', *Jerusalem Studies in Arabic and Islam*, 17, 204–43.
Owens, J. (1990) *Early Arabic Grammatical Theory: Heterogeneity and Standardization*, Philadelphia, PA: John Benjamins.
de Sacy, S. (1829) *Anthologie grammaticale arabe*, Paris: Imprimerie Royale.
Troupeau, G. (1973–74) 'La *Risālat al-Kitāb* de Sībawayhi', *Mélanges de l'Université Saint-Joseph*, 40, 323–38.
Versteegh, K. (1997) *Landmarks in Linguistic Thought: Vol. III. The Arabic Linguistic Tradition*, London: Routledge.

'THE FIRST GRAMMARIAN' (TWELFTH CENTURY)

'The First Grammarian' is a name traditionally applied to the author of an anonymous, untitled Icelandic text written in Old Norse and known as the 'First Grammatical Treatise' (FGT). Textual evidence indicates that it was probably composed between 1125 and 1175 CE. The topic of FGT is the writing system of Icelandic. In seven dense manuscript pages, the First Grammarian proposes and justifies specific reforms of the then-contemporary Latin-based orthography of Icelandic, and along the way reveals his conceptualization of the sound properties of the language. Despite its apparently narrow compass, the FGT is noteworthy in the history of linguistics for a number of reasons. It is a valuable source of data in Germanic paleography and philology (Benediktsson 1972: 108–88). It augments our understanding of the medieval European grammatical tradition, with which the First Grammarian was clearly acquainted and which he applied ingeniously to Icelandic (Law 2003: 199–201). It has been presented as precociously anticipating key concepts and methods of twentieth-century phonology; but such precursorist readings of the FGT have been challenged on grounds that raise important linguistic–historiographical issues. As a result, the First Grammarian's brief, modest text casts a remarkably long shadow, falling across varied domains in the study of language.

The name 'First Grammatical Treatise' calls for explanation. It derives from the fact that the text is positioned as the first of four independent grammatical expositions that, together with a preface, are included in a mid-fourteenth-century manuscript known as the 'Codex Wormianus' (which also includes the *Prose Edda*, a famous collection of Norse mythology and instructions for poets). The Codex Wormianus is named for the Danish physician, natural philosopher and collector of curiosities Ole Worm (1588–1654), who once possessed the manuscript and had it cleaned. The text of the FGT contains scribal errors that indicate that the Codex Wormianus version (which is our only source of the FGT) is a copy and not the original; that copy also shows the scribe occasionally substituting mid-fourteenth-century Icelandic for the Old Norse in which the First Grammarian presumably wrote. Following the FGT in the Codex Wormianus are the similarly untitled Second, Third and Fourth Grammatical Treatises, copied by the same hand but apparently composed by different authors subsequent to the FGT. Only the First and Fourth are preserved uniquely in the Codex Wormianus, and only the FGT has been extensively examined by modern scholars (cf. Hovdhaugen 1987: 73–76).

The identity of the First Grammarian is a matter of speculation; Benediktsson (1972: 201–3) cites about ten candidates. Regardless of who the author was, we can deduce something about his background from the text itself (*ibid.*: 22–33; 189–201). It is clear that he was familiar with the Latin pedagogical grammars of **Aelius Donatus** and **Priscian of Caesarea**, in addition to certain commentaries on those works that were part of *grammatica*-based medieval education. The text refers to facts about Irish, Hebrew, English and Greek, but without necessarily implicating the author's first-hand foreign-language competence (except, arguably, for English; Haugen 1950/1972: 74–75). The First Grammarian was not attuned to the theoretical concerns of the **Speculative Grammarians**, who were approaching their heyday in Paris when the FGT was probably written. The proposed date of composition for the FGT in the mid-twelfth century is determined on the basis of sketchy internal evidence (style, spelling, scant references to other scholars or to datable cultural artefacts) and even sketchier external evidence, granted the apparent failure of the First Grammarian's orthographic reform initiatives.

That is what we can glean about the author of the FGT. We know little more about the history of the text. The Danish scholar Rasmus Rask (1787–1832), on whose work **Jacob Grimm** built, published the contents of the Codex Wormianus in 1818. An 1848 edition by another scholar was the first to separate the relevant section into a preface plus the first, second, third and fourth treatises (Benediktsson 1972: 14–15). For the next hundred years, the FGT remained part of the specialist literature in Germanic philology. Then, in 1950, the Norwegian-American linguist Einar Haugen (1906–94), remembered for his research on Scandinavian languages, bilingualism and language planning, and for his contributions to post-Bloomfieldian linguistics, published a translation of the FGT with commentary that highlighted what he perceived as its parallels in modern phonological theory.

Haugen's (1950) edition, revised in 1972, stimulated other editions, translations and commentaries. Some followed Haugen's lead (e.g. Benediktsson 1961, 1972; Einarsson 1953); others contested Haugen's reading of the FGT (e.g. Albano Leoni 1975; Perridon 1985; Markey 1998). The boom in FGT studies drew the attention of historiographers, some of whom have objected to Haugen's interpretation of FGT as anachronistic (Ulvestad 1976; Koerner 1997).

At the base of this controversy is the text itself. The First Grammarian's goal was straightforward: to persuade readers – presumably scholars, not students – to adopt new orthographic standards for writing Old Norse. The text falls into three unmarked subsections by topic: short introductory remarks, and then separate analyses of the spelling of vowels and of consonants. Haugen depicts the style of the original as 'rambling' interspersed with 'vivid and homespun' examples (Haugen 1950/1972: 10; 6); in translation, the First Grammarian presents a well organized and disarmingly earnest case for reform. The author shows common sense in anticipating and countering readers' objections, and thoughtfully (sometimes playfully) illustrates his proposals.

The FGT begins by motivating the legitimacy of reform, observing that different languages employ different letters. English uses Latin orthography, but removes some letters and adds others to fit the profile of English. Tailoring the Latin orthography to Icelandic requires adding vowels and revising the inventory of consonants. The First

Grammarian noted that vowels differ from consonants because consonants cannot be named or pronounced alone without a supporting vowel. Therefore vowels are more basic, and he addressed them first. Latin *a*, *e*, *i*, *o* and *u* are insufficient for Icelandic; four new symbols are needed, each associated with a sound 'spoken with the mouth more [or less] open' relative to specific other vowels (trans. Haugen 1950/1972: 15). The First Grammarian then claimed it was necessary to 'split off from these nine vowels thirty-six distinctions, each of which changes the meaning if they are precisely distinguished', because each of the nine can also be 'spoken in the nose', and can be either long or short (*ibid.*: 15, 17). The author illustrated that nasality and length vary independently by embedding words that instantiated those distinctions in invented sentences to show that nasality and length contrast. For example, he marked nasalized vowels with a superscript dot, then cited the sentence: '*Hair* (*har*) grows on living creatures, but the *shark* (*hår*) is a fish' (*ibid.*: 17).

This first substantive section ends with remarks about the pronunciation of two adjacent vowels, then moves to consonants. The First Grammarian proposed to rename consonants whose conventional names did not reveal their pronunciation. Moreover, 'so that the writing may be less and quicker, and the parchment last the longer' (*ibid.*: 25), he proposed substituting a single small upper-case letter for geminate consonants (B for *bb*, F for *ff*, etc.). Among other innovations, he introduced a new character to represent the 'friendly union' of *n* and *g*, because '*n* which comes before a following *g* in the same syllable is spoken less in the nose and more in the throat than other *n*'s' (*ibid.*: 27). He admitted þ without distinguishing voiced ð from voiceless θ (which, in modern terms, were allophones in Old Norse), but dispensed with *k* and *q* in favour of *c*, on the grounds that *k* and *q* marked no distinctive sound (*ibid.*: 25).

No-one disputes that the FGT is perceptive and ingenious. But some modern readers go further: 'the principles of analysis which the author applies are fundamentally the same as those of modern phonemics, so that the treatise may be said to bear a greater resemblance, in methodology, to linguistics in the 20th century than in any other period' (Benediktsson 1961: 237). The warrant for this claim is varied. Some perceived parallels are – as Benediktsson states – methodological. For example, the First Grammarian seemed to anticipate the modern technique of establishing meaningful distinctions by citing minimal pairs: he argued for expanding the orthographic inventory of vowels because of contrasts like *har* (hair)/*hår* (shark), where the latter has a nasal vowel. He assembled multiples like *sar*, *sǫr*, *ser*, *sęr*, *sor*, *sør* (where the novel nuclei mark what we now recognize as the effect of umlaut), emphasizing that each distinctive vowel 'supported by the same letters and placed in the same position, makes a different sense, and in this way give examples ... of the most delicate distinctions' (trans. Haugen 1950/1972: 17).

Another perceived parallel between the FGT and modern phonology goes beyond the normal scope of methodology. Essential to the First Grammarian's exposition is the term *'stafr'* (Benediktsson 1972: 42ff). *Stafr* is usually translated as 'letter', and identified with the medieval concept of *'littera'*, which in the Latin grammatical tradition Donatus defined as the smallest element of articulated sound. *Littera* is comprised of three qualities: *nomen* 'name', *figura* 'shape', and *potestas* 'power'. Likewise, the First Grammarian analyses *stafr* into a triad of attributes variously translated as 'name'; 'shape'/'letter'/'appearance'; and 'speech value'/'sound'. Both Haugen (1950/1972: 53) and Benediktsson (1972: 45–50) make the case that in the FGT *stafr* is an abstraction, an emergent notion of the concept of phoneme. They point out that the author's criterion for identifying a *stafr* isn't purely phonetic, since he employed *þ* for both [ð] and [θ]; rather, he relied on evidence that a sound 'changes the meaning' (Haugen 1950/1972: 17; sometimes translated as 'changes the discourse'; *ibid.*: 52) in the way that nasalization of the vowel distinguishes *har* from *hàr*.

Not all modern readers have found these parallels persuasive. Ulvestad (1976), building on Albano Leoni's (1975) dissenting edition of the FGT, pointed out that precursorist exegeses balance on terms translated as 'distinction' and 'change the discourse/meaning'. According to Ulvestad, those translations misrepresent the FGT and exaggerate its resemblance to modern linguistics. Koerner (1997: 228) similarly rejected the FGT as an antecedent to contemporary phonology: 'modern scholars have been misled in their assessment ... probably because they could not or did not divest themselves of their own twentieth-century structuralist background', and as a result they have 'misread, distorted, or at least overinterpreted' a medieval manuscript that has humbler aims than Haugen and Benediktsson recognize. Koerner conceded that the general 'temptation to read modern-day concerns and notions into [older] texts' is a danger that 'every serious historian of linguistics has struggled with' (*ibid.*: 233–34). It is easier to pick out what appears familiar in a medieval text than it is to discern implicit assumptions that separate it from twenty-first-century language science. But to abandon that struggle risks missing opportunities to experience how truly different a different intellectual culture can be.

The orthographic reforms that the First Grammarian proposed were largely unsuccessful. Even the FGT itself does not employ the revised spelling it advocates, except in examples cited by the author, and there only irregularly. However, the FGT has contributed to the history of the language sciences in ways that transcended its author's goals.

Editions of the 'First Grammatical Treatise'

Snorra-Edda ásmat skáldu og þarmeð fylgjandi Ritgjörðum, 1818 (R. Rask, ed.), Elmén, Stockholm.

First Grammatical Treatise: The Earliest Germanic Phonology. An Edition, Translation and Commentary, 1950 (E. Haugen, ed.), Language Monograph 25 (revised 2nd edn 1972, Longman).

The First Grammatical Treatise: Introduction, Text, Notes, Translation, Vocabulary, Facsimilies, 1972 (H. Benediktsson, ed.), University of Iceland Publications in Linguistics 1, Institute of Nordic Linguistics, Reykjavík.

Il primo trattato grammaticale islandese, introduzione, testo, traduzione e commento, 1975 (F. Albano Leoni, ed.), Il Mulino, Bologna.

Further reading

Benediktsson, H. (1961) 'The earliest Germanic phonology', *Lingua*, 10, 237–54.

Einarsson, S. (1953) Review of *First Grammatical Treatise: The Earliest Germanic Phonology*, E. Haugen, ed., *Journal of English and Germanic Philology*, 52, 570–71.

Hovdhaugen, E. (1987) 'The first vernacular grammars in Europe: The Scandinavian area', *Histoire Épistémologie Langage* 9, 73–89.

Koerner, E. F. K. (1997) 'Einar Haugen as a historian of linguistics', *American Journal of Germanic Linguistics and Literatures*, 9, 221–38.

Law, V. (2003) *The History of Linguistics in Europe: Plato to 1600*, Cambridge: Cambridge University Press.

Markey, T. (1998) 'Some thoughts on Konrad Koerner's "Einar Haugen as a historian of linguistics"', *American Journal of Germanic Linguistics and Literatures*, 10, 91–103.

Perridon, H. (1985) 'Neutralization, archiphonemes and the First Grammatical Treatise', *Amsterdamer Beiträge zur älteren Germanistik*, 23, 71–96.

Ulvestad, B. (1976) '*Grein sú er máli skiptir*: tools and tradition in the First Grammatical Treatise', *Historiographia Linguistica*, 3, 203–23.

THE SPECULATIVE GRAMMARIANS
(*fl. c.* 1250–1400)

From the mid-1200s until the early 1400s, scholars teaching at the medieval universities of Paris, Bologna and Erfurt (west of Leipzig) developed a distinctive approach to the study of language. Despite some heterogeneity of outlook among them, as a group these men, trained in logic, philosophy, theology, rhetoric and the classical grammatical tradition, have come to be called the 'Speculative Grammarians', using the term 'speculative' in the sense of 'theoretical'. The Speculative Grammarians' key contribution is that they redefined the study of grammar as an investigation into the general principles of language, rather than the features of any one tongue. Their work has also been cited as the first attempt in Europe to formulate a syntactic theory. Some of the most important names associated with Speculative Grammar are William of Conches (c. 1085–post-1154) and Peter Helias (c. 1100–post-1166) of France; Siger of Courtrai (c. 1280–1341) from Belgium; the Danes Boethius of Dacia (1240/50–post-1277) and Martin of Dacia (1250/60–1304); Robert Kilwardby (1215–79), who was the Archbishop of Canterbury; and Thomas of Erfurt (fl. 1300), whose origins are unclear. Generally, little is known about the lives of the Speculative Grammarians. Most were teachers, but as was typical for medieval scholars, many also held positions of religious authority. It was not uncommon for them to fall into disfavour with the church hierarchy at some point in their lives.

Until Speculative Grammar altered people's notions of what it meant to study language, *grammatica* was largely the analysis and memorization of Latin, using pedagogical texts descended from those by **Aelius Donatus** and **Priscian of Caesarea**. Students pored over lists of Latin vocabulary items, patterns for the conjugation and declension of words, and grammar rules. Capping these activities were exercises in which students inched over a text, identifying the properties and subclass memberships of words one by one. Then, starting in the 1100s, translations of the works of **Aristotle** and commentaries on Aristotle originally written in Arabic began to circulate, stimulating intellectual life in Europe in several ways. When Aristotle's *Posterior Analytics* and other works were rediscovered, scholars recognized that the study of language in traditional terms could never achieve the status of a science because, according to Aristotle, science inquired into general principles rather than simply collected and classified phenomena. The newly established medieval universities were committed to the pursuit of scientific and theoretical knowledge – that is, knowledge that led to universal and essential truths – and not mere practical knowledge. Therefore the study of grammar in this new context had to be reconceptualized as the study of whatever was essential, or universal, in language.

In order to discover what is essential or universal in language, a twenty-first-century scholar might begin by surveying many languages comparatively, asking 'What do all human languages seem to have in common?' But twelfth- and thirteenth-century scholars took a different approach. They considered that only the languages of scholarship (Greek, Latin, Hebrew) have the requisite fixity and regularity to serve as legitimate objects of study, and among them only Latin was widely known. Medieval scholars believed Latin to be the most highly developed language, a kind of archetype for all languages. Therefore they assumed they could discover what was essential to human languages by looking deeply into a single exemplar, namely Latin.

Speculative Grammarians searched for universal truths about language by writing commentaries, often in question-and-answer format, on grammatical treatises about Latin such as Priscian's sixth-century *Institutiones Grammaticae*. A typical such text started with a metagrammatical introduction, then launched into analysis of the *partes orationis* ('sentence constituents' or 'parts of speech') of Latin, followed by sections on morphology and on syntax. This much was conventional. But Speculative Grammarians – especially a group known as the Modistae, associated with the University of Paris, which included Martin of Dacia, Boethius of Dacia, Siger of Courtrai and Thomas of Erfurt – went on to assert what they determined to be the essential properties of language. For example, the Modistae treated the classical eight *partes orationis* as universal, even in the face of the awkward fact that Greek, but not Latin, has definite articles. This point is one of the few where they addressed actual cross-linguistic data (Covington 1984: 26–27). For the most part, the Modistae deduced universals of syntax and semantics from their assumption that language, thought and reality necessarily mirror each other. In the words of Boethius of Dacia, who wrote a commentary on Priscian's grammar around 1270, 'There is but one logic for all tongues, and hence also just one grammar' (trans. Henry 1980: 86).

The Modistae went on to develop complex theories of the relationships between words, concepts and the real-world objects that words signify (Pinborg 1982; Rosier 1983; Libera and Rosier 1992). Their trademark theoretical concept was that of the *modi significandi* (hence the name 'Modistae'), sometimes translated as 'modes of signifying', essentially those aspects of meaning that distinguish the different *partes orationis*. Boethius of Dacia famously illustrated the point by explaining that the concept of *dolor* 'pain' can be signified under a range of *modi significandi*: either as *dolor* 'pain'; *dolere* 'to feel pain';

dolenter 'painfully'; or *heu* 'alas' (i.e. 'ouch!') (trans. McDermott 1270/ 1980: 51). In addition, different *modi significandi* distinguish pronouns from nouns, common nouns from proper nouns, given names from family names, and so forth. The various modes derive indirectly from the properties of things in the world, so that (for example) the *modus* identifying nouns exists because substances exist. That derivation is indirect because our concept of substance mediates between words and things. Thus the Modistae accommodated the fact that we have nouns, such as 'nothingness', for which a concept exists without there being any real-world substance corresponding to 'nothingness'.

As the Modistae's penetration into the intricacies of grammar increased, they developed more and more complicated inventories of modes and classes of modes to account for the complex relationships they perceived between language, thought and reality (Bursill-Hall 1971). In addition, they defined syntactic principles that combined words in part according to their associated *modi significandi*. Modistic syntax is built up out of pairs of 'consignifying' words sensitive to such requirements as transitivity, government, the congruence of the words' *modi significandi*, and dependency relationships holding between agents and patients. The Modistae, and Speculative Grammarians in general, derived the universality of their syntactic principles by linking them to concepts in Aristotelian logic, such as the 'four causes' (four factors bearing on the make-up of things: material cause, out of which the thing arises; formal cause, the essence determining its creation; efficient cause, or productive force; and final cause, or purpose) and 'ten categories' (ten kinds of being a predicate can assert: substance, quantity, quality, relation, etc.). Aristotle's writings made it possible to take for granted the unity of grammar, thought and reality: because people's conceptions of the shared material world in his terms were taken to be the same, therefore it was assumed that grammar is necessarily the same across all languages. As the early or pre-modistic grammarian Magister Jordanus (*fl.* mid-1200s) wrote, 'Though words in and of themselves may not be the same for all people, nonetheless they are the same for all people with regard to the way they are put together and the meaning they convey' (trans. Covington 1984: 20).

Speculative Grammar thus grew out of the existing grammatical tradition, but turned language scholarship away from classification and pedagogy toward ontological issues and the articulation of universals. But as an increasingly elaborate superstructure of theoretical proposals grew up, a new generation of scholars criticized it as uneconomical and arcane. (Speculative Grammar developed alongside medieval

47

scholastic philosophy, which has long been parodied as arguing superfluously about angels and the heads of pins.) By the beginning of the fourteenth century, the English scholastic philosopher William of Ockham (*c.* 1285–*c.* 1347) and other scholars identified with the rise of medieval nominalism began to attack Speculative Grammar. Around 1330, the Averroist (one whose philosophy was influenced by the Muslim scholar Ibn Rushd [1126–98]). Johannes Aurifaber gave a series of public lectures in Erfurt aimed at debunking the claims of the Modistae. Critics dispensed with the *modi significandi* as unexplanatory, and rejected the unity of grammar, thought and reality on the grounds that mental language contains only aspects of meaning that bear on the truth value of a proposition, not purely formal features such as grammatical gender (Covington 1984: 121–26). Gradually, the glamour of Speculative Grammar faded. Grammarians returned to the work of transmitting the traditional analysis of Latin as a body of descriptive knowledge, the purpose of which was to ensure that subsequent generations had access to classical literature and scholarship.

Today, Speculative Grammar is most remembered as an early, ultimately unsuccessful, attempt to build a theory about what is universal in language within the intellectual context of the European Middle Ages. In the late 1960s, **Noam Chomsky**'s book *Cartesian Linguistics* identified the work of seventeenth-century French 'rationalist' grammarians **Claude Lancelot** and **Antoine Arnauld** as precursors to modern generative grammar. In response, reviewers such as Salmon (1969) pointed out that as early as the thirteenth century, the Speculative Grammarians had tried to define a universal grammar, thus attempting to accomplish some of the work that Chomsky attributed to scholars in the 1600s.

Howsoever one sees the outcome of this modern controversy, and despite the failure of the Speculative Grammarians' overall project, they contributed to western language science. Their writings developed and popularized the notion of the syntactic relationship of government (*regimen*), and their propensity to view grammatical relations in terms of agent/patient rather than subject/predicate roles influenced humanist grammars into the early Renaissance. Moreover, the Speculative Grammarians' conceptualization of what is essential and universal in human language was deeply shaped by their assumptions about the perfection of Latin, and about the self-evident irrefutability of Aristotle's logic. This fact serves as a useful reminder of how local cultural boundaries can limit our capacity to imagine even what we presuppose to be universal.

Bibliography

Modern editions and translations of the writings of Speculative Grammarians include: *Godfrey of Fontaine's Abridgement of Boethius of Dacia's* Modi significandi sive quaestiones super Priscianum maiorem, 1980 (A. C. Senape McDermott, ed. and trans., John Benjamins, Philadelphia, PA); *Quaestiones Alberti de Modis Significandi*, 1977 (L. G. Kelly, ed. and trans., John Benjamins, Philadelphia, PA); *Grammatica Speculativa of Thomas of Erfurt*, 1972 (G. L. Bursill-Hall, ed. and trans., Longman, London); 'Traduction d'un extrait de la syntaxe du traité *De Modus Significandi* de Martin de Dacie' (I. Rosier, *Archives et Documents de la Société d'Histoire et d'Epistémologie des Sciences du Langage*, 3, 1983, 59–99). Excerpts from the writings of Speculative Grammarians appear in *Notices et extraits de divers manuscrits latins pour servir à l'histoire des doctrines grammaticales au moyen âge*, 1868 (C. Thurot, ed., Imprimerie Impériale, Paris; repr. Frankfurt: Minerva, 1964).

Further reading

Bursill-Hall, G. L. (1971) *Speculative Grammars of the Middle Ages: The Doctrine of* Partes Orationis *of the Modistae*, The Hague: Mouton.

Chomsky, N. (1966) *Cartesian Linguistics*, New York: Harper & Row (3rd edn 2009, Cambridge University Press).

Covington, M. A. (1984) *Syntactic Theory in the High Middle Ages*, Cambridge: Cambridge University Press.

Henry, D. P. (1980) 'Two medieval critics of traditional grammar', *Historiographia Linguistica*, 7, 85–107.

Libera, A. de, and Rosier, I. (1992) 'La pensée linguistique médiévale', in S. Auroux (ed.), *Histoire des idées linguistiques: Vol. 2. Le développement de la grammaire occidentale*, Liège: Mardaga.

Pinborg, J. (1982) 'Speculative grammar', in N. Kretzmann, A. Kenny and J. Pinborg (eds), *The Cambridge History of Later Medieval Philosophy: From the Rediscovery of Aristotle to the Disintegration of Scholasticism 1100–1600*, Cambridge: Cambridge University Press.

Rosier, I. (1983) *La grammaire spéculative des Modistes*, Lille: Presses Universitaires de Lille.

Salmon, V. (1969) 'Pre-Cartesian linguistics', *Journal of Linguistics*, 5, 165–87.

KING SEJONG THE GREAT (1397–1450)

King Sejong (also 'Seycong', 'Seijong') was the much celebrated fourth monarch of the Joseon, or Yi, dynasty of Korea, traditionally dated from 1392 to (in some accounts) Japan's annexation of Korea in

1910. Sejong's reign (1418–50) is depicted as a progressive era during which a self-confident, neo-Confucian civil and military bureaucracy ruled an agricultural society. Sejong was an intellectually gifted, hands-on king. He promoted cultural, scientific and technological advances. His consummate achievement was the invention of the Korean alphabet now known as *hangeul* (also '*hankul*', '*han'gŭl*'). *Hangeul* is a marvel among the world's writing systems, an orthography of 'rarified elegance and mathematical consistency' (Ramsey 1992: 50). Controversial during Sejong's day, *hangeul* has displaced other writing practices as the officially sanctioned orthography of both North and South Korea, granted certain usage differences between north and south, and granted certain modifications to accommodate 550 years of language change. In addition to its felicitous linguistic design, and its specific value to Korean speech communities, *hangeul* contributes to the general study of language by disrupting eurocentric assumptions about the nature of writing systems.

One unusual facet of *hangeul* is that it emerged fully developed, without local precedent, from an identifiable source. Tradition attributes full responsibility to Sejong: he created *hangeul* in the twenty-fifth year of his reign, spent three years refining it, then promulgated it publicly on 9 October 1446 (King Seijong Memorial Society 1970: 61). In modern times, the unique authorship of *hangeul* by Sejong is disputed (Lee 1997; Yeon 2008). Whether Sejong (alone or not) relied on an external model, and if so, whether that model was Mongolian '*Phags-pa* or one of the Indic scripts brought to Korea with Buddhism, is also debated (Ledyard 1966/1998).

Less controversial is that Sejong exceeded his duty as a monarch and model of neo-Confucian virtue in applying his talents to the country's practical problems. Ascending the throne at age twenty-one, he reduced the threat of Japanese piracy and strengthened Korea's borders against Manchuria. He reorganized the *Jiphyeonjeon* ('Hall of Worthies'), a kind of fifteenth-century royal think-tank that assembled the country's brightest and most enterprising young scholars. In addition to serving as advisors, the *Jiphyeonjeon* compiled texts on topics such as geography ('Geographical Descriptions of the Eight Provinces'), pharmaceuticals ('The Great Collection of Native Korean Prescriptions'), and agriculture ('Straight Talk on Farming') (Hejtmanek 1992: 24). Sejong and his advisors also patronized the arts, reformed court music, rationalized tax and penal codes, publicized examples of moral behaviour, and introduced technological innovations, including rain gauges, water clocks, sundials and improved printing techniques.

Sejong's innovations in printing and his invention of *hangeul* demonstrate his concern with spreading literacy. Fifteenth-century Korean scholars already had at their disposal two scripts derived from Chinese orthographic tradition. Chinese characters, however, are an unpromising foundation for writing Korean because of the vast typological differences between Chinese (an isolating, SVO, Sino-Tibetan tone language with highly constrained syllable structures) and Middle Korean (an agglutinative, morphophonemically elaborate, SOV language, probably Altaic, with complex syllables and vowel harmony). Nevertheless, China's long-sustained cultural dominance as East Asia's 'Middle Kingdom' invested Chinese orthography with irresistible prestige. In Sejong's day, the *Jiphyeonjeon* and dynastic historians employed a writing system called *idu* ('clerk readings'), based on Chinese (Ledyard 1966/1998: 31–83). Texts written in *idu* represented Korean lexical stems (nouns and verbal nuclei) with translation equivalents in Chinese characters. The inflectional elements and grammatical particles of Korean were represented by matching each one to a Chinese character perceived as having similar sound properties, regardless of the character's meaning. To render texts written in Chinese interpretable in Korean, another technique developed. Scholars abbreviated Chinese characters to create elements called *gugyeol*, reducing their graphic complexity and disassociating them from their meanings. *Gugyeol* were interpolated into the sequence of characters in a Chinese text to represent the inflectional or functional elements essential to Korean, making it possible to read Chinese in Korean.

Idu and *gugyeol* made writing and reading highly complex, specialized skills. Korean scribes shared their experience with the Japanese, who faced parallel problems in adapting Chinese orthography to their own highly inflected, agglutinative language. Japanese scribes developed analogies to Korean *idu* and *gugyeol*, then went on to create a syllabary, a set of 48 symbols that represent minimal Japanese syllables. Cultural, historical and linguistic factors led the Japanese to continue complexifying their orthographic practices beyond what they learned from Koreans, while remaining tethered to the prestigious but uncongenial Chinese model. The result is a multi-layered system of stunning intricacy, the mastery of which poses formidable cognitive challenges.

In fifteenth-century Korea, however, King Sejong took a different path. Recognizing that mastering *idu* and *gugyeol* required a commitment that exceeded what could be expected of the general population, Sejong created *hunminjeongeum* ('the correct sounds for the instruction of the people'; also *hunmin chŏng'ŭm*) – later renamed *hangeul* ('Korean [or "great"] script') by linguist Chu Sigyŏng (1876–1914) (Kim-Renaud 1997a: 1). Sejong introduced his invention of *hangeul* thus:

> The sounds of our country's language are different from those of the Middle Kingdom and are not smoothly adaptable to those of Chinese characters. Therefore, among the simple people, there are many who have something they wish to put into words but are never able to express their feelings. I am distressed by this, and have newly designed twenty-eight letters. I desire only that everyone practice them at their leisure and make them convenient for daily use.
>
> (trans. Ledyard 1966/1998: 277)

Sejong's original design for the twenty-eight letters used sparse, stiff lines juxtaposed symmetrically, favouring right angles. Later, their shapes were adapted to the dynamics of brush-writing. *Hangeul* forms a true alphabet, not a Japanese-style syllabary, because individual symbols represent separate vowels or consonants. However, individual letters are assembled into blocks that constitute syllables. For example, the syllable '*nim*' is comprised of independent symbols for *n*, *i* and *m*, integrated around the vowel nucleus into a visually coherent rectangular unit, parsed from left to right and top to bottom (with successive syllable blocks arrayed in columns, *right to left* and top to bottom). By synthesizing individual phonemes into syllable blocks, then assembling syllables into words, *hangeul* resolves the stream of speech into units at multiple levels. With this, *hangeul* represents psycholinguistic reality more richly than Chinese or Japanese orthographic traditions. Moreover, Middle Korean was a pitch-accent language; *hangeul* records the High, Low or Rising tone of each syllable by the placement of a dot within the margins of the syllable block. This captures another facet of the sound properties of language uninstantiated in Chinese or Japanese (King 1996).

Sejong distinguished vowels from consonants. He defined the inventory of vowels using three cosmologically salient symbols: a dot standing for heaven, associated with the Chinese concept of *yang* 'bright/heavy'; a horizontal line for earth, associated with *yin* 'dark/lightweight'; a vertical line for man, who stands between heaven and earth. *Hangeul* vowels strategically juxtapose these three elements with reference to the categories of vowel harmony. In Middle Korean, the vowels in an inflection or particle attached to a root must harmonize with the character of the root vowel. Sejong therefore divided the vowels into two subclasses. *Yang* vowels – *o*, *a*, *ʌ* – pattern together harmonically. The fact that they form a set is signalled by the appearance of a heavenly dot either below an earthly horizontal line, or left of a vertical line standing for man, somewhere inside their specific graphic shape. *Yin* vowels – *u*, *ə*, *i* – likewise form a harmonic set, which is signalled by the appearance of a heavenly dot either above an earthly horizontal, or right of a vertical standing for man. In this way, a vowel's shape encodes information about its harmonic subclass membership. *Hangeul* diphthongs and vowel-plus-glide constructions likewise respect phonological patterning. They also graphically register fine phonetic perceptions according to Korean cosmological semiotics (Kim-Renaud 1997b: 170–75).

Sejong's treatment of the consonants shows familiarity with Chinese phonological theory alongside original analysis of the sound properties of Korean. He cross-classified *hangeul* consonants according to place of articulation and 'strength' (Ledyard 1966/1998: 209–32). Roughly, there are five places of articulation: molar (dorsal or velar); lingual (apical); labial; incisor (dental); and laryngeal. 'Strength' has four values: 'wholly clear' (tense, unaspirated stops); 'partly clear' (tense, aspirated stops); 'wholly eluvial' (lax, preglottalized stops); and 'neither clear nor eluvial' (nasals; *h*, *l*, *z*). Voicing is not distinguished. Not every cell in the implied 5 × 4 matrix is filled in, and certain data require additional subclassification. Incomplete historical knowledge hampers our full reconstruction of Middle Korean phonetics. But Sejong's phonological analysis is remarkably cogent. What is more remarkable is that *hangeul* reveals refined phonetic and articulatory insight. Sejong invested wholly clear consonants with default status. Adding a strategically placed single horizontal stroke to a 'wholly clear' consonant such as *k* yields a parallel 'partly clear', aspirated consonant, *kʰ*. Doubling the shape of *k* yields the 'wholly eluvial', preglottalized consonant *k'*. In this way, the shapes of *hangeul* reveal their phonetic relationships across different values for strength, while holding place of articulation constant.

But perhaps the most remarkable fact about *hangeul* was not recognized until 1940. In that year, a long-lost essay by Sejong's *Jiphyeonjeon*, entitled *Hunminjeongeum Haerye* (*Explanations and examples of the correct sounds for the instruction of the people*), was rediscovered. This text indicates that *hangeul* consonant shapes are deliberately iconic: the symbol for 'molar' (velar) *k* is a miniature diagram of the base of the tongue in contact with the velum; 'incisor' (dental) *s* illustrates a raised tongue tip; labial *p* depicts rounded lips, etc.

Sampson (1985) labels *hangeul* a 'featural' orthography, which analyses the elements of speech at the level of features such as place of articulation, aspiration and tone, then synthesizes features into phonemes, and phonemes into syllables. Moreover, a consonant's shape graphically illustrates its articulatory basis, uniquely synthesizing form and meaning.

In Sejong's century, *hangeul* met intransigent opposition from scribes who felt it threatened their cultural hegemony (Lee 1997). Eventually, the ingenuity of the system won the day, although even modern writers mix *hangeul* with Chinese characters in some contexts. The Republic of Korea commemorates Sejong's invention annually on 9 October, Hangeul Day.

British linguist Roy Harris (b. 1931) has written extensively about the linguistics of writing systems across time. From **Aristotle** or earlier, the notion that writing represents speech runs through western language study; Harris (1986: 29–56) shows that **Ferdinand de Saussure**, **Leonard Bloomfield**, **Ludwig Wittgenstein** and many others take for granted that writing visibly records (idealized) speech. To Harris, this assumption devalues orthography as a source of insight into language. It also leads to the 'tyranny of the alphabet', one aspect of which is the depreciation of non-alphabetic writing systems as underdeveloped relative to alphabetic systems.

Korean *hangeul*, however, does not record speech. Rather, it records the constituent features of speech. Moreover, its iconic basis disrupts an alphabetic/non-alphabetic dichotomy insofar as the individual symbols non-arbitrarily represent articulatory gestures rather than (components of) sounds. For these reasons, *hangeul* deserves more attention in the study of orthography. Harris (2000: 137) equates unthinking prioritization of the alphabet to belief that 'the best kind of drawing of a jet of water must be one in which each droplet is separately shown'. *Hangeul* analyses jets of language into sub-droplet particles, wherein the shapes of particles are not accidental. In doing so it challenges eurocentric assumptions about writing and speech from outside western linguistic tradition.

Sejong's major works

The classic source in English for Sejong's linguistic work is G. K. Ledyard's 1966 University of California at Berkeley dissertation, *The Korean Language Reform of 1446* (1998, Singu Munhwasa, Seoul). An Appendix to Chapter 4 translates the *Hunminjeongeum* and *Hunminjeongeum Haerye*.

Further reading

Harris, R. (1986) *The Origin of Writing*, La Salle, IL: Open Court.
——(2000) *Rethinking Writing*, Bloomington, IN: Indiana University Press.
Hejtmanek, M. (1992) '*Chiphyŏnjŏn*', in Y.-K. Kim-Renaud (ed.), *King Sejong the Great: The Light of Fifteenth Century Korea*, Washington, DC: International Circle of Korean Linguistics.
Kim-Renaud, Y.-K. (ed.) (1997a) *The Korean Alphabet: Its History and Structure*, Honolulu: University of Hawai'i Press.
——(1997b) 'The phonological analysis reflected in the Korean writing system', in Y.-K. Kim-Renaud (ed.), *The Korean Alphabet: Its History and Structure*, Honolulu: University of Hawai'i Press.
——(ed.) (1992) *King Sejong the Great: The Light of Fifteenth Century Korea*, Washington, DC: International Circle of Korean Linguistics.
King, R. (1996) 'Korean writing', in P.T. Daniels and W. Bright (eds), *The World's Writing Systems*, Oxford: Oxford University Press.
King Seijong Memorial Society (1970) *King Seijong the Great: A Biography of Korea's Most Famous King*, Seoul: King Seijong Memorial Society.
Lee, K.-M. (1997) 'The inventor of the Korean alphabet', in Y.-K. Kim-Renaud (ed.), *The Korean Alphabet: Its History and Structure*, Honolulu: University of Hawai'i Press.
Ramsey, S. R. (1992) 'The Korean alphabet', in Y.-K. Kim-Renaud (ed.), *King Sejong the Great: The Light of Fifteenth Century Korea*, Washington, DC: International Circle of Korean Linguistics.
Sampson, G. (1985) *Writing Systems: A Linguistic Introduction*, Stanford, CA: Stanford University Press.
Yeon, J. (2008) 'Queries on the origin and the inventor of *Hunmin chŏngŭm*', *SOAS–AKS Working Papers in Korean Studies*, 1.

ANTOINE ARNAULD (1612–94) AND CLAUDE LANCELOT (1615–95)

Antoine Arnauld and Claude Lancelot surely could not have foreseen the reputation they would achieve in twenty-first-century language science. Both were devoted members of a religious community southwest of Paris known as Port-Royal, a community buffeted by sectarian and political strife in mid seventeenth-century counter-Reformation France (Sainte-Beuve 1840–59/2004). Arnauld attained high renown as a theologian, philosopher and ardent defender of their controversial Jansenist religious sect. Lancelot kept a lower profile as teacher and textbook-writer for the 'Little Schools' operated by the Port-Royal abbey for local children. Together, the two were responsible for creating the 1660 *General and Rational Grammar*, or 'Port-Royal grammar', addressed to young French-speaking foreign-language learners. Though hardly revolutionary, this and other Port-Royal textbooks introduced innovations that remained influential into the 1800s. Then – in words used to preface a 1975 translation into English – Arnauld and Lancelot's *Grammar* 'would slowly have fossilized into an item in the archeology of linguistic history had it not been generously summoned to the life of controversy as a declared ancestor of transformational grammar by Noam Chomsky' (Danto 1975: 11). Surely Arnauld and Lancelot would have been surprised that their *Grammar* attained this second life, three hundred years later.

Arnauld descended from a prominent family of soldiers and lawyers who had a history of conflict with the powerful and well connected religious order of Jesuits. The family were major supporters of a convent in Port-Royal associated with Jansenist reformers, who were inspired by the theology of Augustine of Hippo (354–430 CE) and Dutch theologian Cornelius Jansen (1585–1638). Jansenists attracted the bitter enmity of Jesuits on theological and political grounds. At the beginning of the eighteenth century, Jansenist positions on divine grace and free will were declared heretical, resulting in the forced disbandment of the Port-Royal community. But during Arnauld's prime, Jansenists were a major force: they attracted the support of some courtiers and of mathematician Blaise Pascal (1623–62), and they educated the future playwright Jean Racine (1639–99). Among participants in the Port-Royal community were most of Arnauld's nine older siblings (including a sister appointed abbess at age eleven), cousins, nieces, nephews, uncles, and even his widowed mother. Arnauld's greatest fame rests in his theological writings, but he also co-authored a Jansenist-inspired exposition of logic, which shares common ground with the *Grammar* and displays skills he acquired in his first career as a lawyer.

Arnauld's collaborator Lancelot came from a pious, unpretentious background. Lancelot studied under Jean du Vergier de Hauranne, the Abbot of Saint-Cyran (1581–1643), spiritual director of Port-Royal and friend of Cornelius Jansen. Later, Lancelot wrote an account (1663/2003) of his teacher Saint-Cyran, which is infused with the author's humility and guilelessness. Above all, Lancelot was a gifted teacher, especially of children. He wrote *A New Method for Learning with Facility the Latin Tongue* (1653/1816), and similar learner's grammars of Greek, Italian and Spanish. As he narrated in the Preface to the *General Grammar* (Arnauld and Lancelot 1660/1975: 39), that experience led him to puzzle over what is universal versus what is particular to certain languages. He consulted Arnauld, whose responses to his questions seemed so inspired that Lancelot recorded them in what became the *General and Rational Grammar*. The *Grammar* is revealingly subtitled 'Containing the foundations of the art of speaking explained in a clear and natural manner; The reasons for what is common to all languages, and for the principal differences among them; And several new remarks concerning the French language'. The book is at once a pedagogical grammar directed at explaining language as an 'art', a general grammar addressing what we now call language universals, a rational grammar that seeks the reasons for universals, and a particular grammar of French. It defines speaking as 'explaining one's thoughts by signs', then treats two aspects of signs: in Part 1, their 'sounds and [written] characters' and in Part 2, 'their signification' (*ibid.*: 41). Chapters I–V of Part 1 separately address vowels, consonants (including comparison of Latin and French versus Greek and Hebrew consonants), syllables, word stress, and sound–symbol correspondences. Chapter VI argues for introducing child learners first to the sounds associated with the letters of the alphabet, rather than their names. Part 2 opens with a chapter of meta-theoretical orientation, followed by twenty-two chapters addressing specific parts of speech, their subclasses (relative pronouns, impersonal verbs), and morphological features (gender, case). A final chapter comprises a few pages on syntax.

In the topics it covers, their order, and the amount of attention distributed across them, the *Grammar* follows tradition: sounds are not segregated from their orthographic representations, with this section appearing at the beginning; syntax is covered briefly, at the end; individual parts of speech are treated individually and in a sequence familiar since **Aelius Donatus**' *Ars Minor*. Moreover, in the place of 'what is common to all languages', Arnauld and Lancelot often end up presenting an inventory of the details of French, with a few cross-linguistic remarks woven in. For example, the chapter 'On pronouns' (pp. 92–97) opens with the full paradigm of French pronouns. Arnauld and Lancelot cite a few forms in Latin, and mention gender-marked second-person Hebrew pronouns. But otherwise the discussion revolves around problems of pronoun usage in French. Later, the *Grammar* ethnocentrically idealizes French as 'fond of clarity and of expressing things as much as possible in the most natural and least encumbered fashion, although at the same time, French is second to none in either beauty or elegance' (p. 175).

If, by today's standards, Arnauld and Lancelot's commitment to cross-linguistic comparison seems limited, it was still distinctive in its time. Moreover, the *Grammar* adopted an educational philosophy

specifically tailored to Jansenist philosophy, as set forth in the introduction to Part 2 (pp. 65–68). Jansenists emphasized education as the
best means of rescuing humans from original sin, and placed language at
the centre of their curriculum. Grammar not only opened up the
opportunity to read sacred literature, but also enhanced one's 'judgement'. 'Judging' (affirming the properties of something) was one of
three essential mental operations, along with 'conceiving' (attending
or imagining), and 'reasoning' (deducing a conclusion from judgements). Propositions consist of a subject, predicate, and connection
between the two, most essentially a copula. Subjects and predicates –
the 'objects of thought' – expressed by nouns, articles, pronouns,
participles, prepositions and adverbs, represent the operation of conceiving. The connection between the two – the 'manner of
thought' – expressed by verbs, conjunctions and interjections, represents the operation of judging. (Reasoning is an extension of judging,
not addressed separately.) Therefore Lancelot and Arnauld first treated
the parts of speech signifying the objects of thought, followed by
those signifying the manner of thought, since (as they asserted)
manner of thought depends on the objects signified.

Lancelot and Arnauld's classification of words into these categories
was not without precedent, but their motivation for adopting it was
novel. And by focusing on propositions, they brought attention to
larger and more complex units, compared with the traditional analysis
of language into a collection of words. In addition, Lancelot and
Arnauld brought attention to the phenomenon of ellipsis: underlying
any nominative form, they claimed, some verb is associated with it,
even if that verb is not overt; likewise, 'there can be no adjective
which is not related to a substantive' and 'never a genitive ... which is
not governed by another noun' (pp. 171–72). They identified ellipsis
as a variety of figurative language, and therefore a surface perturbation
of the regularity of grammar where, at base, every element is present
and in its place (p. 173).

This depiction of Lancelot and Arnauld's ideas goes beyond the
content of the *Grammar*. For the details of particular issues, they
repeatedly referred readers to Lancelot's pedagogical works, especially
the Latin *Method* (1653/1816). At face value, the general grammar
was a repository of what languages have in common, factoring out
material that would otherwise be repeated in each particular grammar, the business of which was to communicate the distinctive features of Latin, Greek, Italian or Spanish. But the actual content of the
Grammar versus individual grammars cannot be so cleanly separated:
the *Grammar* has some of the complexion of a particular grammar of

French in cross-linguistic context; conversely, the Latin *Method* text fleshes out some claims about universals that the *Grammar* makes in passing. Lakoff (1969: 348–50), among others, pointed out that Lancelot's treatment of ellipsis in the third edition of the Latin *Method* goes beyond its representation in the *Grammar*. The *Method* claims that Latin inchoatives – verbs marked aspectually to express the beginning of an action or state – for which there is no corresponding synchronically-attested stative, must arise from statives that no longer exist. These inchoative verbs are therefore abstract with respect to the contemporary language. In contrast, the *Grammar* assumed that structures underlying figures of speech had to be well formed (and in this sense, the *Grammar* rejected abstraction). Thus, according to Lakoff, the *Method* better reveals Port-Royal rationalism than does the *Grammar*, since it assumes the regularity of underlying forms beyond what is attested on the surface of the language. Lakoff attributes Lancelot's more abstract analysis of ellipsis in the Latin *Method* to his exposure to the Spanish grammarian Sanctius (Francisco Sánchez de las Brosas, 1523–1601).

Ellipsis is a minor topic in Port-Royal grammatical works, but one that figures in the *Grammar*'s second life. **Noam Chomsky** (1966) raised the *Grammar* from obscurity in arguing that it reveals a rationalist outlook, which he labelled 'Cartesian'. He traces Cartesian linguistics from the 1600s through **Wilhelm von Humboldt**. According to Chomsky, it re-emerged in modern generative grammar after a hiatus during the era of comparative-historical linguistics and American structuralist linguistics. He identified four parallels between Port-Royal rationalism and late-twentieth-century generative grammar: (1) recognition of the creativity of language; (2) acknowledgement of a distinction between underlying ('deep') grammatical structures and surface facts; (3) commitment to explanation over description; (4) rationalist orientation to language acquisition and use. With reference to (2), Chomsky (1966: 33–34) analysed the *Grammar*'s treatment of the sentence 'Invisible God created the visible world'. Lancelot and Arnauld remark that with this one proposition 'three judgments pass through [one's] mind', 'without being expressed in words' (*ibid.*: 99–100): that God is invisible; that God created the world; and that the world is visible – alongside a more explicit alternative proposition: 'God *who* is invisible created the world *which* is visible.' Chomsky construed this rather sparse discussion to indicate that the *Grammar* postulates an underlying deep structure related to surface structure through optional, transformation-like operations that reduce relative clauses.

These and others of Chomsky's (1966) interpretive and historio-graphical claims ignited tremendous controversy. Lakoff (1969) objected that Chomsky's Cartesian linguistics actually has greater historical depth, going back as far as Sanctius; other critics have pushed its origins further back in time, or in other directions. Some, like Percival (1972), doubt that there is a coherent 'Cartesian linguistics' with anything resembling the meaning Chomsky imputes to the term; still others dispute the specific similarities between Cartesian rationalism and generative grammar that Chomsky identified. (Thomas [2004: 104–19] reviews these and other arguments.)

Whatever the fate of 'Cartesian linguistics' as a concept, Chomsky brought attention to the work of the Post-Royal grammarians. Arnauld and Lancelot were not strangers to controversy, albeit unexpected parties to this controversy, in this century.

Arnauld's and Lancelot's major works

Arnauld, A. and Lancelot, C., *General and Rational Grammar*, 1975 (J. Rieux and B. E. Rollins, trans.), Mouton, The Hague (original work published 1660).

Arnauld, A. and Nicole, P., *Logic or the Art of Thinking*, 1996 (J. V. Buroker, ed. and trans.), Cambridge University Press, Cambridge (original work published 1662).

Lancelot, C., *A New Method of Learning with Facility the Latin Tongue: Vols 1–2*, 1816 (T. Nugent, trans.), Wingrave & Collingwood, London (original work published 1653).

Lancelot, C., *Mémoires Touchant la Vie de M. de Saint-Cyran*, 2003 (D. Donetzkoff, ed.), Nolin, Paris (original work *c.* 1663).

Further reading

Chomsky, N. (1966) *Cartesian Linguistics*, New York: Harper & Row (3rd edn 2009, Cambridge University Press).

Percival, W. K. (1972) 'On the non-existence of Cartesian linguistics', in R. J. Bulter (ed.), *Cartesian Studies*, Oxford: Blackwell.

Danto, A. C. (1975) 'Preface', in Arnauld, A. and Lancelot, C., *General and Rational Grammar* (J. Rieux and B. E. Rollins, trans.), The Hague: Mouton.

Lakoff, R. (1969) Review of the book *Grammaire générale et raisonnée, ou la grammaire de Port-Royal*, H. H. Brekle, ed., *Language*, 45, 343–64.

Sainte-Beuve, C. A. (2004) *Port-Royal: Livres I à VI* (two vols) (P. Seillier, ed.), Paris: Laffont (original work published 1840–59).

Thomas, M. (2004). *Universal Grammar in Second Language Acquisition: A History*, New York: Routledge.

JOHN WILKINS (1614–72)

John Wilkins' intellectual leadership as a cleric and educator was a moderating influence during a tumultuous interval in English political, religious and academic life. Through the Civil War and Restoration, Wilkins modelled political and religious tolerance. He also promoted scientific inquiry as both of material benefit to society, and a common ground on which even his peers with very polarized views could meet and work constructively. Wilkins' relevance to the history of language study derives from the single book he wrote about language – his 'Darling' (Shapiro 1969: 220) – which he hoped would help overcome the discord of his times. The book was an ambitious, imaginative attempt to invent a universal language, complete with its own invented orthography. Wilkins organized the words of his 'Philosophical Language' to reflect what he considered their scientific relationships. He then created for each word a unique written character, the shape of which (he claimed) would transparently communicate its meaning to readers of any language background. Wilkins developed his project in assiduous detail but, not surprisingly, it failed on both linguistic and cultural grounds. Only rarely was it ever put to communicative use. Nevertheless, the intricate organizational scaffolding of Wilkins' universal language is a linguistic curiosity that illustrates the concerns of language scholars in his day.

Wilkins was son of a goldsmith, and on his mother's side, grandson of a well-known Puritan clergyman. He grew up in the environs of Oxford and was educated in theology at Oxford's Magdalen Hall. Throughout his life, he assumed various ecclesiastical roles as vicar, preacher or private chaplain to important figures in seventeenth-century British public life. He also wrote books on religious topics directed to his fellow preachers. By conviction, Wilkins was a moderate nonconformist. But he maintained the friendship and respect of powerful people across the board, eventually being appointed to the role of Bishop of Chester.

Alongside Wilkins' career in the church, he also served as an administrator and educational reformer at both Oxford and Cambridge, where he consistently advocated religious tolerance and openness to scientific knowledge. Wilkins exploited his 'unique talent for enlisting friendly cooperation among the best brains of his day in the face of bitter ideological, social, and political conflicts' (Shapiro 1969: 3) to organize working groups that addressed scientific issues, both in Oxford and in London. In the 1650s he helped found the Royal Society, a private learned society for the promotion of science that remains a force in the twenty-first century. The Royal Society sponsored lectures, projects and experiments, and incubated both theoretical and practical scientific inquiry. Under its auspices, Wilkins worked on such topics as devices for the improvement of hearing; cultivation of potatoes to alleviate famine; acquisition of naval timber; animal-to-human blood transfusion; and spontaneous generation of insects (Shapiro 1969: 195–98). He published books for the general public that explained scientific discoveries. One was a popularization of the work of Copernicus and Galileo, which assured readers that ideas such as heliocentrism were not inconsistent with biblical authority. Another explained the structure and practical applications of simple machines such as levers or pulleys.

Among projects sponsored by the Royal Society, what most captured Wilkins' imagination was the creation of a universal language. The topic had been an object of fascination in Europe since the beginning of the 1600s. Some of the most renowned figures of the century evinced interest in universal languages: French philosopher René Descartes (1596–1650), German scholar Gottfried Wilhelm Leibniz (1646–1716), and Czech educational reformer Comenius (1592–1670). The popularity of the topic rests on several socio-historical facts (Knowlson 1975; Slaughter 1982). Latin had lost value as a language of learning and communication across national boundaries because Protestants associated it with the Roman church. Seventeenth-century scientists' avid attention to the natural world required them to coin new terms, and to define those terms' relationships to each other and to new superordinate concepts. Many believed that the political and especially religious strife of the day was at least partially caused by linguistic ambiguity or miscommunication across factions; the hope was that miscommunication could be corrected by adopting a shared 'philosophical' (i.e. scientific) language. Moreover, Wilkins had long advocated that preaching be purged of elaborate rhetorical structures and ornate classical or literary allusions to make way for a style he considered simple and direct. A universal language would provide basic building blocks for this reform effort.

Many scholars discussed the desirability of a universal language in these terms, but few actually attempted to create one. Wilkins accepted the challenge. At first he collaborated with Scottish schoolmaster and fellow Royal Society member George Dalgarno (1626–87), but the two reached an intellectual impasse and parted ways to work separately, leaving it unclear who initiated material and who borrowed material from whom. Dalgarno published his proposal first, in 1661, as the *Ars Signorum*. Wilkins had started work on his in the 1650s at Oxford, but invested more time in it after he moved to

London in 1660. In 1666, parts of the manuscript were destroyed at the printer's during the Great Fire of London. But Wilkins persevered, finally publishing his work in 1668 as *An Essay Towards a Real Character, and a Philosophical Language.*

Following the front matter, the *Essay* consists of four substantive parts. Part 1, the Prologomena, provides a mid-seventeenth-century perspective on the origin of language in the Garden of Eden and its multiplication at Babel (see **Language in the Bible**); documents the gradual corruption of languages over time; and gives an exposition of the redundancies and deficiencies of written and spoken language, granted that 'Neither Letters nor Languages have been regularly established by the rules of Art' (p. 19). Wilkins aimed to remedy those defects, starting with the assumption that words label mental notions that are consistent cross-linguistically:

> That *conceit* which men have in their minds concerning a Horse or Tree, is the Notion or *mental Image* of that Beast, or natural thing, of such a nature, shape, and use. The *Names* given to these in several Languages, are such arbitrary *sounds* or *words*, as Nations of men have agreed upon, either casually or designedly, to express their Mental notions of them ... So if men should generally consent upon the same way or manner of *Expression*, as they do agree on the same *Notion*, we should then be freed from the Curse in the Confusion of Tongues ...
>
> (Wilkins 1668: 20)

Part 2, the longest section, introduces Wilkins' 'Universal Philosophy' for organizing words into a three-tiered branching taxonomy, which employs **Aristotle**'s logical terms, seventeenth-century natural-historical systematics, and folk categories (Slaughter 1982). He first 'enumerat[ed] and describ[ed] all such things and notions as fall under discourse' (p. 22) into forty Genera. Wilkins regarded the first six Genera as categories of universal or transcendental notions, subsuming such lower-order terms as 'discourse', 'length', 'sufficiency', etc. The remaining thirty-four Genera are distributed into a truncated version of Aristotle's categories, namely substance, quantity, quality, action and relation. Wilkins subdivided each of the forty Genera into Differences (usually six per Genus, excepting the more prolific cases of plants and animals), then Differences into Species. Much of Part 2 is taken up specifying these categories, displayed in Tables that branch to the right, visually recording a complex superstructure of domination and inclusion from Genus through Difference to Species.

Because Wilkins' Tables articulate the characteristics of phenomena at each taxonomic level, definitions of the lowest-level elements can be construed by linking together the characteristics of the relevant Genus, Difference and Species. Thus 'The word *Diamond* doth by its place in the Tables appear to be a Substance, a Stone, a pretious Stone, transparent, colourless, most hard and bright' (p. 289). At the Species level of organization, Wilkins recorded synonyms and derivatives. At the Difference level, he often juxtaposed pairs of antonyms. Insofar as possible, the Tables traffic in substantives, from which other parts of speech derive. Wilkins, however, conceded that the imperfection of language disrupts that ideal (p. 299). Therefore, the Genus 'Transcendental Mixed relations' subsumes the Difference 'Length', which in turn subsumes the Species *lengthen, longitude, prolong, protract, eke out, extend, tedious, prolixness*. 'Length' is juxtaposed to 'Shortness', which subsumes *brevity, conciseness, abbreviate, curtail, abridge, restrain, compendious, succinct* (p. 33). Nouns appear as Species alongside verbs and adjectives.

Wilkins' Tables comprise more than half of the 454-page *Essay*. Part 3 turns to grammar. Not surprisingly, granted Wilkins' goal to create a universal language mirroring the structure of reality, his grammatical proposals sometimes parallel those of the **Speculative Grammarians** (Salmon 1975). For example, Wilkins rejected verbs as independent *partes orationis*. In this he followed Modistae like Thomas of Erfurt (*fl.* 1300), whose grammar Wilkins acknowledged (p. 297; but, as was conventional, he misattributed the work to Johannes Duns Scotus, *c.* 1265–1308). So-called 'verbs' are adjectives that co-occur with the copula *be*, or subsume it. Therefore the copula 'serves for the uniting of the Subject and Predicate in every Proposition' (pp. 303–4): 'I read' is equivalent to 'I am reading' (cf. 'I am happy'). Part 3 also proposes an inventory of eight vowels and twenty-six consonants as a provision for representing personal or place names, which, lacking meaning, cannot be assigned Real Characters. Wilkins analysed the articulatory properties of these thirty-four vowels and consonants, which are 'commonly known and used in these parts of the World' (p. 383), and invented an orthographic shape for each one – a vertical line modified by loops or hooks – alone or in a consonant-plus-vowel structure (p. 376).

Part 4 presents Wilkins' Real (in the sense of 'correlated with nature') Characters, where shape and pronunciation are designed to be transparently derivable from meaning, by reference to the taxonomy worked out in Part 2. The Characters are essentially permutations of a short horizontal line that identify their referents at the Genus level.

Those lines were then elaborated by modifying their shapes on the left or right to identify their referents at the levels of Difference and Species. In principle, the meanings of the characters should be recognizable without recourse to spoken language, by associating each one and its modifications with a specific position within Wilkins' Tables. The *Essay* defined 2030 characters in this way. Wilkins went further, to create a system of pronunciation for the Real Characters by assigning a two-letter sequence to each Genus, a single consonant to each Difference, and a vowel or diphthong to each Species (all ordered according to his taxonomy). For example, *de* signified the Genus 'element'; *deb* the first Difference under that Genus, 'fire'; and *deba* the first Species under that Difference, 'flame' (p. 415). Thus Wilkins associated each character with a pronounceable word, the meaning of which was discernible by recognizing the associations between its shape and the ordered entries in his three-tiered taxonomy.

The reception of Wilkins' *Essay* was mixed from the start. A few of his contemporaries took it up and tried to refine its details. Others evinced scepticism. Its faults are obvious: to succeed, Wilkins' universal language would require perfect, immutable, comprehensive, pan-cultural knowledge of the world and human experience – a state unlikely to be realized in any century. (For instance, when the whale was discovered to be a mammal, not a fish, its taxonomic position would have to be reassigned, as would its pronunciation and orthographic representation; Emery 1948: 182.) Wilkins' work did have some delayed effects: his systematic construction of definitions was a novelty that became an undercurrent in English lexicography (Dolezal 1985: 111); the influence of the Tables was felt on the organization of Peter Mark Roget's (1779–1869) famous *Thesaurus* (Hüllen 2004). However, assessed against Wilkins' bold goal to create a 'Real Character, and a Philosophical Language' in seventeenth-century terms, the *Essay* was an ingenious failure. Failures, too, are part of the history of the language sciences.

Wilkins' major works

An Essay Towards a Real Character, and a Philosophical Language, 1668, Gellibrand and Martyn, London (available through Early English Books Online).

Further reading

Dolezal, F. (1985) *Forgotten But Important Lexicographers: John Wilkins and William Lloyd*, Tübingen: Niemeyer.

Emery, C. (1948) 'John Wilkins' universal language'. *Isis*, 38, 174–85.
Hüllen, W. (2004) *A History of Roget's* Thesaurus: *Origins, Development, and Design*, Oxford: Oxford University Press.
Knowlson, J. (1975) *Universal Language Schemes in England and France, 1600–1800*, Toronto: University of Toronto Press.
Salmon, V. (1975) '"Philosophical" grammar in John Wilkins' *Essay*', *Canadian Journal of Linguistics/Revue canadienne de linguistique*, 20, 131–59 [repr. in J. L. Subbiondo (ed.) (1992) *John Wilkins and 17th-Century British Linguistics*, Philadelphia, PA: John Benjamins].
Shapiro, B. J. (1969) *John Wilkins 1614–1672: An Intellectual Biography*, Berkeley, CA: University of California Press.
Slaughter, M. M. (1982) *Universal Languages and Scientific Taxonomy in the Seventeenth Century*, Cambridge: Cambridge University Press.
Subbiondo, J. L. (ed.) (1992) *John Wilkins and 17th-Century British Linguistics*, Philadelphia, PA: John Benjamins.

JOHN LOCKE (1632–1704)

John Locke was one of the most important early English empiricist philosophers, whose ideas powerfully influenced the European Enlightenment. In addition to writing about politics, religion, economics and education, he was deeply involved in the political and religious turmoil of his day, which spanned the aftermath of the English Civil War, the Restoration and the 'Glorious Revolution' of 1688. During this period, England was overtaken by debate about the roles of the monarchy versus parliament, and about the power and privileges of Catholics versus Protestants. Locke served behind the scenes as an advisor to key players, and several times was appointed to public office. His positions evolved over his lifetime, but he is now best known for rejecting the divine authority of kings, supporting religious toleration, and championing liberalism in the sense of freedom of speech and thought. Locke's writings are often cited as having helped shape the Constitution of the United States.

Locke's involvement in public affairs existed alongside his career as a scientist and scholar. He befriended some of the late-seventeenth-century's greatest scientists, including Robert Boyle and Isaac Newton. His thinking was influenced by the empiricism of Francis Bacon (1561–1626) and Thomas Hobbes (1588–1679), who prioritized observation and direct experience as sources of knowledge. Locke 'wanted to get away from the imagination, ... away from all private visionary insights down to the plain, measurable, publicly verifiable facts' (Cranston 1957: 163).

Locke made significant contributions to what we would now call the philosophy and psychology of language. He wrestled with what he perceived as the inadequacies of language as an instrument for communicating knowledge. He argued that to evade misunderstanding, complex ideas must be analysed into the simple, definable ideas out of which complex ideas are constructed. Probably the most famous facet of Locke's epistemology is the claim that the mind is created as a blank slate, devoid of innate ideas, on which sensory experience is then inscribed. This position implicates him in the controversy that surrounds **Noam Chomsky**'s historiography of linguistics, which contrasts the views of 'rationalists' versus 'empiricists' about the nature of mind and language. To Chomsky, modern generative grammar is part of a rationalist tradition that acknowledges an innate language faculty, a tradition he attributes to the French mathematician and philosopher René Descartes (1596–1650) and general grammarians **Antoine Arnauld** and **Claude Lancelot**. Locke's rejection of innate ideas would seem to assign him to the opposing camp in a history of linguistics that contrasts rationalists and empiricists in these terms. But the full story is not so clear-cut.

John Locke was born in Somerset, in southwest England, to a Puritan family. His father was a lawyer, his mother the daughter of a tanner. When his father's employer ended up on the winning side of the Civil War, the elder Locke was rewarded for his loyalty by the admission of his son to Westminster School, adjacent to the famous abbey in central London. The adolescent Locke excelled in his studies, even as the culture and traditions of the school challenged his religious upbringing and probably led him, much later, to criticize harsh disciplining of schoolchildren. From Westminster, Locke proceeded to Christ Church at Oxford in 1652. By 1660 he had earned his Bachelor's and Master's degrees, and was elected to the position of tutor, overseeing the education of younger students.

The curriculum at Oxford emphasized philosophy, theology, and classical languages and literatures. The path of least resistance would have been for Locke to prepare for ordination. But although he held strong religious commitments, he hesitated. He left Oxford for some months in 1665 for a diplomatic post in Germany, during which time he struggled with vocational questions. Eventually, Locke's fascination with science, and specifically with the intellectual foundations of experimentation, led him to abandon theology in favour of medicine.

Back at Oxford, Locke made a concerted study of science and medicine. He also met Anthony Ashley Cooper (1621–83), the future first Earl of Shaftesbury, a man whose patronage shaped Locke's fate intellectually, politically and socially. In 1667, Shaftesbury invited Locke to join his retinue as his private physician. The next year, Locke successfully removed a cyst from Shaftesbury's liver, earning Shaftesbury's lasting gratitude. As the Earl's fortunes alternately waxed and waned in late-seventeenth-century English politics, so did Locke's; when Shaftesbury was forced to flee to Holland in 1682 (where he died), Locke followed. During his exile in Holland, Locke was expelled from Oxford by King James II, who had converted to Catholicism. But in 1689 the political tide turned, and James was deposed in favour of his Protestant daughter Mary and her husband William. Locke accompanied the queen-to-be as she returned from Holland to England to take up the throne.

Henceforth, however, Locke was less involved in political affairs and more in scholarly writing. He never returned to live at Oxford, but rather moved back and forth between London, where he had some residual public duties, and Oates, the Essex estate of Lady Damaris Masham (1658–1708), daughter of the philosopher Ralph Cudworth, with whom Locke enjoyed a long-standing intellectual (and, before her marriage, possibly romantic) relationship. As Locke's asthmatic lungs gradually gave out, he found more reasons to avoid the fog and pollution of London in favour of Oates. He died there, attended faithfully by Lady Masham.

In addition to his private letters and notes, Locke left behind books on education and economics, and other works that had appeared anonymously in the last fifteen years of his life (*Two Treatises on Government*; *A Letter Concerning Toleration*; *The Reasonableness of Christianity*). Arguably his most influential work is the one most relevant to language, *An Essay Concerning Human Understanding*. Locke began writing this very long text in 1671 while he was living in Shaftesbury's household, then continued working on it in Holland. The *Essay* went through at least three drafts before being published in 1690. Locke's goal was to develop an epistemology coherent with the scientific orientation he had first encountered at Oxford, which sought truth via direct sensory experience, rather than deducing truth from traditional maxims or general principles.

The *Essay* is comprised of four books. In Book I, Locke denies that the mind is endowed with innate principles, either speculative (e.g. 'the whole is bigger than a part') or 'practical' (that is, moral principles, e.g. 'men should keep their compacts'), or innate ideas ('redness'; 'God'). He addresses, and rejects, various arguments in support of innateness. For example, that all people might immediately accept a particular proposition on first encountering it did not, to Locke, indicate that it is innate, since that would admit far too much under the definition of innateness. Locke further rejected a compromise notion that propositions could be innate, but only come to be known through the exercise of reason, on the grounds that reason does not dawn in the mind until experience has furnished the mind with ideas. Moreover, to identify as 'innate' any ability that humans can develop – in Barnes' (1972: 205) example, 'the ability to tell burgundy from claret' – would empty the term of meaning; and Locke found unintelligible the claim that innate ideas may exist implicitly but require stimulation from the environment to be activated.

Locke further argued that if principles are innate, the ideas out of which they are constructed must be innate as well. However, new-born infants do not possess ideas, since they do not possess terms that name those ideas. He allowed that infants perceive hunger or thirst, but that fact does not indicate that they know what hunger and thirst are. True ideas such as 'sin' or 'equality' cannot exist in the absence of linguistic abilities that infants patently lack.

Finally, Locke pointed out that purportedly innate speculative and moral principles are not present in all human societies. He cited missionaries' and travellers' reports of behaviour such as infanticide and cannibalism that challenged seventeenth-century European assumptions about human nature.

> He that will carefully peruse the History of Mankind, and look abroad into the several Tribes of Men, and with indifferency survey their Actions, will be able to satisfy himself, That there is scarce that Principle of Morality to be named, or *Rule* of *Vertue* to be thought on ... which is not, somewhere or other, *slighted* and condemned by the general Fashion of *whole Societies* of Men, governed by practical Opinions, and Rules of living quite opposite to others.
>
> (Locke 1690/1975: I.iii.10)

Book II of Locke's *Essay* addresses the inevitable question: if, indeed, the mind is 'white Paper, void of all Characters, without any *Ideas*; [then] How comes it to be furnished?' (*ibid.*: II.1.2). For Locke, ideas (and hence propositions) have two sources. Their major source is sensation, through the operation of the five senses on objects in the world. Secondarily, ideas can derive from reflection, that is, from our perception of the workings of the mind. Thus:

External Objects furnish the Mind with the Ideas *of sensible qualities,* which are all those different perceptions they produce in us: And the *Mind furnishes the Understanding with* Ideas *of its own Operations.* These ... contain all our whole stock of *Ideas;* and we have nothing in our Minds, which did not come in, one of these two ways.

(*ibid.*: II.i.5)

Locke's *Essay* was not unanimously accepted. Some readers were enthusiastic, causing the publisher to issue four successive editions in Locke's own lifetime. Others suspected that, notwithstanding his personal piety, his ideas were subversive to religion, and on these grounds strongly opposed his anti-innatism. Locke's epistemology had provocative political ramifications, too, since 'the elimination of innate ideas had the effect (and intention) of upsetting hierarchies and establishing assent on the basis of evidence and probable reasoning' (Carey 2006: 38). To Aarsleff (1982: 175), Locke's position coheres with his support for religious toleration, since if there is no transcendental human nature, no one group can assert its 'natural' superiority over another.

The seventeenth-century religious and moral context that rendered Locke's epistemology controversial in his day has passed. However, questions remain about what, if anything, is innate in human cognition and language. Psychologists such as Spelke (1994) argue that infants are born with elaborate, domain-specific cognitive resources; linguists such as Crain (1991) report experimental evidence that children possess intricate grammatical knowledge that they cannot have gleaned through experience. Research of this sort supports Chomsky's conclusion that an innate human language faculty shapes children's emerging native-language grammars. However, it is significant that in Chomsky's many discussions of how empiricism in the history of language science contrasts with 'Cartesian' rationalism (which embraces innate mental faculties), Chomsky only rarely adverts to Locke, even though Locke's *Essay* is the conventional touchstone for anti-innatism. In fact, insofar as Chomsky cites Locke (e.g. Chomsky 1965: 49, 203), surprisingly, he attributes to Locke a position close to that of Descartes with respect to innatism, while still holding fast to the dichotomy between empiricists and rationalists. Some critics, such as Aarsleff (1982: 170–76), seem to agree that Locke's anti-innatism has been misrepresented, but interpret this as a challenge to Chomsky's stark separation of empiricism from rationalism. Other critics, such as Yolton (1956: 26), have pointed out that even in Locke's own day – long before the controversy over

Chomsky's historiography – some readers of the *Essay* expressed difficulty identifying who actually supported the innatism that Locke attacked. Although the historical status and specific content of his doctrine remains controversial, Locke raised issues about the sources of linguistic and cognitive capacities that continue to animate scholarship in our own time.

Locke's major works

An Essay Concerning Human Understanding, 1975 (P. H. Nidditch, ed.), Oxford University Press, Oxford (original work published 1690).

Further reading

Aarsleff, H. (1982) *From Locke to Saussure*, Minneapolis, MN: University of Minnesota Press.

Barnes, J. (1972) 'Mr. Locke's darling notion', *The Philosophical Quarterly*, 22, 193–214.

Carey, D. (2006) *Locke, Shaftesbury, and Hutcheson: Contesting Diversity in the Enlightenment and Beyond*, Cambridge: Cambridge University Press.

Chomsky, N. (1965) *Aspects of the Theory of Syntax*, Cambridge, MA: MIT Press.

Crain, S. (1991) 'Language acquisition in the absence of experience', *Behavioral and Brain Sciences*, 14, 597–650.

Cranston, M. (1957) *John Locke: A Biography*, London and New York: Macmillan.

Spelke, E. (1994) 'Initial knowledge: six suggestions', *Cognition*, 50, 431–45.

Yolton, J. W. (1956) *John Locke and the Way of Ideas*, Oxford: Oxford University Press.

SAMUEL JOHNSON (1709–84)

Samuel Johnson was a major British literary figure who achieved towering stature as a critic and as a bold, trenchant and witty essayist. He was also a poet, biographer and political writer. Johnson contributed directly to the study of language through his authorship of an English dictionary that indelibly influenced both language attitudes and lexicographical practice. 'Dr Johnson's dictionary' was only superseded a century later by **James Murray**'s *Oxford English Dictionary*, which capitalized on Johnson's accomplishment. In addition, Johnson's prose style has been celebrated as a model of rhetorical grace and power, setting a standard for what it means to write and speak effectively in English.

Johnson had an inauspicious start (Boswell 1791–94/1925; Bate 1975). Born the son of a bookseller in the West Midlands town of Lichfield, about halfway between London and Liverpool, he probably contracted scrofula (tuberculosis of the lymph nodes that results in disfiguring abscesses and scarring around the neck) from a wet-nurse. Perhaps as a side effect, both his eyesight and hearing were damaged. From early adulthood, he exhibited uncontrollable tics and obsessive stereotypical gestures of his face and limbs, plausibly diagnosed in retrospect as symptoms of Tourette's syndrome (Wiltshire 1991: 24–34). Moreover, years of poverty, professional rejection, and bouts of overwhelming self-doubt and despair often lent his person and manners a rawness incongruous with his eloquence and refined intellectual sensibilities.

Johnson's gifts were apparent early. He supplemented his education at a local grammar school by reading Latin classics and English poetry in his father's bookshop. As an adolescent, he sharpened his conversational skills with a sophisticated and much older cousin. In 1728 he went up to Oxford, where he impressed others as being brash and preoccupied, probably disguising a sense of being out of his depth socially and financially, if not academically. After a little over a year he ran out of money and had to return to Lichfield. He tried to get work as a schoolteacher, but without a degree, failed. This exacerbated the first of several severe psychological, spiritual and financial crises he underwent periodically from young adulthood. Johnson initiated various writing projects, including editing, translation and poetry. Occasional modest successes boosted his confidence. In 1735 he married a widow 20 years older than himself. Although the marriage turned sour for both parties, Johnson was heartbroken when his wife died years later.

Eight years after leaving Oxford, Johnson moved to London to eke out a living as an editor and writer. His poems, political essays and biographies gradually earned him a reputation as a scholar with strong conservative, nationalist, political views, a devout Christian, a self-assured moralist – and, above all, a skilled writer and arbiter of taste.

In 1746, a coalition of London booksellers commissioned Johnson to produce a dictionary that would provide English speakers with the benefits of dictionaries then being produced in France and Italy, and remedy the faults of existing English dictionaries: imprecise definitions, focus on rare or 'hard' words, and thoughtless copying of material from one text to another. A goal of the new dictionary would be to 'fix' the language for a speech community that sought authoritative linguistic standards (Sledd and Kolb 1955; Reddick 1996).

Johnson promised to finish the dictionary in three years. He first composed a *Plan* (published in 1747 and reprinted in Johnson 2005, Vol. XVIII: 1–59) that outlined his proposed lexicographic practices. Johnson declared that he would select as headwords both common and obscure terms (*horse* as well as *crocodile*) – since 'who shall fix the limits of the reader's learning?' (p. 34) – and also specialist words readers might plausibly encounter. Granted the unsettled orthography of English in his day, he would favour spellings that preserved distinctions, even at the expense of admitting gaps between written and spoken forms. But he would not introduce new spellings. In matters of pronunciation, the dictionary would indicate 'accentuation' (p. 38; i.e. stress assignment) in polysyllabic words, and record the contrast of vowels in monosyllables like *flow* versus *brow* (p. 39). But Johnson did not take responsibility for the pronunciation of every headword.

Under 'Etymology or derivation', Johnson's *Plan* declared that he would evade the confusion of existing dictionaries by (in some undefined way) recording derivational relationships (*action, actionable, active, activity*, etc.; p. 40). But he stressed the irregularity of English inflections, which spans words 'thrown together by negligence, by affectation, by learning, or by ignorance' (p. 43). Likewise, English grammar seemed so unruly to Johnson that it is best conceived of as collocations between specific words (*die OF x*, but *perish WITH y*; p. 45). He also indicated that his dictionary would trace words back to their origins in foreign languages, by which he hoped to 'secure our language from being over-run with *cant*, [and] from being crowded with low terms' (p. 42).

Johnson elaborated on the semantic content of the dictionary, taking a middle road on the issue of whether a dictionary should provide encyclopedic information or simple definitions. He would order entries with the 'natural and primitive' senses of headwords coming first, followed by semantic extensions, then increasingly metaphorical and poetic senses, and finally idiosyncratic uses by specific writers (p. 47). The dictionary would also record the connotations of near synonyms. Johnson decided to include rare or obsolete terms only if they had been in circulation since the accession of Elizabeth in 1558, and to include 'barbarous or impure' words but 'brand [them] with some note of infamy' (p. 53). Most distinctively, Johnson added that he would illustrate the usage of words by quoting passages by 'writers of the first reputation', organized chronologically. He hoped that these quotations would also 'give pleasure or instruction by conveying some elegance of language, or some precept of prudence, or piety' (p. 55).

Addressing Lord Chesterfield, whose support he hoped to attract, Johnson concluded:

This, my Lord, is my idea of an English dictionary, a dictionary by which the pronunciation of our language may be fixed, and its attainment facilitated; by which its purity may be preserved, its use ascertained, and its duration lengthened. And though, perhaps, to correct the language of nations by books of grammar, and amend their manners by discourses of morality, may be tasks equally difficult; yet as it is unavoidable to wish, it is natural likewise to hope, that your Lordship's patronage may not be wholly lost; that it may contribute to the preservation of the antient, and the improvement of modern writers; that it may promote the reformation of those translators, who for want of understanding the characteristical difference of tongues, have formed a chaotic dialect of heterogeneous phrases; and awaken to the care of purer diction, some men of genius, whose attention to argument makes them negligent of stile, or whose rapid imagination, like the Peruvian torrents, when it brings down gold, mingles it with sand.

(Johnson 2005, Vol. XVIII: 57–58)

Johnson's method was first to search through books written in English by authors he admired (including translations of classical literature and the King James Bible), marking potential headwords and their contexts in pencil. **John Locke** is among authors frequently cited. He hired a corps of helpers to copy the relevant passages and organize the headwords alphabetically. Johnson then construed definitions on the basis of the assembled quotations, while also relying heavily on reference works and earlier dictionaries.

The 1755 edition, a labour of nine years, included 43,000 headwords and 114,000 illustrative quotations. Johnson's *Preface* (*ibid.* Vol. XVIII: 63–113) acknowledged numerous social and language-internal reasons why 'tongues … have a natural tendency to degeneration' (p. 109), hinting that his experience as a lexicographer eroded the confidence he had expressed in his *Plan* that it is possible to 'fix' a language. These doubts did not prevent him from trying to 'discourage some words by applying a kind of linguistic weed-killer' (Wimsatt 1959: 66) in labelling them 'cant' or 'low'. But despite the reputation of Johnson's dictionary as a landmark of prescriptivism, modern scholars debate the extent to which, in the end, its author self-confidently wielded linguistic authority (Lynch and McDermott 2005: 92–128).

Johnson's was neither the first nor the largest English dictionary, although it was the first in English to use illustrative quotations. His etymologies are often shallow and occasionally ridiculous, as when he derives 'doodle' from *do little*, or 'saunter' from French *aller à la SAINTE TERRE* 'go to the Holy Land', after idlers who rove around France collecting alms ostensibly for that purpose. But Johnson's choice of headwords was intuitively sound, and he had such a good instinctive feel for the language that his definitions are still admired today as perspicuous. In addition to their high literary value, Johnson's definitions and his choice of illustrative quotations exhibit a plucky, unabashed subjectivity that has charmed readers for centuries. He made free with his prejudices against the adoption of foreign (especially French) vocabulary into English, his aversion for words he disliked, and his general cultural antipathy for the Scots. Johnson also broadcast his nationalism and his religious views. But even those opposed to his beliefs usually found the dictionary engaging.

Aside from the dictionary, Johnson's other major linguistic legacy is his distinctive prose style (Wimsatt 1941; DeMaria 1986). Complex, multiply embedded parallelism, often subsuming rhetorical antithesis or inversion, is one outstanding trait of Johnson's writing. In a typical line from the *Plan*, Johnson stated '[as [it is unavoidable to wish], [it is natural likewise to hope,]] that your Lordship's patronage [may not be wholly lost]; that it [may contribute to [the preservation of the antient], and [the improvement of modern writers]]]'. His sentences are long and syntactically elaborate, and his diction abstract and philosophical, but often illuminated by a streak of bright sensory detail, as when (in the same passage) he analogizes a gifted mind hampered by poor writing skills to 'Peruvian torrents, [which] when it brings down gold, mingles it with sand.' Some readers found Johnson's style pompous or affected, even as it seemed to grow more colloquial as he aged. Some parodied his habitual rhetorical triples. But Johnsonian style was also immensely admired, lending authority and erudition to his critical opinions on Shakespeare (reprinted 1968) and his biographies of English poets (1779–81). Johnson is still cited admiringly as an epitome of literary taste by present-day 'language mavens' (e.g. Simon 1980: 81, 198).

Although Johnson mingled with the literary and intellectual elite of his day, he constantly gave money to the poor even as he lived on the edge of financial ruin. Johnson adopted and personally cared for numerous waifs and aged, destitute or abandoned persons, so that his home became a refuge where (in the words of a friend) 'the lame, the blind, the sick, and the sorrowful found a sure retreat from all the evils whence his little income could secure them' (Bate 1975: 501). Johnson's personal generosity and lack of elitism balance his reputation as a literary arbiter and inkhorn language scholar.

Johnson's major works

A Dictionary of the English Language, 1755, Strahan, London (Times Books facsimile, 1979).
The Lives of the English Poets: Vols 1–3, 1967, (G. Birkbeck, ed.), Octagon, New York (original work published 1779–81).
Yale Edition of the Works of Samuel Johnson: Vols I–X, XIV–XVIII, XXI–XXIII, 1958–, Yale University Press, New Haven, CT and London. (Volume XVIII, *Johnson on the English Language,* published 2005, reprints Johnson's Plan for the dictionary, prefaces to editions of the dictionary and related works, and essays on the history and grammar of English printed in the dictionary.)

Further reading

Bate, W. J. (1975) *Samuel Johnson,* New York: Harcourt Brace Jovanovich.
Boswell, J. (1925) *The Life of Samuel Johnson, LL.D.* (R. Ingpen, ed.), Boston, MA: Lauriat (original work published 1791–94).
DeMaria, R. Jr (1986) *Johnson's* Dictionary *and the Language of Learning,* Chapel Hill, NC: University of North Carolina Press.
Lynch, J, and McDermott, A. (eds) (2005) *Anniversary Essays on Johnson's Dictionary,* Cambridge: Cambridge University Press.
Reddick, A. (1996) *The Making of Johnson's Dictionary 1746–1773* (rev. edn), Cambridge: Cambridge University Press.
Simon, J. (1980) *Paradigms Lost: Reflections on Literacy and its Decline,* New York: Clarkson N. Potter.
Sledd, J. H. and Kolb, G. J. (1955) *Dr. Johnson's Dictionary: Essays in the Biography of a Book,* Chicago: University of Chicago Press.
Wiltshire, J. (1991) *Samuel Johnson in the Medical World,* Cambridge: Cambridge University Press.
Wimsatt, W. K. M. Jr (1959) 'Johnson's Dictionary', in F. W. Hilles (ed.), *New Light on Dr. Johnson,* New Haven, CT and London: Yale University Press.
——(1941) *The Prose Style of Samuel Johnson,* repr. 1972, Hamden, CT: Archon.

ÉTIENNE BONNOT, ABBÉ DE CONDILLAC (1714–80)

Étienne Bonnot was born in Grenoble to a family of the provincial nobility. His father purchased lands in southeast France in the area known as Condillac when Étienne was six years old. Étienne was ordained a priest in 1741, but despite the title *abbé* (abbot), seems not to have exercised a clerical role; he is now conventionally identified by the single name 'Condillac'. An admirer of **John Locke**, Condillac became a celebrated philosopher in his day. His major contribution to the study of language concerns a topic of keen interest in mid-eighteenth-century Europe, the origin of language. Condillac's 1746 *Essay on the Origin of Human Knowledge* is sometimes viewed as having opened debate about glottogenesis, a debate which – in some accounts – closed in 1770 with the submission of **Johann Gottfried Herder**'s prize essay 'Treatise on the origin of language'.

Condillac left no autobiography, no journal and few letters, so we know relatively little about him as a person. But his contemporaries also knew little about him, because he led an essentially solitary life, 'always serious, brooding, and preoccupied' (Baguenault de Puchesse 1910: 20). He got a slow start educationally, apparently not learning to read until he was twelve, in part due to the poor eyesight that burdened him throughout his life. Eventually he travelled to Paris to study theology at the Sorbonne, but later wrote that on finishing his studies he felt so dissatisfied that he then began his education anew by immersing himself in independent reading. In the late 1740s, Condillac sometimes appeared at fashionable salons of the Parisian intelligentsia, but evidently lacked the self-aggrandizing temperament, or at least the verve, to make much of an impression. He was on friendly terms with *philosophes* of the French Enlightenment such as Jean-Jacques Rousseau (1712–78) and Denis Diderot (1713–84), who openly admired, even echoed, his ideas. However, Condillac kept his personal and intellectual distance. In Rousseau's *Confessions* (1770/ 1959: 347), for example, the author mentions an occasional amiable dinner with Condillac, adding that the two split the expenses for their meals. One can imagine a circumspect and reserved Condillac maintaining careful boundaries between himself and a turbulent personality like Rousseau.

Starting in 1758, Condillac lived for nine years in Parma, Italy, where he served as a tutor to the grandson of Louis XV. Returning to France, he was elected to the Académie Française in 1768. Soon afterward he retired to a chateau in the countryside near Orléans, from which he made only occasional trips to Paris. By his request, Condillac was buried without fanfare in the local cemetery. Appropriately for a man who lived largely in his mind, nothing now marks the site of his physical remains (Gilot and Sgard 1981: 105–6).

Condillac occupies an intriguing niche in the history of French philosophy. In his early years in Paris, he rejected René Descartes' (1596–1650) rationalism and the doctrine of innate ideas. Instead, he found a home in the writings of the English empiricists, particularly Locke. Condillac also admired Isaac Newton (1643–1727), Francis Bacon (1561–1626) and George Berkeley (1685–1753), working from summaries and translations into French of their works. The philosophical issues that absorbed him were (in modern terms) mostly psychological: the mind, senses, perception, memory, consciousness and thought. As was common in his century, he sought out the origins of things on the assumption that beginnings provided unique insight into the nature of things. He also participated in then-popular curiosity about differences between humans and animals, the ramifications of deafness and blindness, and the experience and mental status of feral children – all of which were grist for eighteenth-century reflection on the nature of human nature.

Condillac is sometimes identified as having adopted a 'mechanistic' philosophy. However, the connotations of this term may be misleading, granted that his writings consistently assume the relevance of a human soul alongside the full superstructure of biblical authority, including (for example) Adam and Eve's expulsion from the Garden of Eden. Moreover, as Aarsleff (2001: xv) points out, Condillac's writing favoured organic over mechanical metaphors. The epithet 'empirical sensationalist' may better represent Condillac's stance in his best known work, the 1754 *Treatise on the Sensations*. In this text, Condillac experimentally imagined a statue of a human being, in which he hypothesized the presence of a human soul but no perceptual capacities or mind, much less any Cartesian innate ideas (*Philosophical Writings*, Vol. 1: 155–339). He then imagined the successive endowment of the statue with each of the five senses, exploring what he argued would be a resulting gradual awakening of the statue's consciousness and mental faculties, stimulated by input from each of the senses or combinations thereof. Condillac's point was to demonstrate that all functions of the mind, including attention, memory, judgement, imagination, etc., could be viewed as deriving from sensory experience. In this he went a step further than Locke in claiming that even reflection is a product of the senses.

The famous image of a statue that was gradually brought to life through incremental opening of its senses probably constitutes Condillac's most striking contribution to eighteenth-century discussion of human cognition. But he did not extend his thought-experiment as far as the acquisition of language, because the capacities that the statue gradually acquired were, to Condillac, only precursors to human linguistic abilities.

The text in which Condillac wrote most extensively about language came earlier, in his first publication, the *Essay on the Origin of Human Knowledge* (*Philosophical Writings*, Vol. 2). Although his ideas evolved between the 1746 *Essay* and the 1754 *Treatise*, and his independence from the influence of Locke grew, both texts emphasized analysis as a method of discovery. In the case of the statue, Condillac broke down constructs such as consciousness and memory into what he perceived to be their constituent parts, speculating about how each such part derived from the senses. In the *Essay*, Condillac presented language as the prime tool for analysis. Speakers gain control over their experiences through language, because in order to communicate a thought or experience through words, a speaker has to analyse it into ordered components. Thus for Condillac language imposes an analysis on experience, and analysis is the basic means by which we achieve understanding.

The analytical character of language is, however, distinctive to what Condillac calls instituted or artificial language, that is, language purposely created by humans. Natural language, such as the involuntary expressive sounds that animals as well as humans make (grunts, cries, exclamations of pain, fear, surprise, etc.), does not impose an analysis on experience, but rather represents it holistically. Therefore it is crucial for Condillac to explain how voluntary, instituted language arose out of natural language. He devoted the second and final part of the *Essay* to speculation about the origin of language, which – of course – he approached through analysis. First, Condillac conscientiously exempted Adam and Eve from participating in the creation of language, since God had set them apart, separately providing for their linguistic and cognitive capacities. He then went on to speculate about the experience of 'two children, one of either sex, sometime after the deluge, [who] had gotten lost in the desert before they would have known the use of any sign' (Condillac 1746/2001: 113). Unlike Condillac's statue, these children's senses would be intact, and thus they had access to consciousness, attention, memory and imagination. But as yet they had no language, and therefore no means by which to analyse their experience or control their cognitive operations.

One day the sensation of hunger made these children call to mind a tree loaded with fruit which they had seen the day before. The next day this tree was forgotten, and the same sensation called to mind some other object. Thus the exercise of the imagination was not within their power. It was merely the effect of the circumstances in which they found themselves.

When they lived together they had occasion for greater exercise of these first operations, because their mutual discourse made them connect the cries of each passion to the perceptions of which they were the natural signs. They usually accompanied the cries with some movement, gesture, or action that made the expression more striking. For example, he who suffered by not having an object his needs demanded would not merely cry out; he made as if an effort to obtain it, moved his head, his arms, and all parts of his body. Moved by this display, the other fixed the eyes on the same object, and feeling his soul diffused with sentiments he was not yet able to account for to himself, he suffered by seeing the other suffer so miserably. From this moment he feels that he is eager to ease the other's pain, and he acts on this impression to the extent that it is within his ability. [...]

The frequent repetition of the same circumstances could not fail, however, to make it habitual for them to connect the cries of the passions and the different motions of the body to the perceptions which they expressed in a manner so striking to the senses. The more familiar they became with the signs, the more readily they were able to call them to mind at will. ... [Thus] little by little they succeeded in doing by reflection what they had formerly done only by instinct.

... [W]hen they had acquired the habit of connecting some ideas to arbitrary signs, the natural cries served as a model for them to make a new language. They articulated new sounds, and by repeating them many times to the accompaniment of some new gesture that indicated the objects to which they wished to draw attention, they became accustomed to giving names to things.

(*ibid.*: 114–16)

In this way, Condillac imagined how a language of instituted signs could be created out of a language of action and of natural signs. His influence on debate about the origin of language was powerful. His immediate contemporaries, and the *Idéologues* of revolutionary France, greatly admired his work. Even those who challenged Condillac seemed to start from the same premises. Herder's famous essay is often taken as having closed the book on the topic of the origin of language, even as some of the pages in that book attributed to Herder might more accurately be attributed to Condillac (Aarsleff 1982: 149–52). Joly (1985), among others, has similarly argued that there is more to Condillac's thinking than is presented by those who see him as wholly in Locke's shadow, or who dismiss him together with Locke as a foil to Cartesian rationalism.

After Condillac's day, preoccupation with the origin of language was displaced by comparative-historical analysis of the evolution of individual languages and their relationships. By 1865, the constitution of the Linguistic Society of Paris famously declared that it would entertain no discussion of the origin of language. However, inquiry into the topic has returned in twenty-first-century linguistics, framed in the terms of modern anthropology, evolutionary science and 'biolinguistics' (Trabant and Ward 2001; Aitchinson 2004). The debate to which Condillac made a prominent contribution in the eighteenth century now again engages scholars, for different reasons. It has not yet been resolved.

Condillac's major works

Philosophical Writings of Etienne Bonnot, Abbé of Condillac: Vols 1–2, 1982–87 (F. Philip, trans.), Lawrence Erlbaum, Hillsdale, NJ.
Essay on the Origin of Human Knowledge, 2001 (H. Aarsleff, ed. and trans.), Cambridge University Press, Cambridge (original work published 1746).

Further reading

Aarsleff, H. (1982) From Locke to Saussure, Minneapolis, MN: University of Minnesota Press.
——(2001) 'Introduction' in Étienne Bonnot de Condillac, Essay on the Origin of Human Knowledge (H. Aarsleff, ed. and trans.), Cambridge: Cambridge University Press.
Aitchinson, J. (2004) 'Recent developments in language origin', European Review, 12, 227–34.
Baguenault de Puchesse, G. (1910) Condillac: sa vie, sa philosophie, son influence, Paris: Plon-Nourrit.
Gilot, M, and Sgard, J. (eds) (1981) Corpus Condillac: Vol. 1. Biographie, Geneva: Slatkine.
Joly, A. (1985) 'Cartesian or Condillacian linguistics?', Topoi, 4, 145–49.
Rousseau, J.-J. (1959) Les Confessions, in Oeuvres Complètes: Vol. 1 (B. Gagnebin and M. Raymond, eds), Paris: Gallimarde (original work completed c. 1770).
Rousseau, N. (1986) Connaissance et langage chez Condillac, Geneva: Droz.
Trabant, J., and Ward, S. (eds) (2001) New Essays on the Origin of Language, Berlin and New York: Mouton de Gruyter.

JOHANN GOTTFRIED HERDER (1744–1803)

Johann Gottfried Herder would probably have rejected depiction of himself as a philosopher, historian or literary critic. In modern terms he was all these, as well as a teacher and Lutheran clergyman. But he would have objected to the fragmentation of experience implied by these labels, and found such categories incoherent. Another incongruity between Herder's self-perception and our view of him is that he was painfully conscious of the gap between his actual accomplishments and his raging ambitions. Instead of seeing what he could have achieved, but didn't, today we recognize that he initiated many important modern ideas about language. Herder would also probably not have imagined that, in linguistics, he would now be best remembered for his early and hastily composed *Treatise on the Origin of Language*.

Herder was born in the small city of Mohrungen in East Prussia to a poor, pious family. His father gave up the trade of weaver to become a schoolteacher. To make ends meet, he farmed out his only son as a domestic servant to the local school supervisor. Young Herder made the most of the situation by reading the books in his master's library. At 18, a surgeon attached to the Russian army that occupied Mohrungen recognized his precocity. The surgeon took Herder to Königsberg, supported his enrolment in medical school, and arranged for the first of several operations that Herder was to endure, before the advent of anaesthesia, to correct a disfiguring fistula to the tear gland under his right eye.

The operation failed, but the university in Königsberg opened to Herder a new world. Switching from medicine to theology, he met the philosophers Immanuel Kant (1724–1804) and Johann Georg Hamann (1730–88). Kant awed Herder, although in the short run influenced him less than the erudite but independent, enigmatic and mystically religious Hamann. Hamann was sceptical of Enlightenment rationalism, and transmitted to Herder a fascination with 'primitive' poetry and a drive to harmonize all branches of learning and to integrate sense-experience with knowledge. Herder later quarrelled with Hamann, as he did with all his friends. But Hamann modelled to Herder what it meant to be a scholar at a time when Herder was probably particularly susceptible to a charismatic intellectual mentor.

By early adulthood, the main themes of Herder's life emerged: his keen, critical, untrammelled mind; his breadth of knowledge, scope of interests and urge to synthesize; his sincere if unconventional religious commitments; his irony and sense of entitlement; his difficulty managing personal, vocational and financial obligations; and the physical suffering that no doubt contributed to his characteristic bitterness (Clark 1955). He found solace in marriage to a pragmatic and loyal woman, Caroline, and joy in fatherhood. But Herder's was not a happy life.

During his two years in Königsberg, Herder began writing reviews and newspaper articles. He then moved to teach in Riga, where he was ordained in 1767, worked as a minister, and published an important book on German literary criticism. Herder abruptly left Riga to travel to France and Holland, where he met with literary and philosophical stars but returned as dissatisfied and agitated as before. He served as a tutor and travelling companion, struck up a tumultuous friendship with Johann Wolfgang von Goethe (1749–1832), and planned numerous writing projects in philosophy, criticism, aesthetics and history. He settled for five years in Bückeberg as a preacher, then finally moved in 1776 to Weimar, where he was appointed chief pastor to the court. In this last phase of his life, Herder was relatively productive as a scholar and somewhat more at peace intellectually with himself and others. He began publishing his major work, *Outlines of a Philosophy of the History of Man*, in 1784. Although never finished, it came closest to his goal of a synthetic survey of history, philosophy and science, with forays into language, government and literature.

Herder's chief contribution to the study of language is his *Treatise on the Origin of Language*. Written during the unstable period between Riga and Bückeberg, he hurriedly created this text in late December 1769, to submit to a contest sponsored by the Berlin Academy of Sciences by their 1 January 1770 deadline. The Academy offered a prize for the best essay on the following topic:

> Supposing that men are abandoned to their natural faculties, are they in a position to invent language? And by what means might they arrive at this invention by themselves? What is required is a hypothesis which will explain the matter clearly and satisfy all the difficulties.
>
> (trans. Stam 1976: 117)

Among thirty entries the Academy received, Herder's took the prize. The topic had already been debated in Europe for some decades, raising as it did giant and timely questions about God, history, science and the human mind. Before Herder's day, **John Locke**, Giambattista Vico (1668–1744), **Condillac** and Jean-Jacques Rousseau (1712–78) had notably contributed their different opinions, directly or indirectly; during and after his day, so would Hamann, **Jacob Grimm, Friedrich Schlegel, Wilhelm von Humboldt, Max Müller** and many others. Herder perceived the Academy to have framed the question as an invitation to critique two existing proposals: the claim that language is of divine origin, a position that some scholars still held; and the claim (identified, accurately or not, with Condillac and Rousseau) that language originates 'naturally' or 'mechanically' just as animals come forth with their characteristic vocal sounds. Herder's essay not only challenged these two answers to the question of how language arose, but also seemingly challenged the legitimacy of the question itself.

The essay has two parts, each headed by one of the questions the Academy posed. But Herder hardly exploits this organizational superstructure. Instead, he spirals discursively from subtopic to subtopic in an oracular, exclamatory style ornamented with rhetorical questions, classical allusions and multiple varieties of emphasis, which **Edward Sapir** characterized (perhaps wryly) as 'warm, enthusiastic diction' (Sapir 1907: 137). The essay begins by asserting that humans express emotions via 'natural sounds'. 'The languages of all ancient and savage peoples' preserve such sounds, as 'the juices which enliven the roots of language' (Herder 1772/2002: 68–69). But these sounds are not the main substance of human language. Herder distinguished human language from animal sounds, because humans lack animals' specialized instincts. The trade-off is that humans have vastly broader, if less articulated, potential:

> The bee hums just as it sucks, the bird sings just as it makes a nest ... But *how does the human being speak by nature? Not at all! –* just as he does little or nothing through sheer instinct as an animal. [...] Born with such a dispersed, weakened sensuality, with such indeterminate, dormant abilities, with such divided and weakened drives, obviously dependent on and directed to a thousand needs, destined for a large sphere – and yet so orphaned and abandoned that it does not even enjoy the gift of language with which to express its shortcomings ... No! Such a contradiction is not nature's way of organizing her household. There must, instead of instincts, be other hidden powers sleeping in the human child! *Born dumb,* but [the child will perhaps itself create a language for itself]!
>
> (*ibid.*: 80–81)

What humans lack in localized instincts, they make up for in range, most particularly by their generalized endowment for *Besonnenheit,* 'reflection'. Through reflection, humans associate experiences and objects with words. Herder used the example that observation of the sounds a sheep makes might lead an early language-maker to identify the animal as 'the bleating one', forging an object/name relationship (*ibid.*: 88–89) – although later he declared that the first words were verbs, not nouns (*ibid.*: 101). Thus, although some languages incorporate natural, expressive cries, they are not the foundation of language: Condillac erred in making animals into humans, and Rousseau in making humans into animals (*ibid.*: 77). Furthermore, Herder mocked Condillac's imaginary tableau, in which two isolated children purportedly invent language by associating their thoughts with sounds, calling it a 'hollow explanation', on the basis that it is unclear how children could have thoughts in the absence of language (*ibid.*: 76).

Herder also addressed the position that language is a gift outright from God. Near the beginning of the essay, he refuted a claim that had been brought forth as evidence for divine origin, namely that the sounds of all languages are universally reducible to twenty letters. As counterevidence, he cited the difficulties European missionaries and explorers expressed at capturing the sounds of Abenaki, 'Peruvian' or Siamese (*ibid.*: 70). This is one of the few places where Herder adverted to actual linguistic data (albeit only in passing). It is also worth noting that, whereas the claim itself was framed in terms of 'twenty *letters*', Herder countered it with observations about the *sounds* of languages. Later in the text, he emphasized the advantages of sound as a basis of language, arguing that the sense of hearing ideally subserves communication.

Herder objected to divine origin theories on other grounds as well. For example, he asked 'How can the human being learn language through divine instruction if he has no reason? And of course he has not the slightest use of reason without language' (*ibid.*: 91–92). Moreover, he asserted that belief in the divine origin of language, 'as pious as it may seem, is entirely irreligious' because 'it diminishes God'; whereas, if language is of human origin, this 'shows God in the greatest light: *His work, a human soul, creating and continuing to create a language through itself because it is His work, a human soul*' (*ibid.*: 163).

Herder's essay ends by conceding that instead of supplying the Academy with a new hypothesis about the origin of language, he refuted two popular hypotheses, then asserted that language has no discrete 'origin', but rather is a product of human reflection. The human 'centre of gravity' falls on reflection 'as with the bee it falls immediately on sucking and building'; therefore, humankind's '*first moment of taking-awareness ... was also the moment for the inward emergence of language'* (*ibid.*: 128).

The Academy responded enthusiastically to Herder's essay. His old mentor Hamann, however, wrote a biting, typically cryptic review. Herder himself seems to have had second thoughts, in that he told his publisher and Caroline that he did not want the essay published (Stam 1976: 131). Many readers detect Herder's tone veering from playful, to ironic, to caustic. In retrospect, what the *Treatise* minimally accomplished was to discredit divine origin theories, even if it did not settle the issue of the origin of language to the satisfaction of all parties.

Herder's work is now rarely cited directly in linguistics, although his influence comes down to the present day. Trabant (1990) claims that Herder's emphasis on hearing as the basis of language instilled the 'phonocentrism' into modern language science that French philosopher Jacques Derrida (1930–2004) criticized; Marchand (1982) and Taylor (1991) explicate aspects of Herder's legacy to language philosophy. In addition, Herder's contributions include an emphasis on language as a repository of the 'genius' of its speakers and shaper of their thought, and the value he placed throughout his work on the capacity of history to reveal the inner nature of a people. The former idea arguably anticipated the 'Sapir–Whorf hypothe sis', while the latter gave impetus to nineteenth-century comparative-historical linguistics. Both ideas were developed by Wilhelm von Humboldt, apparently through the influence of Herder.

Herder's major writings

Herders Werke in fünf Bänden, 1969 (W. Dobbek, ed.), Aufbau, Berlin.
'Treatise on the origin of language', 2002, in *Johann Gottfried von Herder: Philosophical Writings* (M. N. Forster, ed. and trans.), Cambridge University Press, Cambridge (original work published 1772).
Outlines of a Philosophy of the History of Man, 1800 (T. Churchill, trans.), Bergman, New York (original work published 1784–91).

Further reading

Clark, R. T. Jr (1955) *Herder: His Life and Thought*, Berkeley: University of California Press.
Marchand, J. W. (1982) 'Herder: Precursor of Humboldt, Whorf, and modern language philosophy', in *Johann Gottfried Herder: Innovator Through the Ages* (W. Koepke, ed.), Bonn: Bouvier.
Sapir, E. (1907) 'Herder's "Ursprung der Sprache"', *Modern Philology*, 5, 109–42.

Stam, J. H. (1976) *Inquiries into the Origin of Language: The Fate of a Question*, New York: Harper & Row.

Taylor, C. (1991) 'The importance of Herder', in *Isaiah Berlin: A Celebration* (E. Margalit and A. Margalit, eds), Chicago: University of Chicago Press.

Trabant, J. (1990) 'Herder's discovery of the ear', in *Herder Today: Contributions from the International Herder Conference*, November 5–8, 1987, Stanford, CA (K. Mueller-Vollmer, ed.), Berlin and New York: Walter de Gruyter.

AUGUST WILHELM VON SCHLEGEL (1767–1845) AND KARL WILHELM FRIEDRICH VON SCHLEGEL (1772–1829)

Only a fraction of the voluminous writings of each of the brothers Schlegel (as they are often referred to) is directly relevant to linguistics. Both brothers should probably be characterized principally as literary critics and leaders in the emergence of nineteenth-century German Romanticism. The older brother, Wilhelm, met his greatest success as a translator and critic, while the younger, Friedrich, lectured and wrote extensively on literature, art and philosophy. However, both Schlegels contributed insights about language that proved influential: Wilhelm in the field of typology and as a scholar of Sanskrit, and Friedrich as the author of a text now recognized as a founding document of comparative linguistics.

The Schlegels grew up the sons of a Lutheran pastor in Hanover, in what is now northwestern Germany (Morrison 1946; Eichner 1970). Wilhelm and Friedrich studied at Göttingen, and the latter more extensively at Leipzig. Both lived in Jena in the late 1790s, but then moved independently around Europe throughout early adulthood in pursuit of the various means by which intellectuals in their day supported themselves: by serving as tutors, presenting series of public lectures, or attaching themselves to patrons. At different times, Wilhelm also held professorships in Jena and Bonn, while Friedrich eventually entered the Austrian civil service.

The two brothers had complementary personalities and talents, but their careers started out associated with the same literary-cultural movement. In this, Friedrich took the lead. He was an ambitious, restless spirit who lived the romantic life of one who seeks transcendent meaning in literature, religion and art. As a scholar, Friedrich aimed to define aesthetic and moral principles for evaluating artistic merit. His search for a comprehensive critical theory passed through several distinct stages. His first publications were appreciative analyses of Greek and Roman literature. Later, he wrote poetry, a novel and a play. In Jena at the end of the century, the brothers Schlegel founded the literary journal *Athenäum*, which became an intellectual home for scholars and writers who rejected Enlightenment rationalism and variously lionized imagination, sentiment, irony, 'naturalness', and Medieval literature and spirituality. In some of these trends, they carried forward ideas of **Johann Gottfried Herder**. The *Athenäum* group became known as 'Romantics', with Friedrich as their intellectual pioneer, and Wilhelm skilled at simplifying for the public the movement's complexities and paradoxes. The group gathered around the vivacious dinner table of a house briefly shared by both Schlegels and their wives. Brilliant though this circle of friends and colleagues was, dissent, death, interpersonal friction and financial exigency dispersed its members by 1801. Both brothers moved on, although German Romanticism survived.

Wilhelm's gifts as a translator were apparent early. He began turning Shakespeare's plays into German while he was still living in Jena. Published over a thirteen-year interval, his translations are still admired today for their craftsmanship. In the first decade of the 1800s, he went on to translate works by the seventeenth-century Spanish dramatist Calderón, and poetry from Italian, Spanish and Portuguese. Wilhelm also published an essay comparing Euripides and Racine, which caused a splash in Paris. During this period he met Madame de Staël (1766–1817), whose famous literary-political salon shifted between Paris and Geneva in reaction to the chaotic events of the French Consulate and First Empire, and in particular according to the vicissitudes of her antagonistic relationship with Napoleon. Wilhelm assisted Madame de Staël in her writings, tutored her children, and travelled around Europe as her companion. Then, in 1814, he took up the study of Sanskrit in Paris. A few years later he proposed a typology of languages, to which we return below. After Madame de Staël's death, Wilhelm settled in Bonn to teach Sanskrit. Returning to his early successes, he translated the *Bhagavad Gita* into Latin. Wilhelm established a press that could print the Indian *devanagari* script, briefly edited a journal that promoted Indian studies, and in other ways was instrumental in spreading access to the literature of India in Europe.

In his mid-life turn to Sanskrit and language typology, Wilhelm went further down a path Friedrich had blazed immediately after the heady days in Jena. The younger Schlegel settled in Paris around 1801, a move that proved important in the history of linguistics. There Friedrich encountered Alexander Hamilton (1762–1824), a

Scotsman who had served with the British army in Calcutta, where he had become intrigued by Indian culture and languages. Hamilton was temporarily stranded in Paris due to hostilities between France and Britain, so he whiled away the time organizing books on Sanskrit at the Imperial Library. Those books had been accumulating since the 1700s: manuscripts sent back by Jesuit missionaries, and the works of French scholars and British colonial administrators. Among other materials, Hamilton must have introduced Friedrich to the famous 'philologer's passage' in a speech by the British jurist and scholar of Sanskrit and Persian Sir William Jones (1746–94). Jones founded the Asiatic Society of Bengal. In his third anniversary address to the society in 1786, Jones speculated that Sanskrit was related to Latin, Greek and other European languages. This became one of the most quoted statements in the history of linguistics because, in the absence of hard evidence, Jones had anticipated the conclusion that a subsequent generation of philologers eventually reached by painstakingly assembling proof of the existence of an Indo-European language family.

When Friedrich Schlegel arrived in Paris, he already knew that Herder and others had dabbled in Indian literature and championed India as the cradle of civilization. But through his work with Hamilton, Friedrich became one of the first Europeans to actually learn Sanskrit outside India. In 1808, he published *On the Language and Wisdom of the Indians*. This text contains an ambitious digest of Indian philosophy, a section purporting to trace all ethnic groups back to an original Indian source, and eighty pages of Sanskrit poetry in translation. But it is the book's first section that is most important to the history of linguistics. Friedrich opened by acknowledging Jones' speculations about Sanskrit and the familiar European languages, then went on to accomplish what Jones had not – to ground the purported relatedness of Sanskrit to the European languages by comparative analysis. Citing data principally from German, Latin, Greek and Persian, Friedrich compared dozens of words and roots cross-linguistically, then highlighted parallels in (what we would now call) verbal and nominal morpho-syntax. On this basis he asserted:

> The old Indian language, *Sanscrit*, that is, the *formed* or perfect, and *Gronthon*, the dialect employed in writing and literature, has the greatest affinity with the Greek and Latin, as well as the Persian and German languages. This resemblance or affinity does not exist only in the numerous roots, which it has in common with both those nations, but extends also to the grammar and

internal structure; nor is such resemblance a casual circumstance easily accounted for by the intermixture of the languages; it is an essential element clearly indicating community of origin. It is further proved by comparison, that the Indian is the most ancient, and the source from whence others of later origin are derived.

(trans. Millington, 1808/1977: 428–29)

Friedrich more guardedly declared the relatedness of Sanskrit to 'the Armenian, the Sclavonian, and the Celtic', while excluding Coptic, Hebrew, Basque and 'the great undefined variety of the northern and southern Asiatic and the American languages' (*ibid.*: 429). Thus, in the inventory of languages he proposed to be related to Sanskrit, Friedrich proved more accurate than Jones. However, unlike Jones, he erred in attributing to Sanskrit the role of the original source language, rather than (as later scholars proved) the role of an unusually conservative collateral descendant of an extinct proto-language. Sanskrit is the cousin, not the mother, of the European languages.

Friedrich's exercise in comparative grammar – a term he 'brought into the field of genealogical comparison' (Timpanaro 1977: xxxiv) – now seems strikingly successful for a novice. It was, however, only his starting point. He used language to develop the case for India as the origin of civilization, and asserted that Sanskrit's regularity and consistency signalled its nature as an 'organic', as opposed to a 'mechanical' language. Organic languages create words and signal grammatical relations by inflecting roots internally. Mechanical languages, on the other hand, exploit particles, affixes and word order distinctions. Organic languages may decay over time, adopting other grammatical strategies as their inflectional regularity erodes. To Friedrich, this was attested in the descent of European languages from Sanskrit, but somehow did not challenge the strict dichotomy he established.

Friedrich's organic/mechanical typology is significant on several grounds. Although earlier scholars had classified languages on various bases, it was probably the first attempt to create a comprehensive morphological typology. Moreover, to Friedrich, organic languages are different in kind from mechanical languages, and intrinsically superior. This committed him to polygenesis, since although their exquisite regularity might be lost over time, organic languages could not have arisen from gestures or from inadvertent vocal sounds: organic and mechanical languages must have had separate origins. Positing this disjunction was congenial to Friedrich's notion of an original Indian homeland from which descended the languages later called Indo-European (or 'Aryan', a term later made notorious more with reference to ethnic than linguistic stock).

Like any purported single key to cross-linguistic variation, Friedrich's typology lacked refinement. But subsequent scholars built upon it. Among them was his brother Wilhelm, who in an essay on Provençal (1818/1971: 14–18) suggested a three-way classification of languages as monosyllabic versus affixing versus inflecting. Monosyllabic languages such as Chinese consist essentially of roots, but 'sterile' roots that render such languages intellectual liabilities. Wilhelm conceded some unspecified virtues to affixing languages (to which class he assigned Native American languages and Basque), but predictably reserved his highest praise for the copiousness and 'organicism' of inflecting languages. The latter class he subdivided into 'analytic' languages, whose independent auxiliaries, articles and case-marking prepositions apparently drift in the direction of Chinese, and 'synthetic' languages, which seemingly resist developing away from the core properties of inflecting languages. Sanskrit he identified as strictly synthetic.

The Schlegels' typological proposals influenced much nineteenth-century language scholarship, including that of **Wilhelm von Humboldt**. Moreover, Friedrich's 1808 book attracted considerable attention, inspiring among others **Franz Bopp** to take up the study of Sanskrit.

In the same year that *On the Language and Wisdom of the Indians* appeared, Friedrich scandalized some of the public by converting to Catholicism. Coincidentally or not, he then ceased his research into Indian language and literature. Wilhelm, on the other hand, steadily continued to promote the study of Sanskrit in his writing and teaching in Bonn. Thus we can attribute more responsibility for the transforming expansion of Sanskrit studies in Europe in the nineteenth century to the older Schlegel brother. Friedrich, however, was probably more intellectually original. He was also less able to satisfy his ambitions. Fittingly, he died before Wilhelm of a stroke suffered while writing, in the early morning hours, a sentence about 'entirely perfect and complete understanding' – a state 'for which he had striven throughout his life' (Eichner 1970: 143).

August Wilhelm von Schlegel's major writings

Course of Lectures on Dramatic Art and Literature, 1846 (J. Black, trans.), Henry G. Bohn, London (original work published 1809–1811; reprinted by AMS Press, 1965).

Observations sur la langue et la littérature provençales, 1818, Librairie Grecque-Latine-Allemande (reprinted by Tübinger Beiträge zur Linguistik, 1971).

Friedrich von Schlegel's major writings

Über die Sprache und die Weisheit der Indier: Ein Beitrag zur Begründung der Altertumskunde, 1808, Mohr and Zimmer, Heidelberg (new edition prepared by E. F. K. Koerner, including 1849 translation by E. J. Millington as *On the Language and Wisdom of the Indians*, John Benjamins, Amsterdam, 1977).

Further reading

Eichner, H. (1970) *Friedrich Schlegel*, New York: Twayne Publishers.
Koerner, E. F. K. (1989) 'Friedrich Schlegel and the emergence of historical-comparative grammar', in *Practicing Linguistic Historiography*, Amsterdam: John Benjamins.
Morpurgo Davies, A. (1998) *History of Linguistics: Vol. IV. Nineteenth-Century Linguistics* (G. Lepschy, ed.), London: Longman.
Morrison, A. J. W. (1946) 'Memoir of the literary life of Augustus William von Schlegel', in A. W. Schlegel, 1809–1811/1946.
Timpanaro, S. (1977) 'Friedrich Schlegel and the beginnings of Indo-European linguistics in Germany' (J. P. Maher, trans.), in F. Schlegel, *Über die Sprache und die Weisheit der Indier: Ein Beitrag zur Begründung der Altertumskunde*, Heidelberg: Mohr and Zimmer, 1808 (new edition prepared by E. F. K. Koerner, Amsterdam: John Benjamins, 1977).

WILHELM VON HUMBOLDT (1767–1835)

Wilhelm von Humboldt was an unusual man, who led an unusual life. His writings on language are also unusual in that their interpretation varies fundamentally from one reader to another, like a shifting scene viewed through a kaleidoscope. To some, Humboldt's work was foundational to one or more domains of nineteenth-century language science, including language typology; conceptualization of the relationship of language, thought and culture; and basic theoretical questions about the nature of language. Others conceive of Humboldt's work as atypical in his day in that, for example, he avidly studied a range of non-Indo-European languages in an era when such interest was rare among European scholars. In addition, some have found in Humboldt's writings support for specific positions or claims, while still others reject the evidence that he held those positions or intended to make those claims.

At least three related factors contribute to the equivocal nature of Humboldt's legacy. First, he found the act of writing onerous, rarely revised what he wrote, and seemed not to conceive of writing as an instrument for sharpening his own thought. Not surprisingly, generations of readers have found his work dense and obscure, in the original German as in translation. Humboldt produced long, complex sentences, adopted new terms, or extended familiar ones without specifying their referents, and seemed sometimes to shift his position with respect to an issue without acknowledging an apparent change of mind. Second, Humboldt turned to language studies late in life, published little (on language or any topic) in his lifetime, and although he was personally acquainted with many top European scholars of his day (including **Johann Gottfried Herder**, the **Schlegels**, **Franz Bopp**, Johann Wolfgang von Goethe [1749–1832], and Friedrich Schiller [1759–1805]; and through correspondence, with the Americans John Pickering [1777–1846] and Peter Stephen Duponceau [1760–1844]), he wasn't part of a school whose communal legacy might help us interpret his writings, or make sense of how they evolved. Third, Humboldt's commitment as a scholar was to cultivate his own talents, not to communicate his findings for the benefit of others – and he belonged to a social class that could afford such an indulgence. In his writings, therefore, one gets the sense that to Humboldt 'the reader was a barely tolerated presence' who confronts what 'is rather like a long and private meditation that in a series of *aperçus* points toward a center that is never reached' (Aarsleff 1988: xvii–xviii).

Humboldt was born into the second tier of aristocracy surrounding the Prussian royal household, acquiring early the courtly manners that variously assisted his progress through life. He and his younger brother Alexander (1769–1859), who achieved international fame as a geologist, natural historian and explorer of Latin America, were educated first by tutors, and subsequently through attending private lectures by scholars in Berlin. Wilhelm proceeded to the university in Göttingen, then returned to Berlin to assume the sort of civil-service position for which he had been groomed. But his education had opened to him intellectual and personal values that proved more formative than his career preparation. Humboldt's exposure to Classics inspired a lifelong attachment to ancient Greek ideals, including the nobility of self-cultivation and a penchant for metaphysical speculation. In addition, he had joined a social circle that bound its members to seek moral perfection above all else, in the context of sentimentalized pacts of friendship. After thirteen months of what seemed to be the beginning of a brilliant career, Humboldt requested a leave of absence in 1791, married a wealthy young woman within that social circle, and retreated to the countryside to invest his full attention in his own *Bildung* ('formation, [self-] cultivation'). For about a decade, he conceived and abandoned numerous writing projects, rarely finishing any; visited and entertained friends; travelled; observed the rapidly shifting political landscape; and struggled with his ideas about government, freedom, morality, history, philosophy, aesthetics, literature and differences between the sexes. He and his wife also started what became a family of seven children. Humboldt collected a little language data during a visit to the Basque country in 1801, and translated some of Pindar's poetry. But instead of being an interlude of serene, private *Bildung*, his early adulthood was spent roaming over a huge intellectual terrain without seeming to find a satisfactory home (Sweet 1978–80).

Humboldt re-entered the civil service in 1802. After serving as Prussia's envoy to the Vatican for six years, he was recalled to Berlin and spent twelve years working at high levels in government administration, and representing Prussia in Vienna and London. The achievement for which Humboldt is most remembered today is his reform (from elementary through university level; *ibid.*, Vol. 2: 14–105) of what became the most admired educational system in Europe. Berlin's Humboldt University was eventually named to honour his commitment to open, humanistic education.

Humboldt wielded administrative and diplomatic power effectively and with obvious relish. However, when some who opposed or felt threatened by his liberal values ousted Humboldt from public service in 1819, he readily reassumed a private life centring on *Bildung* and the pursuit of his long-suspended intellectual interests. Those interests had gradually converged on language, inspired by the emergence of comparative-historical linguistics.

Although one of his first acts after retiring at age fifty-two was to plunge into Sanskrit, Humboldt was especially intrigued by the indigenous languages of the Americas. In Rome, he had examined the Vatican's collection of New World missionary grammars. His brother the explorer also collected linguistic materials for him. Eventually, Humboldt worked with Basque, ancient Egyptian, Chinese and Malayo-Polynesian. In his last years he studied Kawi, an extinct Austronesian language relexicalized with Sanskrit loanwords, which was still used for literary purposes in parts of Indonesia.

A series of lectures to the Prussian Academy of Sciences, beginning in 1820 (translated as *Essays on Language* [1820–29/1997]), communicate Humboldt's approach and assumptions. But his most-cited text is a book-length introduction (Humboldt 1836/1988) to his last major work, a three-volume grammar of Kawi. It records his mature philosophy of language, illustrated with references to (*inter alia*) Delaware, Burmese, Arabic, Chinese, Greek, Sanskrit and Malayan languages. Humboldt accepted the importance of detailed empirical study of individual languages. He seemed to take for granted that all languages share principles of organization: in an 1822 letter to **Wilhelm Schlegel**, he declared that 'My point of departure is that there really is something universal in the grammar of all languages' (Sweet 1978–80, Vol. 2: 503). However, Humboldt was most committed to investigating how languages differed, an interest that underlies two of his most noted contributions: his studies in language typology, and his speculations about the relatedness of language, thought and culture.

In his work on typology, Humboldt rejected **Friedrich Schlegel**'s categorical distinction between organic and mechanical languages. In contrast to isolating languages such as Chinese (where words consist of bare roots) and inflecting languages such as Sanskrit (where words are formed by internal modification of a root), he coined – or probably coined; *ibid.*, Vol. 2: 404) – the expression 'agglutinative' to characterize languages whose words are built up by attaching prefixes or suffixes to a root. Not all of Humboldt's writings maintained this tripartite distinction, which he represented as tendencies rather than rigid categories. An 1822 lecture, for example, illustrated both agglutinative and inflectional features in Native American languages, adding that 'attributing agglutination to some languages and inflexion to others no longer seems tenable' (Humboldt 1820–29/1997: 37). By recognizing the possibility of mixed-category languages, and by acknowledging that languages could evolve from one type to another, Humboldt departed significantly from Schlegel's typology.

On the other hand, Humboldt shared with Schlegel a conviction that inflecting languages confer special intellectual capacities. Again, not all his writings are of one accord, but the impression is that to Humboldt (as to many of his contemporaries), languages are not equal vehicles for intellectual development or expression. This belief implicates another major Humboldtian theme – the relationship of language, thought and culture. In the same 1822 lecture, he claimed that inflecting languages predispose their speakers to formal analysis. While languages are rarely exclusively of one type, speakers of languages in which inflection plays a minor role do not participate in the 'general clarity and precision' afforded by inflecting languages, and will unconsciously find it 'difficult … to escape from this obscuring of the purely formal aspect' of thought (*ibid.*: 47–48). Thus, according to Humboldt, the particular character of a language affects its speakers' intellectual capacities, and even their perception. Brown (1967) analysed Humboldt's characteristically ambiguous writings on this issue, concluding that he contributed to the emergence of linguistic relativity, a version of which developed in mid-twentieth-century

American linguistics as the Sapir–Whorf hypothesis (see **Edward Sapir; Benjamin Lee Whorf**).

Language typology and linguistic relativity drifted somewhat out of fashion after Humboldt's death, such that **William Dwight Whitney** (1872: 273) famously characterized Humboldt as one to whom scholars typically paid homage without actually reading his works. However, in the next century **Noam Chomsky** (1964: 17–21; 1966: 19–31) brought renewed attention to Humboldt by attributing to him a key role in the lineage linking the French general grammarians **Antoine Arnauld** and **Claude Lancelot** to modern generative grammar. Chomsky cited Humboldt's statement in passing that language is 'no product (*Ergon*), but an activity (*Energeia*)' (Humboldt 1836/1988: 49), interpreting this as having anticipated generative grammar's view of language as not a static corpus, but rather a generative process. Chomsky has repeatedly cited Humboldt's representation of the capacity of language to make 'infinite use of finite means' (Chomsky 1966: 20; cf. Humboldt 1836/1988: 91) as an expression of the generative creativity of language. Moreover, Chomsky found one of Humboldt's more enigmatic terms, the '*Form*' of a language (Chomsky 1966: 22; cf. Humboldt 1836/1988: 48–54), congenial to his own mid-1960s notion that a language consists essentially of language-specific rules that interact with universal linguistic principles, rather than consisting of a list of words, sounds and patterns.

Capitalizing on these remarks by Humboldt, as well as on Humboldt's little-specified acceptance of the existence of language universals, Chomsky built a modern reputation for Humboldt as a visionary precursor of generative grammar. Some scholars have found Chomsky's reading persuasive (Andrews 1979; Losonsky 1999). Others, especially historians of linguistics, reject it as inaccurate and misleading (Baumann 1971; Leppin 1977), on the grounds that Chomsky has distorted Humboldt's ideas to force them into congruence with his own. Humboldt's ideas are notoriously difficult to specify. For example, it has been argued that his claim that language makes 'infinite use of finite means' means that human thought is unbounded, yet communicable through the bounded instrument of language. Chomsky, however, employs the expression to characterize the unlimited productive capacity of a grammar.

This matter of interpretation, among others, remains unsettled. At the very least, Chomsky has engaged another generation in his admiration for Humboldt, a generation that may endorse at least part of Whitney's (1872: 273) declaration that we need a guide who 'penetrates the mysteries, unravels the inconsistencies, and expounds the dark sayings, of that ingenious and profound but unclear and wholly unpractical thinker', Wilhelm von Humboldt.

Humboldt's major works

On Language: The Diversity of Human Language-Structure and Its Influence on the Mental Development of Mankind, 1988 (P. Heath, trans.), Cambridge University Press, Cambridge (original work published 1836).

Essays on Language, 1997 (T. Harden and D. Farrelly, eds and trans.), Peter Lang, Frankfurt (texts of lectures originally presented 1820–29).

Cowan, M., *Humanist Without Portfolio*, 1963, Wayne State University Press, Detroit, MI (anthology of Humboldt's writings, in translation, on political, social and natural science, philosophy, education, language; some auto-biographical texts).

Further reading

Aarsleff, H. (1988) 'Introduction', in W. von Humboldt, *On Language: The Diversity of Human Language-Structure and Its Influence on the Mental Development of Mankind*, Cambridge: Cambridge University Press.

Andrews, I. (1979). 'Some critics of Chomskyan theory reviewed', *Studies in Language*, 3, 439–52.

Baumann, H.-H. (1971) 'Die generative Grammatik und Wilhelm von Humboldt', *Poetica*, 4, 1–12.

Brown, R. L. (1967) *Wilhelm von Humboldt's Conception of Linguistic Relativity*, The Hague: Mouton.

Chomsky, N. (1964) *Current Issues in Linguistic Theory*, The Hague: Mouton.

——(1966) *Cartesian Linguistics*, New York: Harper & Row (3rd edn 2009, Cambridge: Cambridge University Press).

Leppin, J. (1977) 'Some observations on the Chomskyan interpretation of Wilhelm von Humboldt', *Archivum Linguisticum*, 8, 46–59.

Losonsky, M. (1999) 'Introduction', in W. von Humboldt, *On Language: On the Diversity of Human Language Construction and Its Influence on the Mental Development of the Human Species* (M. Losonsky, ed and P. Heath, trans), Cambridge.

Sweet, P. R. (1978–80) *Wilhelm von Humboldt: A Biography: Vols. 1–2*, Ohio State University.

Whitney, W. D. (1872) 'Steinthal on the origin of language', *North American Review*, 114, 272–308.

JACOB GRIMM (1785–1863)

Jacob Grimm's lifelong preoccupation was to preserve and document the language-based creations of German-speaking people. He wrote about the laws of German speakers, their mythology, folk literature and, above all, language. Thus he helped define what was 'German' before there was a German nation. Starting in 1812, with his younger brother Wilhelm (1786–1859), Grimm published three volumes of folktales that have been integrated on many levels into western popular culture and literature. The Grimms' *Nursery and Household Tales* recorded, with minimal literary embellishment, traditional stories told by common people in their own voices: fishermen, nannies, soldiers, children. Later, the brothers began work on a historical dictionary of German that was not completed until the mid-twentieth century. But Jacob's philological interests ran deeper than his brother's, so that he alone is responsible for the *Deutsche Grammatik*, which many view as having initiated scientific study of German. This text also contains Jacob's signature contribution to linguistics, his formulation of what came to be called 'Grimm's Law'.

Jacob and Wilhelm lived and worked closely together almost all their lives. The two oldest sons of a large family, they carried considerable responsibility for their siblings' and mother's welfare after their father, a lawyer, died young. They were educated together in Marburg, and together moved away from the study of law when, under the influence of scholars on the fringes of the Romantic movement that centred on **Friedrich** and **Wilhelm von Schlegel**, they first encountered medieval German texts. Both Grimms were employed for years as librarians and archivists, working to preserve manuscripts and valuable older books from fire and from the ravages of the Napoleonic wars. Jacob also served as secretary to the legation of his ancestral state of Hesse, in which role he participated in the Congress of Vienna in 1814 to 1815, and visited Paris to try to retrieve books confiscated from Hessian libraries. He found travel rewarding, but political intrigue tiresome. In letters he sent home, he seems to have counted the days until he could return to his family and antiquarian studies (Michaelis-Jena 1970).

Later, Wilhelm and Jacob accepted professorships in Göttingen. They were abruptly removed from their positions in 1837, as members of a group nicknamed 'the Göttingen Seven', for protesting the King of Hanover's abrogation of constitutional guarantees of civil and academic freedom. Eventually, supporters of the Grimms found them new positions in Berlin that involved a little teaching and good opportunities to pursue their philological research. By the end of their lives, the Grimms' reputations were established and their work internationally celebrated – although for the retiring Jacob, this entailed having to suffer time spent away from his beloved books, accepting honours and being fêted by visitors.

Jacob's 4000-page *Deutsche Grammatik* ('German Grammar', but more accurately 'Germanic Grammar') partially occupied him for more than twenty years, and became a model that others emulated in producing grammars of Romance and Slavic. Published in four volumes and two editions (Volume 1 in three editions), it is a historically informed comparative grammar of the Germanic languages. It addresses the sound systems of Germanic languages in their historical contexts; morphology and word formation; and an array of morpho-syntactic phenomena. A final section on complex sentence structure was never completed. Grimm assembled and analysed data from Gothic, Old and Middle High German, Old Norse, and a range of modern Germanic languages, including English, making abundant comparison with other Indo-European languages, especially Latin, Greek, Sanskrit and Slavic. The text cites page after page of examples (and counter-examples) of the features of Germanic languages, meticulously gleaned from grammatical and literary works.

Tradition has it that Grimm was influenced to write his grammar in reaction to a critical 1815 review by Wilhelm von Schlegel of the first volume of a journal the Grimms published. Schlegel was not captivated by folk literature, and dismissed some adventurous etymologies that Jacob had proposed. He further declared that what was needed instead was close, disciplined analysis of older texts. Grimm took up the challenge, attending to the smallest details of German and their reflexes in related languages over time. He adopted an anti-prescriptivist stance, although, along with German Romantics in general, he maintained that earlier forms of a language gave unique access to its nature and to the culture of its speakers.

Another formative influence on Grimm's *Deutsche Grammatik* was the work of the Danish philologist Rasmus Kristian Rask (1787–1832). In his preface to the first edition, Grimm admiringly depicted Rask's work on Icelandic, to which he had just gained access as Volume 1 went to press. In the 1822 second edition of Volume 1, Grimm developed Rask's discoveries about sound correspondences between Germanic and other Indo-European languages. In fact, he built upon his predecessor's work so closely that some (like **Otto Jespersen**) wanted to rename Grimm's famous statement 'Rask's Law.' Rask pointed out sound correspondences between certain Germanic words and their Greek and Latin cognates, but Grimm organized and systematized those findings in the wider context of Indo-European languages. The key correspondences are, in brief, that Proto-Indo-European voiceless stops p, t, k, k^w correlate with proto-Germanic voiceless fricatives f, θ, $h(x)$, hw; voiced stops b, d, g, g^w

correlate with voiceless stops p, t, k, k^w; and voiced aspirated stops bh, dh, gh, g^wh correlate with plain voiced stops b, d, g, g^w. As a single example for each case, compare Sanskrit *pitár-* with Gothic *fadar* 'father'; Latin *duo* with Gothic *twái* 'two'; Sanskrit *dhā* 'put' with the English verb *do*. Expressed in the terms of modern linguistics, the generalization is that Proto-Indo-European plosive consonants as a set can be related to Germanic consonants by shifting specific features for manner of articulation, voicing or aspiration, while preserving their features for place of articulation. Grimm's statement of these relationships was made even more compact by his treatment of both Sanskrit *bh* (etc.) and what we now call fricatives, as 'aspirates'.

This tripartite set of sound correspondences that Grimm articulated constitutes what Germanic linguists now call the First Sound Shift. Grimm conceived it not as an array of individual sound-to-sound correspondences, but as a relationship of subsystems to subsystems; and those subsystems displace each other in a circular chain shift, 'like a game of musical chairs played by the non-sonorant phonemes' (Gessman 1990: 3). The First Sound Shift remains a key to the development of Germanic languages, and a showpiece of historical linguistics, even though the extent of interdependence among its three parts, as well as its impetus, dating, geographical locus and direction of spread, remain controversial (Collinge 1985: 63–76). Grimm conflated the First Sound Shift with what is now treated separately as the Second Sound Shift, an additional set of correspondences (also anticipated by Rask) in which the relationship of Proto-Indo-European to Gothic consonants is mirrored in the relationship of Gothic to Old High German consonants. In other words, in the evolution of Old High German, certain consonants participated twice in the same game of musical chairs, each time revolving an additional step, so that (for example, using Grimm's notation) what appear as Proto-Indo-European b, d, g surface in Gothic as p, t, k, and later surface in Old High German as f, z, ch.

As with the First Sound Shift, the dating and impetus for the Second Sound Shift are obscure. But to nineteenth-century philologists, these correspondences made miraculous sense out of an ocean of bafflingly near-identical words in many languages.

On closer inspection, however, Grimm's Law as articulated in 1822 may be rather *too* miraculous. One problem is that it rests uneasily on the fact that Grimm was 'fortunate in his ignorance of phonetics' (Lehmann 1967: 47): he mostly articulated his principles in terms of letters rather than sounds, and his statement of correspondences conveniently obfuscated differences between aspirates and fricatives.

Another problem is that Grimm displayed a happy knack for landing on examples that fit rather than challenged his principles, so that although he conscientiously acknowledged certain counter-examples, he still under-represented the actual range of non-conforming data.

Some non-conforming data, however, eventually proved tractable. In the hands of the next generation of philologists, what were at first taken as exceptions to Grimm's Law reinforced rather than refuted it. One set of apparent counter-examples was resolved by the recognition that Grimm's Law does not apply to the second of two adjacent consonants. Another potential threat to the generality of Grimm's Law was eliminated by the mathematician and Sanskrit scholar Hermann Grassmann (1809–77). Grassmann discovered that when two aspirated consonants appear in a Sanskrit or Greek word, as a rule the first loses its aspiration. This fact explains the apparent mis-correspondence of Germanic *b* to certain words with Sanskrit *b*, where, according to Grimm's Law, one would expect Sanskrit *bh*. ('Grassmann's Law' apparently emerged separately in Sanskrit and Greek, and is also attested in other language families.) Another set of apparent counter-examples was accounted for by the Danish scholar Karl Verner (1846–96). 'Verner's Law' made sense of a subset of medial consonants which at first defied Grimm's Law, such as the *p* in Sanskrit *saptá* or Latin *septum*, which surfaces in Gothic as *b* (in *sibun* 'seven'), not *f* as expected. The key here turns out to be that the second syllable is accented in Sanskrit, a feature presumably retained from Proto-Indo-European. Verner's Law states that unaspirated voiceless stops and fricatives that precede an accented syllable diverge from the predicted pattern, appearing in Germanic as voiced.

Thus Grimm's Law was refined in ways that heightened rather than threatened its prestige. To many scholars, this stream of work was so successful that by the end of the nineteenth century the Neogrammarians (see **Karl Brugmann**) presented Grimm's Law as the parade case for the unexceptionality of sound laws – even granted that it had been substantially retouched since 1822. Grimm's insight still retains its glamour, as indicated by the many attempts to update or rethink it in the diverse terms of subsequent decades (Collitz 1926; Weinstock 1968; Emonds 1972).

Grimm made additional contributions to Germanic linguistics. Again working from insights of Rask, he analysed the phenomenon of umlaut, the anticipatory fronting of a vowel – Grimm called it 'clouding' – when the following syllable contains a front vowel (Grimm 1822/1999: 7–10). Grimm noted that fronted vowels may be retained even after historical loss of the syllable that triggered umlaut.

He also discussed the concept of ablaut, the vowel alternation within a root illustrated in Modern English *sing, sang, sung*. Grimm invested symbolic meanings in the alternation of vowels, meanings which (in the fashion of the day) he mined for truths about the nature of the early Germanic language stock. He considered the three vowels *a, i, u* as 'basic' to the vocalic inventories of all languages (Benware 1974).

Finally, the Grimms' historical (rather than normative or prescriptive) dictionary advanced Germanic lexicography. Although they both died before the project advanced beyond the letter F, their goal was to include every German word, however obsolete, to create a comprehensive resource for the study of older literature. In this sense, the dictionary was consistent with Jacob's style of scholarship. Unlike his contemporaries, who dealt with expansive theories, Grimm was most at home handling the humblest data: folktales, not high-culture epics; voiced versus voiceless stops, not grandiose language typologies. An 1822 letter to a friend justifying his grammatical work seems to epitomize Grimm's mindset. He wrote, 'The Lord made small things as well as big ones, and everything man looks at closely, is full of wonder' (Michaelis-Jena 1970: 86).

Jacob Grimm's major writings

Deutsche Grammatik: Vol. I (1st edn), 1819; *Vol. I* (2nd edn), 1822; *Vol. II*, 1826; *Vol. III*, 1831; *Vol. IV*, 1837, *Vol. I* (3rd edn), 1840, Dieterich, Göttingen (reprinted in *Foundations of Indo-European Comparative Philology, 1800–1850*, R. Harris, ed., Routledge, 1999). Lehmann (1967: 46–60) translates the exposition of Grimm's Law from Vol. I (2nd edn).
(with W. Grimm) *Kinder- und Hausmärchen: Vol. I*, 1812; *Vol. II*, 1815; *Vol. III*, 1822; Georg Reimer, Berlin (numerous subsequent editions, including English translations as *Grimm's Fairy Tales*).
(with W. Grimm *et al.*) *Deutsche Wörterbuch: Vol. I*, 1854; *Vol. II*, 1860; *Vol. III*, 1864, Hirzel, Leipzig. Continued by R. Hildebrandt, K. Weigand *et al.* to Vol. XVI (reprinted 1965).

Further reading

Antonsen, E. H. (ed). (1990) *The Grimm Brothers and the Germanic Past*, Amsterdam: John Benjamins.
Benware, W. A. (1974) *The Study of Indo-European Vocalism in the 19th Century*, Amsterdam: John Benjamins.
Collinge, N. E. (1985). *The Laws of Indo-European*, Amsterdam: John Benjamins.
Collitz, H. (1926). 'A century of Grimm's Law', *Language*, 2, 174–83.

Emonds, J. (1972) 'A reformulation of Grimm's Law', in M. Brame (ed.), *Contributions to Generative Phonology*, Austin: University of Texas Press.

Gessman, A. M. (1990) 'Grimm's Law: Fact or fiction?', *Language Quarterly*, 28, 2–16.

Lehmann, W. P. (ed. and trans.) (1967) *A Reader in Nineteenth-Century Historical Indo-European Linguistics*, Bloomington, IN: Indiana University Press.

Michaelis-Jena, R. (1970) *The Brothers Grimm*, London: Routledge & Kegan Paul.

Weinstock, J. (1968). 'Grimm's Law in distinctive features', *Language*, 44, 224–29.

FRANZ BOPP (1791–1867)

Franz Bopp's painstaking work in comparative grammar was foundational to one of the key linguistic achievements of the nineteenth century. Building on previous scholars' recognition that the modern European and classical languages must be related to 'Oriental' languages such as Sanskrit, Old Persian or 'Zend' (Avestan), Bopp assembled, piecemeal, a vast corpus of evidence for parallel morphological patterns among those languages and the ancestors of modern European languages such as Latin, Gothic, 'Old Sclavonic' or Old Prussian. Moreover, he synthesized his observations of similarity and divergence to infer properties of languages for which he had no actual evidence. In doing so, Bopp developed techniques for analysing grammatical correspondences and reconstructing unattested languages. Bopp not only modelled how to do comparative analysis, but also identified specific cross-linguistic correspondences. The validity of some of those correspondences has endured through subsequent language research.

Bopp was born in Mainz, on the Rhine River in southwestern Germany. A year later, when the French revolutionary army occupied his home town, his family fled east to Aschaffenburg. Bopp was educated in Aschaffenburg. His teacher Karl Joseph Windischmann (1775–1839), an admirer of **Friedrich von Schlegel**, influenced him to focus on the languages of India and the Near East. In 1812 Bopp travelled to Paris, the European centre of Sanskrit studies, on a grant from the king of Bavaria that Windischmann helped him obtain. Like both Friedrich and **Wilhelm von Schlegel**, Bopp pored over manuscripts held at the Imperial Library and worked through Sanskrit literature with scholars such as Antoine Léonard de Chézy (1773–1832). He continued in Paris until 1816, serenely absorbed in his books and seemingly oblivious to the surrounding social and political chaos as Napoleon's empire disintegrated. The immediate material product was his celebrated early work, the 'Conjugationssystem' (Bopp 1816/1975). The first half of this text analyses correspondences between Sanskrit and other Indo-European languages. The second half consists of translations of Sanskrit literature.

After Paris, Bopp went to London to consult additional manuscripts, with the support of the Bavarian Academy. His sojourn in England marked an intellectual turning point. He revised the *Conjugationssystem* and published a new version of the first half in English (Bopp 1820/1989). From London, Bopp moved to the University of Göttingen, where he was awarded a doctorate. Because he had attracted the attention of **Wilhelm von Humboldt** when both men were in London, Bopp hoped Humboldt would find him a position in the up-and-coming university in Berlin that Humboldt had founded. Eventually this did come to pass, although not until Bopp had secured the permission of his longtime benefactor the king of Bavaria (Park 2006). Bopp was made professor of Oriental Literature and General Philology in Berlin in 1821. He remained affiliated with the university until his death. His publications include translations of excerpts of the Indian epic the *Mahabharata*; a grammar of Sanskrit; a Sanskrit–Latin glossary; a study of accentuation in Greek and Sanskrit; an analysis of Malayo-Polynesian proposing that it was part of the Indo-European language family; and, notably, a six-volume comparative grammar of Indo-European languages, the second edition of which was translated into English as Bopp (1833–52/1856).

Going back to his days in Paris, and even earlier to his study with Windischmann, an early stimulus of Bopp's interest in Sanskrit had been Friedrich von Schlegel's *On the Language and Wisdom of the Indians*. Bopp's 1816 *Conjugationssystem*, like Schlegel's 1808 book, contained both comparative grammatical material and examples of Indian literature. In the 1820 English version of the *Conjugationssystem*, however, Bopp dropped the Indian texts and, in his comparative material, separated himself from some of Schlegel's views. Bopp rejected Schlegel's assertion that European languages derive from Sanskrit. Rather, he argued that they are collateral descendents from a common source, on the grounds that although Sanskrit does, indeed, preserve certain otherwise unattested properties attributable to an ancestral language, 'there are instances where the reverse is the case, where grammatical forms, lost in the Sanskrit, have been preserved in Greek or Latin' (Bopp 1820/1989: 15). Bopp's position is now taken as fact.

Moreover, Bopp (*ibid.*) respectfully criticized Schlegel's binary typology of languages into the 'organic' or inflecting type, which expresses morphological relationships by modifying roots internally – and which, according to Schlegel, included Sanskrit and the idealized Indo-European languages – versus the 'mechanical' type, which modifies roots through affixation, particles or compounding. Bopp followed Indian grammarians in insisting that Sanskrit roots are monosyllabic. That limits their ability to be modified, because 'such languages cannot display any great facility of expressing grammatical modification by the change of their original materials without the help of foreign additions', and are constrained to changes of the monosyllabic vowel or to reduplication (*ibid.*: 20–21). Instead, Bopp asserted that 'both methods [of modifying roots] are adopted in the formation of all languages ... and that the second, by use of significant suffixes, is the method that predominates in them all' (*ibid.*: 20).

With this, Bopp seemed to reject Schlegel's value-laden division of languages into organic versus mechanical types, and to clear the way for a more technical, descriptive analysis of cross-linguistic variation. For the most part, that is the tone of his work. Still, Bopp's *Comparative Grammar* proposed in passing a tripartite language typology, which he identified with Wilhelm von Schlegel: (1) the Chinese type, which has bare roots 'without the capacity of composition, and hence without organism, without grammar' (to Bopp 'organism' seemed to mean grammatical arrangement derived from agglutination; Delbrück 1882: 18); (2) the Sanskrit type, whose monosyllabic roots 'are capable of combination, and obtain their organism and grammar nearly in this way alone'; and (3) the Semitic types, with disyllabic roots that are modified internally to form words (Bopp 1833–52/1856: 102–3). To the Sanskrit family alone, Bopp attributed:

> a great superiority ... in the judicious, ingenious selection and application of [forms combined with roots], and the accurate and acute defining of various relations, which hereby becomes possible; finally, in the beautiful adjustment of these additions to a harmonious whole, which bears the appearance of an organized body.
>
> (*ibid.*: 103, trans. Eastwick)

Despite the evidence that Bopp conceptualized language in these terms, the *Comparative Grammar* does not otherwise dwell on typological issues or on the differential value or beauty of specific languages. Rather, it is almost completely taken up with patient and sober cross-linguistic comparison. Bopp privileged the position of Sanskrit by

organizing his discussion around its features and forms, and by pointing out parallels and gaps between Sanskrit and Zend, Gothic, Greek,
Latin, etc. The text begins with an inventory of 'Characters and
sounds' but quickly moves on to morphology (the structure of roots;
case; the inflection of adjectives, numerals and pronouns). The
remainder of Bopp's *Comparative Grammar* is divided between analysis
of verbal morphology (agreement, tense, mood, voice, etc.) and word
formation in general (participles and infinitives, affixation, compounding, indeclinable word classes), all presented with copious
examples. Throughout, Bopp demonstrated how comparison of linguistic forms builds the case for relatedness of languages. For example,
Sections 148 to 157 discuss singular nominative and accusative nouns
across masculine, feminine and neuter genders. Bopp started out by
noting that 'In neuters, throughout the whole Sanskrit family of languages the nominative is identical with the accusative' (*ibid.*: 161). He
then examined examples across various declensional classes, first from
Sanskrit and then from Zend, Lithuanian and Gothic. A chart (*ibid.*:
163–64) compares twenty-six nominative singular nouns in these
languages, plus Greek and Latin, calling attention to parallel structures
among lexical cognates and to parallel patterns of inflectional morphology. Moving on to the accusative case, Bopp generalized that 'The
character of the accusative is *m* in Sanskrit, Zend, and Latin; in Greek
v for euphony' (*ibid.*: 164). He then discussed diverse instantiations of
the basic accusative *m*, the source of which he attributes to a pronoun
(*ibid.*: 171) – the same source he posits for case and agreement endings in general. Bopp illustrated how Sanskrit modifies accusative *m*
following monosyllabic or consonant-final stems, where it takes a
'precursory vowel' (*ibid.*: 166). He worked through residual irregularities, and speculated about whether Sanskrit accusative *m* had earlier
been attached to neuter stems ending in −*i* or −*u*, while the much
larger class of neuter stems ending in −*a* dropped *m* to neutralize the
difference between nominative and accusative. Thus Bopp engaged in
internal reconstruction of Sanskrit and cross-linguistic comparative
analysis, demonstrating the value of moving back and forth between
the two. He cleared the way for the bolder reconstructions of later
scholars such as August Schleicher (1821–68).

Bopp's contribution, therefore, was not to theorize language comparison or to generalize about types of languages, but rather to demonstrate how comparative analysis could be carried out. Nevertheless,
the Preface to the *Comparative Grammar* (*ibid.*: v) declares that its
objective was to inquire into the 'physical and mechanical laws' of
languages. By 'physical law' Bopp meant what we now call 'phonetic'

laws, a domain that is not his strong suit since virtually all of the *Comparative Grammar* is taken up in dissection of morphology. Bopp did, however, elaborate on 'mechanical laws', such as his 'law of gravity', by which he accounted for apparently anomalous alterations of verbal roots. Bopp noted that 'Before light terminations extensions are frequent, which, before the heavier, are withdrawn' so that in some instances 'the entire body of the root can only be maintained before light terminations, but, before the heavy, mutilation occurs' (*ibid.*: 669). Bopp pointed out examples of this feature in Sanskrit, then explored its presence or absence in other Indo-European languages (*ibid.*: 669–87).

However, for Bopp a 'law' was not an exceptionless, across-the-board rule. Contrasting Bopp's conception of a law to that of the Neogrammarians, Delbrück (1882: 21) quoted Bopp as writing that 'We must expect to find no laws in language which offer more resistance than the shores of rivers and seas'. Delbrück cited numerous examples where Bopp readily admitted exceptions or at least looseness in the application of 'laws', concluding that 'Even the admission of wholly isolated cases of [irregularities] does not terrify him' (*ibid.*: 22).

Bopp's conception of laws governing language structure, then, was part of what Neogrammarians such as **Karl Brugmann** sought to overturn. Bopp also sometimes represented language as a living, 'organic' phenomenon, rhetoric he probably inherited from Schlegel; this was another target of the Neogrammarians' criticism. Bopp did not develop the 'organic' metaphor to the extent that Schleicher would do. But insofar as he did, Morpurgo Davies (1987) argued that its adoption provided Bopp with a notion of language change – since everything 'organic' cycles through birth, decay, and death – that was sufficient for his purpose, which was to identify correspondences across languages over time. Bopp was a comparativist more than a historian, although comparative-historical linguistics regards him as a founding figure.

Bopp's major works

Über das Conjugationssystem der Sanskritsprache in Vergleichung mit jenem der griechischen, lateinischen, persischen und germanischen Sprache, 1816 (K. J. Windischmann, ed.), Andreäische Buchhandlung, Frankfurt am Main (reprinted by George Olms, Hildesheim, 1975).
Analytical Comparison of the Sanskrit, Greek, Latin and Teutonic Languages, Shewing the Original Identity of Their Grammatical Structure, 1989 (K. Koerner, ed.), John Benjamins, Philadelphia, PA (original work published 1820).

Vergleichende Grammatik des Sanskrit, Zend, Griechischen, Lateinischen, Litthauischen, Altslawischen, Gothischen und Deutschen, Vols 1–6, 1833–52, F. Dümmler, Berlin (reprinted in *Foundations of Indo-European Comparative Philology 1800–1850, Vols 10–11,* R. Harris, ed., Routledge, 1999). 2nd edn published as *A Comparative Grammar of the Sanskrit, Zend, Greek, Latin, Lithuanian, Gothic, German and Sclavonic Languages, Vol. 1–3* (E. B. Eastwick, trans.), Williams and Norgate, London, 1856.

Further reading

Delbrück, B. (1882) *Introduction to the Study of Language: A Critical Survey of the History and Methods of Comparative Philology of the Indo-European Languages* (E. Channing, trans.), Leipzig: Breitkopf and Härtel.

Guigniaut, M. (1877) 'Notice historique sur la vie et les travaux de M. François Bopp', *Mémoires de l'Académie des Inscriptions et Belles-Lettres,* 29, 201–24 (reprinted in Bopp, F., *Analytical Comparison of the Sanskrit, Greek, Latin and Teutonic Languages, Shewing the Original Identity of Their Grammatical Structure* (K. Koerner, ed.), John Benjamins, Philadelphia, PA, 1989 (original work published 1820).

Hoenigswald, H. M. (1993) 'On the history of the comparative method', *Anthropological Linguistics,* 35, 54–65.

Morpurgo Davies, A. (1987) '"Organic" and "organism" in Franz Bopp', in H. M. Hoenigswald and L. F. Wiener (eds), *Biological Metaphor and Cladistic Classification,* Philadelphia, PA: Unversity of Pennsylvania Press.

Park, P. K. J. (2006) 'Return to Enlightenment: Franz Bopp's reformation of comparative grammar', in D. L. Hoyt and K. Oslund (eds), *The Study of Language and the Politics of Community in Global Context,* Lanham, MD: Lexington.

Verburg, P. A. (1950) 'The background to the linguistic conceptions of Bopp', *Lingua,* 2, 438–68.

FRIEDRICH MAX MÜLLER (1823–1900)

A portrait of Max Müller's reputation would be a study in chiaroscuro, contrasting light and shadow. As an Oxford professor, exponent of Indo-European philology and the Sanskrit classics, and interpreter of Indian religions and of world mythology to Victorian England, Müller produced a stream of translations, editions, essays, historical and biographical analyses, commentaries and memoirs, some reprinted multiple times. He presented several lecture series on language, religion and mythology that brought him great popular acclaim. Numerous European governments honoured Müller for his scholarship and role as a public intellectual. To his great satisfaction, Queen Victoria made him a member of the Privy Council, while Indians revered him as a champion of their culture despite his having never visited India.

However, during his own lifetime Müller's views were also challenged or rejected, his scholarship belittled, and his acceptance of the British Raj criticized as inconsistent with his (not unqualified) respect for Indian culture and civil rights. In the century since his death, his work has been dismissed as dated and superficial, or simply ignored (Masuzawa 2003). Likewise, Müller's personal life comprised light and darkness, triumph and nobility contrasting with tragedy and egoism.

Müller was German, born in the capital of the duchy of Anhalt-Dessau (Müller 1901; Chaudhuri 1974). His father (a teacher and minor poet) died young, but the older Müller's reputation and social connections helped sustain his son through years of poverty and isolation as he struggled to establish himself. Although music was his first and enduring preoccupation, he studied languages, including Sanskrit, in Leipzig. He was awarded a doctorate precociously at age twenty-one. Müller could then have settled into the life of a civil servant or teacher. Instead, he published his translation of the *Hitopadesha* (a collection of Sanskrit fables) and resolved to devote his life to philology.

Müller met **Franz Bopp** and **Wilhelm von Humboldt** in Berlin in 1844. He then proceeded to Paris, where a letter from Humboldt's brother, the naturalist Alexander von Humboldt, gained him access to the collection of Indian texts at the Bibliothèque Nationale (Bosch 2002: 30). Müller studied and copied Vedic literature by day and observed Parisian high culture by night as an impoverished outsider. Eventually, French scholars recognized his talents. With their encouragement, he decided to edit the monumental *Rigveda*, comprising 1028 Sanskrit hymns, along with its fourteenth-century commentary by Sayana.

In 1846, Müller travelled to London to consult manuscripts and scholars at East India House. Two years later, he moved to Oxford to supervise publication of his edition, underwritten by the East India Company. To make ends meet, he accepted a teaching position. In 1858 Müller was appointed a Fellow of Oxford's All Souls College, but he never became fully at ease in Oxford's labyrinthine ecclesiastical, social and political subcultures. He bitterly resented being passed over for appointment as the Boden Professor of Sanskrit (Bosch 2002: 80–84). However, in 1861 Müller gave nine celebrated lectures on 'The Science of Language' for a non-specialist audience at the Royal Institution of Great Britain. A published version (Müller 1861–64/1875) went through fourteen editions, with translations into six foreign languages, bringing him international fame. Müller's repeat lecture series in 1863 was also successful.

Subsequently he gave addresses at numerous prestigious venues, to great public applause, even as some academics complained that his genial armchair scholarship did not do justice to philological niceties, or that his popularization of the field misrepresented other academics' positions or misappropriated their work. Müller's publications on world religions and mythology were likewise controversial on various grounds, with some parties suspecting him of apostasy and others of surreptitious Christian proselytism. Nevertheless, Oxford named Müller Professor of Comparative Philology in 1868. He was gratified but, still harbouring a grudge over the Boden Professorship, remained ambivalent in his attachment to Oxford.

As a backdrop to these professional highs and lows, Müller endured dramatic personal upheaval in the high style of nineteenth-century romantics, including an agonizingly problematic love affair that culminated in an ecstatic marriage. Later he suffered the deaths of two young-adult daughters, a decade apart. These experiences brought his intellectual work to a standstill (Chaudhuri 1974: 265–86). Eventually, he found the strength to move forward. Müller attributed his recovery to his lifelong commitment to Christianity, although his writings show that he also took inspiration freely from Indian philosophy and religious thought.

The response to Müller's edition of the *Rigveda*, published in instalments over twenty-five years, illustrates the lights and shadows of his scholarly reputation. Müller's work remains an important resource for twenty-first-century Indologists, as do his translations (a selection of *Rigveda* hymns; the *Upanishads*, philosophical texts that culminate the Vedas; the Buddhist scripture *Dhammapada*) and the fifty-volume *Sacred Books of the East* that Müller edited. But Müller drew on European philological techniques and Indian interpretive traditions in a balance that does not always strike present-day scholars as apt (Dodson 2007). Nor does Müller's combination of global admiration for the ancient Vedic (and hence, proto-Indo-European) world with distaste for aspects of Indian scholarship and culture always satisfy modern readers (Tull 1991). During Müller's life, his most sweeping critic was American Sanskritist **William Dwight Whitney**. Even granted Whitney's propensity to find fault, his dissatisfaction with Müller was extreme: Whitney found Müller's translations 'tame and spiritless'; the apparatus 'greatly wanting in pertinence'; the notes showing 'heedless lavishness'; overall the work amounted to a 'severe disappointment' that was 'unfortunate and ill-judged' (Whitney 1873: 138–48). Whitney and Müller sparred for years, creating a notorious trans-Atlantic academic feud driven in part by real differences of orientation (Joseph 2002), and probably also in part by a rivalry for the role of interpreter of Sanskrit literature to the Euro-American public.

Detractors notwithstanding, Müller's lectures to the Royal Institution cemented his fame. The 1861 title is significant: Müller surveyed mid-nineteenth-century European philology as a '*science* of language'. He declared that 'the science of language can declare itself completely independent of history' in the sense that, although language is deeply connected to the culture and history, still 'languages can be analyzed and classified on their own evidence ... without any reference to the individuals, families, clans, tribes, nations, or races by whom they are or have been spoken' (Müller 1861/1875: 79, 82). He stressed what he saw as three stages in the development of the science of language: empiricist, classificatory and theoretical. In a single chapter on the empiricist science of language, Müller recounted how ancient Greek and Roman grammarians identified and named the constituents of language. Müller devoted the bulk of his lectures to the classificatory science of language. He communicated the excitement of scholars' recent reconstruction of the Indo-European language family, and summarized their findings. Reflecting his own expertise and the English public's fascination with India, Müller provided detailed information about Sanskrit and its role in genealogical studies. But he also addressed Semitic and Ural-Altaic (or 'Turanian') languages, with some references to other non-Indo-European families. As an additional classificatory tool, Müller referred to three by-then familiar morpho-logical classes of languages, which he organized hierarchically from 'radical' (isolating) to 'terminational' (agglutinative) to 'inflectional' (*ibid.*: 286–96). Languages may develop in this order or become 'arrested' at a point where they (in some undefined sense) 'settle'. Müller argued on this basis that there was no necessity to reject monogenesis. Curiously, he asserted monogenesis to be consistent with theories of the origin of language derived from both biblical and Darwinian authority (*ibid.*: 326–42), although he evinced strong scepticism regarding the latter while exploiting Darwinan terms to depict language change (Alter 1999: 79–96).

Under the rubric of a theoretical science of language, Müller included a chain of perennial questions about the origin of language, child language acquisition, and whether humans are unique among animals in possessing language. He named, and rejected, the 'bow-wow' (mimetic) and 'pooh-pooh' (interjectionist) theories of the origin of language, coining terms that generations of introductory textbooks on linguistics have repeated ever since (Müller 1861/1875: 358–69).

Müller closed his lectures by returning to the theme of language growth. He proposed that language evolved from a set of roots that are the original constituents of all languages, 'produced by a power inherent in human nature' (*ibid.*: 384). Languages have variously eliminated, expanded and combined them, but some 400 to 500 of these roots are still attested. Müller claimed that the processes by which roots are modified are neither wholly predictable nor arbitrary, nor due to human design, but that looking at language change historically makes it comprehensible.

> The building up of language is not like the building of the cells in a beehive, nor is it like the building of St. Peter's by Michael Angelo. It is the result of innumerable agencies, working each according to certain laws, and leaving in the end the result of their combined efforts freed from all that proved superfluous or useless. From the first combination of two such words [in Chinese] as *gin*, man, *kiai*, many, to form the plural *gin kiai*, to the perfect grammar of Sanskrit and Greek, everything is intelligible as a result of two principles of growth [namely,] [w]hat is antecedent to the production of roots is the work of nature; what follows after is the work of man, not in his individual and free, but in his collective and moderating, capacity.
>
> (*ibid.*: 388–89)

This passage reveals something of the tone that contributed to Müller's success, which invites readers to participate in the author's disarming self-assurance. At times Müller writes extravagantly or anecdotally, but always invitingly. He may have played a role in Europe in the mid- to late-1800s parallel to the role Mario Pei (1901–78) played in the United States in the mid 1900s. Pei was born the year after Müller died; he immigrated from Italy to New York; studied Sanskrit, Germanic and Romance languages at Columbia University; was appointed to the faculty there; faced his share of criticism and participated in his share of controversies (Huebener 1972). When Pei retired in 1952 as Professor of Romance Philology, he left a bibliography the size of Müller's. Notably, Pei published hugely popular books (*The Story of Language*, 1949; *The Story of English*, 1952), which successfully engaged a generation of non-specialist readers in the drama and romance of language science as practised in his day.

Pei never achieved the public profile of Müller, 'the Victorian world's most celebrated linguistic savant' (Alter 1999: 4). But one might say about them both that they 'wrote too quickly and too much', to quote Müller's own critique of another scholar (Bosch 2002: 55). Both men carried the day with the public, and the attention they brought to the study of language was at least as consequential as the specifics of their own views.

Müller's major works

Rigveda Samhita. *The Sacred Hymns of the Brahmans together with the Commentary of Sayanacarya: Vols 1–6*, 1849–74 (F. M. Müller, ed. and trans.), W. H. Allen, London.

Lectures on the Science of Language: Vols 1–2, 1875, Scribner, Armstrong & Co., New York (original work published 1861).

Sacred Books of the East: Vols 1–50, 1879–1910 (F. M. Müller, ed.), Clarendon Press, Oxford.

Chips from a German Workshop: Vol. I–IV, 1869–75, Charles Scribner's Sons, New York (compilation of shorter works; revised and expanded with new contents 1894–95).

My Autobiography: A Fragment, 1901, Charles Scribner's Sons, New York.

Further reading

Alter, S. G. (1999) *Darwininsm and the Linguistic Image*, Baltimore, MD: Johns Hopkins University Press.

Bosch, L. P. van den (2002) *Friedrich Max Müller: A Life Devoted to the Humanities*, Leiden: E. J. Brill.

Chaudhuri, N. C. (1974). *Scholar Extraordinary: The Life of Professor the Rt. Hon. Friedrich Max Müller, P. C.*, London: Chatto & Windus.

Dodson, M. S. (2007) 'Contesting translations: orientalism and the interpretation of the *Vedas*', *Modern Intellectual History*, 4, 43–59.

Huebener, T. (1972) 'Mario A. Pei', in J. Fisher and P. A. Gaeng, *Studies in Honor of Mario A. Pei*, Chapel Hill, NC: University of North Carolina Press.

Joseph, J. E. (2002) '"The American Whitney" and his European heritages and legacies', in *From Whitney to Chomsky: Essays in the History of American Linguistics*, Philadelphia, PA: John Benjamins.

Masuzawa, T. (2003) 'Our master's voice: F. Max Müller after a hundred years of solitude', *Method and Theory in the Study of Religion*, 15, 305–28.

Müller, G. (ed.) (1902) *The Life and Letters of the Right Honorable Friedrich Max Müller: Vols 1–2*, London: Longmans, Green & Co.

Stone, J. R. (ed.) (2002) 'Introduction', in J. R. Stone (ed.), *The Essential Max Müller*, New York: Palgrave.

Tull, H. W. (1991) 'F. Max Müller and A. B. Keith: "Twaddle", the "stupid" myth, and the disease of Indology', *Numen*, 38, 27–58.

Whitney, W. D. (1873) *Oriental and Linguistic Studies*, New York: Scribner, Armstrong & Co.

PAUL BROCA (1824–80)

French surgeon and physical anthropologist Paul Broca was, on all accounts, a gifted, intellectually lively and energetic scientist. Not a language scholar, his legacy to this field lies in his study of the human brain. Broca is conventionally credited with proving, or sometimes even with discovering, the localization of particular language functions in a part of the brain now referred to as 'Broca's area'. That claim probably exaggerates Broca's role, but he deserves recognition for his important contributions to nineteenth-century research on language and the brain.

Broca was the son of a country doctor, born into a family of Huguenot rationalists in southwest France. At age eight, he entered a Calvinist school, where he excelled in languages and mathematics. But he abandoned his plan to study engineering to accede to his parents' desire that he become a doctor. Broca was only seventeen when he travelled to Paris to begin a heady, intense medical school education. He quickly moved up through the hierarchy of competitive classes, tests and appointments that exposed him to a range of medical specialties. Early in his career, Broca made significant discoveries about muscular dystrophy, rickets, and the use of microscopes in treating cancer. But his keenest interest was in surgery. In 1853, he demonstrated his brilliance and ambition in a series of public examinations, the culminating exercise of his medical education. Broca collected numerous awards, and the respect of the medical community, for his erudition, high scientific standards and prodigious capacity for work (Schiller 1979).

It was integral to Broca's success that his career took place amidst the political and social tumult of post-Napoleonic France. During the revolution of 1848, while he was still only a student of medicine, he was drafted into treating royalist as well as republican casualties in Paris's overcrowded and wholly inadequate hospitals. Working for days on end without sleep, he got to see at close range the consequences of runaway political ambition from the point of view of the wounded. One effect on Broca was to increase his scepticism of civil and religious authority. The experience may also have sparked an interest in public health, manifested in his writings on infant mortality and population development. After Broca's death, the story was told of how, during a climax of civic confusion and instability in 1870, he had single-handedly preserved the financial basis of Assistance Publique, the institution that supported French public hospitals. Broca concealed its treasury of 75 million francs in old suitcases under a cartload of potatoes; he had the cart safely and inconspicuously wheeled out of Paris a day before insurgents looted the institution's home office (Schiller 1979: 244–46).

In the terms of the era in which he lived, Broca's political and intellectual commitments were coherent: he was a republican, rationalist, free-thinker, 'materialist' and champion of Darwinian evolution. Like his educational and social-class peers, he blithely assumed that different racial and ethnic groups were intrinsically unequal in intellectual capacity. Those assumptions emerge in Broca's research on physical anthropology, which led him to found the Société d'Anthropologie in Paris in 1859, and to pioneer new techniques of measuring human brains. Broca accepted that brain size correlated with intelligence, and moreover that intelligence was differently distributed across the races – even in the face of embarrassing evidence that some peoples assumed to be inferior ('Eskimos, Lapps, Malays, Tartars'; Gould 1996: 119) had larger brains than Europeans.

Most of the latter half of Broca's professional life was taken up with study of the brain, from the clinical as well as anthropological perspectives. Measurement of brain size was one important research trend. Scholars also debated whether the front versus back parts of the brain played different roles, and some questioned whether specific convolutions of brain tissue could be identified as the seats of specific faculties. However, most were reluctant to imagine that the right versus left hemispheres of the brain could have significantly different roles, granted the overwhelming physiological evidence that paired organs assume identical functions. Progress in this field was slow and insecure, given that scientists were limited to observing 'nature's experiments' in the symptoms of living patients, or reconstructing unrecorded symptoms post-mortem, and then (where possible) conducting technologically simple autopsies. Broca was among those who doubted that all parts of the brain functioned identically. He sought new data to bear on this controversy, data that would meet his standards for reliability and richness of detail.

A watershed event in Broca's career is recorded in the minutes of the April 1861 meeting of the Société d'Anthropologie, when he presented for examination the brain of a recently deceased patient who had lost nearly all capacity for speech some twenty years earlier. In a famous paper published later that year in the *Bulletin de la société anatomique de Paris*, he described the case:

> On the eleventh of April, 1861, to the general infirmary of the Bicêtre, to the service of surgery, was brought a man 51-years-old

called Leborgne who had a diffused gangrenous cellulitis of the whole right inferior extremity, from the foot to the buttocks. To questions which one addressed to him on the next day as to the origin of his disease he responded only by the monosyllable '*tan*', repeated twice in succession and accompanied by a gesture of the right hand. I tried to find out more about the antecedents of this man, who had been at Bicêtre for 21 years. […] Since his youth he was subject to epileptic attacks, but he could become a last-maker at which he worked until he was 31 years old. At that time he lost the ability to speak, and that was why he was admitted at the Hospice of Bicêtre. […] He understood all that was said to him. His hearing was actually very good. Whatever question one addressed to him, he always answered '*tan, tan,*' accompanied by varied gestures, by which he succeeded in expressing most of his ideas.

(trans. von Bonin 1960: 60–61)

Leborgne died six days after his admission to Broca's practice. The autopsy showed clear evidence of pathology in the third frontal convolution of the left hemisphere. In conjunction with Leborgne's documented symptoms of aphasia, Broca interpreted this finding to suggest localization of speech in the left third frontal convolution (roughly, under the topmost edge of the left ear, later called 'Broca's area'). Broca was not the first to propose localization of speech. But his analysis of Leborgne lent his substantial prestige to the idea, supported by his characteristically observant and meticulous report of the details of the case. A few months later, Broca studied an eighty-three-year-old man who suddenly collapsed, and on recovering was able to speak only five specific words. Twelve days later, the man died. His age, medical history, and the length of time for which he suffered aphasia differed radically from Leborgne. But autopsy again showed a clear-cut left hemispheric lesion in Broca's area.

On the basis of these and a few other cases that Broca reviewed, evidence for anatomical localization of the faculty of speech grew, and became identified with Broca's name. In a paper published in 1865 (trans. Berker *et al.* 1986), Broca proposed localization of speech in the left frontal hemisphere. Since the late nineteenth century, Broca's claims have been variously challenged or developed, although never wholly abandoned. One question is whether Broca was really the first to recognize hemispheric asymmetry (Young 1970). A paper by a provincial doctor named Marc Dax (1770–1837), written thirty years earlier but not circulated until 1863, made the same claim on the basis of forty cases of aphasia (though without the support of post-mortem anatomical analysis). It is unclear whether Dax's work had influenced Broca (Cubelli and Montagna 1994). Second, other research began to refine the association of Broca's area with speech deficits, eventually associating specific aphasic symptoms with damage to other specific areas. Leborgne's symptoms constitute an extreme example of what came to be called Broca's aphasia, conventionally characterized as slow, laboured, agrammatic speech without deficits in compre-hension or generalized motor skills. By 1874, German neurologist Carl Wernicke (1848–1905), among others, had distinguished differ-ent varieties of aphasia (Eggert 1977). These included sensory or Wernicke's aphasia, in which patients exhibit deficits in comprehen-sion alongside fluent but semantically disordered speech, replete with phonotactically plausible jargon and neologisms. Wernicke accepted the principles of localization and lateralization of language in the brain, then accounted for a constellation of symptoms very different from those of Broca's aphasia by associating those symptoms with damage to a different left-hemispheric site posterior to Broca's area.

Thus, from the late nineteenth century onward, physicians and neurologists gradually built up our understanding of the relationship between the brain and language. Adding to their work in recent decades are the results of research by contemporary psycholinguists, cognitive scientists and aphasiologists. The advent of modern medical technology has opened vast new frontiers, because we now have non-invasive neuro-imaging techniques that allow us to view the normal brain at work, and to gain insight into the brain functioning of people who exhibit many kinds of non-normal language. Not surprisingly, these techniques convince us that the relationship of brain to language is very complex. Many scientists are now disabused of their confidence that any one deficit can be predictably and uniquely mapped onto damage at any one location in the brain, or *vice versa*. Some doubt whether it makes sense to classify patients into groups on the basis of their symptoms, or according to the site of cerebral dys-function, arguing that there is too much poorly understood individual variation to make secure generalizations. Against this backdrop, what is surprising is the robustness of the insight of scientists in Broca's and Wernicke's generation. Grodzinsky (1991: 563), for example, rejected conceptual and empirical challenges to the existence of agrammatism of the sort described by Broca, concluding that 'the intuitions of the great neurologists of the 19th century were not far-fetched'. Likewise, an analysis by Kreisler et al. (2000: 1117) of 107 patients' records concluded that 'Most clinical–radiological correlations supported the classic anatomy of aphasia'. (For opposing views, see Dronkers *et al.* 2000 and works cited by Grodzinsky 1991 and Kreisler *et al.* 2000; Grodzinsky and Amunts 2006 synthesize research on Broca's area by neurologists, psychologists, linguists and cognitive scientists.) Despite our modern access to how brains function, and our new conceptions of the structure of language, nineteenth-century scholars' basic principles of lateralization and localization arguably still stand.

Bibliography

An English translation of Broca's 1861 paper on Leborgne is available in its entirety in von Bonin (1960: 49–72). Berker *et al.* (1986) translate the 1865 paper that famously asserts that 'we think with the left brain', and Eling (1994) provides extracts from several of Broca's other papers. Schiller's (1979) biography cites many passages from Broca's unpublished letters, and presents a bibliography of almost 500 texts Broca published between 1847 and 1880.

Further reading

Berker, E. A., Berker, A. H. and Smith, A. (1986) 'Translation of Broca's 1865 report: localization of speech in the third left frontal convolution', *Archives of Neurology*, 43, 1065–72.

von Bonin, G. (trans). (1960) *Some Papers on the Cerebral Cortex*, Springfield, IL: Charles C. Thomas.

Cubelli, R. and Montagna, C. G. (1994) 'A reappraisal of the controversy of Dax and Broca', *Journal of the History of Neuroscience*, 3, 215–26.

Dronkers, N. F., Redfern, B. B. and Knight, R. T. (2000) 'The neural architecture of language disorders', in M. S. Gazzaniga (ed.), *The New Cognitive Neurosciences* (2nd edn), Cambridge, MA: MIT Press.

Eggert, G. H. (1977) *Wernicke's Works on Aphasia: A Sourcebook and Review*, The Hague: Mouton.

Eling, P. (ed). (1994) *Reader in the History of Aphasia*, Amsterdam: John Benjamins.

Finger, S. (2000) *Minds Behind the Brain: A History of the Pioneers and their Discoveries*, New York: Oxford University Press.

Gould, S. J. (1996) *The Mismeasure of Man* (revised edn), New York: W. W. Norton.

Grodzinsky, Y. (1991) 'There is an entity called agrammatic aphasia', *Brain and Language*, 41, 555–64.

Grodzinsky, Y. and Amunts, K. (eds) (2006) *Broca's Region*, New York: Oxford University Press.

Kreisler, A., Godefroy, O., Delmaire, C., Debachy, B., Leclerq, M., Pruvo, J.-P. and Leys, D. (2000) 'The anatomy of aphasia revisited', *Neurology*, 54, 1117–22.

Schiller, F. (1979) *Paul Broca: Founder of French Anthropology, Explorer of the Brain*, Berkeley, CA: University of California Press.
Young, R. M. (1970) *Mind, Brain, and Adaptation in the Nineteenth Century*, Oxford: Clarendon Press.

WILLIAM DWIGHT WHITNEY (1827–94)

If the development of western language science were unified enough be represented on a tree diagram of the sort used to depict genealogical relations in biology or linguistics, William Dwight Whitney's work might be placed at a fork where one distinctively American branch radiates out from the European trunk. On one hand, Whitney was European-trained, taken seriously by European scholars, and, along with many of his European peers, studied Sanskrit as a prime comparative-historical tool. Unlike later American scholars such as **Edward Sapir** (or earlier ones such as Peter Stephen Duponceau [1760–1844] and John Pickering [1777–1846]), Whitney did not focus on Native American languages. In these ways Whitney's work held close to the trunk of European scholarship. On the other hand, Whitney contributed to, and wielded his influence over, the institutionalization of the study of language specifically in America. He achieved considerable honour within the American academic community as the country's first Professor of Sanskrit, and considerable public attention as the editor (and hence local arbitrator of correctness) of the *Century Dictionary*, a watershed in American lexicography. Moreover, in much of his writing Whitney emphasized the social basis of language – not a popular theme in Europe in his day but one that, arguably, later developed into characteristically American empirical studies of language variation associated with different social groups.

Use of a tree metaphor to depict Whitney's career is made apt by historical and biographical coincidence: historical, because Whitney worked during the era when biology and linguistics both discovered the utility of tree diagrams in representing relationships of priority and mutual descent; and biographical, because as a young adult Whitney occupied himself with natural-historical studies. Whitney was born to a patrician family in the central Massachusetts town of Northampton. He graduated from Williams College first in his class at age eighteen. For a few years after college, he collected bird and plant specimens and accompanied his naturalist brother Josiah on geological expeditions as far away as Colorado. He happened upon his calling when, on the advice of the family pastor, he picked up a Sanskrit grammar Josiah had brought back from Germany. Eventually Whitney moved to Yale University in New Haven, Connecticut and from there to Berlin (where he studied with **Franz Bopp**) and Tübingen to pursue philology, especially Sanskrit. He began what became a major life project, preparation of an edition and translation of the *Atharva-veda*.

Whitney interrupted his research in Europe to return to Yale in 1853 to accept a professorship in Sanskrit created explicitly for him, although he wasn't awarded a doctorate until 1861 (from the University of Breslau). At Yale he also taught other courses on philology and, to support what became his family of six children, French and German. Whitney became very involved in the promotion of language study through his work with the American Oriental Society and the American Philological Association, groups in which he held long-sustained roles, including that of president. Half of the texts published in the *Journal of the American Oriental Society* between 1857 and 1885 were written by Whitney (Seymour 1894/1967: 412).

In March 1864, Whitney gave a series of six lectures at the Smithsonian Institution, which became the basis for his book *Language and the Study of Language*, addressed to the general reader. The lectures and book form a counterpoint to Oxford popularizer **Friedrich Max Müller**'s 1861 lecture series and book, critiqued by Whitney (1873). Whitney's notorious, long-smouldering feud with Müller became a motif in his writings on both general linguistic topics and Vedic scholarship. Whitney rarely lost a chance to make a testy remark or tart counter-riposte by way of objecting to what he viewed as Müller's loose grasp of philological fact, obliviousness to self-contradiction, and tendency to pander to the masses.

Whitney similarly scourged other scholars whose views he opposed, including **Wilhelm von Humboldt**'s disciple Heymann Steinthal (1823–99) (Whitney 1873), but Müller's interests were probably so close to those of Whitney, while his assumptions and orientation so distant, as to make their rivalry unavoidable. For example, Whitney admitted Darwinian evolution as a plausible analogy for language change, writing that naturalists' questions about species-specific variation, natural selection and the origin of species 'all are closely akin with those [questions] which the linguistic student has constant occasion to treat'; moreover, 'The dialects, languages, groups, families, stocks set up by the linguistic student, correspond with the species genera, and so on, of the zoölogist' (Whitney 1867/1971: 46–47). In contrast, Müller maintained a sceptical distance from Darwin on the grounds that language represented an insuperable barrier between humans and animals. However, parallels between language and natural phenomena were to Whitney only analogies, since he insisted that 'Language is, in fact, an institution ... the product of a series of changes, effected by the will and consent of men, working themselves out under historical conditions' (ibid.: 48). Because Whitney considered language a social institution, he treated its study as just the kind of historical activity that Müller had denied in arguing for a science of language. Whitney wrote:

> Speech is not a personal possession, but a social; it belongs not to the individual, but to the member of society. No item of existing language is the work of an individual; for what we may severally choose to say is not language until it be accepted and employed by our fellows. The whole development of speech, though initiated by the acts of individuals, is wrought out by the community.
>
> (ibid.: 404)

Therefore children learn language by observation and imitation of language use in the environment, and as a result of adult instruction:

> ... we speak English because we were taught it by those who surrounded us in our infancy and growing age. ... [W]e were born, not indeed into the possession of it, but into the company of those who already spoke it, having learned it in the same way before us. We were not left to our own devices, to work out for ourselves the great problem of how to talk ... [T]here was no development of language out of our own internal resources ...
>
> (ibid.: 11)

As Whitney's reputation grew, an invitation from Harvard in 1869 moved Yale, in a counter-offer, to increase his salary and tailor his teaching more to his actual expertise. He published another book for a general readership in 1875. In it, abuse of Müller was more subdued, and Whitney further developed his assertion that language has a social basis. Although child language learning was not a major preoccupation in the 1875 book, it is the first substantive topic he addressed and one he returned to periodically. He materialized language as a kind of asset that child learners come to possess, in the way that one might come to possess a silver table service, namely by inheriting it from an earlier generation (although Whitney himself did not use this metaphor). He insisted that the learner simply 'goes over and appropriates, step by step, what others have wrought out' (Whitney 1875: 14), and therefore 'gets his language ... in the most openly external fashion' (ibid.: 26). This sober, no-nonsense perspective on language learning is characteristic of Whitney, and similarly infuses his treatment of the book's major topic, language change.

Whitney's contributions to Sanskrit philology probably overshadow his writings on general linguistics topics. He returned to Germany in 1875 and 1878 to work with scholars and materials there. His much admired grammar of Sanskrit (Whitney 1879/1941) employs modern analytical categories and labels rather than the traditional classes and terms, and includes older forms of Sanskrit (without comparing it with other languages), thus providing an alternative to the conventional reliance on **Pāṇini**'s grammatical authority. Whitney's edition and translation of the *Atharva-veda* (1855–56/1905) was not completed until after his death. But in the process of carrying out this work and the *Sanskrit Grammar*, he published or contributed to numerous supplementary materials that became valuable aids to specialists (a dictionary, lists of roots, an edition of a treatise on phonetics).

Whitney's last accomplishment was the 7046-page, 500,000-entry *Century Dictionary and Cyclopedia*. Due to illness he was unable fully to complete his editorial responsibilities, but the first version appeared before his death. It significantly advanced American lexicography in its vast coverage and fine-grained treatment of terms and concepts, serving as an important resource for **James Murray**'s later creation of the *Oxford English Dictionary*.

Whitney's legacy to modern linguistics varies. His Vedic research certainly moved that field forward. The professional societies he nurtured still thrive in the twenty-first century. His work on general topics was avidly translated during his lifetime, and his scholarship has been cited admiringly by later linguists, including the Neogrammarians, **Ferdinand de Saussure** and **Leonard Bloomfield**. In particular, Saussure's work has been analysed for evidence that Whitney's notion that language is a social institution, not a natural phenomenon, influenced the development of structuralism (Joseph 2002).

On the other hand, Whitney's common-sense orientation does not always satisfy modern linguists, receptive as many are to theoretical abstraction and the idealization of linguistic data. A telling contrast on the topic of child language learning calls attention to the century of differences that separate Whitney and **Noam Chomsky**'s generative grammar. In *Language and the Study of Language*, Whitney provocatively remarked that although children's linguistic environments vary, in every case, the 'amount and style of [adult] speech' in their surroundings that serves as input 'surpass[es children's] acquirements' (Whitney 1867/1971: 12). That is, to Whitney, child learners encounter a superabundance of linguistic evidence, in both quantity and quality, so that what they acquire is a subset of the wealth of language available to them. That assertion contrasts with Chomsky's claim that children face a 'poverty of the stimulus' in the course of language learning. To Chomsky, input to language learners is impoverished in the sense that simple exposure provides an insufficient and misleading basis for children to project mental representations of the language surrounding them (Chomsky 1980: 42). Far from appraising language in the child's environment in Whitney's terms as rich in both 'amount and style', Chomsky appraises it as finite and degenerate, and therefore incommensurate on both grounds with the unbounded and highly structured knowledge of language that children exhibit.

Chomsky (1966: 90) highlighted his differences with Whitney, quoting Whitney as having written in an anti-Humboldt (anti-Steinthal, and probably anti-Müller) vein that language is a historical product, 'the sum of words and phrases by which any man expresses his thought', and moreover that 'the infinite diversity of human speech ought alone to be a sufficient bar to the assertion that an understanding of the powers of the soul involves the explanation of speech' (Whitney 1873: 372, 360). One can only imagine the animadversions that might arise in an imaginary debate between Whitney and Chomsky, both brilliant American linguists, and opponents well matched in polemical talent and tenacity.

Whitney's major works

Language and the Study of Language, 1867, Scribner, New York (reprinted by AMS Press, 1971).
Oriental and Linguistic Studies, 1873, Scribner, Armstrong & Co., New York.
The Life and Growth of Language: An Outline of Linguistic Science, 1875, D. C. Appleton, New York (reprinted 1898).
A Sanskrit Grammar, 1879, Breitkopf and Härtel, Leipzig (2nd edn reprinted by Harvard University Press, 1941).
Atharva-Veda Saṁhitā: Vols 1–2, 1905 (C. R. Lanman, ed.; W. D. Whitney, trans.), Harvard University Press, Cambridge, MA (Vol. 1 originally published 1855–56).
Century Dictionary and Cyclopedia: Vols 1–10, 1889–91 ('Prepared under the superintendence of William Dwight Whitney'), Century.
Whitney on Language, 1971 (M. Silverstein, ed.), MIT Press, Cambridge, MA (selected essays complementing those in Whitney 1873).

Further reading

Alter, S. G. (2005) *William Dwight Whitney and the Science of Language*, Baltimore, MD: Johns Hopkins University Press.

Chomsky, N. (1966) *Cartesian Linguistics*, New York: Harper & Row (3rd edn 2009, Cambridge University Press).

Chomsky, N. (1980) 'Rules and Representations', *Behavioral and Brain Sciences*, 3, 1–15, 42–61.

Joseph, J. E. (2002) *From Whitney to Chomsky: Essays in the History of American Linguistics*, Amsterdam and Philadelphia, PA: John Benjamins.

Nerlich, B. (1990) *Change in Language: Whitney, Bréal, and Wegner*, London and New York: Routledge.

Lanman, C. R. (1897) *The Whitney Memorial Meeting*, Boston, MA: Ginn and Company (*Journal of the American Oriental Society*, 19; contains Whitney bibliography, biographical material, assessment by Whitney's peers).

Seymour, T. D. (1894) 'Willam Dwight Whitney', *American Journal of Philology*, 15, 271–98 (reprinted in T. A. Seboek (ed.), *Portraits of Linguists: Vol. 1*, Bloomington, IN: Indiana University Press, 1967).

Tetel Andresen, J. (1990) *Linguistics in America 1769–1924*, London and New York: Routledge.

JAMES A. H. MURRAY (1837–1915)

James Murray was the most prominent of the editors of the *New English Dictionary on Historical Principles*, commonly known as the *Oxford English Dictionary* (*OED*). From conception to publication of the first edition, production of the *OED* spanned more than seventy years, six senior editors, and several thousand assistants and volunteer contributors. Nevertheless, it was Murray whose standards, methods and intellectual orientation set the tone for this massive project. Murray's influence continues to the present day, with the second edition of the *OED* still regularly updated and accessible online as well as on paper and CD-ROM. A third edition, authorized in 1990, is now under way.

Murray had the temperament of a lexicographer (inquisitive, exacting, relentless) but an atypical background. The son of a tailor, he was raised in the Borders, an area of rolling pastures and small towns in extreme southeastern Scotland. Murray showed precocious interest in languages and in natural history, especially geology and botany. Before he left the village school at age fourteen, he had acquired some Latin, French, Italian and German, and a reputation for having a lively mind. Murray continued studying independently, hoping eventually to qualify for admission to the university.

But at age seventeen he suspended those plans to take a job as a schoolmaster. He delighted in the opportunities that teaching children gave him to satisfy his broad curiosity – about science, literature, art, history, geography and, above all, languages – and to collect and classify such things as stamps, botanic specimens and antiquities (Murray 1957).

Gradually, Murray's attention focused on archaeology and on philology, including dialectology and the study of Anglo-Saxon. He helped found a local society of amateur archaeologists, enthusiastically presenting papers at its meetings and reorganizing the society's collection of artefacts. After 1862, Murray's life took a new trajectory when he married and moved south to London, to a climate presumed to be more favourable to his wife's health. Of necessity, he accepted a tedious job as a bank clerk. But he soon established friendships with others who shared his interests, and who recognized his intellectual gifts despite his lack of formal educational credentials. Although his wife died after three years in London, Murray stayed on to continue his study of dialectology. He was invited to help edit texts for the Early English Text Society, and to deliver a series of lectures to the London Philological Society that were published in 1873 as *The Dialect of the Southern Counties of Scotland*.

In 1870, Murray accepted a position as teacher at the Mill Hill School, ten miles outside central London. The school provided a wholesome environment for Murray, his second wife Ada, and what became their eleven children, while allowing him to continue participating in the Philological Society. In 1874, Edinburgh University awarded him an honorary doctorate, establishing his scholarly reputation (K. M. E. Murray 1977: 118).

At this point Murray's life took another turn. Since 1857, the Philological Society had been discussing the creation of a new dictionary of English. **Samuel Johnson**'s dictionary was by then one hundred years old. It was still held in high regard, and readers appreciated the utility of Johnson's use of illustrative quotations. But the Philological Society disagreed with Johnson about the role of a lexicographer as an arbiter of usage and style. The Society perceived the lexicographer's task as historical, namely to document how the forms and senses of words changed over time. Moreover, they aimed to inventory *all* English words, not just those deemed 'correct'. The Society solicited volunteers among British and American readers, asking them to cut out or copy onto a half-sheet of paper passages from nineteenth-century or earlier texts in English that, in the reader's judgement, aptly illustrated the usage of a particular word. The range of sanctioned source texts was wide, including newspapers, published letters, criticism, drama and sermons, as well as novels, poetry, history, and political and scientific publications. The Society optimistically imagined that its dictionary would emerge in a few years' time by amassing and editing these slips, inductively arriving at the meanings of headwords by examining their use in context, then organizing alternative meanings (and forms) according to the date of publication of the source. The result would be a dictionary that documented the evolution of each English word.

Public response was enthusiastic. By 1860, volunteer readers had already submitted hundreds of slips of paper. After a couple of false starts, it became clear that the project required vigorous and consistent leadership. Murray was recruited for the job in 1879, with **Henry Sweet** urging Oxford University Press to publish the dictionary under Murray's editorship. After protracted negotiations (in which **Max Müller** played a role as one of the Delegates of the Press), Murray contracted to complete the project within ten years. In the end, production of the dictionary demanded far more time, money and human energy than either party to the original agreement could have foreseen. The first edition took up ten volumes, encompassing over 400,000 headwords and 1.8 million citations. It was published in fascicles, with the first – covering 'A' through 'Ant' – appearing in 1884. The last instalment appeared in 1928, thirteen years after Murray's death.

Murray invested his phenomenal vitality and dedication over the remaining thirty-six years of his life to the *OED*, enduring, among other trials, protracted and painful struggles to sustain the support of Oxford University Press. He first worked at Mill Hill in a specially built shed he called the 'Scriptorium'. Along with a few assistants, he started by sorting the slips sent in by volunteer readers into more than a thousand pigeonholes, organized alphabetically. He published a call for more readers to capture both ordinary words and words 'rare, obsolete, old-fashioned, new, peculiar, or used in a peculiar way' (K. M. E. Murray 1977: 347). The response was so great that even the initial mechanical task of sorting slips by headword became enormous. All of Murray's eleven children were recruited as sorters; the youngest were paid a penny an hour, with the rate going up to sixpence for the oldest children (*ibid.*: 179).

To expedite production of the *OED*, Murray resigned his teaching position in 1885, moved his family to Oxford to be closer to the Press, and erected a new Scriptorium. He now worked full time on the dictionary, relinquishing all other occupations. Although he eventually conceded to having other editors work alongside him, over half of the text of the *OED* can be attributed directly to Murray, and the project in its entirety evinces his philosophy and taste.

One facet of Murray's influence was the criteria for inclusion of words, since even the most ambitious dictionary must impose boundaries. In the 'General explanations' that prefaced the first fascicle, Murray identified the core responsibility of the *OED* as the 'nucleus or central mass' of 'Common Words' of English, both literary and colloquial; a circle of words that 'has a well-defined centre but no discernible circumference' (Murray 1884/1971: x). Murray presented a diagram showing five categories of words radiating away from the circle: words of foreign provenance; slang; 'dialectal' words; scientific terms; technical terms. Especially with reference to scientific and technical terms, Murray's disposition was to include as many as the Delegates of the Press would allow him space to include, even though in principle his policy was to exclude rarefied specialist vocabulary. Thus *abietate* (from Chemistry), *acanthophorus* (Botany), *acanticone* (Mineralogy), *adiabatic* (Physics), and *albedo* (Astronomy) all found places in the first fascicle. Murray's practice of admitting scientific terms challenged not only the pragmatic constraints imposed by his publishers, but also the original design for the dictionary drawn up by the Philological Society, some of whose members were slower than Murray to adopt the results and language of late-nineteenth-century scientific discoveries.

Murray's touch was also evident in the typography and layout of the *OED*. He aimed to meet a high aesthetic standard and to achieve maximal technical clarity so that readers could easily discriminate the elements of entries, while still conserving as much space on the printed page as possible. Murray's typography was so successful, in fact, that many of his decisions about typeface and layout remain intact in the modern *OED Online*. In addition, Murray struggled with questions about how to represent the pronunciation of dictionary entries: which 'accent' of English to assume; how finely to record pronunciation variants; and what phonetic symbols to use. He ended up creating his own phonetic notation (which proved relatively easy to convert into the International Phonetic Alphabet in later versions of the *OED*) to capture educated British speech, and to specify a range of stylistic variants (MacMahon 2000).

In matters of pronunciation, as elsewhere, Murray rejected the role of lexicographer as one who fixes standards. Rather, he resolutely championed descriptivism, and viewed the *OED* as a record of how English speakers have developed and used the language's resources over time. As he acquired a public profile as a lexicographer, many people wrote to Murray asking him to adjudicate questions of usage. He patiently explained that 'I am not the editor of the English language', and calmly sanctioned variability (such as in the pronunciation of the first syllable in the word *either* to rhyme with *fry* versus *free*) as a natural expression of taste. 'No wise person would wish to impose his or her taste on others'; 'Some people wear turned-down collars, & some wear stand-up collars; why should they not? Is not speech as free as dress, when the pronunciations are equally well-grounded?' (Mugglestone 2005: 144–45). Likewise, Murray declined to take a stand on whether the expression *different from* was intrinsically superior to *different to*, or whether the spelling *disyllable* should be preferred over *dissyllable* (*ibid.*: 145; 149).

Another basis on which Murray's work contrasted with some earlier lexicography is in the role it assigned to etymology. Murray's goal was to 'furnish a biography of each word', documenting its ancestry, birth, variants and (if relevant) death (Murray 1900: 47). But he separated etymology from meaning, rejecting speculation that tried to wrest the meaning of a word from its origin or form – a favourite preoccupation of language scholars going back at least to **Plato**'s *Cratylus*. 'Etymology is simply ... a record of the *facts* which *did* happen, not a fabric of conjectures as to what may have happened' (*ibid.*: 44). Murray assumed that to understand the meaning of a word, it was necessary to start with its origins, but that meaning was to be induced not from etymology but from the contexts in which speakers have used the word over time (supplemented by the advice of specialists whom Murray consulted).

Murray was knighted in 1908. Because he simultaneously thrived on, and was embittered by, obscurity and adversity, he seemed uncomfortable with the implication that the public had noticed and valued his work. Perhaps more meaningful to him would be the fact that a century after his death, the *OED* has furnished the biographies of more than 500,000 words, using 2.5 million citations. Its scope now extends to varieties of English worldwide, and its accessibility extends everywhere through the internet.

Murray's major works

The Dialect of the Southern Counties of Scotland: Its Pronunciation, Grammar, and Historical Relations, 1873, Asher & Co., London.
A New English Dictionary on Historical Principles (1st edn), 1884–1928, Clarendon, Oxford (2nd edn 1989; 3rd edn 1990–).

'General Explanations', Preface to the first fascicle of the *Oxford English Dictionary*, 1884 (reprinted in *The Compact Edition of the Oxford English Dictionary*, Clarendon, 1971).

The Evolution of English Lexicography, 1900, Clarendon, Oxford.

Sir James A.H. Murray: A Self-Portrait, 1957 (G. F. Timpson, ed.), John Bellows.

Further reading

Bailey, R. W. (2000) '"This unique and peerless specimen": the reputation of the *OED*', in L. Mugglestone (ed.), *Lexicography and the* OED, Oxford: Oxford University Press.

Brewer, C. (2007) *Treasure-house of the Language: The Living* OED, New Haven, CT: Yale University Press.

MacMahon, M. K. C. (2000) 'Pronunciation in the *OED*', in L. Mugglestone (ed.), *Lexicography and the* OED, Oxford: Oxford University Press.

Mugglestone, L. (ed.) (2000) *Lexicography and the* OED, Oxford: Oxford University Press.

Mugglestone, L. (2005) *Lost for Words: The Hidden History of the* Oxford English Dictionary, New Haven, CT: Yale University Press.

Murray, K. M. E. (1977) *Caught in the Web of Words: James A. H. Murray and the* Oxford English Dictionary, New Haven, CT: Yale University Press.

Willinsky, J. (1994) *Empire of Words: The Reign of the* OED, Princeton, NJ: Princeton University Press.

HENRY SWEET (1845–1912)

Henry Sweet was a crusty and independent-minded British language scholar whose work had broad impact, especially in the fields of phonetics, English philology and language pedagogy. Sweet's bibliography has a wide scope: manuals and annotated texts for learners of Old and Middle English; a handbook for beginners in phonetics; books analysing the history of English grammar and phonology; works on shorthand, spelling reform and teaching English to non-native speakers; a comprehensive plan for the improvement of foreign language pedagogy; and linguistic exegeses of Anglo-Saxon texts. Sweet's career was unconventional in that he never achieved academic status commensurate with his international reputation as a scholar. Over time, he became increasingly entrenched as an institutional outsider. Even as this role vexed him, it suited his personality and, moreover, freed him to indulge in criticism of his peers – a habit that, not surprisingly, resulted in his further isolation.

Sweet's professional unconventionality began early. Born and educated to adolescence in London, he taught himself Old English and
Old Icelandic. At eighteen, he travelled to Heidelberg for a one-year
course in German philology. On returning to London, he continued
his studies independently while employed in business. At the late age
of twenty-four, he won a scholarship to Oxford's Balliol College,
initiating a lifelong contentious institutional relationship. Sweet studied Classics. He found Oxford an impediment to his education, so he
later wrote that, on graduating, 'Plato and Aristotle had so interfered
with my own proper studies that my knowledge of Old English was
at a lower ebb than it had ever been during the preceding five years'
(Sweet 1888: vi). Disaffection was mutual: Sweet was granted a
scandalous fourth-class degree, a rare outcome 'generally reserved for
those about whom the examiners cannot decide whether they are
fools or geniuses' (Anderson 1985: 171–72). Nevertheless, while still an
undergraduate, Sweet had presented three papers to the Philological
Society; published an edition of an Old English manuscript and nine
reviews; and written a book-length article that appeared in the
Transactions of the Philological Society.

After graduating, Sweet began supporting himself (and, later, his
wife) through his publications, supplemented by work as a private
tutor in phonetics. Early in this period, he was active in the Philological
Society, serving as President in 1876–78. Sweet's writings soon spread
his fame to continental Europe, where he was granted several signal
honours and awards, and eventually offered teaching positions. But
Sweet was tenaciously nationalistic, and had fixed his mind on raising
the level of philological scholarship specifically in England, where,
paradoxically, his reputation stagnated (MacMahon 2006). On three
occasions, Sweet expected to be offered prestigious teaching positions
(at University College London in 1876; twice at Oxford in 1885 and
1901). But to his increasing chagrin, he was passed over in favour of
appointees he considered intellectually inferior. Finally, he was named
Reader in Phonetics at Oxford, a role he accepted with some bitterness. Wrenn (1946: 195) retells the story of Sweet's accidental
encounter on the street with **James Murray**, celebrated editor of the
Oxford English Dictionary and among those Sweet had come to resent.
Murray greeted him mildly with 'Good morning, Dr. Sweet', to
which Sweet responded 'Damn you, Murray.'

Against this chequered professional backdrop, Sweet wrote and
published steadily. In 1877, his landmark *Handbook of Phonetics*
appeared, an appropriate early work for a scholar to whom phonetics
was 'the indispensable foundation of all study of language' (Sweet

1877/1970: v). Sweet admired the pioneering work of Alexander Melville Bell (1819–1905), a Scottish phonetician (and father of Alexander Graham Bell, purported inventor of the telephone). As a tool for teaching the deaf, Bell had invented 'Visible Speech', a system of notation that recorded the component articulatory gestures of speech, using novel symbols that mimic the positions of the tongue, lips, glottis, etc. Sweet, however, considered it too dependent on phonetic facts that still remained to be specified (ibid.: 100–101). Another influence on Sweet was the phonetic notation of the somewhat eccentric independent scholar Alexander John Ellis (1814–90), which included inverted letters, digraphs and small upper-case letters. Sweet's interest in orthography also extended to his invention of a system of phonetically informed shorthand (MacMahon 1981).

The *Handbook* improved on Bell's articulatory phonetics with a better organized, more comprehensive, and more phonetically sophisticated analysis of the mechanics of speech. It also introduced two related innovations. First, in the decade between the introduction of Visible Speech and the development of the International Phonetic Alphabet by French phonetician Paul Passy (1859–1940) and others, Sweet invented a two-level phonetic notation, 'Broad Romic' and 'Narrow Romic'. The two names derive from the fact that (unlike Visible Speech) both employ Roman alphabetic characters, but differ with respect to the nature of the sound properties they represent. Broad Romic records 'only those broader distinctions of sounds which actually correspond to distinctions of meaning in language, and indicates them by letters that can be easily written and remembered' (Sweet 1877/1970: 103). Narrow Romic cleaves closely to phonetic detail by recording fine variation in pronunciation – variation that, in modern terms, is allophonic rather than phonemic. For example, Sweet represented 'They came back the same day' in Broad Romic as '–dhei keim bækdhə seim dei \', or in Narrow Romic as '–dhei. keiıhm bækdhʌᵉ seiıhm deiıh \' (ibid.: 113, 114). Sweet's notational techniques captured the prosodic features of utterances, dividing the stream of sounds into segments according to the distribution of stress and rhythm rather than conventional word boundaries. His conventions also recorded variation in pitch (ibid.: 106–8). The goal was to create a system that could be adapted to transcribe any language, at two levels of resolution, as relevant to the transcriber's purposes.

Differences between Broad and Narrow Romic are not, however, simply differences in fidelity to phonetic detail. A second innovation of the *Handbook* is that Sweet came close to articulating a notion of the phoneme, a breakthrough that has been attributed to Sweet's contemporary **Jan Baudouin de Courtenay**, among others. Sweet's Broad Romic recorded 'only the practically necessary distinctions of sound in each language, [...] in the simplest manner possible, omitting all that is superfluous' (Sweet 1910: 9). What counts as superfluous varies from language to language. Considering distinctions like those between 'narrow' versus 'wide' short vowels, 'the distinction between ['narrow', i.e. tense] i and ['wide' i.e. lax] i is a significant one in Danish and Icelandic; [...] while in French it does not exist at all. In English there is the distinction, but it is not an independent one, being associated with quantity' (Sweet 1877/1970: 104). Thus Sweet conceived Broad Romic 'as a kind of algebraic notation, each letter representing a group of similar sounds' (Sweet 1888: x), the identity of which is predictable within the sound system of a particular language. Thus Broad Romic captures what resembles the modern phonemic differences, and Narrow Romic, allophonic variation.

In his later work, Sweet supplanted Narrow Romic in favour of a revised version of Visible Speech as a tool for specifying fine phonetic distinctions, but still relied on Broad Romic wherever it was 'convenient to have a more general notation' (*ibid.*: 13). Sweet's tacit conceptualization of the phoneme is perceptible throughout his work on the history of English, spelling reform and language pedagogy. Although he did not fully bring the notion to fruition, Sweet's clear and comprehensive presentation of the articulatory basis of speech made him the man who 'taught phonetics to Europe and made England the birthplace of the modern science' (Wrenn 1946: 182).

Sweet's philological work on English is also impressive. Even in his precocious undergraduate publications, he showed independence and self-confidence, for example by labelling the highly inflected stage of the language 'Old English' in place of the 'barbarous' label 'Anglo-Saxon' (Sweet 1874: 157). He proposed to divide the history of English into periods that have since become conventional, determined according to the status of vowels in unstressed inflections: Old English names the language when inflections were fully present; Middle English as they were levelled; and Modern English once they were lost (*ibid.*: 160). In his philological publications, as in the other domains, Sweet typically produced works separately for his peers and for novices, so that he authored technical treatises as well as readers, primers, and a dictionary for student use. In this way, his influence spread widely despite his lack of a formal academic position.

Another domain in which Sweet's influence spread was language teaching. His 1885 textbook for German-speaking learners of English,

Elementarbuch des gesprochenen Englisch, written entirely in phonetic transcription, and his less uncompromising *The Practical Study of Languages* (1899/1964), are classics of Europe's nineteenth-century Reform Movement, which replaced grammar-translation teaching methods by prioritizing spoken language and connected texts (Howatt 1984). In particular, Sweet established the importance of phonetics, and of learning a foreign language in integrated natural sentences rather than as words to be assembled into sentences (Atherton 1995).

In 1887, a schoolteacher in Silesia (now Poland), Hermann Klinghardt, conducted an empirical test of Sweet's teaching methods, exposing fourteen-year-old learners to unanalysed sentences of English exclusively in phonetic notation. For administrative reasons, Klinghardt had to compromise aspects of Sweet's idealized teaching programme, but the results were still remarkably successful (Howatt 1984: 173–75). By the time Sweet wrote *The Practical Study of Languages,* he had conceded some use to explicit grammar study, and even translation. But he did so always with a philologist's critical eye (and in his usual succinct rhetorical style):

> ... the question still remains ... , Is it worth while referring [a particular linguistic fact] to a rule, or is it better to learn it simply as an isolated fact?
>
> The usefulness of a rule depends: (1) on its extent – that is, the number of examples included under it; (2) on its efficiency – that is, the number of exceptions it has to admit, the rule that has the fewest exceptions being the most efficient; (3) its definiteness, clearness, and simplicity – that is, the ease with which it is learnt and applied, independently of its extent and efficiency.
>
> (Sweet 1899/1964: 92)

Sweet is among the few linguists to have achieved fame in popular culture, even inadvertently. Irish playwright George Bernard Shaw (1856–1950) identified Sweet as his inspiration for the role of phonetician Professor Henry Higgins in Shaw's play *Pygmalion* (Shaw 1916/1999: 109–13), on which the 1964 musical film *My Fair Lady* was based. Shaw knew Sweet personally, was intrigued by phonetics, and supported Sweet's work on spelling reform. In Act II, Shaw had Higgins cite Broad Romic and Bell's Visible Speech. Still, Shaw insisted that 'Higgins is not a portrait of Sweet' (*ibid.*: 112). Certainly, Higgins' mere high-handedness is no match for Sweet's intractable incapacity to suffer fools. Collins and Mees' (1998: 97–103) biography of **Daniel Jones** argues that Higgins was inspired by Jones, not Sweet, and that Shaw suppressed his actual source for fear of libel, or perhaps at Jones' request. The matter remains unsettled. Comparing the two, Jones' mild manners seem less likely to have kindled Shaw's dramatic imagination than Sweet's characteristic fire and ice. But whatever fictional shadows either man cast, they both advanced the study of language.

Sweet's major works

'A History of English Sounds', 1874, *Transactions of the Philological Society for 1873–1874*, Series D, Trübner & Co., London.
A Handbook of Phonetics, 1877, Clarendon Press, Oxford (reprinted by McGrath, College Park, MD, 1970).
Elementarbuch des gesprochenen Englisch, 1885, Clarendon Press, Oxford.
A History of English Sounds, 1888, Clarendon Press, Oxford.
New English Grammar, 1891, Clarendon Press, Oxford.
The Practical Study of Languages, 1899, J. M. Dent & Co., London (reprinted by Oxford University Press, 1964).
The Sounds of English (2nd edn), 1910, Clarendon Press, Oxford (1st edn 1907).
Collected Papers of Henry Sweet, 1913 (H. C. Wyld, ed.), Clarendon Press, Oxford.
The Indispensable Foundation: A Selection from the Writings of Henry Sweet, 1971 (E. J. A. Henderson, ed.), Oxford University Press, Oxford.

Further reading

Anderson, S. R. (1985) *Phonology in the Twentieth Century*, Chicago, IL: University of Chicago Press.
Atherton, M. (1995) 'Grasping sentences as wholes: Henry Sweet's idea of language study in the Early Middle Ages', *Neuphilologische Mitteilungen*, 95, 177–85.
Collins, B. and Mees, I. M. (1998) *The Real Professor Higgins: The Life and Career of Daniel Jones*, Berlin: Mouton de Gruyter.
Howatt, A. P. R. (1984) *A History of English Language Teaching*, Oxford: Oxford University Press.
MacMahon, M. K. C. (1981) 'Henry Sweet's system of shorthand', in R. E. Asher and E. J. A. Henderson (eds), *Towards a History of Phonetics*, Edinburgh: Edinburgh University Press.
——(2006) 'Henry Sweet (1845–1912)', *Oxford Dictionary of National Biography*, Oxford: Oxford University Press (online edn).
Shaw, B. (1916) 'Pygmalion', in *Androcles and the Lion; Overruled; Pygmalion*, New York: Brentano's (reprinted by Reprint Services, Temecula, CA, 1999).
Wrenn, C. L. (1946) 'Henry Sweet', *Transactions of the Philological Society*, 45, 177–201.

JAN BAUDOUIN DE COURTENAY (1845–1929)

Jan Baudouin de Courtenay was a Polish philologist and language scholar descended from impoverished French aristocrats who had immigrated to Poland generations before his birth. His work anticipates certain features of twentieth-century structuralist linguistics: he developed an early psychological notion of the phoneme; disputed the Neogrammarians' claims about the exceptionlessness of sound laws; and called attention to the value of studying living languages. He also analysed varieties of morphophonemic alternations, especially among the Slavic languages, and wrote about language change, dialectal variation and language typology. Baudouin is a central figure of the 'Kazan School' of linguistics, named for the city 450 miles east of Moscow (now the capital of the Republic of Tartarstan) where he taught for eight years early in his career. Moreover, he was an untiring social critic, who publicly objected to many varieties of linguistic, national, intellectual and religious chauvinism.

Baudouin was born and died in Poland, although he lived abroad for most of his life. After obtaining a master's degree in Slavic philology in 1866 in Warsaw, he travelled to Berlin, Prague and Jena for postgraduate study. As Poles were forbidden to teach in Poland while it remained part of the Russian empire, in 1868 he accepted a teaching post in comparative grammar at the University of St Petersburg. Two years later, Baudouin collected a doctorate from Leipzig for work on the concept of analogy, and another master's degree from St Petersburg for research on Old Polish. After a few years' fieldwork in Austria and Italy, he published an analysis of Slovenian dialects that won him a doctorate from St Petersburg (Stankiewicz 1972). Baudouin's cosmopolitan graduate education exposed him to a range of topics and of late-nineteenth-century academic milieux. Those experiences also probably stimulated his restless, outspoken spirit and committed him to supporting the language rights of oppressed ethnic and national minorities. This periodically got Baudouin into political trouble with the authorities – as did his religious agnosticism, with other authorities.

The next step after St Petersburg was a sojourn teaching in Kazan (Radwańska-Williams 2006). Baudouin chafed against the provinciality of the locale, but attracted a group of bright and ambitious scholars. Among them was Mikołaj Kruszewski (1851–87), who was in turn Baudouin's student, colleague, and successor in Kazan once Baudouin had moved on, all before Kruszewski died at age 36. Baudouin wrote an extraordinary posthumous review of Kruszewski's work that mixed praise, sober analysis, and disgruntled complaints that his former student was 'deluded as to his originality and independence' (Baudouin 1888–89/2005: 40), in particular, deluded about his independence from Baudouin's own ideas.

In 1884 Baudouin took up a chair in Comparative Slavic Grammar in Dorpat, Estonia, a city now known as Tartu. Then, in 1893, he moved to Jagiellonian University in Kracow, which was at that point under Austro-Hungarian rule. He made himself unwelcome in Kracow by publishing a critique of local administrative corruption (Stankiewicz 1972: 10). In addition, the breadth of his linguistic interests caused some to suspect him of pan-Slavism, a suspicion that evinces ignorance of his lifelong, adamant anti-nationalism. With his contract in Kracow not renewed, Baudouin returned to St Petersburg. In addition to his linguistic scholarship, he continued to champion minorities' language rights. In this, Baudouin posed enough of a threat to tsarist Russia that, in 1913, he was sentenced to two years' imprisonment. He was released after serving only two months, and in 1918 returned to newly independent Poland as Chair of Indo-European Linguistics at the University of Warsaw. In 1922 a coalition of minority groups in the Polish senate nominated Baudouin to the presidency of Poland, collecting 20 per cent of the first ballots in a four-way contest (Rothstein 1975: 402–3). He was not elected, but remained active as a scholar and social critic until his death at age 84.

Baudouin wrote voluminously about language, but few of his publications have been translated from Russian or Polish. It is commonplace to remark that his work has not received the attention it deserves. What attention it has attracted often measures the distance between his views and those of his (near-) contemporaries, such as the Neogrammarians, **Ferdinand de Saussure** and **Roman Jakobson**. Although to do so may not sufficiently acknowledge Baudouin's intellectual independence, it is nonetheless revealing to describe his views in that context.

Baudouin had studied alongside Neogrammarian August Leskien (1840–1916) in Jena, and later corresponded with **Karl Brugmann**. Comparative philology and language change were central both to his education and to the Neogrammarians, but Baudouin rejected the Neogrammarians' famous assertion of the exceptionlessness of sound laws. Although he accepted their thesis that language resides in individuals, he wrote in a 1910 essay that this had led to a 'confusion of the idea of individual language with that of average language … [so that] proponents of this theory, which confuses individual evolution with the history of an entire ethnic group … treat these changes as if they were taking place in a colossal brain of a single man' (trans. Stankiewicz 1972: 274), thus slighting the social dimension of language. Baudouin also rejected the view that phonetic changes result from the innovations of a single individual whom others imitate, in favour of a concept he called 'collective individuality', whereby change is introduced by the 'simultaneous beginning of a certain tendency, a certain trend in different places and in different minds' (trans. Stankiewicz 1972: 275–76). He felt that a 'sound law' could hold only over very small, 'microscopic' domains, whereas the Neogrammarians (mis)applied that term to macroscopic statements of historical regularity which actually constitute 'an epiphenomenal result of countless deterministic occurrences', deriving from 'the interaction of a multitude of factors (including morphological and semasiological ones, as well as the state of the linguistic system at a given time)' (Adamska-Sałaciak 1997: 914).

In rejecting the Neogrammarians' sound laws, Baudouin walked the same path as Saussure. In fact, the two scholars had met in Paris in 1881, and there is direct evidence that Saussure appreciated both Baudouin's and Kruszewski's writings (Jakobson 1971: 420–21). Baudouin's work prefigures several conceptual innovations associated with Saussure. For example, he acknowledged the 'interplay of statics and dynamics', or synchrony and diachrony (Stankiewicz 1972: 16) in his research on cross-linguistic influence and dialectal variation across time. More generally, Baudouin dealt in many of the linguistic dichotomies that Saussure made famous (e.g. social/individual; paradigmatic/syntagmatic; form/substance; internal/external; *langue/parole*; see **Ferdinand de Saussure**), although he conceived of them less starkly, in less irreconcilable terms (Stankiewicz 1972: 7).

Minissi (1989: 150) went so far as to assert 'an extraordinary parallelism' between Baudouin and Saussure. Schogt (1966: 18), on the other hand, considered Baudouin's and Saussure's works complementary, because the former's strength in phonology makes up for the underdevelopment of that area in the latter. Certainly, phonology and morphophonemics were central to Baudouin and the Kazan School; together with Kruszewski, Baudouin theorized at length about the relationship between phonetic distinctions and meaning. Along the way, they coined a large technical vocabulary, including the terms 'anthropophonetic' (pertaining to the purely physical aspect of sound systems; Stankiewicz 1972: 246) and 'psychophonetic' (viewing sounds 'from the morphological, psychological standpoint [and their] significance in the mechanism of language and for the "feeling" of a given speech community'; Stankiewicz 1972: 85).

A major preoccupation for Baudouin was the analysis and classification of morphophonemic alterations, a rich resource in Slavic languages. In an 1894 monograph, translated by Stankiewicz (1972: 144–212), he established three kinds of alteration: (1) 'divergences', which are alterations due to anthropophonetic facts, that is, the influence of one sound on its neighbours, such as the voicing of consonants that occur between vowels; (2) 'traditional alterations', which record divergences inherited from earlier states of a language, where the anthropophonetic basis of the alteration can be discovered in the history of the language (Baudouin cites Polish palatal softening/hardening; Stankiewicz 1972: 185); and (3) 'correlations', where an anthropophonetic distinction comes to represent a psychophonetic distinction: Anderson (1985: 65–66) provided as an example English pairs like *cloth/clothe* or *calf/calve*, in which voicing of the final fricative carries the weight of the semantic distinction between noun (e.g. *cloth*) and denominal verb (*clothe*). Baudouin subclassified these three types of alternation and explored their historical relations, asserting that a divergence can become fixed into a traditional alteration, eventually evolving into a correlation. He also argued that correlations can become traditional alterations insofar as their psychophonetic content erodes over time.

Baudouin's terms 'anthropophonetic'/'psychophonetic' are no longer current (although his coinages of the terms 'morpheme' [Stankiewicz 1972: 153] and 'grapheme' [*ibid.*: 281] remain in use). However, they figure in another of his major contributions, namely his provocative definition of the 'phoneme'. In his 1894 monograph, Baudouin wrote:

The phoneme [is] a unitary concept belonging to the sphere of phonetics which exists in the mind thanks to a psychological fusion of the impressions resulting from the pronunciation of one and the same sound; it is the psychological equivalent of a speech sound. The unitary concept of the phoneme is connected (associated) with a certain sum of anthropophonetic representations which are, on the one hand, articulatory ... and on the other hand, acoustic ...

(trans. Stankiewicz 1972: 152)

Baudouin's definition of the phoneme evolved over the course of his career. Stankiewicz quotes an earlier lecture, from 1881, in which Baudouin had written that a phoneme can be arrived at only by "'purging it of the accidence of divergence" which splits the unified sound into its anthropophonetic varieties. This unified, discrete sound is the result of "abstraction" and of "phonetic generalization," or "the sum of generalized anthropophonetic properties"' (*ibid.*: 25). Seven years later, in his review of Kruszewski's work, Baudouin took his ex-student to task for treating phonemes as acoustically indivisible units (Baudouin 1888–89/2005: 46–47). By 1910, he characterized pho-nemes as 'not like separate notes, but like chords composed of several elements' (trans. Stankiewicz 1972: 28). Baudouin labelled two kinds of psychological elements at a subphonemic level: articulatory 'kinemes' and acoustic 'acousmemes'.

Baudouin's decomposition of phonemes brings to mind Roman Jakobson's notion of distinctive features. Baudouin never met Jakobson, but Baudouin's influence was felt in Moscow (where Jakobson was studying) during Baudouin's second residence in St Petersburg. Much later, Jakobson's colleague and Prague School co-founder Nikolaj Trubetzkoy (1890–1938) wrote enthusiastically of Baudouin's phonological research. Baudouin's kinemes and acousmemes, how-ever, differ starkly from Jakobsonian distinctive features in their embeddedness in a thoroughly psychological theory of language. For Baudouin, subphonemic units might not appear in speech: they are 'representations of acoustic–articulatory attributes that are divorced from the actual speech-sounds and are unified into a "sound-image" only in the mind' (Stankiewicz 1972: 29). Writing in 1960, Jakobson criticized this facet of Baudouin's 'antiquated psychologism' as a 'dis-advantageous transfer of phonological problems from the firm ground of linguistic analysis to the hazy area of introspection' (Baudouin 1960/1971: 419). Definitions of the phoneme had evolved away from those pioneered by Baudouin, and they would continue to evolve.

Baudouin's major works

Mikołaj Kruszewski, His Life and Scholarly Work, 2005 (W. Browne, trans.; A. Adamska-Sałaciak and M. Smoczyńska, eds), Uniwersytet Jagiellonski, Krakow (original work published 1888–89).
A Baudouin de Courtenay Anthology: The Beginnings of Structural Linguistics, 1972 (E. Stankiewicz, ed. and trans.), Indiana University Press, Bloomington, IN.

Further reading

Adamska-Sałaciak, A. (1997) 'Baudouin de Courtenay on *Lautgesetze*,' in R. Hickey and S. Puppel (eds), *Language and Linguistic Modelling: A Festschrift for Jacek Fisiak on His 60th Birthday*, Berlin, New York: Mouton de Gruyter.

——(1998) 'Jan Baudouin de Courtenay's contribution to linguistic theory,' *Historiographia Linguistica*, 25, 25–60.

Anderson, S. R. (1985) *Phonology in the Twentieth Century*, Chicago: University of Chicago Press.

Jakobson, R. O. (1971) 'The Kazan School of Polish linguistics and its place in the international development of phonology,' in *Roman Jakobson: Selected Writings: Vol. II*, The Hague: Mouton (original work published 1960).

Koerner, E. F. K. (1978) 'Jan Baudouin de Courtenay: his place in the history of linguistic science,' in *Toward a Historiography of Linguistics*, Selected Essays, Amsterdam: John Benjamins.

Minissi, N. (1989) 'F. de Saussure, J. Baudouin de Courtenay and the linguistics of the time,' in J. Rieger and M. Szymczak (eds), *Jan Niecisław Baudouin de Courtenay a Lingwistyka Światowa: Materiały z konferencji międznarodowej Warszawa 4–7 IX 1979*, Warsaw: Polish Academy of Sciences.

Radwańska-Williams, J. (2006) 'Examining our patrimony: The case of the Kazan School', *Historigraphia Linguistica*, 33, 357–90.

Rothstein, R. A. (1975) 'The linguist as dissenter: Jan Baudouin de Courtenay,' in V. Erlich (ed), *For Wiktor Weintraub: Essays in Polish Literature, Language, and History Presented on the Occasion of his 65th Birthday*, The Hague: Mouton.

Schogt, H. G. (1966) 'Baudouin de Courtenay and phonological analysis.' *La Linguistique* 2, 15–29.

Stankiewicz, E. (1972) 'Baudouin de Courtenay: His life and work,' in E. Stankiewicz (ed. and trans.), *A Baudouin de Courtenay Anthology: The Beginnings of Structural Linguistics*, Bloomington, IN: Indiana University Press.

KARL BRUGMANN (1849–1919)

Karl Brugmann was a key member of a group of scholars, centred in Leipzig in the late 1800s, whose work not only advanced the reconstruction of the Indo-European languages, but also lastingly influenced western language science in general. The group accepted the label '*Junggrammatiker*', usually translated as 'Neogrammarians', although this term loses the 'Young Turk' connotation of the German original. Brugmann was the youngest of the core Neogrammarians, the first generation of which also included August Leskien (1840–1916), Berthold Delbrück (1842–1922) and Hermann Osthoff (1847–1909). Brugmann was responsible for a brash programmatic text now read as the Neogrammarians' manifesto. Its publication in 1878 offended some readers as much as it inspired others. He went on to write an authoritative five-volume comparative grammar of the Indo-European languages (which he called 'Indo-Germanic').

Morpurgo Davies (1986: 151–52) made the important point that Brugmann was one of the first generation of nineteenth-century German language scholars who followed a seemingly modern career path. In this, Brugmann's life contrasts with the lives of earlier scholars such as the largely self-supporting **Wilhelm von Humboldt** (whose contributions followed from lifelong avocational study of language), or the **Schlegel** brothers and **Jacob Grimm**, none of whom held a stable academic post, or even **Friedrich Max Müller**, who left Germany for the life of an expatriate scholar in England. **Franz Bopp** did obtain a professorship in Berlin, but only after Humboldt's intervention, and after years of depending on grants from the King of Bavaria. Brugmann and his generation, however, worked in a climate where comparative–historical linguistics was an established discipline, represented at major German universities and even at some smaller ones. The Neogrammarians' careers developed in this context, where conventions of study and a traditional approach to historical linguistics already existed, and from within which they could declare the need for renewal.

Karl Brugman was born in Wiesbaden, in southwestern Germany, to a middle-class family who changed the spelling of their name to 'Brugmann' in 1882 (so that Brugmann's early publications appeared under the name 'Brugman'). He was educated at local schools, then travelled to northeast Germany to study philology, first at the university in Halle and then nearby at Leipzig. Brugmann quickly and methodically ascended the ranks of German academic life. By 1877, he had achieved the status of *Privatdozent* in Sanskrit and comparative linguistics, having presented and defended a postgraduate *Habilitation* thesis. He became Professor *extraordinarius* in 1882, spent a few years teaching in Freiburg, then returned to Leipzig as Professor *ordinarius* to accept the new Chair in Indo-European linguistics, in which position he remained for the rest of his life.

The Neogrammarian manifesto was not Brugmann's first controversial publication. In 1876, he published a paper that proposed to solve certain irregularities in the conventional reconstruction of Proto-Indo-European by positing the existence of syllabic *n* and *m* (that is, syllables formed by a nasal alone, without an accompanying vowel). Syllabic *r* and *l* had already been proposed, if not fully accepted, but Brugmann's syllabic *n* and *m* stimulated considerable debate. Syllabic *n* and *m* were not attested in any early Indo-European language but, as Brugmann argued, postulating their

existence would clear up many puzzling irregularities in the reconstruction of the parent language and its descendents. The idea also
played a role in the intellectual relationship between Brugmann and
his most famous Leipzig student, **Ferdinand de Saussure**.

With the publication of the 1876 paper, Brugmann fell out of
favour with a former teacher, Georg Curtius (1820–85), who, along
with Brugmann, also co-edited the journal in which the paper
appeared. Far from backing down in the face of this threat to the
legitimacy of his work, Brugmann went forward to co-found a new
journal, in the pages of which he and Osthoff would articulate
Neogrammarian positions. The famous manifesto appeared in the
preface to the first issue, written by Brugmann and co-signed by
Osthoff. Speaking on behalf of the new movement, Brugmann
declared that, in opposition to 'the older linguistics' (Brugmann
1878/1967: 198), which seems in particular to have tacitly included
the work of August Schleicher (1821–68), Neogrammarians adopted
'a two-fold concept, whose truth is immediately obvious' (*ibid*.: 204).
Neogrammarians rejected the romantic and Schleicherian representation of language as an independent natural phenomenon subject to its
own inherent laws. Rather, they asserted that language exists only as a
human product, with a 'true existence only in the individual' (*ibid*.:
204). Language change is therefore due to change in speakers'
language behaviour, not to the drift of language as an independent,
external entity. Brugmann also asserted that the forces acting on
present-day speakers are the same as those that acted on speakers in
the past. This 'uniformitarian' assumption (Christy 1983) had several
consequences: it led Neogrammarians to reject the notion that languages decay over time, and it sanctioned their interest in dialectology
and speech errors as potential keys to language change.

By placing the responsibility for language change in the hands of
individual speakers, and by assuming that language in the past was
subject to the same forces as operate on it in the present, the way was
opened for Brugmann to articulate two key principles of the
Neogrammarian movement:

> First, every sound change, inasmuch as it occurs mechanically,
> takes place according to laws that admit no exception. That is,
> the direction of the sound shift is always the same for all the
> members of a linguistic community except where a split into
> dialects occurs; and all words in which the sound subjected to the
> change appears in the same relationship are affected by the change
> without exception.

Second, since it is clear that form association, that is, the creation of new linguistic forms by analogy, plays a very important
role in the life of more recent languages, this type of linguistic
innovation is to be recognized without hesitation for older periods, too, and even for the oldest. This principle is not only to be
recognized, but also to be utilized in the same way as it is
employed for the explanation of linguistic phenomena of later
periods.

(Brugmann 1878; trans Lehmann 1967: 204)

Brugmann's deliberately provocative rhetoric made it clear that he
considered it timely to make a clean sweep of the field of comparative linguistics as it existed in the 1870s. In fact, he implied that such a
clean sweep had already occurred, in writing triumphantly that the
Neogrammarian movement 'fortunately ... has already done away
with some of the fundamental errors which dominated the entire
older linguistics' (*ibid.*: 199). From his point of view, only a comparative linguist who 'emerges from the hypotheses-beclouded
atmosphere of the workshop in which the original Indo-European
forms are forced ... can arrive at a correct idea of the way in which
linguistic forms live and change' (*ibid.*: 202).

Neither the twofold Neogrammarian reconceptualization of language (as a human product, subject to uniformitarianism), nor the
famous principles of the unexceptionality of sound laws and of
the role of analogy, were entirely novel or sharply distinguished
Neogrammarians from their predecessors. Schleicher, for example,
had prepared the way for the notion of unexceptionality. Moreover,
to Brugmann the correct way to understand language change admitted evidence from the diversity of contemporary languages and dialects, not only reconstructed forms from earlier languages. Study of
living languages certainly already existed in the Neogrammarians' day;
what Brugmann pointed out was that this study could contribute to
the understanding of how languages evolve. On the other hand, for
Brugmann the goal was still to explain linguistic change. In this, he
did not go as far as Saussure in balancing the value of synchronic
study of language (study of the features and relationships of languages
at any single point in time) against the value of diachronic study of
language (study of how languages change over time).

Likewise, the Neogrammarians' claims about sound laws and analogy were not without precedent. What was novel was their attempt
to define new roles for these two key concepts. Brugmann criticized
earlier comparative linguistics for too readily admitting exceptions to

sound laws, that is, for positing many special cases where an otherwise across-the-board change would not apply to a specific word or class of words, or where the change resulted in an idiosyncratic result. Neogrammarians rejected this leniency, insisting instead that sound laws be considered mechanical and exceptionless, even as Brugmann conceded that the movement was not yet in a position to provide alternative accounts for recalcitrant data. The complementary concept of analogy also needed to be assigned a new role, according to Brugmann. He considered analogy a major source of language change, as had others. But he also insisted that analogy had always been a major source of language change. Brugmann cited the example of Greek *híppoi* and Latin *equi* 'horses [nominative plural]', forms that diverge from other Indo-Germanic nominative plurals ending in −*s* (Brugmann 1878/1967: 207). Rather than attempting to reconcile these differences by postulating elaborate exceptions to rules of language change, Brugmann suggested that *híppoi* and *equi* derived by analogy with the pronominal endings −*oi*, which, he later argued in his comparative grammar, spread from pronouns to nouns in five branches of the Indo-Germanic family (Brugmann 1886–93/1972, Vol. 3: 352–53). Fortified by the argument that analogy operated throughout the evolution of a language, rather than being the sign of modern degeneration, Neogrammarians could commit themselves to the exceptionlessness of sound laws.

Brugmann's manifesto stirred up considerable debate in his day, some of it quite bitter. Old-school comparative linguists complained variously that Neogrammarians shortsightedly overstated the success of their principles in dealing with the complexities of language change; that their approach was narrow or mechanistic and offered no insight into the cause of change; or that they had exaggerated, in combative terms, working assumptions commonplace in their day. The Neogrammarian controversy remains 'permanently "up-to-date"' (Wilbur 1977: vii), in the sense that it altered the landscape within which debate about language change takes place. The claim that sound laws are exceptionless, rightly or wrongly labelled with the Neogrammarian name, continues to be debated. Kiparsky (1988), for example, argued that exceptionless sound laws may be said to operate, but only alongside gradual word-by-word spread of changes due to lexical diffusion. **William Labov** treated the Neogrammarian controversy as a touchstone in his exhaustive discussion of internal factors bearing on principles of linguistic change. Labov's work is based on diverse sources, including data collected in Brugmann's era and data from contemporary studies of urban American dialects of English; he concluded that 'On the whole, the findings of [Labov's research] show that the Neogrammarian characterization of language structure is essentially correct' (Labov 1994: 604). There as yet is no sign of closure in the controversy that Brugmann's manifesto opened.

Brugman(n)'s major works

'Nasalis sonans in the original Indo-European language' [excerpt], in W. P. Lehmann (ed. and trans.), *A Reader in Nineteenth-Century Historical Indo-European Linguistics*, 1967, Indiana University Press, Bloomington, IN (original work published 1876).

'Preface' to *Morphological Investigations in the Sphere of the Indo-European Languages I*, 1967 (with H. Osthoff), in W. P. Lehmann (ed. and trans.), *A Reader in Nineteenth-Century Historical Indo-European Linguistics*, Indiana University Press, Bloomington, IN (original work published 1878).

Grundriss der vergleichenden Grammatik der indogermanischen Sprachen, trans. as *Elements of the Comparative Grammar of the Indo-Germanic Languages: Vols 1–5*, 1972 (J. Wright, trans.), Chowkhamba Sanskrit Series Office, Varanasi, India (original work published by Trübner, 1886–93).

Further reading

Christy, T. C. (1983) *Uniformitarianism in Linguistics*, Amsterdam and Philadelphia, PA: John Benjamins.

Jankowsky, K. R. (1972) *The Neogrammarians*, The Hague: Mouton.

Kiparsky, P. (1988) 'Phonological change' in F. J. Newmeyer (ed.), *Linguistics: The Cambridge Survey: Vol. I. Linguistic Theory: Foundations*, Cambridge: Cambridge University Press.

Labov, W. (1994) *Principles of Linguistic Change: Vol. 1. Internal Factors*, Oxford: Blackwell.

Morpurgo Davies, A. (1986) 'Karl Brugmann and late nineteenth-century linguistics', in T. Bynon and F. R. Palmer (eds), *Studies in the History of Western Linguistics*, Cambridge: Cambridge University Press.

——(1992) *History of Linguistics: Vol. IV. Nineteenth-Century Linguistics*, London: Longman.

Wilbur, T. H. (1977) 'Preface' in T. H. Wilbur (ed.), *The Lautgesetz-Controversy: A Documentation*, Amsterdam and Philadelphia, PA: John Benjamins.

FERDINAND DE SAUSSURE (1857–1913)

Ferdinand de Saussure is traditionally depicted as having articulated the foundational principles of twentieth-century structuralist linguistics. He developed assumptions about the nature of language that were emerging into scholarly consciousness; defined and juxtaposed concepts in innovative ways; and introduced novel theoretical distinctions. Facets of Saussurean structuralism spread from linguistics to the humanities, social sciences and beyond. As a result, Saussure is probably the figure whom both linguists and scholars in other fields are most likely to recognize as a key thinker. A hundred years after his death, the intellectual influence attributed to Saussure is pervasive in the language sciences, so that modern linguists in general presuppose the essential systematicity of language, viewed at any point in time – a recognizably Saussurean stance.

Saussure's biography is unusual in that his reputation as an architect of structuralism came as a posthumous accessory to a career in Indo-European comparative-historical grammar. He was born, and lived most of his life, in Geneva, the oldest of nine offspring of a prominent Swiss Protestant family with a tradition of scientific and academic accomplishment. His early fascination with language was fostered by family friend Adolphe Pictet (1799–1875), a linguist, novelist, aesthetician and inventor of military technology. Saussure was educated privately and at various institutions in Geneva, where he studied classical languages and was exposed to scholarship on Indo-European. In 1876, he moved to Leipzig to study with the Neogrammarians, including **Karl Brugmann** and Hermann Osthoff (1847–1909). He also spent some months in Berlin advancing his study of Sanskrit. Saussure was a motivated and well grounded student, respectful of authority. But he showed strong intellectual independence and expressed certain doubts about the Neogrammarians' work. In private, for example, he criticized Brugmann for his incomplete understanding of ablaut (Godel 1960: 23).

In 1877, Saussure began publishing on technical topics in Indo-European historical grammar, subsuming phonology and etymology (collected in Saussure 1922). Just before he turned twenty-one, he finished an essay that brought him lasting acclaim. His *Mémoire sur le système primitif des voyelles dans les langues indo-européennes* ('The original vowel system of the Indo-European languages'), published in early 1879, analysed the distribution and relations of vowels in the ancient parent language and its descendents, focusing on the vowel *a*. He argued that certain instances of *a* in daughter languages actually derive from a 'nasal sonorant', *n̥*, acknowledging Brugmann's recently circulated assertion that Proto-Indo-European featured syllabic *n* and *m*. Saussure, however, secretly felt he had discovered the *a ~ n̥* correspondence years earlier. (The full story is complex; see Joseph, in press.) The *Mémoire* goes on to posit the existence of two additional elements Saussure called 'sonorant coefficients', which no longer appear in daughter languages. In specific contexts, each had functioned sometimes as a vowel, sometimes as a consonant; their presence had predictable consequences for the length and quality of surrounding vowels.

Saussure worked through the evidence for his claims with preternatural self-possession. Some readers expressed startled admiration for the *Mémoir*. Others accepted it only grudgingly, or even flat-out misconstrued it. But gradually support mounted for the validity of Saussure's claims. Danish scholar Hermann Möller (1850–1923) extended them to hypothesize that the sonorant coefficients were varieties of laryngeal consonants, that is, speech sounds produced in the larynx. In 1927, Polish linguist Jerzy Kuryłowicz (1895–1978) recognized in Hittite, the most archaic Indo-European language extant (unanalysed until 1911), laryngeals that exactly instantiated Saussure's hypothesized sonorant coefficients. This spectacular finding cemented Saussure's reputation as having initiated 'laryngeal theory'.

In 1880, Saussure completed a doctoral dissertation on the genitive absolute construction in Sanskrit. It lacked the glamour of the *Mémoire*, but earned him his degree. He then left Leipzig for Paris, where he participated in meetings of the Linguistic Society of Paris, eventually serving for a decade as its secretary. In 1881, Saussure was named a lecturer at the École Pratique des Hautes Études in Paris, where he taught Gothic and Old High German, with additional courses in Lithuanian and in Latin/Greek comparative grammar. He seems to have succeeded as a teacher and established his presence in the intellectual life of the city, although he published little aside from short observations of specific facts in Greek, Gothic, Sanskrit, Lithuanian, etc.

In 1891, Saussure left Paris to accept a professorship in comparative grammar at the University of Geneva. Five years later, he was promoted to a Chair in Sanskrit and Indo-European languages, a position he held until his death. In Geneva, as in Paris, Saussure gained the respect of his colleagues and students. There is evidence that he intended to prepare some of his research and lectures for publication, as others urged him to, but his actual output was rather slight. At the beginning of January 1907, Saussure took over teaching a course on general linguistics and comparative Indo-European. He repeated it in 1908–9 and 1910–11, remodelling the course content each time. Most of the curriculum surveyed the history and features of Indo-European languages, but Saussure also devoted lectures each year to his attempts, apparently long-incubated, to clarify what he viewed as basic principles and concepts for the study of language. It is in this material that Saussure's greatest reputation lies.

After Saussure's premature death in 1913, two of his Geneva colleagues, Charles Bally (1865–1947) and Albert Sechehaye (1870–1946), moved to publish the material covered in Saussure's lectures on general linguistics. But it turned out that Saussure left very little in writing relevant to the course. Bally and Sechehaye instead assembled notes taken by eight students who had enrolled in the course in different years, to create a conglomerate text synthesizing all three successive versions, as reconstructed from student notebooks. As recognition of the importance of Saussure's ideas spread, an extensive hermeneutic industry grew up, producing numerous translations of Bally and Sechehaye's *Cours de linguistique générale* (*Course in General Linguistics*, e.g. Saussure 1916/1983); a critical edition (Engler 1967–74); three published volumes of Saussure's students' notes (Komatsu and Harris 1993; Komatsu and Wolf 1996, 1997); and a collection discovered in 1996 of notes and short texts written in Saussure's hand, some pertinent to the famous course (excerpts published as Saussure 2006). There is also a vast literature of commentary and interpretation.

The unconventional textual basis on which scholars must reconstruct Saussure's proposals complicates their assessment, to be sure. Bally and Sechehaye's text has a labyrinthine character, incorporating vivid images and analogies that have achieved classic status (such as a comparison of the structure of language with the rules of chess; Saussure 1916/1983: 87–89) with bare, oracular assertions and unacknowledged gaps and contradictions. Nevertheless, there is agreement that Saussure introduced concepts and terms – conventionally discussed as contrasting pairs – that have proved very consequential to language scholarship.

Among the most significant is Saussure's distinction between *diachronic* study of language, that is, analysis of textual evidence for how languages change over time, and *synchronic* study of language, analysis of language as a static, self-contained phenomenon, the systematicity of which is presupposed at every historical point. Synchronic study of language certainly already existed in Saussure's day – for example, in **William Dwight Whitney**'s work, which Saussure admired – but by naming it, he recognized it as a counterpoint to the dominant comparative-historical school. Over time, valorization of synchronic study of language has had massive impact beyond linguistics, in the humanities, social sciences, even public life (Harris 2001: 194–213), insofar as it legitimated the study of the synchronic state of a language (or of a discipline, institution, etc.) as 'the only relevant psychological reality for current speakers of the language' (*ibid.*: 197).

A second important Saussurean distinction was between '*langue*' and '*parole*', the former translated non-technically as 'grammar' or 'language', the latter as 'speech'. For Saussure, *langue* is a system of signs shared by a speech community, of which each community member possesses an identical copy. It is 'the social part of language, external to the individual, who by himself is powerless either to create it or to modify it. It exists only in virtue of a kind of contract agreed between the members of a community' (Saussure 1916/1983: 14). *Parole* comprises a speaker's execution of *langue*. Language change is initiated by individuals, and originates in *parole*. Saussure famously contrasted the two in writing that 'one may compare a language to a symphony. The symphony has a reality of its own, which is independent of the way in which it is performed'; the independence of *langue* and *parole* mirrors the fact that 'mistakes which musicians may make in performance in no way compromise that reality' (*ibid.*: 18). To Saussure, *langue*, rather than *parole*, was the central object of the study of language. (He also sometimes employed a third term, *langage* or *faculté du langage* ['language faculty'], to label an individual speaker's access to the socially defined system of signs that is *langue* [Koerner 1973: 228–37]).

Among other broadly influential contributions of Saussure's course in general linguistics is his discussion of the nature of the linguistic sign. *Langue* is comprised of a network of signs, each of which has two faces: the 'signifier' (a specific psycholinguisticly salient sound pattern, not sounds themselves) and the 'signified' (the psycholinguistic concept that the sign 'stands for', not the thing itself). Staking out a radical position, Saussure declared that the relationship of signifier and signified is entirely arbitrary, that is, there exists no necessary connection between signifier/signified pairs (Saussure 1916/1983: 67–69). In addition, Saussure asserted that linguistic signifiers are linear in the sense that they unfold along only one dimension, namely, time (as opposed to, say, nautical signals; *ibid.*: 69–70) and that a linguistic system is essentially negative in that it comprises only differences among signifiers and differences among signified elements – not similarities (*ibid.*: 118–20).

Saussure also distinguished between two classes of relationships among linguistic units. *Syntagmatic* relationships hold between items that 'must be arranged consecutively in spoken sequence' (*ibid.*: 121), such as the relationships of root to affix, specifier to head, matrix to subordinate clause. *Associative* or *paradigmatic* relationships, in contrast, are the diverse meaning- and form-based associations among items, such as how (in modern terms) the word 'kitchen' primes 'chicken';

'kitchenette'; 'eat'; 'stove'; 'bedroom', etc. The significance of the syntagmatic/paradigmatic distinction is that it labelled structural relationships, which, to Saussure, constitute the heart of language, as opposed to conceiving language as a collection of sounds, words or sentences.

Saussure's provocative exposition of these foundational ideas, even imperfectly refracted through his students' notes, eventually displaced his reputation as an Indo-Europeanist. Conceptualization of language as a synchronically analysable system of signs, among which structural relationships hold, inspired linguists (and anthropologists, literary critics, psychologists, mathematicians, etc.) to rethink key disciplinary assumptions. Saussure's influence has not been received uncritically: **Roman Jakobson**'s distinctive features contested the linearity of the linguistic sign, and his analyses of iconicity and markedness contested Saussurean arbitrariness; both **Otto Jespersen** and **J. R. Firth** were unconvinced of the value of distinguishing *langue* from *parole*; Roy Harris (b. 1931) argued against treating writing as a secondary manifestation of language relative to speech, a deep-seated tradition in which Saussure participated (Harris 1986: 40–41). Saussure's influence has also sometimes been received infelicitously: the parallels **Noam Chomsky** identified between *langue/parole* and competence/performance seem not to respect the social-centeredness of *langue* (Joseph 1990).

Critics notwithstanding, Firth remarked that by 1950 linguists could 'almost be classified by using the name of de Saussure', into 'Saussureans, anti-Saussureans, post-Saussureans, or non-Saussureans' (Firth 1950/1957: 179).

Saussure's major works

Mémoire sur le système primitif des voyelles dans les langues indo-européennes, 1968, Georg Olms, Hildesheim (original text published 1879).
Recueil des publications scientifiques, 1922 (C. Bally and L. Gautier, eds), Editions Sonor, Genève.
Course in General Linguistics, 1983 (C. Bally and A. Sechehaye, eds; R. Harris, trans.), Duckworth, London (original text published 1916).
Writings in General Linguistics, 2006 (S. Bouquet and R. Engler, eds; C. Sanders and M. Pires, trans.), Oxford University Press, Oxford (original texts *c*. 1891–1911).

Further reading

Culler, J. (1976) *Ferdinand de Saussure*, New York: Penguin.
Engler, R. (1967–74) *Ferdinand de Saussure Cours de linguistique générale, Édition critique: Vols 1–3*, Wiesbaden: Harrassowitz.

Firth, J. R. (1950) 'Personality and language in society', *The Sociological Review*, 42, 37–52 (reprinted in *Papers in Linguistics 1934–1951*, Oxford University Press, 1957).

Godel, R. (1960) 'Souvenirs de F. de Saussure concernant sa jeunesse et ses études,' *Cahiers Ferdinand de Saussure*, 17, 12–25.

Harris, R. (1986) *The Origin of Writing*, La Salle, IL: Open Court.

——(2001) *Saussure and his Interpreters*, New York: New York University Press.

Joseph, J. E. (1990) 'Ideologizing Saussure: Bloomfield's and Chomsky's readings of the *Cours de Linguistique Générale*', in J. E. Joseph and T. J. Taylor (eds) *Ideologies of Language*, London: Routledge.

——(in press) 'Les "Souvenirs" de Saussure revisités', *Langages*. Available in English at www.cerclefds.unical.it/seminaire/download/joseph.pdf; see also J. E. Joseph (2011) *Saussure*, Oxford: Oxford University Press.

Koerner, E. F. K. (1973) *Ferdinand de Saussure: Origin and Development of his Linguistic Thought in Western Studies of Language*, Braunschweig: Vieweg.

Komatsu, E. (ed.) and Harris, R. (trans.) (1993) *Saussure's Third Course of Lectures on General Linguistics (1910–1911)*, Oxford: Pergamon.

Komatsu, E. (ed.) and Wolf, G. (trans.) (1996) *Saussure's First Course of Lectures on General Linguistics (1907)*, Oxford: Pergamon.

——(1997) *Saussure's Second Course of Lectures on General Linguistics (1908–1909)*, Oxford: Pergamon.

Sanders, C. (ed.) (2004) *The Cambridge Companion to Saussure*, Cambridge: Cambridge University Press.

OTTO JESPERSEN (1860–1943)

The Danish scholar Otto Jespersen published his autobiography in 1938 under the title *En Sprogmands Levned*, literally '*A Language-man's Life*'. The Foreword to the English edition points out that the Danish word '*sprogmand*' is not really equivalent to either 'philologist' or 'linguist'. Although the translator adopted the latter term, it seems fitting that this independent-minded scholar's self-representation does not fall into any established category. Personally, Jespersen led a conventional life for a successful European academic and administrator in the early twentieth century. But intellectually, his allegiance was not to any school, approach or topic. Rather, Jespersen was a self-defined 'language-man', who had the good fortune to be able to follow his broad and boundary-crossing curiosity about language into many subfields, and to freely develop his many creative and original insights. Randolph Quirk (b. 1920), in the Foreword to the tenth edition of Jespersen (1905/1982), depicted him as 'indeed the most distinguished scholar of the English language who has ever lived'.

Jespersen's upbringing encouraged independence. The seventh of ten children born to a family of lawyers and public servants in Jutland (the westernmost, peninsular portion of Denmark), he was orphaned at age 13. To attend school, he moved to a town northwest of Copenhagen, where his Jutland dialect was the object of ridicule. Jespersen worked his way through the University of Copenhagen with the help of relatives, scholarships and part-time jobs (principally as a language tutor but also as shorthand stenographer in the Danish Parliament). After completing almost four years of courses in Law, he abruptly abandoned that field to embark on the riskier, less practical study of languages. As a result, it took him a decade to obtain a Master's degree, in French. Those extra years probably fixed Jespersen's habits of wide and self-motivated study of Germanic and other European languages, and of phonetics, comparative-historical linguistics, and language teaching. Jespersen's attenuated student life also gave him time to establish personal contacts with linguists all over Europe, to become active in professional societies and informal study groups, and to solidify his attachment – albeit often a critical one – to the University of Copenhagen. These experiences sustained him throughout his life.

After a year of travel, during which he studied in Berlin and met (among others) phoneticians **Henry Sweet** in England and Paul Passy (1859–1940) in France, Jespersen submitted a doctoral dissertation on English grammatical case. Two years later, in 1893, he was appointed Copenhagen's first regular professor of English language and literature. He married in 1897 and raised a son, Frans. Jespersen travelled throughout Europe and spent nine months lecturing in the United States in 1909 (at Berkeley and Columbia). Otherwise, his entire career was played out at the University of Copenhagen, as professor, dean and eventually vice chancellor.

A number of interconnected themes emerge in Jespersen's wide-ranging work. Two of his first and most formative interests were phonetics and foreign language teaching. He combined them in urging (along with Sweet, Passy, and the Germans Felix Franke [1860–86] and Wilhelm Viëtor [1850–1918]) that modern language teachers train students in articulatory phonetics, and teach phonetic transcription to both first- and second-language learners. Jespersen criticized stilted, artificial learners' texts and downplayed teaching methods that relied on translation, memorization, and rules and exceptions. In *How to Teach a Foreign Language*, he championed speech-based practice modelled on 'sensible communications' (Jespersen 1901/1904: 11), and summarized the recommendations of a fellowship of phoneticians and educators to which he belonged (labelled the 'Reform Movement'; Howatt 1984). Perhaps Jespersen's underpaid and insecure years supporting himself as a language tutor licensed him to think critically about then-current instructional practices, which extended the traditions of Latin pedagogy to modern languages. But even later, when as a faculty member and administrator he had rather more to lose, Jespersen continued to try to reform the university's language teaching and teacher-education programmes.

The Reform Movement influenced language pedagogy in Europe and even the USA. Jespersen's work in phonetics, on the other hand, had its impact in Denmark. He created a notational system still used for the study of dialectal variation in Danish, and wrote several treatises on descriptive phonetics for language teachers and students of linguistics. His major work in this field, *Fonetik* (1897–99), has not been translated into English.

Jespersen's writing started out strongly in phonetics and language teaching, but soon expanded. *Progress in Language* (1894), an extension of his PhD thesis, represents another theme maintained throughout his career: the conviction that historical change is a process of incremental 'gain in clearness and simplicity' (Jespersen 1905 [9th edn]: 190), not decay or cyclic evolution. Jespersen's notion of 'progress' in language was, in part, a rejection of the prevailing nineteenth-century assumption that erosion of morphological inflections represents a natural deterioration of languages over time. Using the history of English as his chief example, Jespersen argued that linguistic change is a process through which communicative efficiency increases; English, in his view, profited from its loss of nominal and verbal inflections and reduction of irregularity. *Progress* also displays some of the hallmarks of Jespersen's approach, in particular his abundant use of illustrations from literature and common speech. Jespersen insisted on building his analyses out of attested language data, which, throughout his life, he meticulously copied by hand, numbered, and annotated on eight-by-six-inch slips of paper. He mistrusted what he viewed as rarified, abstract argumentation or theorizing in the absence of empirical evidence. In this, he was at odds with his younger compatriot **Louis Hjelmslev**.

Jespersen's views of historical change and his empirical stance are also displayed in *Growth and Structure of the English Language* and, most elaborately, in *Modern English Grammar on Historical Principles*, a monument of exacting and sensitive scholarship whose value still stands a century after the appearance of the first of its seven volumes. The latter work was published over a forty-year period and, although somewhat confusingly laid out, contains a wealth of perspicuous observations about English, richly exemplified. Francis (1989: 93–94) noted parallels between Jespersen's *Modern English Grammar* and

James Murray's *New English Dictionary on Historical Principles* – similarities of title, ambition, reliance on painstakingly culled linguistic examples, and even similarity in their protracted dates of publication. Jespersen seems to have designed his grammar as a companion to the *Oxford English Dictionary*.

In keeping with his insistence that theory be rooted in observed language data, it was in the course of preparing the *Modern English Grammar* that Jespersen wrote his most theoretical work, *The Philosophy of Grammar*. In this book, he developed terms and concepts that appeared in his earlier publications, which together constitute another overall theme of his scholarship. Some are still prominent today, if not necessarily associated with Jespersen's name. One key concept is what he called 'the three ranks', the claim that in 'combinations' of words 'there is a certain scheme of subordination' (Jespersen 1924 [reprinted 1958]: 96) such that one is primary, alongside at least two other possible levels of nested relationships (note that Jespersen lacked the concepts of grammatical 'phrase' and 'phrasal head'). Thus in *a furiously barking dog*, '*dog* is primary, *barking* secondary, and *furiously* tertiary' (*ibid.*: 97). Jespersen generalized these terms beyond conventional word classes to clauses, so that 'the "part of speech" classification and the "rank" classification represent different angles from which the same word or form may be viewed' (*ibid.*: 107). Furthermore, Jespersen distinguished the 'more rigid or stiff' relationship of a primary to a secondary, which he called 'junction', from the 'more pliable' relationship of a primary to a tertiary, which he called 'nexus' (*ibid.*: 116). With these terms in hand, Jespersen analysed many varieties of juncture and nexus covering a wide swath of traditional syntactic phenomena, both in the 1924 book and in more detail in *Modern English Grammar*.

Two other important works also exemplify Jespersen's independence and creativity. *Language* (1922) contains a long section on child language learning, not a standard topic of linguistic interest in his day. Jespersen's position contrasts with, for example, **William Dwight Whitney**, for whom language learning was simply a product of imitation and adult instruction. Jespersen characteristically noticed what is extraordinary about the ordinary: he recognized, for example, the problem posed by the emergence of children's questions such as 'Why you smoke, Father?' in a context where adults model normal subject–auxiliary inversion in English questions, and he remarked on children's incongruous imitation of adult statements like 'You mustn't eat that' as 'Not eat that' (Jespersen 1922 [reprinted 1964]: 136). On these grounds, he evinced doubt that children are taught language or merely passively absorb it. Rather, learning a language 'demands extraordinary labour on the child's part'; along the way the child 'creates something never heard before by us or by anybody else' (*ibid.*: 128, 129).

A final major theme in Jespersen's scholarship carried his creativity to the limit. Jespersen, a pacifist, opposed nationalism and observed with anguish the violence that overwhelmed Europe in the early twentieth century. Although international auxiliary languages had long intrigued him, political events increased his sense of the urgency of developing a language that might foster international cooperation. Jespersen became a force in collaborative efforts to assess existing auxiliary languages such as Esperanto or Volapük. World War I interrupted those efforts, but in what he characterized as 'what many may regard as the greatest folly of my life' (Jespersen 1995/1938: 147), he persisted after the war, gradually becoming disaffected with the existing auxiliary languages. Jespersen decided to invent his own, 'Novial'. Novial turned out no more or less successful than its competitors. However, its existence testifies to Jespersen's daring and creativity.

Jespersen remained active as a scholar until his death at age eighty-three. Since then, generations of students have found his erudition leavened with a clarity, warmth and sprightliness of style that make his writing a genuine pleasure. Regard for Jespersen's achievements has nevertheless proven capricious. Falk (1992) reports an absence of references to Jespersen among American structuralists, with the exception of **Leonard Bloomfield**. Bloomfield abundantly and appreciatively cited Jespersen, even as Bloomfield took issue with what he perceived as Jespersen's pernicious psychological assumptions. It is a tribute to Jespersen's complexity as a scholar that two of his modern champions are **James McCawley** and **Noam Chomsky**. Chomsky (1977) admiringly revisited *The Philosophy of Grammar* in commemorating the fiftieth anniversary of the Linguistic Society of America. He highlighted Jespersen's assertion that syntax does not merely reflect semantics, an issue about which Chomsky and McCawley were engaged in a notorious controversy. McCawley likewise wrote admiringly of Jespersen, frequently referring to his grammatical insights, and reviewing books about and by Jespersen. As ever, Jespersen the *sui generis* 'language-man' does not readily fit into any obvious category or school.

Jespersen's major writings

Listed here by initial publication date or initial publication in English. Almost all of Jespersen's writings have been reissued multiple times, in multiple editions. Citations in the text above indicate both edition and page.

Progress in Language, 1894, Macmillan, New York.

Fonetik: en systematisk fremstilling af læren om sprogglyd, 1897–99, Schubothe, Copenhagen.

How to Teach a Foreign Language, 1904 (S. Y.-O. Bertelsen, trans.), Macmillan, New York (original work published 1901).

Growth and Structure of the English Language, 1905, Teubner, Leipzig.

A Modern English Grammar on Historical Principles, Part I: Sounds and Spellings, 1909, Winter, Heidelberg; *Part II: Syntax Vol. 1*, 1914, Winter, Heidelberg; *Part III, Syntax Vol. 2*, 1927, Winter, Heidelberg; *Part IV, Morphology*, 1942 (with the assistance of P. Christophersen, N. Haislund and K. Schibsbye), Munksgaard, Copenhagen.

Language: Its Nature, Development and Origin, 1923, George Allen and Unwin.

The Philosophy of Grammar, 1924, George Allen & Unwin, London.

An International Language, 1928, George Allen & Unwin, London.

Selected Writings of Otto Jespersen, 1962, George Allen & Unwin, London.

A Linguist's Life: An English Translation of Otto Jespersen's Autobiography with Notes, Photos and a Bibliography, 1995 (A. Juul, H. F. Nielsen and J. E. Nielsen, eds; D. Stoner, trans.), Odense University Press, Odense (original work published 1938).

Further reading

Chomsky, N. (1977) 'Questions of form and interpretation' in *Essays on Form and Interpretation*, New York: North-Holland.

Falk, J. (1992) 'Otto Jespersen, Leonard Bloomfield, and American structural linguistics', *Language*, 68, 465–91.

Francis, W. N. (1989) 'Otto Jespersen as grammarian', in A. Juul and H. F. Nielsen (eds), *Otto Jespersen: Facets of His Life and Work*, Amsterdam and Philadelphia, PA: John Benjamins.

Howatt, A. P. R. (1984) *A History of English Language Teaching*, Oxford: Oxford University Press.

Juul, A. and Nielsen, H. F. (1989) *Otto Jespersen: Facets of His Life and Work*, Amsterdam and Philadelphia, PA: John Benjamins.

DANIEL JONES (1881–1967)

David Abercrombie (1909–92), prominent student of British phonetician Daniel Jones, marked the centenary of Jones' birth with a memorial lecture at the University of Leeds that was both appreciative and critical. 'Jones was not a profound thinker, and he did not pretend to be', Abercrombie (1985: 15) declared outright. Others have also tempered their praise for Jones, noting that his abiding practicality made him 'suspicious of theoretical abstraction, and [...] preoccup[ied] with surface phenomena' (Gimson 1977: 151), or reacting to what they have viewed as 'over-subtlety' and 'excessive academicism' (Lewis 1980: 346, 347) in his attention to phonetic distinctions. Moreover, Jones' responsibility for popularizing the term and notion of Received Pronunciation (RP) as a model for learners of English appeared to ally him with a narrowly prescriptivist position in debate about language standards, even though he made explicit his regard for other dialects.

Whatever his limits, Jones unquestionably played a key role in the development of phonetics. Among his notable accomplishments are his specification and systematization of eight 'Cardinal Vowels' as a technique for characterizing the vowel inventories of languages; meticulous descriptive work on English phonetics, much of it directed at second-language learners or teachers; promotion of a utilitarian concept of the phoneme; pioneering explorations into the phonetic facts of languages as varied as Cornish, Sindhi (spoken in Pakistan), and Gã (spoken in Ghana); application of phonetics to the improvement of orthography in various languages; and – through all this work – successful institutionalization of the study of phonetics in England. In addition, Jones' unusual linguistic-perceptual talents and his capacity to analyse fine acoustic and articulatory distinctions made him a legendary figure in the history of the discipline.

Jones came from an upper-class London family. His barrister father was by avocation a lawn tennis enthusiast, who helped to codify the rules of the game and to establish the Wimbledon tournament. Following the conventions of his social class, Jones was tutored at home and then sent to boarding school before entering King's College Cambridge. (Before entering Cambridge he also briefly attended a London day school, incidentally gaining exposure to a different sociolinguistic context.) Jones graduated with a mediocre degree in mathematics, then dutifully prepared for a career in law. But vacation travels to Europe had aroused his curiosity about modern languages. In 1901, he spent several weeks in Marburg attending a German language immersion course taught by an enterprising and lively instructor who emphasized phonetic training. Jones was captivated (Collins and Mees 1998).

Three years later, when his health deteriorated while preparing for the bar examinations, Jones persuaded his parents to send him to Paris to regain his strength. Perhaps a stronger motivation was to reprise his Marburg experience by enrolling in courses in French phonetics. He lived with the extended family of phonetician Paul Passy (1859–1940), founder of the International Phonetics Association, and co-designer of the International Phonetic Alphabet (IPA). Jones abandoned law to become Passy's protégé, eventually marrying one of Passy's nieces.

In 1907, Passy helped Jones secure a part-time lectureship in phonetics at University College in London. The timing was good because, although phonetics already had a long tradition in Britain pre-dating **Henry Sweet**, academic interest in it had recently soared, especially as a technique for improving the speech of second-language learners of English. Jones capitalized on this trend. His role at University College expanded, while he produced a torrent of publications on phonetics, and transcriptions of diverse languages and dialects that demonstrated how phonetics can record prosodic features as well as vowels and consonants. Many of Jones' lifelong professional preoccupations surfaced early, including orthographic reform, the phonetics of Shakespeare and Chaucer, and the phonetics of Bantu (with his attention later spreading to East Asian, Indo-Iranian and other languages). Jones' reputation grew internationally in the 1910s. In 1921, he was named Britain's first Professor of Phonetics. He personally built up the University College Department of Phonetics – including through the aftermaths of both World Wars – and remained at its head until retiring, reluctantly, in 1949.

While Jones was not the first to analyse the articulation of vowels, his exposition of the Cardinal Vowels is probably the most famous. He defined the eight Cardinal Vowels (in order: *i, e, ɛ, a, ɑ, ɔ, o, u*) according to their bases in specific gestures of the tongue and lips. He conceived them as schematically arrayed on the far edges of a trapezoidal space, the boundaries of which represent the natural limits of movement of the tongue from a neutral position along two axes: high versus low; back versus front. Jones insisted on the utmost articulatory precision, so that his students underwent long, repetitious, individualized tuition in ear-training and articulatory gymnastics. The goal was to be able to exploit the Cardinal Vowels as points of reference in identifying and reproducing vowels in diverse natural languages. Jones' writings tirelessly explain the features of the Cardinal Vowels and their utility as a descriptive technique, before addressing other vowels and consonants (e.g. Jones 1918/1956: 29–48).

According to Jones, the ideal is to acquire the system of Cardinal Vowels by sustained face-to-face practice with a trained teacher. Failing that, he had photographs taken of his own lip movements (*ibid.*: 33), X-rays of his tongue positions (Jones 1909/1950, frontispiece), oscillograms of his voice (Jones 1950/1962, frontispiece), and in 1956 recorded his pronunciation of the Cardinal Vowels on gramophone records. The latter are now accessible as sound files on the internet (see 'Recordings'), fixed as a kind of public standard against which phoneticians can still, across the ages, calibrate their production of vowels to those of Daniel Jones.

Among Jones' other contributions are his many forays into descriptive phonetics. His 1916 collaboration with a gifted native speaker of Tswana is particularly impressive for its recognition that the language employs complex tonal features, including downstep (i.e. the lowering of a high tone when it follows a low tone, in a context where the low tone is not phonetically realized; Jones 2002, Vol. 6). He also published substantive analyses of French, Spanish, Italian, Russian and Cantonese (*ibid.*, Vols 4–6). But most of all, Jones worked on English. The utility of his 1917 *English Pronouncing Dictionary* has been proven to generations of learners and media personnel. The seventeenth edition, published in 2006, specifies both British and American pronunciations of 80,000 words, including geographical and personal names and loanwords into English. A CD-ROM accompanies the text, a Jonesian touch.

The *Pronouncing Dictionary* and Jones (1918/1956) brought to the foreground the matter of which version(s) of English pronunciation a phonetician should model, an issue that attracted comment in Jones' day, as in the present. Jones unflinchingly employed as the standard his own RP speech, which is to say the upper-class, southern British pronunciation cultivated among schoolboys in the public (i.e. boarding) schools. At the same time, Jones expressed the opinion that what made speech 'good' was a speaker's intelligibility, not the choice of dialect:

> The sounds of London dialect (Cockney), for instance, are not in themselves bad. Words pronounced in Cockney fashion are perfectly intelligible to others who speak with local London pronunciation. Users of RP sometimes find London dialect pronunciation difficult to understand, but their difficulty is to be attributed to unfamiliarity with that manner of speech and not to any inherent 'badness' in the sounds.
>
> (Jones 1909/1950: 5)

Furthermore, he continued:

> ... what is 'pleasing' to one person is not necessarily pleasing to another. People's ideas as to what is pleasing or displeasing are often determined by associations with circumstances under which

certain kinds of pronunciation are used, and not by any inherent goodness or badness of the sounds uttered.

(*ibid.*)

While Jones expressed seemingly modern tolerance ('Above all it appears to me important that *no other person should ever disparage the pronunciation of another*'; Jones 1937: 208, his emphasis), he still disingenuously selected RP as his phonetic model as if it possessed obvious, natural priority. Nowhere did Jones address the sociocultural consequences of setting as a public target a variety of English spoken by only a tiny minority of the relevant speech community (Macaulay 1988).

One additional facet of Jones' work highlights his inveterate pragmatism, namely, his writings on the concept of the phoneme. In articles from the latter half of his career (collected in Jones 2002, Vol. 7; see also Jones 1950/1962), Jones presented three definitions of the term: what he took as **Jan Baudouin de Courtenay**'s mentalistic version (phonemes as abstract sounds that surface differently in different phonetic contexts); Jones' favoured physical definition (phonemes as families of sounds, each appropriate to a specific phonetic context); and the Prague School's phonological conception (phonemes as speech features that distinguish the meanings of words). Jones found the mentalistic definition attractive, but adopted the physical definition because of its ready applicability to language teaching (Jones 2002, Vol. 7: 9). As his student Abercrombie (1985: 23) wrote, 'Jones' phoneme concept had the minimum of theory behind it. [He] always said that there was no such thing as phonology as a subject separate from phonetics' – and, one might add, Jones' phonetics aimed at phonetic exactitude (and hence relevance to language pedagogy) over theoretical elegance or breadth of generalization. Thus he rejected a phonological conception of the phoneme which incorporated duration or pitch. Instead, Jones distinguished prosodic features from phonemes, coining the term 'chroneme' to denote differences in length, and 'toneme' differences in pitch (Jones 2002, Vol. 7: 3).

Because of Jones' leadership in institutionalizing the study of phonetics, it is also important to understand his historical role. Henry Sweet was the best known linguist in Britain when Jones launched his career. Jones heard Sweet lecture in 1907 and sought out private lessons from him. But although many of their interests coincided, and despite his admiration for Sweet, Jones was more influenced by his experiences learning phonetics in France and Germany. Jones' relationship with Sweet contrasted with his relationship with his nearer contemporary **J. R. Firth**. Jones hired Firth at University College in 1927, and supported his work until Firth moved to the School for Oriental and African Studies (SOAS). But Jones' practicality, his emphasis on ear-training, his hostility to linguistic theory and (despite the X-rays and oscillograms) his mild antipathy toward experimental technology all contrasted with Firth's orientation. Even when both worked at University College, their intellectual paths crossed little. After Firth hired away to SOAS some of Jones' colleagues and favourite students in 1944–45 (Collins and Mees 1998: 355–56), Jones considered Firth a rival.

In an intriguing exploration of Jones' phonetic claims, Ladefoged (1967: 50–142) submitted to modern acoustic analysis recordings of the Cardinal Vowels produced by phoneticians trained by Jones (or by students of those phoneticians) – recordings that Jones himself had evaluated and deemed accurate. Ladefoged's results show only modest convergence in the acoustic properties across different subjects' renditions of any one vowel. In another experiment, Ladefoged found that the same phoneticians' identification of the vowels of novel Gaelic words with respect to Jones' Cardinal Vowels coincided only moderately. These findings cast some doubt on the empirical basis of Jones' phonetics, but leave intact his reputation as one who moved the discipline forward.

Jones' major works

The Pronunciation of English (3rd edn), 1950, Cambridge University Press, Cambridge (1st edn published 1909).
English Pronouncing Dictionary (17th edn), 2006 (P. Roach, J. Hartman and J. Setter, eds), Cambridge University Press, Cambridge (1st edn published 1917).
An Outline of English Phonetics (8th edn), 1956, Dutton, New York (1st edn published 1918).
The Phoneme: Its Nature and Use (2nd edn), 1962, W. Heffer & Sons, Cambridge (1st edn published 1950).
Daniel Jones: Selected Works: Vols 1–8, 2002, B. Collins and I. M. Mees (eds), Routledge, London.
Recordings of Jones' voice demonstrating the Cardinal Vowels: http://www.let.uu.nl/~audiufon/data/e_cardinal_vowels.html (Universiteit Utrecht, Studierichting Fonetiek).

Further reading

Abercrombie, D. (1985) 'Daniel Jones' teaching', in V. A. Fromkin (ed.), *Phonetic Linguistics: Essays in Honor of Peter Ladefoged*, Orlando, FL: Academic Press.

Collins, B. and Mees, I. M. (1998) *The Real Professor Higgins: The Life and Career of Daniel Jones*, Berlin: Mouton de Gruyter.

Gimson, A. C. (1977) 'Daniel Jones and standards of English pronunciation', *English Studies*, 58, 151–58.

Jones, D. (1937) 'On "Received Pronunciation"', *American Speech*, 12, 207–8.

Kemp, J. A. (2001) 'The development of phonetics from the late 18th to the late 19th century', in S. Auroux, E. F. K. Koerner, H.-J. Niederehe and K. Versteegh (eds), *History of the Language Sciences: Vol. 2*, Berlin/New York: Walter de Gruyter.

Ladefoged, P. (1967) *Three Areas of Experimental Phonetics*, Oxford: Oxford University Press.

Lewis, J. W. (1980) 'Daniel Jones (1881–1967)', *Zeitschrift für Anglistik und Amerikanistik*, 29, 343–48.

Macaulay, R. (1988) 'RP R.I.P.', *Applied Linguistics*, 9, 115–24.

EDWARD SAPIR (1884–1939)

A trait often attributed to Edward Sapir is 'brilliant'. An internet search conflating that word with Sapir's name turns up more citations than all the results of similar searches for 'brilliant' plus the names of near-contemporary linguists **Otto Jespersen, Leonard Bloomfield** and **Benjamin Lee Whorf** combined. Sapir was a brilliant linguist, brilliant anthropologist, brilliant lecturer, brilliant writer; an 'intoxicating' man (Mandelbaum 1949: xii). Despite having lived while anthropological linguistics was just emerging in the United States, and when public funding for its basis in fieldwork was erratic (and despite having died young, at age fifty-five), Sapir's star shone brightly during his lifetime and continues to attract the attention of modern scholars.

Sapir immigrated to the United States at age five, with his family, from what was then Prussia, now Lebork, Poland. His first language was Yiddish. His father served as a cantor in orthodox Jewish congregations, first in Virginia, then New York City, although the family was not religiously observant. By high school, Sapir was already recognized as brilliant, and earned a scholarship that he used to graduate from Columbia University in three years with a degree in Germanic. He took courses in music and in Gothic, Icelandic and Sanskrit, becoming well versed in Indo-European comparative-historical philology. Then, in his junior year, Sapir took a graduate anthropology course on Native American languages with Franz Boas (1858–1942), the father figure of American anthropology (Darnell 1990: 8–11).

Boas had done ethnographic fieldwork with Inuit peoples and indigenous groups in the Pacific Northwest. He was instrumental in founding both the American Anthropological Association and the nation's first doctoral programme in Anthropology. Boas conceived the discipline as comprising physical, cultural, archaeological and linguistic branches – although neither he nor most other early anthropologists had depth of exposure to linguistics. Sapir entered the field with solid training in Indo-European linguistics, becoming in succession Boas' student, disciple and colleague. He eventually surpassed Boas in his expertise in Native American languages, bringing comparative-historical techniques to bear on them. Sapir also recognized how comparative-historical linguistics could benefit from what anthropologists were learning about the indigenous languages of the Americas. In his 1905 Master's thesis on **Johann Gottfried Herder**'s essay about the origin of language (published in 1907), Sapir pointed out how data from Native American languages enhanced understanding of the fundamental properties of language in general.

Both before and immediately after he completed his doctorate in 1909, Sapir carried out linguistic and ethnographic fieldwork in Washington, Oregon, California and Utah. His dissertation was a grammar of Takelma. He then took a short-term job at the University of Pennsylvania, during which interval he gathered data on Southern Paiute (still spoken today in southwestern Utah by fewer than 2000 people). Sapir worked with an unusually talented young native speaker, Tony Tillohash, who attended the Carlisle Indian School in Carlisle, Pennsylvania. The collaboration with Tillohash resulted in some of Sapir's most celebrated publications. These included ethnographic studies of Paiute myth and music (*Collected Works* Vol. 4), but probably more importantly, his confirmation, on the grounds of phonological correspondences, of the status of Southern Paiute within the Uto-Aztecan stock (*Collected Works* Vol. 5), and a grammar, dictionary, and texts elicited from Tillohash (*Collected Works* Vol. 10). Moreover, Sapir's classic 1933 article 'would immortalize [Tillohash's] understanding of his native language' (Darnell 1990: 34) in arguing for the psychological reality of the phoneme. Sapir discovered that Tillohash perceived the sounds of Southern Paiute not with respect to their surface properties, but with respect to the roles those sounds played within an overall system of the language. Sapir had anticipated that conclusion in a 1925 article:

> ... [the sounds of a language] belong together in a definite system of symbolically utilizable counters. Each member of this

system is not only characterized by a distinctive and slightly variable articulation and a corresponding acoustic image, but also – *and this is crucial* – by a psychological aloofness from all other members of the system. The relational gaps between the sounds of a language are just as necessary to the psychological definition of these sounds as the articulations and acoustic images which are customarily used to define them. A sound that is not unconsciously felt to be 'placed' with reference to other sounds is no more a true element of speech than a lifting of the foot is a dance step unless it can be 'placed' with reference to other movements that help to define the dance.

(Sapir 1925: 39–40)

In 1910, Sapir began a fifteen-year appointment in Ottawa as chief anthropologist for the Geological Survey of Canada. Although the job included responsibility for ethnological as well as linguistic material, Sapir prioritized the study of numerous indigenous languages. On his meticulous and insightful – in fact, brilliant – synchronic analyses he built a controversial diachronic synthesis of North American indigenous languages. Sapir reclassified the received fifty-five linguistic stocks to six (Eskimo-Aleut, Algonkin-Wakashan, Na-Dene, Penutian, Hokan-Siouan, Aztec-Tanoan), in a move that shocked his contemporaries but has been at least partially sustained by subsequent scholars.

In addition, Sapir accumulated vast linguistic expertise that shaped his perspective on language as a psychological and cultural phenomenon. During the Ottawa years, he wrote his book *Language*, which retains to this day its reputation as an engaging and sensitive introduction to the field directed at non-specialists. A passage from a chapter on language change, or 'drift' (Sapir 1921: 156–63), exemplifies the book's character. The topic is the distribution of *who* versus *whom*; Sapir remarked that most English speakers 'feel that it is quite "incorrect" to say *Who did you see?*' But while we acknowledge *Whom did you see?* as the officially correct form, 'there is something false about its correctness … [so that] the majority of us are secretly wishing [we] could say *Who did you see?*' Sapir proposed four reasons for our 'curious reluctance to use locutions involving the word *whom*, particularly in its interrogative sense'. First, *whom* as the objective case-marked member of the pair *who/whom* is 'psychologically isolated' because the other English words similarly marked for objective case (*me, him, her, us, them*) are all personal pronouns – a coherent class that excludes the otherwise uninflected class of interrogative and relative pronouns (*which*, *what*, *that*) to which *who/whom* belong. Second, *who/whom* also participate in another word class, the interrogative adverbs (*where*, *when*, *how*); like *who/whom* they can bear emphasis, but unlike *who/whom* they are invariant with respect to case. Third, the existing subjective (i.e. nominative)/objective pronoun pairs *I/me*, *he/him*, *she/her*, etc. also differ in their syntactic distribution, as the subjective-case member of the pair precedes the verb, and the objective-case member follows: *I saw HER*; *SHE saw ME*. With interrogative *who/whom*, however, inversion places the objective-case member of the pair before the verb, as in *WHOM did you see?* Fourth, Sapir claimed that the heavy final consonant in *whom* is prosodically clumsy juxtaposed to the initial voiced stop in *did*, adding to the psychological anomaly of *Whom did you see?* For all these reasons, 'there is something unesthetic about the word. It suggests a form pattern that is not filled out by its fellows. The only way to remedy the irregularity of form distribution is to abandon the *whom* altogether ... We do not secretly chafe at *Whom did you see?* without reason.'

Sapir's *Language* abounds in keen observations, adroitly expressed. It communicates the author's wide erudition, and the sensibility of a man who published more than 200 poems in his lifetime and for whom music composition and performance was a serious avocation. Despite the inevitable aging of the book's cultural references and political outlook, it retains the status of a classic.

Language also displays Sapir's 'unabashed preference for the subjective' (Darnell 1990: 105), which distinguishes his orientation from the school of American structuralism that was to follow, materialized in Bloomfield's drive to establish linguistics as a science. But that contrast emerged later. During Sapir's Ottawa days, and even more so after he left to teach at the University of Chicago (from 1925 to 1931), and subsequently at Yale (1931 to 1939 as Sterling Professor in both linguistics and anthropology), his prestige was high. Sapir's personal and intellectual charisma attracted many to the study of language, and his style of fieldwork-based anthropological linguistics that applied Indo-European philological techniques to Native American languages proved influential in the professionalization of linguistics as an independent field in the United States. Sapir was involved in numerous cross-disciplinary initiatives that brought him in touch with a wide range of scholars and social scientists; he collaborated with Bloomfield and others in the creation of the Linguistic Society of America; and he taught very effectively at the 1937 LSA summer Linguistic Institute, where he deeply impressed **Kenneth Pike**, among other students.

At the end of that summer, however, Sapir suffered a first heart attack, presaging his death two years later. He probably didn't live long enough to recognize that his psychologically sensitive, culturally informed approach to language analysis was being supplanted. Nor did he foresee that what would matter to mid-century American descriptivists was the material distribution of linguistic units, not speakers' intuitions. Sapir would have had to have lived another 30 years to see scholarly opinion on this issue turn around again, or to witness his influence on **Joseph Greenberg** and **Noam Chomsky**.

Another legacy of Sapir is carried forward as the so-called 'Sapir–Whorf hypothesis'. Sapir's training in anthropology ensured that his views of language always addressed its cultural context. During the years at Chicago and Yale, he was drawn to investigating problems of culture and personality, and became involved in studying psychological theories and practices, including psychoanalysis. Sapir taught a course at Chicago and later at Yale on the psychology of culture, which was infused with his research on Native American languages and ethnology. He died before writing the book he had contracted to produce on the topic, but a text reconstructing his ideas about language, mind and society (Sapir 1994) was pieced together from his Yale students' lecture notes. Among those students was Whorf. Whorf developed one thread of Sapir's thought about the relationship of language, thought and culture, a thread conventionally followed back to a passage in a 1928 address:

[Language] powerfully conditions all our thinking about social problems and processes. Human beings do not live in the objective world alone, nor alone in the world of social activity as ordinarily understood, but are very much at the mercy of the particular language which has become the medium of expression for their society. ... [T]he 'real world' is to a large extent unconsciously built up on the habits of the group. No two languages are ever sufficiently similar to be considered as representing the same social reality.

(Sapir 1928/1949: 162)

The claim that language shapes experience, and hence culture, runs alongside other notions of the relationship of language and culture in Sapir's work, even in the same text (Joseph 1996: 378). Whorf picked up this particular thread, however, and wove it into his own intellectual fabric. Subsequent generations have cut and sewn that fabric into a garment that Sapir might have found alien. But no doubt Sapir is not alone among brilliant scholars in being remembered for what he only partially believed, as well as for only part of what he believed.

Sapir's major works

Herder's 'Ursprung der Sprache', *Modern Philology*, 5, 1907, 109–42.
Language: An Introduction to the Study of Speech, 1921, Harcourt, Brace & Co., Orlando, FL.
'Sound patterns in language', *Language*, 1, 1925, 27–51 (reprinted in *Selected Writings*).
'La réalité psychologique des phonèmes', *Journal de Psychologie Normale et Pathologique*, 30, 1933, 247–65 (trans. and reprinted in *Selected Writings*).
Selected Writings of Edward Sapir in Language, Culture, and Personality, 1949 (D. G. Mandelbaum, ed.), University of California Press, Berkeley, CA.
The Collected Works of Edward Sapir: Vols 1–16, 1990– (P. Sapir, editor-in-chief), Mouton de Gruyter, Berlin.
The Psychology of Culture: A Course of Lectures, 1994 (reconstructed and ed. by J. T. Levine), Mouton de Gruyter, Berlin.

Further reading

Cowan, W., Foster, M. K. and Koerner, K. (eds) (1986) *New Perspectives in Language, Culture, and Personality: Proceedings of the Edward Sapir Centenary Conference (Ottawa, 1–3 October 1984)*, Amsterdam and Philadelphia, PA: John Benjamins.
Darnell, R. (1990) *Edward Sapir: Linguist, Anthropologist, Humanist*, Berkeley, CA: University of California Press.
Joseph, J. E. (1996) 'The immediate sources of the "Sapir–Whorf Hypothesis"', *Historiographia Linguistica*, 23, 365–404.
Koerner, E. F. K. (1984) *Edward Sapir: Appraisals of His Life and Work*, Amsterdam and Philadelphia, PA: John Benjamins.
Mandelbaum, D. G. (1949). 'Editor's introduction', in D. G. Mandelbaum (ed.), *Selected Writings of Edward Sapir in Language, Culture, and Personality*, Berkeley, CA: University of California Press.
Spier, L., Hallowell, A. I. and Newman, S. S. (eds) (1941) *Language, Culture, and Personality: Essays in Memory of Edward Sapir*, Menasha, WI: Sapir Memorial Publication Fund.

LEONARD BLOOMFIELD (1887–1949)

Leonard Bloomfield was probably the single most prominent figure in American structuralist (or 'descriptivist') linguistics in the 1920s and 1930s. His is certainly the name most frequently mentioned in characterizing pre-generative study of language in the United States; he 'has become a symbol for an entire period' (Hymes and Fought 1975: 101). Bloomfield's scholarship on Indo-European historical linguistics (especially Germanic), Tagalog and Algonquian is still admired today; his text *Language* served as the handbook for a generation of linguists; he had significant impact on foreign language teaching and learning; and he was instrumental in founding the Linguistic Society of America (LSA), serving as President in 1935. In all his work from the mid-1920s, Bloomfield insisted on identifying linguistics as a science, and modelled what it meant in his day to adopt a scientific orientation in the study of language. His procedure for analysis looked first at linguistic forms and their distributions, and avoided imposing a received inventory of grammatical classes or *a priori* generalizations on the description of languages. Bloomfield also famously rejected mentalism – by which he meant reliance on speakers' intuitions, mental processes or 'feelings' for linguistic form or usage in the depiction of the structure of a language – in favour of a 'mechanistic' stance.

Bloomfield's father (and uncle Maurice [1855–1928], later a renowned scholar of Indo-European and Indic philology, and second President of the LSA) emigrated from Austria. His family bought and operated a resort in rural southeastern Wisconsin, where Leonard and his two accomplished siblings grew up. By the time he was nineteen he had graduated from Harvard; from there he went on to the University of Wisconsin and then the University of Chicago, graduating in 1909 with a doctorate in Germanic and Comparative Indo-European Philology. Bloomfield taught German at the Universities of Cincinnati and Illinois, but interrupted his teaching career in 1913 for a year of study in Leipzig and Göttingen with, among others, **Karl Brugmann**. After returning to America, he moved from Illinois to Ohio State and subsequently to the University of Chicago. The last nine years of his life he spent as Sterling Professor of Linguistics at Yale, where he filled some of the empty space created by the death of **Edward Sapir**.

In character, Bloomfield was modest and retiring. He had little 'stage presence' and lacked Sapir's intellectual verve, although stories about Bloomfield reveal a certain quirky wit. He faced a number of personal trials, including the suicide of his sister at age eighteen, an adverse relationship with one of his two adopted sons, and the deterioration of his wife's mental health after their move from Chicago to New Haven. He seemed to have worked steadily through these difficulties, and others, with characteristic calm self-possession and meticulous attention to detail (Hall 1987, 1990).

Bloomfield's early publications were studies in Germanic philology and Indo-European comparative linguistics. His first book, *An Introduction to the Study of Language*, was intended for novices. He completed it before he adopted anti-mentalism, and in advance of his sojourn in Europe.

In the decade after his return to the USA, Bloomfield initiated his most distinctive work. He collaborated with a native speaker of the Austronesian language Tagalog, who happened to be enrolled in an engineering course at the University of Illinois, eliciting from him a corpus of folk tales and narratives. Bloomfield applied traditional philological techniques to this material to produce a grammar of Tagalog (Bloomfield 1917/1967), the insight of which is still valued. Around the same time, he began seriously studying Algonquian languages, chiefly Menominee, but also Fox, Cree and Ojibwa. He spent the summers of 1921 and 1922 doing fieldwork on a Menominee reservation near his ancestral home in Wisconsin, thanks in part to funding arranged by Sapir. He made many Menominee friends, and later objected with uncharacteristic rancour to the disparagement to which Menominee culture and language were typically subjected (Bloomfield 1970: 211).

Also in the early 1920s, Bloomfield, Sapir and others led a drive to create what became the LSA. Bloomfield wrote a letter arguing for the importance of an association that would promote the scientific study of language, then circulated the letter in soliciting a panel of founding members. Eventually, an essay version of Bloomfield's letter (reprinted in *ibid.*: 109–12) introduced the inaugural issue of the LSA's journal *Language* in 1925.

With Bloomfield's move to Ohio State, he met and befriended the behaviourist psychologist Alfred P. Weiss (1879–1931). Weiss inspired him to try to study language devoid of concepts such as '*mind, consciousness, will*, and the like', which he called 'spectres of our tribal animism' (*ibid.*: 237). Bloomfield associated mentalism with the philosophical grammarians of the past, although he detected it in some contemporary work as well, notably that of Sapir. (Sapir and Bloomfield seem to have respected each other's work, although their contrasting personal and intellectual styles left each wary of the other.) In his pursuit of scientific clarity and disciplinary autonomy, Bloomfield developed an influential 'Set of Postulates for the Science of Language' (*ibid.*: 128–38) that aimed to define the necessary terms and explicate the working assumptions of the discipline.

These varied commitments and experiences enriched Bloomfield's 1933 text *Language*, often cited as his masterwork. The book reviews

American structuralist linguistics from Bloomfield's perspective. It accepted **Ferdinand de Saussure**'s regard for synchrony as well as diachrony, dividing its attention over both the systematicity of linguistic structure and the evolution of languages as they develop historically. It also supported the Neogrammarian hypothesis of the regularity of sound change. Bloomfield drew extensive examples from his own research on Tagalog and Menominee, and worked through his conception of a thoroughly mechanistic science of language. In one famous passage (Bloomfield 1933: 22–26), he analysed a random linguistic event and its context as a behaviourist might see it: an imaginary Jill perceives her own hunger (stimulus); she moves her vocal apparatus to produce a certain pattern of sounds (response); Jill's partner Jack hears the sounds (i.e. they serve as a stimulus to him); Jack then 'vaults the fence, climbs the tree, takes the apple, brings it to Jill, and places it in her hand' (response). Bloomfield's point is that the meaning of Jill's speech can be conceived of mechanically as residing in 'the situation in which the speaker utters it and the response which it calls forth in the hearer' (*ibid.*: 139), dispensing with reference to mental images or psychological concepts.

Despite misconceptions to the contrary, Bloomfield's mechanistic science of language did not try to study language in the absence of reference to meaning by solely examining the distribution and shapes of linguistic units. Bloomfield (*ibid.*: 139–57; 425–43) made it clear that, although he conceded semantics to be 'the weak point in language-study' (p. 140) in the sense that our knowledge of how to represent and classify meaning is underdeveloped, to study words and grammar necessarily means to study 'speech-forms and their meanings' (*ibid.*: 513). For example, the evolution of language over time cannot plausibly be studied without reference to stability or change in the meanings of words. In *Language*, as throughout his writings, Bloomfield was quite conventional in using identity or difference in meaning as a prime criterion for judging the relationships of sounds, words or structures.

Language also evinces Bloomfield's admiration for the tradition of grammatical analysis associated with **Pāṇini**. He shared Pāṇini's drive to be both succinct and thorough in, for example, his analyses of the forms of compound nouns or of zero forms (i.e. in treating plural *sheep* as a singular noun plus a null plural marker – *sheep* + 0 – thus sustaining the parallel to singular *cat* + s yielding plural *cats*). In addition, Bloomfield adopted specific terms and taxonomic devices from Pāṇinian tradition (Rogers 1987).

In Bloomfield's later years at Yale, he continued to articulate a science of language and to publish occasional papers on Austronesian and Algonquian. He developed a new interest in applying modern linguistics to elementary-school instruction in reading, although his writings in this field were little appreciated by educators. More effective was Bloomfield's involvement in the Intensive Language Program. This began as an American Council of Learned Societies-sponsored initiative to develop expertise and materials in various world languages. It expanded into a national military priority in 1941 when the USA entered World War II (see **Charles Hockett**). Linguists prepared materials for rapid instruction in more than thirty spoken languages, with Bloomfield responsible for Dutch, Russian and Burmese. He published a pamphlet setting out his ideas about how to elicit and analyse the grammar of a foreign language by working face-to-face with an untrained native speaker (Bloomfield 1942). Teaching methods and materials based on the Intensive Language Program, imbued with Bloomfield's ideas, influenced American foreign-language educational practice into the 1960s (Murray 1994: 144–53).

Bloomfield suffered a stroke in 1946, which ended his life as a productive scholar. He lived for a few more years to observe the development of 'post-Bloomfieldian' linguistics, which dominated study of language in the United States for the next decade. Important post-Bloomfieldians included Bernard Bloch (1907–65, editor of *Language* 1940–65), Zellig Harris (1909–92), **Charles Hockett** and George Trager (1906–92), among others. **Kenneth Pike** worked during the same period but stayed somewhat outside the circle.

The extent of continuity between Bloomfield and post-Bloomfieldians is controversial. Post-Bloomfieldians carried forward Bloomfield's drive to create a science of linguistics and his reticence to generalize descriptive terminology across languages. But although, to Bloomfield, 'characterization of a language should always start from form rather than from meaning' so as to avoid 'introducing irrelevant philosophical apriorisms, or imposing on one language semantic categories actually relevant only for some other' (Hockett 1968: 24), he nonetheless freely used meaning as a device for distinguishing linguistic forms. This contrasts with post-Bloomfieldians, who distinguished linguistic forms by analysing their distributions. Post-Bloomfieldians also went beyond Bloomfield in a self-conscious emphasis on methodological 'rigour'. Some insisted, for example, that linguistic description separate the elements of phonology, morphology and syntax into discrete self-contained levels, each feeding into the next in succession. Conversely, Bloomfield's investment in behaviourism was not commonplace among post-Bloomfieldians.

Even more controversial is the relationship between American structuralist linguists of the 1930s to the 1950s and the generative grammarians who followed them. In the opinion of some historians of linguistics, **Noam Chomsky** downplays the extent to which the work of Bloomfield and even the post-Bloomfieldians influenced him. Fought (1999), for example, sees unacknowledged continuities between Bloomfield's important 1939 paper 'Menomini morphophonemics' and Chomsky's MA thesis, completed in 1951, on modern Hebrew morphophonemics. Murray (1994: 225–47) surveys evidence of other continuities and discontinuities in the emergence of generative grammar; Newmeyer (1986: 4–28) provides a different view.

These ongoing controversies are important in trying to achieve an understanding of Bloomfield's place in the history of American linguistics. Something of that place can be gleaned from the character of his intellectual style, which prioritized a science of linguistics. Hymes and Fought (1975: 114) view Bloomfield's work as including, from its start, 'rejection of teleological explanation, and ethnocentric categories, together with a commitment to empirical validation'; but they acknowledge that Bloomfield's legacy was also constituted of 'patient hours of handling data unstudied by more than two or three others; [and] frank admiration and respect for the qualities of members of minority cultures, including linguistic and narrative skills invisible to others'.

Bloomfield's major works

An Introduction to the Study of Language, 1914 (J. F. Kess, ed.), Henry Holt, New York (reprinted by John Benjamins, 1983).
Tagalog Texts with Grammatical Analysis, 1917, University of Illinois Press, Urbana, IL, (reprinted by Johnson Reprint Corp., 1967).
Language, 1933, Henry Holt, New York.
'Menomini morphophonemics', Études phonologiques dédiées à la mémoire de N. S. Trubetzkoy, 1939 (reprinted in Anthology, 1970).
Outline Guide for the Practical Study of Foreign Languages, 1942, Linguistic Society of America, Baltimore, MD.
A Leonard Bloomfield Anthology, 1970 (C. F. Hockett, ed.), Indiana University Press, Bloomington, IN (reprints many important short works).

Further reading

Falk, J. S. (1992) 'Otto Jespersen, Leonard Bloomfield, and American structural linguistics', Language, 68, 465–91.
Fought, J. (1999) 'Leonard Bloomfield's linguistic legacy: later uses of some technical features', Historiographia Linguistica, 26, 313–32.

Hall, R. A., Jr (ed.) (1987) *Leonard Bloomfield: Essays on His Life and Work*, Philadelphia, PA: John Benjamins.

Hall, R. A., Jr (1990) *A Life for Language: A Biographical Memoir of Leonard Bloomfield*, Philadelphia, PA: John Benjamins.

Hockett, C. F. (1968) *The State of the Art*, The Hague: Mouton.

——(1999) 'Leonard Bloomfield: after fifty years', *Historiographia Linguistica*, 26, 295–311.

Hymes, D. and Fought, J. (1975) *American Structuralism*, The Hague: Mouton.

Matthews, P. H. (1993) *Grammatical Theory in the United States from Bloomfield to Chomsky*, Cambridge: Cambridge University Press.

Murray, S. O. (1994) *Theory Groups and the Study of Language in North America: A Social History*, Philadelphia, PA: John Benjamins.

Newmeyer, F. J. (1986) *Linguistic Theory in America* (2nd edn), New York: Academic Press.

Rogers, D. E. (1987) 'The influence of Pāṇini on Leonard Bloomfield', *Historiographia Linguistica*, 14, 89–138 (reprinted in Hall 1987).

LUDWIG WITTGENSTEIN (1889–1951)

Ludwig Wittgenstein, born in Vienna and buried in Cambridge, England, spent his life struggling with foundational questions of philosophy, especially those basic to logic and mathematics. His work is credited as precipitating 'the linguistic turn', a major mid-twentieth-century reorientation in the history of philosophy. The linguistic turn influenced philosophers to examine language as a key to solving philosophical dilemmas, bringing new attention to linguistic issues. In addition, modern linguists have variously adopted, or been stimulated by, concepts and terms from Wittgenstein's later work, sometimes using them as a foil against which to develop alternatives.

Wittgenstein approached philosophy without formal training or even a broad general education. He was the youngest of eight children of an opulently wealthy and culturally sophisticated Austrian family. His wilful, hard-driving, industrialist father made a fortune in railroads and ironworks. His mother cultivated the children's musical and literary connoisseurship, while tutors instructed them at home in the family's several palaces around Vienna. Wittgenstein's tastes in music (Haydn, Beethoven, Brahms) and literature (Goethe, Schiller, Nietzsche and, later, Tolstoy) were narrowly defined, deeply held, and built on early and sustained exposure (McGuinness 1988).

An apparent mechanical talent first led Wittgenstein to pursue engineering. He left home at seventeen to attend a technical school in Berlin, then proceeded to Manchester, England to study aeronautics.

Wittgenstein was intrigued by applied scientific phenomena, but more so by the mathematical principles behind them. In 1911, he travelled to Cambridge to try to meet Bertrand Russell (1872–1970), England's foremost philosopher of mathematics and one of the founders of analytical philosophy. Wittgenstein's intensity and originality eventually won Russell over. He accepted Wittgenstein as a student, and soon thereafter as a peer. Wittgenstein was a high-strung, self-critical and fastidious scholar who craved solitude and control over his environment to bring forth his ideas, but equally depended on the stimulation of a receptive audience. Many admired his incisive and untrammelled mind, while finding his friendship demanding, at times suffocating.

Wittgenstein published only one major work during his lifetime, the *Tractatus Logico-Philosophicus*. He laboured over it for a decade, beginning in Cambridge and continuing into two years of intermittent solitude in rural Norway. In the politically fateful year of 1914, he volunteered in the Austrian army, probably both out of patriotic duty and to avoid an impasse in his writing. Wittgenstein aggressively sought the most dangerous military assignments, ending up a prisoner of war in Italy. On being released from prison in the aftermath of World War I, he found the political and social conditions of Europe devastating. He reacted by renouncing his inheritance to take a position as a schoolmaster among Austrian peasants, a vocation for which he proved poorly suited.

Throughout the war, Wittgenstein had worked as best he could on the *Tractatus*, convinced that it culminated western philosophy. By 1919, he declared the manuscript complete. He re-established contact with Russell, who helped get the *Tractatus* published. Russell, however, neither agreed with nor understood all of it. Along with Russell's impatience with Wittgenstein's post-war spiritual crisis, this caused a permanent rift between the two men.

Russell's uncomprehending response was not unique, because the *Tractatus* is notoriously difficult and enigmatic. Composed of about 500 spare, unaccommodating, assertions numbered in outline form, it reflects back to readers a huge range of plausible interpretations. The text addresses the nature of logic, science and mathematics, with comments on aesthetics and ethics. There is labyrinthine discussion of (*inter alia*) tautology versus contradiction, propositions versus functions, objects versus facts. Among themes in the *Tractatus* most relevant to language and linguistics is the distinction between *saying* and *showing*, that is, between what can be expressed by meaningful propositions and what can only be revealed through symbols or pictorial representations, not language – or perhaps cannot be communicated at all. That which can only be shown, according to Wittgenstein, includes the existence of objects, and the features and relationships among objects. Moreover, he asserted that many of the difficulties of philosophy derive from philosophers' obliviousness to how conventional language imposes particular logical relationships. As relationships, those should only be able to be shown, not said; nevertheless, to Wittgenstein philosophy was the activity of trying to solve philosophical problems by looking into the logic of language.

This theme in the *Tractatus* helped impel the 'linguistic turn' in philosophy (Rorty 1967). In addition, Wittgenstein's early work became central to the emergence in Vienna in the late 1920s of logical positivism, an informal school of empiricist-minded mathematicians and analytical philosophers who asserted that all knowledge must derive from observation, or inference based on observation. Logical positivism became identified with some varieties of behaviourism in psychology. Although by 1927 Wittgenstein had abandoned school teaching and returned to Vienna, he deflected overtures from the Vienna school – in part because he was reluctant to become reinvolved in philosophy, and in part because he suspected that they misunderstood the *Tractatus*. Wittgenstein was also wary of the Vienna school's rejection of metaphysics and their claim that ordinary language is inadequate to communicate scientific truth (McGuinness 1985).

By 1928, however, Wittgenstein had reconsidered whether the *Tractatus* actually resolved all of philosophy. He gradually returned to his struggles with writing, and to the orbit of Cambridge where, in 1929, he was awarded a doctorate and a position as lecturer. Always ill at ease in academia, Wittgenstein withdrew periodically to Norway, or later, Ireland, and he left the university temporarily for blue-collar jobs during World War II. Coming as Wittgenstein did from a line of wealthy assimilated Jews, Hitler's invasion of Austria catastrophically fractured his family (Monk 1990: 385–400). This further destabilized his peace of mind and his capacity to write.

Through the remainder of his life, Wittgenstein created, revised and reassembled numerous overlapping texts, rarely to his full satisfaction. He found both writing and teaching onerous, so he adopted a habit of dictating his ideas to students and friends. Compilations of students' lecture notes known as Wittgenstein's 'Blue' and 'Brown' books have also survived. The book *Philosophical Investigations*, published after Wittgenstein's death, has various complex relationships to the dictated texts and to his students' notes. It constitutes the most authoritative representation of his later work.

In style and content, *Philosophical Investigations* differs significantly from the *Tractatus*. It is written in informal, vernacular prose; it contains illustrative stories, diagrams, analogies, imagined first-person dialogues with the reader, and all manner of examples. But like the *Tractatus*, it presents formidable hermeneutic challenges. Although individual parts of *Philosophical Investigations* often seem engagingly clear, there remain many questions about how the parts cohere (or whether they cohere); about the overall goals of the text; and about the relationship of Wittgenstein's early to his later writings.

No consensus exists about the relevance of Wittgenstein's work as a whole to the study of language. But several ideas and terms developed in *Philosophical Investigations* have been adopted in linguistics. Among the most famous passages is Wittgenstein's citation of a fifth-century narrative about child language learning from Latin church father and neo-Platonist Augustine of Hippo's (354–430) *Confessions* (I, 8). Augustine claims to have learned language by observing, then imitating, adults labelling objects in his environment. Wittgenstein analysed the limitations of Augustine's conception of language learning in 'remarks' (subsections, noted below as 'R') 1–6 of *Philosophical Investigations*. First, 'ostensive teaching' (Wittgenstein 1953/2001: R6) cannot account for the acquisition of (in modern terms) functional categories such as articles or complementizers – whose meanings cannot be pointed out – or even lexical categories (adjectives, prepositions) aside from nouns. Augustine also provided no basis for the acquisition of grammar, only of isolated nouns. In addition, Wittgenstein found Augustine's narrative inadequate to explain the multiple complex communicative and expressive activities that humans carry out through language, other than the rudimentary task of naming objects.

Wittgenstein used Augustine's narrative to criticize conventional assumptions about language. Since ostensive teaching cannot exhaustively define words, child language learning under Augustine's assumptions must operate like adult foreign language learning, wherein the learner 'already [has] a language, only not this one' (*ibid.*: R32). That is to say, an Augustinian view implies that an inner private language exists, and that ostensive teaching labels its constructs. Wittgenstein rejected this assumption, although the extent to which he offered a satisfactory counter-proposal is open to interpretation. Varieties of the notion of a private language remain alive in the work of modern philosophers of language such as Fodor (1975: 64). Nevertheless, Wittgenstein's citation of Augustine stimulated interest in the nature of language learning before the matter became the topic of empirical research.

Wittgenstein's rejection of private language is, in part, based on his assertion that meaningful discourse requires the participation of a community: in the absence of publicly acknowledged standards, he argued, how can an individual determine whether he or she maintains a consistent definition of a privately defined word? Following philosopher Saul Kripke (b. 1940) (see also Katz 1990), generative grammarian **Noam Chomsky** adverted to this argument with reference to the status of rule-governed knowledge of language, since Wittgenstein seems to challenge the feasibility of tacit, abstract rules or principles constraining human grammar. Chomsky (1986: 221–43) rejected Wittgenstein's scepticism about individual private knowledge on the grounds that individuals' linguistic judgements (for example, of the antecedent of a pronoun in a specific context, or the meaning of 'John is too stubborn to talk to'; *ibid.*: 241–42) are consistent across time. Those judgements are also consistent across individuals, but according to Chomsky, that fact does not necessarily locate their source in a community of speakers.

A related influential Wittgensteinian contribution is the notion of 'language games', the vast array of rule-governed routines and communicative practices that speakers employ. Augustine's child learner engages in the language game of ostensive learning; however, word meanings are imparted to the child not by pointing to their referents, but by the roles that words play in the game of ostensive learning. Language games include 'giving orders, and obeying them – describing the appearance of an object ... reporting an event – speculating about the event ... guessing riddles ... requesting, thanking, cursing, greeting, praying' (Wittgenstein 1953/2001: R23). Words appear deceptively parallel, but their roles in specific language games vary widely, the way knobs on the dashboard of a locomotive may look alike despite the fact that the engineer twists one, switches another, pulls another, moves still another to and fro (*ibid.*: R12). Wittgenstein aimed to clarify philosophy by bringing attention to its constituent language games, and the multifarious roles of words used in them. Despite profound differences in stance and style between Wittgenstein and **J. L. Austin**, Austin also addressed this issue.

Another tool that Wittgenstein used to communicate the complexity of words and their meanings is his concept of 'family resemblance'. In *Philosophical Investigations* (*ibid.*: R66–77), Wittgenstein argued that some words cannot be explained by definitions articulated as necessary and sufficient conditions. He explored a lengthy example using the word 'game', whose various exemplars (tic-tac-toe; board games; Olympic games; poker) do not meet any single inductive definition, but still constitute a recognizable class by forming 'a complicated network of similarities overlapping and criss-crossing: sometimes overall similarities, sometimes similarities of detail' (*ibid.*: R66). Modern psycholinguists have found the notion of family resemblances valuable in modelling the structure of semantic relationships in the human mental lexicon.

Wittgenstein's writings continue to be probed for their relevance to the study of language. Despite the interpretive challenges his work presents, recognizably Wittgensteinian ideas have entered the slip-stream of linguistic discourse.

Wittgenstein's major works

Tractatus Logico-Philosophicus. The German Text of Ludwig Wittgenstein's Logisch-philosophische Abhandlung, 1961 (D. F. Pears and B. F. McGuinness, trans.), Routledge & Kegan Paul, London (original text published 1921).

Philosophical Investigations: The German Text, with a Revised English Translation, 2001 (3rd edn, G. E. M. Anscombe, trans.), Blackwell, Oxford (original text published 1953).

Further reading

Augustinus, Aurelius (1942) *The* Confessions *of St Augustine, Books I–X* (F. J. Sheed, trans.), Sheed & Ward, New York (original work *c.* 399).

Chomsky, N. (1986) *Knowledge of Language*, New York: Praeger.

Fodor, J. A. (1975) *The Language of Thought*, New York: Thomas Y. Crowell.

Fogelin, R. J. (1987). *Wittgenstein* (2nd edn), London: Routledge & Kegan Paul (1st edn 1976).

Katz, J. J. (1990) *The Metaphysics of Meaning*, Cambridge, MA: MIT Press.

McGuinness, B. (1985) 'Wittgenstein and the Vienna Circle', *Synthese* 64, 351–58.

——(1988) *Wittgenstein: A Life. Young Ludwig 1889–1921*, Berkeley, CA: University of California Press.

——(2002) *Approaches to Wittgenstein*, London and New York: Routledge.

Monk, R. (1990) *Ludwig Wittgenstein: The Duty of Genius*, New York: Free Press.

Rorty, R. (ed.) (1967) *The Linguistic Turn: Recent Essays in Philosophical Method*, Chicago, IL: University of Chicago Press.

JOHN RUPERT FIRTH (1890–1960)

J. R. Firth, associated with the University of London's School of Oriental and African Studies (SOAS) and with what has come to be

178

called the London School of linguistics, was a major innovative force in linguistic theory in England in the first half of the twentieth century. Firthian linguistics contrasts starkly with the atheoretical orientation of Firth's one-time colleague **Daniel Jones**; further afield, Firth's work contrasts with post-Bloomfieldians' reticence to use meaning as an analytical tool, and contrasts with generative grammar's pursuit of universals. Some modern scholars characterize Firth's work as simply ahead of its time. For example, Butt (2001: 1807) asserts that contemporary linguistics needs to look beyond its current 'psychologism and universalism' to appreciate Firth's insistence on viewing language in its broadest social context, and his commitment to the centrality of meaning. There has been lively debate about whether, and to what extent, Firthian prosodic analysis can be related to modern autosegmental and metrical phonology. Firth's ideas have been extended to a 'neo-Firthian' school, sometimes identified with his student **Michael A. K. Halliday**, although there is no consensus about the exact relationships between Firth, Halliday and neo-Firthian linguistics.

Firth was brought up in a middle-class Yorkshire family. His academic training in history. He graduated from the University of Leeds in 1911, receiving an MA degree in 1913. After briefly teaching history at Leeds Training College, he self-consciously embarked on what he called his 'de-Europeanisation' (Rebori 2002: 175) by joining the Indian Educational Service. From 1914 to 1915, Firth taught English in rural Punjab. Then, as World War I spread, he enlisted in the British army and spent three years in East Africa, India and Afghanistan.

Firth returned to (what was then) India in 1920 as professor of English at the University of Punjab, in Lahore (Robins 1961: 191). He remained there until 1928, gradually becoming absorbed in the study of Indian languages and the indigenous tradition of language analysis. Firth found **Pāṇini**'s phonetics and its application to Indian vernacular languages especially intriguing. When he went back to London on leave in 1923, he met Daniel Jones and sought out training in phonetics. Firth eventually resigned his position in Lahore for a part-time lectureship under Jones at University College London. He was simultaneously employed at the London School of Economics and at a forerunner of SOAS, teaching phonetics to Indian Civil Service recruits.

In 1937, Firth secured a Leverhulme fellowship to return to India to study Marathi, Gujarati, Urdu and Telugu. Back in London 15 months later, he moved entirely to SOAS, gradually ascending the academic ranks. During World War II, he oversaw a successful intensive course in Japanese, just as **Leonard Bloomfield** was pressed into similar service in America. Firth devoted much of his energy after the war to institutionalizing the study of languages and linguistics at SOAS and, with that in place, building up the status of linguistics in British higher education in general. He enjoyed short-term academic appointments in Egypt, Michigan, Nice and Edinburgh, and in 1957 delayed retirement to retrace his steps from 1914–15 and to serve as a linguistic consultant in what had become Pakistan.

Firth's colleagues sometimes found him hard to work with: generous and energetic, but also blunt, demanding, controlling. Furthermore, he was neither an expert teacher nor a gifted writer. Firth's students at SOAS routinely sought out his teaching assistant, the future historiographer of linguistics R. H. Robins (1921–2000), to help them make sense of Firth's lectures (Rebori 2002: 169). His writing is desultory, rarely presenting a fully intact argument. Perhaps most damaging to the growth of his influence, Firth never produced a thorough summary of his major theoretical innovations. He left only a series of provocative but heterogeneous essays (collected in Firth 1957, 1968) on theoretical (and occasional applied) topics and on Indian languages, alongside two popularizations of modern linguistics for general readers (Firth 1964).

Nevertheless, at least three major initiatives are now conventionally attributed to Firth. First, he developed a linguistic theory that insisted on studying language in its 'context of situation', and that prioritized meaning. By Firth's lights, meaning is the central business of language, and meaning in a very broad sense is embodied at every level of linguistic organization.

> The central concept of the whole of semantics … is the context of situation. In that context are the human participant or participants, what they say, and what is going on. The phonetician can find his phonetic context and the grammarian and lexicographer theirs. And if you want to bring in general cultural background, you have the contexts of experience of the participants. […] But even when phonetician, grammarian, and lexicographer have finished, there remains the bigger integration, making use of all their work, in semantic study. And it is for this situational and experiential study that I would reserve the term 'semantics'.
>
> ('The technique of semantics', Firth 1935/1957: 27)

One source of Firth's notion of meaning, as built up from the many components of the total 'context of situation', is the work of his London School of Economics colleague, the Polish anthropologist

Bronisław Malinowski (1884–1942). Malinowski's fieldwork in Melanesia convinced him that the meanings of Trobriand islanders' individual words cannot be fathomed outside their comprehensive cultural context.

Malinowski/Firthian notions of meaning and of context of situation deliberately cover a huge range. Firth rejected **Ferdinand de Saussure**'s separation of *langue* from *parole* as artificially distinguishing social versus individual phenomena ('Personality and language in society', Firth 1950/1957: 180; 'General linguistics and descriptive grammar', Firth 1951/1957: 227). However, certain other themes in Firth's work have the effect of reducing the scope of what he expected a linguistic theory to account for. For example, Firth wrote about 'restricted languages', that is, different 'situationally appropriate forms of language' ('The treatment of language in general linguistics', Firth 1959/1968: 207) that speakers master for use in different contexts. The speech register used between two teenagers exhibits a constellation of features (phonetic, lexical, grammatical), so that the meaning-bearing components of adolescents' 'restricted language' are to some extent predictable. Likewise, Firth studied what he called 'collocations'. The English word 'time', for instance, tends to co-occur with 'saved', 'spent', 'wasted' or 'flies' because 'in any close social group [collocations] provide the basis for the mutual expectancies of words and sentences' ('Modes of meaning', Firth 1951/1957: 195). In this way, collocations reduce the burden of integrating meaning *ab initio* across the many levels of language. Firth labelled his approach 'polysystemic' in that he analysed the systematicity of multiple small domains of language without positing uniform categories or principles that would unite meaning at all levels. In his view, analyses both within and across languages might be fully independent because language necessarily consisted of multiple, heterogeneous, co-existing systems.

In the latter half of Firth's career, he proposed a complementary phonological theory, prosodic analysis. This constitutes a second major Firthian initiative. He granted the utility of the still novel concept of the phoneme for the purposes of transcribing speech, but argued that phonemes fail to capture the polysystematicity of sound structure. For example, the same phoneme may have different privileges of occurrence, word-initially versus word-finally, and thus cannot really be identified as the 'same' phoneme. Moreover, some phonological properties cannot be attributed to independent phonemes, such as vowel harmony; tone (which, in Chinese for example, is a property of syllables); or palatalization (which derives from juxtaposition of consonants and vowels). In addition, phonological properties may have ties to morphosyntax, further complicating attempts to represent them as autonomous, segmentable units. In place of phonemic analysis, Firth proposed instead that:

[phonological structure] be expressed as a plurality of systems of interrelated phonematic and prosodic categories. Such systems and categories are not necessarily linear and certainly cannot bear direct relations to successive fractions or segments of the time-track of instances of speech. By their very nature they are abstractions from such time-track items. Their order and interrelations are not chronological.

(‘Sounds and prosodies’, Firth 1948/1957: 137)

Firth anticipated frank divergence in the prosodies (and ‘phonematics’, or phonemic inventories) of different languages, as another facet of polysystematicity. This aspect of Firth’s work more than any other energized his students and colleagues to produce a number of remarkable prosodic analyses emphasizing patterns and processes in languages such as Tibetan, Hausa (spoken in Nigeria), Tigrinya (Ethiopia), Tigre (Eritrea), Terena (Brazil) and Sundanese (Java) (Palmer 1970; see also Bazell et al. 1966).

In a review of Firthian linguistics, Langendoen (1968: 76–115) criticized what he saw as the inadequacies of these attempts to apply prosodic analysis to diverse languages, highlighting in particular their free proliferation of rules and categories. From Firth’s point of view, however, polysystematicity is to be expected at every level, in every language, unconstrained by efforts to delimit it or impose uniformity: ‘I do not propose an a priori system of general categories […] Science should not impose systems on languages, it should look for systems in speech activity’ (‘The semantics of linguistic science’, Firth 1948/1957: 144). It is not surprising, then, that Firth did not attempt to articulate linguistic universals. Writing from within early generative grammar, Langendoen found little to recommend in this stance. Anderson (1985: 189–93), however, asserted that the treatment of suprasegmental phenomena in prosodic analysis parallels some of the insights of autosegmental phonology. Anderson cited several of the studies in Palmer (1970) that Langendoen dismissed, while conceding that modern autosegmental phonology provides means for relating multiple prosodic phenomena not accounted for in Firthian prosodic analysis, ‘which has no analog of even simple cases of rule ordering’ (Anderson 1985: 193). John Goldsmith (b. 1951), whose 1976 dissertation initiated autosegmental phonology, likewise described Firth’s work admiringly while pointing out what he considered its intrinsic limits (Goldsmith 1992); Ogden and Local (1994) responded with a critique of Goldsmith's grasp of prosodic analysis.

A third initiative attributed to Firth is that he successfully fostered the growth of language science in the UK. He contributed to national studies of the status of language learning, and was decorated for his wartime service as a language programme director. He worked to place his students in academic posts around the country. Due in part to Firth's efforts, the discipline of linguistics grew both at SOAS and nationwide during his lifetime. It seems appropriate that Firth was appointed to Great Britain's first academic Chair in General Linguistics, in 1944.

Arguably, a fourth initiative might also be attributed to Firth, that of stimulating interest in linguistic historiography. Driven either by his early academic training in history, his exposure to the time depth of Indian reflection on language, or his efforts to secure the future of linguistics in Britain, Firth consistently infused a consciousness of the history of the language sciences in discussion with students and colleagues, in his published papers, and even in his popular writings. His papers typically begin with historical references going as far back as ancient Indian, Greek or Biblical scholarship, sometimes passing forward to **Henry Sweet**, whom he greatly admired. Firth's student R. H. Robins (cited by Swiggers 1997: 62–65; Koerner 2001) recounted how Firth encouraged his curiosity about ancient and medieval language studies. His panoramic *A Short History of Linguistics* (Robins 1967/1997) eventually played a prominent role in the mid-twentieth-century revival of linguistic historiography. Thus Robins' book might be counted as one that Firth never wrote, but for which he nonetheless deserves some credit.

Firth's major works

Papers in Linguistics 1934–1951, 1957, Oxford University Press, Oxford.
The Tongues of Men and Speech, 1964 (reprinted with Preface by P. Strevens), Oxford University Press, Oxford (*Speech* originally published in 1930; *Tongues* in 1937).
Selected Papers of J. R. Firth 1952–59, 1968 (F. R. Palmer, ed.), Indiana University Press, Bloomington, IN.

Further reading

Anderson, S. R. (1985) *Phonology in the Twentieth Century*, Chicago, IL: Chicago University Press.

Bazell, C. E., Catford, J. C., Halliday, M. A. K. and Robins, R. H. (eds) (1966) *In Memory of J. R. Firth*, London and New York: Longman.

Butt, D. G. (2001) 'Firth, Halliday, and the development of systemic functional theory', in S. Auroux, E. K. K. Koerner, H.-J. Niederehe and K. Versteegh (eds), *History of the Language Sciences: Vol. 2*, Berlin and New York: Walter de Gruyter.

Goldsmith, J. A. (1992) 'A note on the genealogy of research traditions in modern phonology', *Journal of Linguistics*, 28, 149–63.

Koerner, E. F. K. (2001) 'R. H. Robins, J. R. Firth, and linguistic historiography', *Henry Sweet Society Bulletin*, 36, 5–11.

Langendoen, D. T. (1968) *The London School of Linguistics*, Cambridge, MA: MIT Press.

Mitchell, T. F. (1975) *Principles of Firthian Linguistics*, London: Longman.

Ogden, R. and Local, J. K. (1994) 'Disentangling autosegments from prosodies: a note on the misrepresentation of a research tradition in phonology', *Journal of Linguistics*, 30, 477–98.

Palmer, F. R. (ed.) (1970) *Prosodic Analysis*, Oxford: Oxford University Press.

Robins, R. H. (1961) 'John Rupert Firth', *Language*, 37, 191–200.

——(1997) *A Short History of Linguistics* (4th edn), London and New York: Longman (originally published 1967).

Swiggers, P. (ed). (1997) *Language and Linguists: Aims, Perspectives, and Duties of Linguistics*, Leuven and Paris: Peeters.

Rebori, V. (2002) 'The legacy of J. R. Firth: a report on recent research', *Historiographia Linguistica* 29, 165–90.

LEV SEMENOVICH VYGOTSKY (1896–1934)

Lev Vygotsky was a Russian scholar, much of whose short career focused on literature, psychology and education. His importance to the study of language lies largely in his influence – hardly felt in Europe or the United States until the late 1970s – on theories of child and adult language learning, and on language pedagogy. Vygotsky emphasized the social and cultural dimensions of language learning and what he viewed as its basis in human interaction. His work has been championed by linguists, psychologists and educators who reject analyses of language learning that (by the light of their reading of Vygotsky) reduce it to a merely cognitive phenomenon, and therefore have a narrowly formal, abstract or mechanical character. In his own day, Vygotsky contrasted his approach with those of a range of his contemporaries, including behaviourists, Freudians, and the Swiss child psychologist Jean Piaget (1896–1980). At present, Vygotsky's work contrasts with a different range of approaches to language learning, among them those associated with generative grammarian **Noam Chomsky**, and with connectionists' computer-based models of language learning.

Vygotsky was born in the north-eastern part of what has become the Republic of Belarus. His family moved south to the town of Gomel, now famous for having suffered the most direct fallout from the 1986 Chernobyl nuclear accident. Vygotsky's father was a banker and supporter of a local library, who had his son tutored at home. He completed his last two years of secondary education at a private Jewish school, where poetry, drama and history captured his imagination. By dint of both stellar exam scores and amazing good luck, Vygotsky was admitted to the Imperial University in Moscow – an exceedingly rare achievement for a Jewish student from the provinces (Levitin 1982: 13–14). He arrived in Moscow in 1913, and quickly transferred from medicine to law. He soon started taking additional classes in the humanities at the improvised Shanyavsky People's University, to which some professors and students had decamped to protest repression at the Imperial University.

In Moscow, Vygotsky plunged into the turbulent intellectual culture of his time. He returned to Gomel in the fateful year of 1917 with degrees from both universities. The Russian revolution rendered his credentials in law useless; however, he got work as a teacher and somehow managed to pursue his interests in drama, art and literature. By the 1920s, in a climate of sociopolitical chaos and increasing economic difficulty, Vygotsky turned more and more to psychology. He eventually taught a course at Gomel Teachers' College that inspired one of his first books, *Pedagogical Psychology*. Not all views he espoused at that time were sustained in his later work, although his conception of thought as internal speech is already intact, as are expressions of his ideological commitment to socialist reform, his 'revolutionary zeal', and his 'almost unlimited faith in the possibility for the improvement of man' (van der Veer and Valsiner 1991: 55–56).

In 1924, Vygotsky gave a presentation (translated in van der Veer and Valsiner 1994: 27–45) at the Second Psychoneurological Congress in Petrograd, promoting the value of studying consciousness by probing people's direct experience of thought. With this he argued against the established view, associated with Russian physiologist Ivan Pavlov (1849–1936), that human behaviour should be analysed as a complex of conditioned reflexes and therefore that 'reflexology' warranted the status of a separate subdiscipline within psychology. Vygotsky's lecture attracted the attention of psychologists trying to rebuild the discipline in the new post-revolutionary sociopolitical context. They recruited Vygotsky to return to Moscow, where he ended up working in various capacities at the Institute of

Psychology, the Institute for the Study of the Handicapped, and the Krupskaya Academy of Communist Education.

Vygotsky's return to Moscow in 1924 initiated a decade-long period of high productivity, interrupted several times by bouts of the tuberculosis that eventually killed him at age thirty-seven. While teaching and working as an editor during the day, he feverishly wrote books, articles and reviews, working until late at night in a corner of the cramped Moscow apartment he shared with twelve family members (G. Vygodskaia, in Lloyd and Fernyhough 1999, Vol. 1: 4–6). Vygotsky's intellectual curiosity covered a wide swath. He contributed to 'defectology' (the study of children with physical or mental defects, including deafness, blindness, and cognitive and social disorders); literary criticism; and psychoanalysis. Moreover, he investigated cognitive development in children and adolescents, including socially disadvantaged populations; perception; attention; play and imagination; psychological processes among Central Asian ethnic groups living outside the scope of urban culture; and the educational implications of all of these topics. Vygotsky read about, observed, and himself conducted a number of what we would call empirical studies, probing psycholinguistic and other cognitive capacities.

Aside from the brevity of his career, there are a number of reasons why Vygotsky's reputation spread slowly. Due to the vicissitudes of Soviet control over intellectual life in Russia, his publications and followers were sometimes publicly celebrated, sometimes repressed during the 1940s and 1950s. Outside Russia, some readers were nonplussed by passages in his writings where Vygotsky applied Marxist thought in assessing psychological theories, or extolled the future classless society under communism. Even though the political content in Vygotsky's writings is relatively restrained, he obviously worked in an intellectual milieu that took Marxist ideology for granted. Thus his writings fell under the general Cold War-era estrangement of Europe and the United States from Soviet scholarship (Toulmin 1978: 51–52). Moreover, not only does Vygotsky freely cite other scholars' work without indicating his sources, but he reports the results of his psycholinguistic and pedagogical studies in summary fashion, omitting the raw data and treating rather casually the information about participants, procedures and outcomes to which modern readers expect to have direct and explicit access. One also notices that, rather than reporting his ideas and findings point-blank, Vygotsky's favoured rhetoric is to work them out discursively, in piecemeal fashion, as if they emerged in the process of communicating with readers – a style consistent with his stance about how learning takes place.

A collection of excerpts from Vygotsky's writings was retranslated into English in 1978. Published to acclaim in the USA as *Mind in Society*, it precipitated what co-editor Michael Cole later called (in Reiber and Robinson 2004: viii) a 'Vygotsky boom' among psychologists and educators. From the panorama of topics that Vygotsky wrote about, two themes in particular have caught the attention of language scholars.

One theme is basic to all of Vygotsky's work, namely his insistence that development operates through the processes by which a learner internalizes aspects of the external cultural and material context, via a series of transformations. Especially relevant to language is his claim that, in one such transformation, thought derives from speech:

An interpersonal process is transformed into an intrapersonal one. Every function of the child's cultural development appears twice: first, on the social level, and later, on the individual level; first, *between* people (*interpsychological*), and then *inside* the child (*intrapsychological*). This applies equally to voluntary attention, to logical memory, and to the formation of concepts. All the higher functions originate as actual relations between human individuals.

(Vygotsky 1930–35/1978: 57; emphases in the original)

Vygotsky's proposal that 'external or communicative speech ... [turns] "inward" to become the basis of inner speech' (*ibid.*: 57) is a cornerstone of the extension of Vygotskian cultural-historical theory to language studies. Young children, unlike animals, recruit external, social speech into egocentric speech as a tool to help them solve problems: Vygotsky cites a four-and-a-half-year-old child accompanying an attempt to reach a piece of candy by talking to herself: 'On the stool ... I can get it from that other stool, stand and get it ... No, that doesn't get it. I could use the stick ... It will move now' (*ibid.*: 25). Children adapt social speech, first used in relation to other people, into egocentric speech, which helps them plan and modulate their behaviour. Eventually, egocentric speech is transformed into internal speech, or thought. With that, children succeed in the crucial task of symbolically representing cultural behaviour and norms in consciousness: 'The internalization of socially rooted and historically developed activities is the distinguishing feature of human psychology, the basis of the qualitative leap from animal to human' (*ibid.*: 57). In a 1929 letter (Levitin 1982: 154), he represented his work as 'attempting to restore the history of the human psyche'.

Vygotsky contrasted his analysis of language and thought with the analysis he attributed to Piaget. According to Vygotsky, Piagetian egocentric speech in young children reflects egocentric thought, but both of these disappear as socialization advances and autism recedes. Piagetian egocentric speech accompanies a child's activity, but has no role in it and is extinguished as socialization proceeds. In contrast, for Vygotsky, egocentric speech is instrumental to children's developing internalization of the social and cultural world; to say it disappears 'is like saying the child stops counting when he ceases to use his fingers and starts adding in his head' (Vygotsky 1934/1986: 230). Vygotsky cited experimental evidence showing that egocentric speech is reduced in contexts where children work alone (*ibid.*: 231), or with deaf-mute children or children who speak other languages (*ibid.*: 233). Moreover, Vygotsky asserted that as children transform egocentric speech into thought, it becomes progressively abbreviated through ellipsis of subjects and modifiers down to bare predicates, which 'we must assume ... to be the basic form of syntax of inner speech' (*ibid.*: 236). Thus from ages three to seven, a child's egocentric speech becomes less intelligible to observers (*ibid.*: 229).

Not all scholars would represent differences between Piaget and Vygotsky in these terms (cf. Lloyd and Fernyhough 1999, Vols 1 and 2). However, both men's work influenced linguistics and education. In Vygotsky's case, a second theme in his work has special relevance to language pedagogy, namely his concept of the 'zone of proximal development' (ZPD). Consistent with Vygotsky's cultural-historical orientation, the notion of ZPD provides a critical role for the social environment in learners' advancement from lower to higher states of development. In the optimal pedagogical context, children interact with adults (or, more generally, learners interact with tutors, including more competent peers), who facilitate their growth by fine-tuning communication to a level just slightly beyond the child's *status quo*. The individually and situationally variable gap between what a child can accomplish independently and what she can accomplish with tutorial assistance constitutes her relevant ZPD. The tutor provides a kind of scaffolding within the ZPD, which 'awakens a variety of internal developmental processes that are able to operate only when the child is interacting with people in his environment [...] Once these processes are internalized, they become part of the child's independent developmental achievement' (Vygotsky 1930–35/1978: 90).

The concept of ZPD has been exploited in foreign language pedagogy both for its contribution to theories of learning, and for its practical applications in language classrooms. For example, some teachers cite the purported efficacy of instruction aimed at learners' ZPD as a warrant for raising the profile of collaborative dialogue and pair-work exercises. More broadly, Vygotsky's cultural-historical theory (sometimes called 'sociocultural theory') has influenced scholars who reject 'cognitive-computational' research (Johnson 2004: 11) on the grounds that the latter artificially abstracts learners' cognitive states and processes out of the interpersonal and cultural experiences that are foundational to language learning. In some applications of Vygotsky's work to the study of language acquisition, sociocultural theory supplants all other approaches. For other scholars, a Vygotskian emphasis on the interpersonal source of language is in a complementary, not oppositional, relation to work that theorizes second-language learners' resulting knowledge of target language syntax, morphology, lexis or phonology.

Vygotsky's major works

Thought and Language, 1986 (A. Kozulin, ed. and trans.), MIT, Cambridge, MA (original work published 1934).

Mind in Society: The Development of Higher Psychological Processes, 1978 (M. Cole, V. John-Steiner, S. Scribner and E. Souberman, eds), Harvard University Press, Cambridge, MA (extracts from papers written between 1930 and 1935).

The Collected Works of L. S. Vygotsky, Vols 1–6), 1987–99 (R. W. Rieber, ed., with A. S. Carton and J. Wollock), Plenum, New York.

Further reading

Daniels, H., Cole, M. and Wertsch, J. V. (eds) (2007) The Cambridge Companion to Vygotsky, Cambridge: Cambridge University Press.

Johnson, M. (2004) A Philosophy of Second Language Acquisition, New Haven: Yale University Press.

Levitin, K. (1982) One is Not Born a Personality: Profiles of Soviet Educational Psychologists (Y. Filippov, trans.), Moscow: Progress Publishers.

Lloyd, P. and Fernyhough, C. (eds) (1999) Lev Vygotsky: Critical Assessments (Vols I–IV), London: Routledge.

Reiber, R. W. and Robinson, D. K. (eds) (2004) The Essential Vygotsky, New York: Kluwer Academic.

Toulmin, S. (1978) 'The Mozart of psychology', New York Review of Books, 25, 51–57.

van der Veer, R. and Valsiner, J. (1991) Understanding Vygotsky: A Quest for Synthesis, Oxford: Blackwell.

van der Veer, R. and Valsiner, J. (eds) (1994) The Vygotsky Reader, Oxford: Blackwell.

ROMAN JAKOBSON (1896–1982)

The impact of Roman Jakobson, even during his lifetime, extended far beyond what is implied by his capsule self-description, 'Russian philologist' (Jakobson, *Selected Writings* VI: x). Jakobson was a major figure in mid-twentieth-century European and American language study, who contributed to both theoretical and applied linguistics: phonology, prosody, poetics, semiotics, translation theory, psycholinguistics, language universals, literary history and criticism, and historical and descriptive linguistics, especially Slavic. He was also a man with a vivid personal and intellectual presence, who attracted friends and collaborators in many countries, and who led a remarkably adventurous life. As a young man, he played a role in the world of *avant garde* literature, art and scholarship in Moscow. In the 1920s and 1930s, Jakobson was instrumental in defining the character of a Prague school of linguistics. Later, he moved to New York and subsequently to Cambridge, Massachusetts, influencing many people along the way and developing his distinctive and ambitious ideas in diverse fields until the very end of a long and productive life.

Jakobson grew up in Moscow as a Russian–French bilingual, precociously coming of age during the turbulent onset of the Russian revolution. As a high-school student, he observed, and soon participated in, the emergence of Futurism, a radical literary and artistic movement that initially allied itself with the political and social transformations sweeping the country (Jakobson 1992). In cafés and lecture halls, an adolescent Jakobson revelled in the new influences of Picasso, Braque, Husserl, Einstein's theory of relativity, experimental theatre, and especially modern poetry. In 1914, he entered the Historical-Philological Faculty of Moscow University, where he studied folklore, cemented his commitment to the linguistic analysis of poetry, and co-founded the Linguistic Circle of Moscow, a forum for debate about language, literature, and culture. As he put it, 'These were impassioned times' (*ibid.*: 12). They were also dangerous times, since Jakobson was not only a Jew, but also sometimes publicly on the 'wrong' side in the complex, shifting political landscape of revolutionary and post-revolutionary Russia.

In 1920, Jakobson moved to Prague, ostensibly as a translator for the Russian Red Cross, but actually more to escape encroaching oppression and widen his intellectual horizons. He struggled with poverty, but quickly became rich in friends, among them Czech and European émigré artists and scholars including Nicolaj Trubetzkoy (1890–1938), Professor of Slavic Philology in Vienna. Jakobson replicated his

experience in Moscow by enthusiastically participating in the founding of the Prague Linguistic Circle in 1926. The first paper he read to
the Circle displayed his emerging self-confidence and laid down some
of the tenets of what became a distinctively Jakobsonian stance.
He expressed his discontent with the Neogrammarians' 'idle agglom-
eration of utterly scattered, atomized linguistic data' (Jakobson,
Selected Writings I: 633) and their failure to explain the social basis of
sound change (*ibid*.: 1). He also challenged **Ferdinand de Saussure**'s
rigid separation of synchrony from diachrony, on the grounds that
historical sound change had to be analysed by the light of a language's
overall system of sounds, and with reference to attested universals
(*ibid*.: 2).

In 1930, Jakobson earned a doctorate from Charles University, and
eventually was offered a professorship in Brno, half way between
Prague and Vienna. Collaboration with the Prague Circle, especially
with Trubetzkoy, continued to be central to his work. The Circle
was more than a group of scholars with similar interests in language,
literary criticism, folklore and history; rather, it self-consciously
adopted the status of a 'school' with an explicit, collective ideology
(Toman 1995). Jakobson either wrote or co-wrote several of the
Prague Circle's manifestos. They were presented to European con-
gresses of linguists or published in the group's working papers in the
late 1920s and early 1930s (e.g. the 1929 'Theses' in Steiner 1982:
3–31). An important theme was the functional basis of language. That
is, Jakobson and his colleagues asserted that human communication
imposes certain patterns and properties on language, which both
synchronic and diachronic study of language should anticipate. This
counted as a two-pronged rejection of Saussure's legacy: rejection
of the isolation of synchrony from diachrony, and rejection of
Saussurean arbitrariness.

With respect to arbitrariness, Jakobson's studies of iconicity and
onomatopoeia explored what he saw as the essential non-arbitrariness
of the linguistic sign. Jakobson challenged a third core Saussurean
principle, the linearity of the linguistic sign, in what many see as his
single most outstanding contribution to linguistics. Saussure had
claimed that language, unlike visual communication, is linear in the
sense that it transmits meaningful elements one at a time. Eighteenth-
century historical-comparativism had been built on analysis of the
linear distributions of individual sounds, often materialized as letters.
Those sounds had little intrinsic order or internal relationship beyond
the inconsistent arrangement imposed on them by the International
Phonetic Alphabet (based, for example, on heterogeneous articulatory

characteristics like 'nasal' or 'bilabial', with different criteria for vowels versus consonants). Jakobson felt that the concept of the 'phoneme' obscured the systematic relationships of sound units. Moreover, his experience in poetics sensitized him to look for relations of opposition and contrast. Starting in his days in Brno, and continuing into the 1950s, he proposed to analyse phonemes as bundles of two-valued features that were partly articulatory, partly acoustic, partly perceptual. For example, the phoneme /b/ could be resolved into seven binary features: [−vocalic], [+consonantal], [−nasal], [−compact], [−continuent], [−tense], and [+grave]. The phoneme /v/ shares the seven features of /b/ and their values except substituting [+continuent] for [−continuent]. Likewise, /p/ shares all the features of /b/ except for [+tense] (Jakobson, *Selected Writings* I: 418–25; 738–42).

If phonemes are comprised of multiple binary distinctive features transmitted simultaneously, Jakobson's analysis flouted Saussurean linearity. But distinctive features provided a flexible and precise tool for specifying relationships among sounds, for describing sound change, for pinpointing differences and similarities within and across languages, and for articulating larger generalizations of (non-)co-occurrence. Jakobson saw the potential of a cross-linguistic inventory of binary distinctive features to contribute to articulating principles of typology and phonological universals. Not all of the Prague Circle followed along. Trubetzkoy, for one, argued that some distinctive features had more than two values. But Jakobson continued to refine his ideas, until a version he co-authored in 1951 with Swedish phonetician C. Gunnar Fant (1981–2009) and Massachusetts Institute of Technology (MIT) linguist (earlier, Jakobson's student) Morris Halle (b. 1923) achieved wide acceptance (Jakobson, *Selected Writings* VIII: 583–654). Jakobsonian binary distinctive features deeply influenced the development of generative grammar, which extended the notion to the representation of morphological, semantic and syntactic properties.

The concept that phonemes could be decomposed into binary distinctive features stands out as a particularly salient product of Jakobson's Prague Circle days. He also began or advanced many other projects during this period, especially on Slavic historical and literary topics. But by the late 1930s, fascism destroyed the conditions under which the Circle had thrived. As the Nazis closed the universities and imposed 'protectorate' status on Czechoslovakia, Jakobson fled with his first wife to Denmark in early 1939. There he was invited to lecture to the Copenhagen Linguistic Circle. A receptive but differently oriented audience led Jakobson to reconsider phonological typology and universals in a renewed light (Jakobson and Pomorska, 1983: 36).

By September 1939, the Nazis' further advance forced Jakobson to Norway, where he stayed until the spring of 1940, when he had to relocate to Sweden. During this unsettled interval he made good use of libraries in Stockholm and the resources of the Academic Hospital of Uppsala University to pursue an interest in working out his claims about phonological universals in two novel domains. Jakobson compared the course of language acquisition in children cross-linguistically with the course of language attrition in people afflicted with aphasia, concluding that the two processes are mirror opposites. This resulted in *Child Language, Aphasia, and Phonological Universals*, originally published in German in Uppsala in 1941, one of Jakobson's best known and most original works.

Jakobson continued to write pioneering analyses of both child language and aphasia, raising the importance of both topics to linguistic theory. In what may be another instance of Jakobsonian binarism, he viewed the two as inversions of each other – the building up of language and its dissolution – processes subject to the same principles, with what was acquired later being lost earlier. Moreover, Jakobson dichotomized aphasia into two contrasting types (Jakobson, *Selected Writings* II: 229–59). One type he labelled 'similarity disorder'. This results from an inability to connect words to their meanings within the network of other word-to-meaning relationships; such patients produce streams of relatively empty speech. The other type of aphasia Jakobson labelled 'contiguity disorder', affecting the capacity to reproduce the propositional context of words, results in the 'telegraphic' speech style famously studied by **Paul Broca**. In his discussion of acquisition, Jakobson emphasized the coherence and systematicity of child language and its basis both in the child's environment and in his or her internal capacities. He wrote that 'the creativity of the child is obviously not … invention out of nothingness; on the other hand, however, neither is his imitation a mechanical or involuntary adoption. The child creates as he borrows' (Jakobson 1941/1968: 13–14).

In 1941, Jakobson had to flee Sweden. He managed to get passage on a boat to the United States, where he settled for the last forty years of his life. In New York, he found support at the Ecole Libre des Hautes Études, a French–Belgian university in exile, then at Columbia University. Ever willing to begin again, he co-founded a Linguistic Circle of New York, although this initiative did not recapture the collegiality of Moscow or Prague. He did, however, get to know French anthropologist Claude Lévi-Strauss (1908–2009) and communicate to him the excitement of post-Saussurean linguistics.

Lévi-Strauss was subsequently instrumental in spreading stucturalism in anthropology.

In 1949, Jakobson accepted a professorship in Slavic Languages and Literatures at Harvard, where he influenced an oncoming generation of linguists, anthropologists and Slavicists until he retired in 1967. In the last twenty-five years of his life, he also held a courtesy appointment at MIT, epicentre of generative linguistics – whose abstention from functional and social contextualization of language he found uncongenial, even as he maintained warm personal relationships with its proponents. To the end, Jakobson sustained his binary focus on literature and language, surrounded simultaneously by the intellectual and social circles of these two institutions.

In Jakobson's memoirs and biographers' accounts of his accomplishments, the sheer fulness of his work and life obscures one intriguing motif. Jakobson developed his wide-ranging and fertile ideas within a context of intense interpersonal give-and-take, often under unpromising external conditions. It is as if, having grown up during a revolution, Jakobson expected to live and thrive amidst rapid, threatening change and sometimes outright danger, stimulated and sustained by his connections to other people. Leaving Poland by boat on his way to Prague for the first time, Jakobson had excitedly solicited a fellow passenger, a stranger, to read some Czech verse aloud to him. The experience inspired him to write about differences between Czech and Russian metre (Jakobson and Pomorska 1983: 22). (Later, on another boat headed for New York, Jacobson discovered philosopher and fellow emigrant Ernst Cassirer [1874–1945] aboard. They spent the crossing in animated conversation, oblivious of Nazi warships.) During his Scandinavian odyssey, Jakobson noted that he arrived in Oslo on 1 September 1939, the official first day of World War II. Unperturbed, he joined 'a close-knit group of Norwegian linguists' and immediately launched an ambitious collaborative phonological atlas of the world (Jakobson and Pomorska 1983: 37–38). In the face of oppression and serial dislocation, Jakobson remained resolutely confident of the importance of what speakers of all languages share.

Jakobson's major works

Selected Writings: Vols I–VIII, 1966–88, Mouton, The Hague.
Child Language, Aphasia, and Phonological Universals, 1968, Mouton, The Hague (originally published 1941 as *Kindersprache, Aphasie und allgemeine Lautgesetze;* reprinted in *Selected Writings*, Vol. I).
My Futurist Years, 1992 (B. Jangfeldt and S. Rudy, eds; S. Rudy, trans.), Marsilio, New York.

Further reading

Armstrong, D. and van Schooneveld, C. H. (1977) *Roman Jakobson: Echoes of his Scholarship*, Lisse: Peter de Ridder.

Halle, M. (1983) *Roman Jakobson: What He Taught Us*, Columbus, OH: Slavica.

Holenstein, E. (1974) *Roman Jakobson's Approach to Language*, Bloomington, IN: Indiana University Press.

Jakobson, R. and Pomorska, K. (1983) *Dialogues*, Cambridge, MA: MIT Press.

Toman, J. (1995) *The Magic of a Common Language: Jakobson, Mathesius, Trubetzkoy, and the Prague Linguistic Circle*, Cambridge, MA: MIT Press.

Steiner, P. (ed.) (1982) *The Prague School: Selected Writings, 1929–1946*, Austin, TX: University of Texas Press.

Waugh, L. R. (1976) *Roman Jakobson's Science of Language*, Lisse: Peter de Ridder.

BENJAMIN LEE WHORF (1897–1941)

Since the mid–1900s, Benjamin Lee Whorf's name has been associated with a long-standing preoccupation in western language science, namely attempts to define the relationship of language, thought and culture. Popular as well as scholarly writings on this topic almost always cite the 'Whorf(ian) hypothesis', sometimes called the 'Sapir–Whorf hypothesis', crediting both Whorf and his teacher, **Edward Sapir**. A range of claims about language, thought and culture have been attributed to Whorf, and his actual position is not easy to specify. But in general, the Whorf hypothesis is taken to assert that language imposes a particular shape on cognition, and that different languages differentially affect cognition. Beyond this signature contribution to linguistics, Whorf was also responsible for a body of original descriptive, historical and philological work on Native American languages, especially Mayan and Hopi, that is still of interest to specialists.

Whorf's biography as a linguist is exceptional. He was born into an old New England family and raised outside Boston amidst a household busily engaged in artistic, intellectual and natural-historical pursuits. He proved a mediocre student at Massachusetts Institute of Technology (MIT), but eventually graduated with a degree in chemical engineering. In 1919 Whorf accepted his first and only job, as fire-prevention engineer in the employ of the Hartford Fire Insurance Company at the firm's home office in Connecticut. He filled roles of increasing responsibility in the division of the company that promoted fire safety by inspecting commercial properties and advising business owners. Whorf displayed creativity and a knack for both working with people and analysing fire-safety problems. He was evidently so well suited to this line of work that he continued in it until his death, while simultaneously committing substantial time and effort to intellectual activities tangential to his formal career (Carroll 1956/1989). By coincidence, another man with an active extra-vocational life, the Pulitzer-winning modernist poet Wallace Stevens (1879–1955), was Vice-President of the company during Whorf's tenure there, although there is no record that the two interacted (Lavery 2000).

Whorf was intrigued with conflicts between science and religion, on which topic he completed an unpublished novel (Rollins 1980: 36–46). This led him to study Hebrew. From here, Whorf came across a book that sought to decode esoteric meanings in the Book of Genesis by a seemingly Kabbalistic analysis of Hebrew roots. Whorf's exploration of linguistics branched off in the mid- to late 1920s into the study of Mayan and Aztec writing systems. He began corresponding in earnest with museum specialists and archaeologists, and in 1928 published a first paper on Aztec philology, in which he speculated about what is now called language typology. On this basis, Whorf was granted a Social Science Research Council fellowship of the sort normally reserved for established scholars with doctorates, to pursue his studies of indigenous languages in Mexico.

Taking a short leave of absence from fire-prevention engineering, and accompanied by his wife and mother-in-law, Whorf travelled to Mexico. He consulted with professionals in the capital, recorded the grammar of native speakers of a descendant of classical Aztec, and had the good fortune to locate some inscriptions that linked Aztec and Mayan writing. Returning to Connecticut, Whorf produced a series of papers on Mayan hieroglyphs. His expertise advanced to a new level when Edward Sapir accepted a professorship at Yale in 1931. Whorf commuted to New Haven to attend Sapir's first course on Native American languages, initiating a discipleship that lasted until Sapir's death in 1939. Although officially Whorf enrolled in Yale's doctoral programme, he never pursued a degree. He seemed to prefer amateur status, even later when he filled in teaching Native American linguistics at Yale as Sapir's health declined.

In the early 1930s, Whorf travelled regularly to New York City to work with a native speaker of Hopi living there. Except for a brief visit to Arizona in 1938, this was the basis of Whorf's first-hand exposure to Hopi. He published a series of notes on Mayan and Aztecan languages, and amassed a collection of unpublished papers

(Whorf 1956/1989: 271–76). Analysing these data drew Whorf's attention to the relationship of language and thought – specifically to the relationship of Hopi verbal categories and Hopi conceptualization of time and space, which he argued contrasted with the conceptualization of time and space in what he called 'Standard Average European' languages. In a volume memorializing Sapir, Whorf wrote:

> Concepts of 'time' and 'matter' are not given in substantially the same form by experience to all men but depend on the nature of the language or languages through the use of which they have been developed. ... Certain ideas born of our own time-concept, such as that of absolute simultaneity, would be either very difficult to express or impossible and devoid of meaning under the Hopi conception ... [in which] there are no formless extensional items; existence may or may not have form, but what it also has, with or without form, is intensity and duration, these being nonextensional and at bottom the same.
>
> (Whorf [1941] 1956/1989: 158)

In this way, Whorf illustrated the 'linguistic relativity principle' with reference to Hopi. However, it was his experience as a fire-prevention engineer that first led him to the idea. Whorf had observed, for example, that people have difficulty recognizing fire hazards in circumstances where language fails to acknowledge their presence, such as when workers freely smoke cigarettes in the vicinity of what they label 'empty gasoline drums' – drums actually filled with highly combustible vapour (*ibid.*: 135).

Whorf was invited to submit his research to the *Technology Review*, MIT's general-interest science journal. In the last two years of his life, he published three essays in the *Technology Review* written for non-specialist readers. This material has been widely cited in discussion of the Whorf hypothesis. It does not always make clear how much scope Whorf intended to give to language in shaping thought. For many readers, his writings admit both the interpretation that he held a weak 'linguistic relativity' position (wherein thought merely bears the imprint of language), and that he held a much stronger position of 'linguistic determinism' (wherein language imposes inescapable limits on thought). Among texts that seemingly take the latter stance is the essay 'Language, mind, and reality', in which Whorf wrote:

> ... the forms of a person's thoughts are controlled by inexorable laws of pattern of which he is unconscious. These patterns are the

unperceived intricate systematizations of his own language. ...
And every language is a vast pattern-system, different from
others, in which are culturally ordained the forms and categories
by which the personality not only communicates, but also ana-
lyzes nature, notices or neglects types of relationship or phenomena, channels his reasoning, and builds the house of his
consciousness.

(Whorf [1942] 1956/1989: 252)

This passage originally appeared in a journal of the Theosophical
Society, a pan-religious organization heavily influenced by the philosophy and spirituality of India, in which Whorf participated (Lee
1996; Hutton and Joseph 1998). He seems to assert that 'the only way
out of the "grooves" of thought which one's native language sets
down is the study of language, which results in a spiritually transcendent experience' (Joseph 1996: 394).

Theosophy, and perhaps more essentially, analytical philosophy
(which advocated close analysis of words as a key to philosophical
insight), may have influenced Whorf's articulation of the relationship
of language, thought and culture, as Joseph (1996) argues. But speculation about this topic runs far back in western language science, albeit
in diverse guises. One account places Whorf in a tradition connecting
Johann Georg Hamann to his student **Johan Gottfried Herder**, to
Wilhelm von Humboldt, to Franz Boas, to Boas' protégé Sapir and
hence to Whorf. Koerner (1995) indicates some of the complexities
of this chain of influence. Lee (1996), who has studied Whorf's published and unpublished writings closely, finds coherence in them that
many readers miss.

Despite the uncertain genealogy and scope of the Whorf hypothesis –
or perhaps abetted by such uncertainties – Whorf's work has currency
in contemporary language science (e.g. Gumperz and Levinson 1991).
Citations of his work in non-specialist literature attest to its continuing popular appeal as well, although not all readers find it persuasive.
A frequent critique is that the weak linguistic relativity version
of the Whorf hypothesis is obviously true, but too vague to be
informative, much less verifiable; and that the strong version, linguistic determinism, would necessarily doom all translation or cross-
linguistic communication – and in fact would make it impossible to
ascertain whether attempts to cross linguistic (and hence cognitive)
boundaries succeed or fail. Other scholars, such as Lucy (1992a; also
Lee 1996), find greater subtlety and refinement in Whorf's work
than is often recognized, pointing out that he explored both covert

and overt means by which language classifies experience; how individual experiences thus classified contribute to larger-scale cognitive structures; and how an analyst might overcome his or her own language-induced biases in order to study the influence of language on cognition.

Most commentators, regardless of their assessment of Whorf's work, agree that the suggestive evidence with which he supported his ideas needs to be supplemented by close empirical study. Empirical results that scholars have so far brought to bear on the Whorf hypothesis are heterogeneous and contradictory. The work of Berlin and Kay (1969) on the universality of colour terminology is often cited as disconfirming linguistic relativity. Berlin and Kay reported that speakers of twenty genetically unrelated languages organize basic colour terms according to the same hierarchy, regardless of how rich or sparse their colour vocabulary is. If speakers of diverse languages similarly prioritize and encode their perceptions of colour, Berlin and Kay concluded that those perceptions must be independent of language differences and thus inconsistent with Whorf's claims.

Lucy (1992a) criticized colour term studies on several grounds, including that Whorf did not preclude the existence of semantic universals, if that is what Berlin and Kay claim to have discovered. Lucy's own research (Lucy 1992b) turned up support for linguistic relativity. He compared the performance of speakers of Yucatec Maya with speakers of English on a cognitive task. The two languages differ in that all Yucatec nouns have properties somewhat like English mass (as opposed to count) nouns. Yucatec nouns are not inherently separated into units, and so necessarily co-occur with classifiers that impose countability on them, in the way that *quart* makes the mass noun *milk* countable in the expression *a quart of milk*. A picture-description recall task showed that English speakers attended more to number and shape, whereas Yucatec speakers attended more to the material composition of objects. Lucy interpreted these results to show that the sensitivities of each group are keyed to the morpho-syntax of their native language.

Everett (2005) added a new twist. In a study of Pirahã, spoken by 150 people in the interior of Brazil, he asserted that Pirahã lacks features taken to be linguistic universals, including quantifiers like *all* or *every*; numbers; colour terms; and syntactic embedding. On the basis of many years' residence among the Pirahã, he offered evidence for the culture's extreme empiricism, in the sense that Pirahã speakers discourage abstraction and shun topics beyond their direct experience. He concluded that Pirahã cultural orientation constrains their grammar. With this, Everett breathed fresh controversy into the discussion of language, thought and culture associated with Whorf's name.

Whorf's major works

'The phonetic value of certain characters in Maya writing', *Papers of the Peabody Museum*, 13, no. 2, 1933.

'The Hopi language, Toreva dialect' and 'The Mila Alta dialect of Aztec', in *Linguistic Structures of Native America*, 1946 (H. Hoijer, ed.), Viking Fund, New York.

Language, Thought, and Reality: Selected Writings of Benjamin Lee Whorf, 1956 (J. B. Carroll, ed.), MIT Press, Cambridge, MA (anthology of Whorf's papers from 1927 to 1941; reprinted 1989).

Further reading

Berlin, B. and Kay, P. (1969) *Basic Color Terms: Their Universality and Evolution*, Berkeley, CA: University of California Press.

Carroll, J. B. (1956) 'Introduction' in B. L. Whorf, *Language, Thought, and Reality: Selected Writings of Benjamin Lee Whorf*, Cambridge, MA: MIT Press.

Everett, D. L. (2005) 'Cultural constraints on grammar in cognition in Pirahã', *Current Anthropology*, 46, 621–46 (including peer commentary and reply by Everett).

Gumperz, J. J. and Levinson, S. C. (1991) 'Rethinking linguistic relativity', *Current Anthropology*, 32, 613–23.

Hutton, C. M. and Joseph, J. E. (1998) 'Back to Blavatsky: The impact of theosophy on modern linguistics', *Language and Communication*, 18, 181–204.

Joseph, J. E. (1996) 'The immediate sources of the "Sapir–Whorf Hypothesis"', *Historiographia Linguistica*, 23, 365–404.

Koerner, K. (1995) 'The "Sapir–Whorf Hypothesis": a historico-bibliographical essay', in *Professing Linguistic Historiography*, Amsterdam and Philadelphia, PA: John Benjamins.

Lavery, D. (2000) 'Imagination and insurance: Wallace Stevens and Benjamin Lee Whorf at the Hartford', *Legal Studies Forum*, 24, 481–92.

Lee, P. (1996) *The Whorf Theory Complex: A Critical Reconstruction*, Amsterdam and Philadelphia, PA: John Benjamins.

Lucy, J. A. (1992a) *Language Diversity and Thought: A Reformulation of the Linguistic Relativity Hypothesis*, Cambridge: Cambridge University Press.

——(1992b) *Grammatical Categories and Cognition: A Case Study in the Linguistic Relativity Hypothesis*, Cambridge: Cambridge University Press.

Rollins, P. C. (1980) *Benjamin Lee Whorf: Lost Generation Theories of Mind, Language, and Religion*, Ann Arbor, MI: University Microfilms International for the Popular Culture Association.

LOUIS HJELMSLEV (1899–1965)

Louis Hjelmslev was the co-founder and mainstay of the Linguistic Circle of Copenhagen, which flourished from 1931. An informal fellowship of scholars modelled on the Linguistic Circle of Prague, the Copenhagen group served as a focus for the development of linguistics in Denmark. Pre-eminent among those developments was Hjelmslev's distinctive style of post-Saussurean structuralism, which, with his collaborator Hans Jørgen Uldall (1907–57), he named 'glossematics'. Glossematics aimed to establish a general linguistic theory, the principles of which apply to the analysis of both sounds and meanings within any language (and some of which could be extended to other semiotic systems, such as sign languages or even nautical flag codes). Working at a high level of abstraction, Hjelmslev and Uldall attempted to deduce from formal principles a set of categories for the description of language, using scrupulously precise terms and stringently logical reasoning. For various reasons, however, the theory was never articulated in satisfactory depth in writing, nor were its virtues adequately displayed in the analysis of specific languages. Glossematics has had its strongest impact in Denmark and in France. Nevertheless, it contributes to the general history of the language sciences as an early twentieth-century school that participated in some of the same intellectual trends that stimulated such divergent scholars as **Ferdinand de Saussure**, **Roman Jakobson**, and American descriptivists/ structuralists of various stripes. Hjelmslev's work is still occasionally cited in modern linguistics, especially semiotics, even if his writings are not widely read.

Hjelmslev was the son of a mathematician who served the University of Copenhagen as a faculty member and eventually as Rector. In 1917, he enrolled at the University to study comparative philology. While an undergraduate, he won a prize for a paper on Oscan inscriptions, then went on to spend a year in Lithuania. Hjelmslev completed his MA thesis on Lithuanian phonetics in 1923, before taking a year's study of comparative-historical linguistics in Prague, and two years in Paris. The latter experience exposed Hjelmslev to the strong influence of Saussure, brought back to Paris from Geneva by Saussure's students and colleagues.

In Paris, Hjelmslev wrote his first book, *Principes de Grammaire Générale*. It was published in 1928, and prefigured some of what became glossematics. Back in Copenhagen, Hjelmslev's mentor at the University, Holger Pedersen (1867–1953), declined to accept *Principes* as a doctoral thesis on the grounds that it was too theoretical (Fischer-Jørgensen

1965: vi). Hjelmslev gamely submitted a more conventional study of Baltic historical phonology, and was awarded the doctorate in 1932.

Hjelmslev's experience of rejection apparently neither blunted his independence nor dissuaded him from wrestling with programmatic matters in the study of language. Although his next major publications were an edition of the writings of the Danish philologist Rasmus Kristian Rask (1787–1832) and a cross-linguistic study of case, he continued to explore language at the high level of abstraction that was congenial to him. Lively evening meetings of the Copenhagen Circle provided both support and critique in the initial stages of working out his ideas. A former student of Hjelmslev described how the group met uninterruptedly throughout the war, even though members had to bicycle home afterwards via back streets, by the light of lanterns wrapped in black paper, to evade a municipal curfew (Fischer-Jørgensen 1997: 28).

In 1934, Hjelmslev left Copenhagen to take up a position as reader in comparative linguistics at the University of Aarhus, on the Jutland peninsula. He returned in 1937 to accept the Chair once held by his mentor Pedersen. He spent the rest of his career at the University of Copenhagen as a faculty member and – following in his father's footsteps – also served in administrative roles at the University and in Danish scholarly societies. He co-founded and edited the journal *Acta Linguistica*, which survives to the present day as *Acta Linguistica Hafniensia*. He also edited the working papers of the Copenhagen Circle. In his heyday, Hjelmslev gave frequent guest lectures on glossematics, and spent the summer of 1952 at the University of Indiana participating in the Linguistic Society of America's summer Linguistic Institute.

One reason why glossematics has had a smaller impact than it might have had is that Hjelmslev and Uldall were separated during World War II and, once reunited, their views had diverged to the point of undermining their capacity to collaborate. Eventually, each published separately a part of the work they had planned together. Having studied with **Daniel Jones**, Uldall's strength was in phonetics, so the two men first articulated their shared project under the rubric of phonology. Later, with Hjelmslev carrying most of the responsibility for developing the theory, its compass expanded.

A second reason for the modest impact of glossematics (at least outside Denmark) lies in Hjelsmlev's failure in promoting his work. The *Prolegomena to a Theory of Language* appeared in Danish in 1943, and in English translation in 1953. Along with two collections of essays (Hjelmslev 1959, 1973), it is the best record of his conception of glossematics; however, it gives only glimpses of the theory

Hjelmslev envisioned. The *Prolegomena* largely consists of a tissue of loosely connected conceptual statements couched in idiosyncratic terminology (idiosyncratic even, apparently, in the original Danish), which offers no extended example of how glossematics might succeed in the analysis of real language, nor a satisfying overview of how its parts cohere. Hjelmslev's posthumously published *Résumé of a Theory of Language* (1975) is a list of terse apothegms that purport to lay out the system of rules and definitions underlying glossematics. It displays Hjelmslev's penchant for eccentric technical vocabulary, but unfortunately does little to answer questions that the *Prolegomena* raises.

Working through these difficulties, one can still appreciate Hjelmslev's achievements. He endorsed the empirical principle that linguistic theory must be internally consistent, exhaustive, and maximally simple. His procedure started with texts – written or spoken corpora – that are to be partitioned and subpartitioned into iteratively smaller units. This approach, which inverts American descriptivists' working habits, Hjelmslev characterized as 'deductive' (although, curiously, sometimes labelling it 'inductive'; Siertsema 1954: 41–53). An important tool in the task of partition is the 'commutation test', essentially a substitution test to determine whether one element can be replaced by another without disturbing its identity. Glossematics insists that its terms and concepts are relevant to all 'planes' of language, that is, to 'expression' (sounds) equally as to 'content' (morphosyntax). Therefore the commutation test distinguishes *ram* from *ewe* on the basis of a single contrasting element on the plane of content, and likewise distinguishes the consonant cluster *sl* from *sn* on the plane of expression (Hjelmslev 1961/1943: 70).

Behind any text (which Hjelmslev calls a 'process') is a system in which an inventory of elements appears in combinations. By iterative partitioning of the distinctive units of the process, a linguist can classify the combinatorial privileges of each unit. The totality of combinations of a particular item constitutes its 'form'. Form is prior to, and manifested in, 'substance'. On the plane of expression, substance refers to sounds or graphemes, or gestures in the case of sign languages; their study Hjelmslev calls 'cenematics', from the Greek word for 'empty', on the grounds that units of expression-substance are empty of meaning. On the plane of content, substance refers to cognitive structures like thoughts or ideas. The study of content-substance Hjelmslev calls 'plerematics', from the Greek word for 'full', since these units are full of meaning (see Hjelmslev 1959: 82, reprinting an essay from 1939).

Starting with these general proposals, Hjelmslev developed a complex web of terms and concepts for the partition of Hjelmslevian 'process', and then defined and labelled the relationships holding among those terms. Glossematics displays the obvious influence of Saussurean structuralism in taking for granted the value of synchronic analysis. It also incorporates Saussurean-inspired dichotomies such as expression/content, system/process, form/substance. The Copenhagen School also felt the influence of the Prague School, especially of Jakobson. Many of the concepts of glossematics parallel those used in the Prague School (whether or not they are actually inspired by the Prague School); ·for example, the distinction between Hjelmslevian 'extensive' versus 'intensive' members of a contrastive pair of units resembles the Jakobsonian distinction between unmarked and marked members of a pair. On the other hand, Hjelmslev and Uldall rejected the Prague School's focus on phonemes and phonetic detail in favour of a more abstract treatment of sounds, which they dubbed 'phonematics'. Hjelmslev aimed to create an explicit linguistic theory that would 'provid[e] a procedural method by means of which objects of a premised nature can be described self-consistently and exhaustively'. By 'objects of a premised nature' he meant a collection of 'the fewest and most general possible premisses' (Hjelmslev 1961/1943: 15) which are 'able to satisfy the conditions for application to a large number of empirical data' (ibid.: 14). Hjelmslev's drive to define the architecture of a linguistic theory also manifested in American descriptive linguistics and, albeit differently, in generative grammar.

As it has come down to us today, however, glossematics does not fully satisfy modern linguistics' search for an explicit theory of language that has been tested against, and found adequate to account for, the properties of diverse human languages. Although the Linguistic Circle of Copenhagen published a *festschrift* for Hjelmslev in 1949 (*Recherches structurales*) illustrating mid-century research inspired by glossematics, the lack of a fully developed application of Hjelmslev's work remains problematic. Hjelmslev's innovative terminology and conceptual apparatus have been stumbling blocks for some readers going back to his own decade: his compatriot and older contemporary **Otto Jespersen** – who kept his distance from the Linguistic Circle of Copenhagen – complained 'I do not yet really understand what it means to approach phonetics deductively, any more than a zoologist can describe carnivorous animals deductively' (trans. Rischel 1989: 56). It is instructive therefore to keep in mind what Hjelmslev, a self-identified linguistic theoretician, considered to be his own goals, as he stated them in an unusually communicative essay that contrasts three subtypes of linguists:

The *specialist* brings bricks to the building of linguistics, but he is unable, without outside assistance, to put the bricks in place; he doesn't define, but asks the others for definitions, which he then usually scraps. The *linguistic philosopher* has more philosophical or metaphysical than actual linguistic aims; his claims are difficult to verify, and when he occurs in a pure breed, he makes it a matter of principle not to define. The *linguistic theoretician* has purely linguistic but often very abstract aims; he overwhelms his audience with definitions and with terminology. Both the linguistic philosopher and the linguistic theoretician help to place the specialist's brick into the building, though the operation is rarely altogether successful. The linguistic philosophers are often inclined ... to place the brick in a certain position without tangible justification. The linguistic theoreticians know well enough where the brick should be; but it is in a new place each day; they are continually rebuilding the edifice. The fate of the specialists is thus a sad one; but they have the great consolation that without them the whole business would be nothing.

('A causerie on linguistic theory', 1941,
reprinted in Hjelmslev 1973: 103)

Hjelmslev's major works

Principes de Grammaire Générale, 1928, A. F. Høst, Copenhagen.
Prolegomena to a Theory of Language, 1961 (2nd edn, F. J. Whitfield, trans.), University of Wisconsin Press, Madison, WI (1st edn 1953, Indiana University Publications in Anthropology and Linguistics; original work published 1943 as *Omkring sprogteoriens grundlæggelse*).
Essais Linguistiques. Travaux du Cercle Linguistique de Copenhague XII, 1959.
Essais Linguistiques II. Travaux du Cercle Linguistique de Copenhague XIV, 1973.
Language: An Introduction, 1970 (F. J. Whitfield, trans.), University of Wisconsin Press, Madison, WI (original work published 1963 as *Sproget: En introduktion*).
Résumé of a Theory of Language, 1975 (F. J. Whitfield, ed. and trans.), University of Wisconsin Press, Madison, WI (original unpublished work entitled *Sprogteori: Résumé*).

Further reading

Badir, S. (2000) *Hjelmslev*, Paris: Les Belles Lettres.
Fischer-Jørgensen, E. (1965) 'Louis Hjelmslev', *Acta Linguistica Hafniensia*, 9, ii–xxii.

——(1997) 'Hjelmslev et le Cercle linguistique de Copenhague', in A. Zinna (ed.), *Hjelmslev Aujourd'hui*, Turnhout: Brepols.

Linguistic Circle of Copenhagen (1949) *Recherches structurales 1949: Interventions dans le débat glossématique, Travaux du Cercle Linguistique de Copenhague* V.

Rischel, J. (1989) 'Otto Jespersen's contribution to Danish and general phonetics', in A. Juul and H. F. Nielsen (eds), *Otto Jespersen: Facets of His Life and Work*, Amsterdam and Philadelphia, PA: John Benjamins.

Siertsema, B. (1954) *A Study of Glossematics*, The Hague: Martinus Nijhoff.

Zinna, A. (ed.) (1997) *Hjelmslev Aujourd'hui*, Turnhout: Brepols.

J. L. AUSTIN (1911–60)

The British scholar John Langshaw Austin was a key figure in the development of 'ordinary language philosophy' at Oxford, beginning in the late 1930s. Ordinary language philosophers (among them the later **Ludwig Wittgenstein**) rejected the assertion that everyday language is ineluctably loose and unruly, and must be converted into the precise terms of logic before it can represent philosophical claims. Austin's special talent was that he was sensitive to subtle differences of meaning among everyday words and within families of words, and could dissect and articulate those differences. One famous essay, for example, explores the contrasting properties of the adverbs 'involuntarily', 'inadvertently', 'by accident', 'by mistake' (Austin 1961/1979: 175–204). Austin's keenest interest was in what he called 'performative' utterances, which superficially resemble garden-variety statements but have distinctive properties: rather than describing states or events, they accomplish actions. For example, by uttering the performative verb 'apologise' in 'I apologise for being late', a speaker *performs* the act of apology. In this way, the meaning properties of performative verbs differ starkly from verbs like 'fasten' or 'memorize'.

Austin lived an apparently tranquil and orderly (if short) life, unobtrusively succeeding at whatever he pursued. The son of an administrator at St Leonard's, an independent school north of Edinburgh, he was raised mostly in Scotland. He won scholarships in Classics to Shrewsbury School, and then Balliol College, Oxford. Austin's study of Latin and Greek branched out into philosophy, inspiring a lifelong interest in **Aristotle**. His education in Classics disposed him to inspect language at close range, and developed his ability to analyse the intricacies of words. Austin suspended his academic career for six years during World War II to apply his powers of analysis in the British Intelligence Corps. Some go so far as to credit much of the success of the Allied invasion of Normandy to Austin's calm and accurate mastery of military intelligence from his position in the War Office (G. J. Warnock, in Fann 1969: 8–10). Indeed, after the war he was decorated by the British, French and Americans. In 1946, Austin returned to Oxford and remained there for the rest of his life. He was appointed to the prestigious White's Professorship of Moral Philosophy in 1952.

Austin published relatively little: seven articles; an edition of a work on Gottfried Leibniz (1646–1716); a translation of Gottlob Frege's (1848–1925) treatise on arithmetic. The major conduit of his influence in his lifetime was through his lectures and face-to-face interaction with students and peers, including his regular hosting of informal Saturday morning discussion groups on selected topics in the philosophy of language (Warnock, in Berlin *et al.* 1973: 31–45). Austin had firm convictions, enjoyed being right, and could be dogged in defence of what he felt was correct. But he displayed no taste for adversarial showmanship, preferring dry wit to bombast or self-indulgent exercise of authority. Both as a writer and lecturer, Austin mastered the vivid, quirky example and the incisive illustration that precisely nailed his point. His ingenuity disarmed audiences.

> You have a donkey, so have I, and they graze in the same field. The day comes when I conceive a dislike for mine. I go to shoot it, draw a bead on it, fire: the brute falls in its tracks. I inspect the victim, and find to my horror that it is *your* donkey. I appear on your doorstep with the remains and say – what? 'I say, old sport, I'm awfully sorry, &c., I've shot your donkey *by accident*'? Or '*by mistake*'? Then again, I go to shoot my donkey as before, draw a bead on it, fire – but as I do so, the beasts move, and to my horror yours falls. Again the scene on the doorstep – what do I say? 'By mistake'? Or 'by accident'?
>
> (Austin 1961/1979: 185)

After Austin's death, three books appeared that assembled his unpublished work. *Philosophical Papers* reprinted articles published during his lifetime, alongside seven other texts on philosophical and linguistic issues from 1939 onward, reconstructed by his colleagues from manuscripts and lecture notes. *Sense and Sensibilia* recapitulates lectures Austin delivered at Oxford between 1947 and 1955, and at the University of California at Berkeley in 1958. The topic is sensory perception, which Austin addresses through a critique of logical positivists' position on the question of whether it is material objects that humans perceive, or sense data. Characteristically, one of Austin's means of investigating the issue is through analysis of the nuances of meaning in ordinary-language expressions such as 'It *looks* blue' versus '*looks like* blue', '*appears* blue', etc. (Austin 1962a: 34–36).

Austin's third posthumously published book, *How to Do Things with Words*, was likewise assembled from notes he collected for lectures at Oxford in the 1950s, and at Harvard University, which he visited in 1955 to present the William James lecture series. *How to Do Things with Words* is Austin's best known work, and the fullest exposition of his research on performatives. Written in an informal style, Austin began by calling attention to performatives such as 'I *apologize* for being late' or 'I *name* this ship the Queen Elizabeth'. Performatives exhibit the conventional grammar of statements, lacking any idiosyncratic formal marker; but as opposed to 'constatives' (such as 'I *take* the bus on Friday'; 'I *opened* the can with a screwdriver'), performatives cannot be designated either true or false; and, most importantly, their utterance (under appropriate circumstances) constitutes an action rather than a description or a statement. Austin pointed out that the performative utterances he presented share certain formal properties – first-person singular subjects, present indicative active verbs – but that these features do not define the class, since 'Passengers *are warned* to cross the track by the bridge only' is performative but 'I *drink* beer' is not (Austin 1962b: 56–57).

In a circuitous manner, Austin (*ibid.*) explored other features of performatives. He asserted that they are characteristically embedded in culturally defined procedures or practices (*marry* a couple, *nominate* a candidate), but conceded that other performatives (*promise, warn, order*) are not so conventionally delimited. Each performative implies a specific context of use that makes its employment, in Austin's term, 'felicitous'. Austin analysed differing grounds on which performatives may be infelicitous (*ibid.*: 14–24). For example, the performative utterance of a promise may 'misfire' if the conditions legitimating its use are not met (for example, because the speaker does not have the authority to issue that promise); or the utterance of a promise may take place, but constitute an 'abuse' of the meaning of the term (for example, because the speaker has no genuine intention of carrying out the promised action).

Austin contextualized his analysis of performatives by introducing a taxonomy of 'speech acts', which labels three facets of an utterance in human communication (*ibid.*: 99–131). First, the act of uttering words associated with particular sense and reference properties Austin calls a 'locutionary act'. Locutionary acts have meaning. Second, an 'illocutionary act' is what a speaker accomplishes by employing a locutionary act: the speaker performs the illocutionary act of warning through the locutionary act of uttering 'I warn you that X'. Austin describes illocutionary acts as having force rather than meaning. Third, a 'perlocutionary act' is accomplished if the force of an illocutionary act registers on the listener – that is if, having been warned, the listener modifies her behaviour to avoid the consequences against which she has been warned – or, alternatively, a contrarian listener recognizes the warning and flouts it. In this sense, to Austin perlocutionary acts are the effects of uptake of illocutionary acts.

Austin used this taxonomy to try to pare away locutionary meanings and perlocutionary effects from utterances in order to focus on illocutionary force, which resides most directly in performative verbs. He then tentatively identified five classes of performatives defined according to their illocutionary force (*ibid.*: 150–62): verdictives (*diagnose*; *convict*); exercitives (*appoint*; *urge*); commissives (*vow*; *oppose*); behabitives (*apologize*; *curse*); expositives (*report*; *argue*).

How to Do Things with Words is the acknowledged fountainhead of Austin's conceptualization of performatives. He was nevertheless cognizant of its limits throughout. For example, he pointed out that the same utterance may be a constative or a performative; that virtually any utterance can plausibly be construed as performative; and that illocutionary force is not the exclusive burden of performatives (since 'You *must do* X' counts as an order although 'do' is not a performative); and that even a particular tone of voice, or a shrug, can carry the weight of illocutionary force.

Since his death, Austin's admirers as well as his critics have taken up the job of elaborating and criticizing his work. Perhaps the best known figure to build on Austin's ideas is the American philosopher of language John R. Searle (b. 1932) of the University of California at Berkeley. Searle studied at Oxford in the 1950s. The nature of his debt to Austin, and where and how the two scholars' work converges or diverges, is controversial (Rajagopalan 2000; Sbisà 2002). Searle developed the notion of speech act, proposing a more finely grained version of Austin's tripartite distinction among locutionary, illocutionary and perlocutionary acts. Searle also elaborated the conditions bearing on felicitous illocutionary acts: for the intended force of 'I promise to do X' to obtain, the context of its utterance has to meet 'preparatory conditions' (the hearer must value the speaker's performance of X); 'sincerity conditions' (the speaker must sincerely intend to do X); and 'essential conditions' (the utterance must count as an obligation of the speaker to do X) (Searle 1969: 57–71). Exploiting these distinctions, and his similarly more articulated notions of the array of illocutionary acts and the bases on which illocutionary acts differ from each other, Searle analysed the range of variation of speech acts. In the opinion of some scholars, Searle offered a more satisfactory inventory of the territory that Austin first surveyed, and moreover, in emphasizing the rule-governedness of speech acts, Searle delimited what was to Wittgenstein the chaotic diversity of 'language games'. In addition, Searle's work on indirect speech acts – a speaker's performance, for example, of the illocutionary act of requesting that a window be closed by saying 'It's chilly here' – connects some of Austin's concerns to those of **H. P. Grice**.

Many commentators have criticized what in retrospect appears as imprecision, sketchiness or inconsistency in Austin's work. It is also evident that his conceptualization of how to do things with words suffers from narrowness, first because it has no empirical basis other than Austin's and his audience's intuitions, and second because it is entirely construed from the facts of English. Since his death, however, anthropological research such as that conducted by Finnegan (1969) and Rosaldo (1982) has extended Austin's work in the analysis of numerous languages. Other disciplines have also capitalized on the notion of speech act, so that Austin's work is cited in fields such as medicine, computer science, management, drama, education, and especially law (Yeager 2006).

It is also part of Austin's legacy that his students and colleagues converge on what counted as his greatest contribution. They describe the experience of thinking aloud with Austin about (for example) 'by accident' versus 'by mistake', and about the relationships of words, deeds and things as 'fun' (G. Pitcher, in Berlin *et al.* 1973: 19), and 'enormously enjoyable' (G. J. Warnock, *ibid.*: 39), and an activity that yielded 'true intellectual happiness' (I. Berlin, *ibid.*: 16).

Austin's major works

Sense and Sensibilia, 1962a, Oxford University Press, Oxford.
How to Do Things with Words, 1962b, Harvard University Press, Cambridge, MA.
Philosophical Papers, 1979 (3rd edn; J. O. Urmson and G. J. Warnock, eds), Oxford University Press, Oxford (originally published 1961).

Further reading

Berlin, I., Forguson, L. W., Pears, D. F., Pitcher, G., Searle, J. R., Strawson, P. F. and Warnock, G. J. (1973) *Essays on J. L. Austin*, Oxford: Oxford University Press.

Fann, K. T. (1969). *Symposium on J. L. Austin*, New York: Humanities Press.
Finnegan, R. (1969) 'How to do things with words: performative utterances among the Limba of Sierra Leone,' *Man*, 4, 537–52.
Rajagopalan, K. (2000) 'On Searle [on Austin] on language,' *Language and Communication*, 20, 347–91.
Rosaldo, M. Z. (1982) 'The things we do with words: Ilongot speech acts and speech act theory in philosophy,' *Language in Society*, 11, 203–37.
Sbisà, M. (2002) 'Speech acts in context,' *Language and Communication*, 22, 421–36.
Searle, J. R. (1969) *Speech Acts*, Cambridge: Cambridge University Press.
Warnock, G. J. (1989) *J. L. Austin*, London: Routledge.
Yeager, D. (2006) *J. L. Austin and the Law*, Lewisburg, PA: Bucknell University Press.

KENNETH L. PIKE (1912–2000)

The American linguist and missionary Kenneth Pike contributed to the study of language in three ways. As a theoretician, Pike wrote about tone and phonemics, and created an ambitious system of grammatical analysis he called 'tagmemics'. As a descriptivist and field linguist, Pike analysed little-known languages, especially those indigenous to Mexico, Peru and Ecuador. Out of these experiences, he produced numerous grammatical studies (often collaboratively), and designed orthographies for languages that lacked written forms. As a faculty member at the University of Michigan and as a leader of a Christian evangelical organization that supports linguistic field work in the service of Bible translation, Pike trained many others to work first-hand with the languages of South America, Asia, Africa and the Pacific.

Pike grew up in rural Connecticut, the son of a doctor who had spent time in Alaska as a missionary. After graduating from Gordon College of Theology and Missions in Boston, Pike hitch-hiked to Arkansas in 1935 to attend 'Camp Wycliffe', a missionary-training programme organized by William Cameron Townsend (1896–1982). Townsend had spent ten years in Guatemala creating an orthography for the indigenous Mayan language Kaqchikel, then translating the Bible into Kaqchikel. Soon Pike was in Mexico doing similar work on Mixtec. When he conceived the need for academic training in linguistics, he enrolled as a doctoral student at the University of Michigan (Pike 1998: 149–51). Pike studied under post-Bloomfieldian Charles Fries (1887–1967) and profited from interactions with **Edward Sapir** and **Leonard Bloomfield** while maintaining his association with Townsend's missionary activities, by then carried out under the name of the Wycliffe-associated Summer Institute of Linguistics (later renamed 'SIL International'). Pike alternated time spent at Michigan with field research, accompanied from 1938 by his wife Evelyn, Townsend's niece, who took up the study of languages alongside her husband. In 1948, Pike accepted a faculty position at Michigan that allowed him to spend generous intervals abroad. From then until the mid-1990s, the Pikes travelled around the globe, lecturing and acting as consultants to literacy, language study and Bible translation projects under the auspices of SIL International. Pike served as president of SIL from 1942 until 1979, and of the Linguistic Society of America in 1961. Until the very end of his life, he indefatigably advised students and colleagues, and published a stream of linguistic and linguistic-anthropological monographs, journal articles, poetry, and reflections on his vocation as a missionary.

Not surprisingly, Pike's experiences as a field linguist informed his theoretical work. As a novice wrestling first with the sounds and tones of Mixtec, his early publications focused on phonetics (Pike 1943/1976). Then he moved on to publish *Phonemics* (Pike 1947/ 1961), subtitled '*A Technique for Reducing Languages to Writing*'. His most ambitious work, Pike (1954–60/1967), communicated an early version of tagmemics. Pike (1982) summarized later developments.

Starting with a term employed by Bloomfield (1933: 166–68), Pike's 'tagmemes' are to grammar what morphemes are to the lexicon, or phonemes to phonology. A tagmeme correlates a grammatical position, or 'slot' (e.g. 'subject'), with a member of the relevant class of 'fillers' (e.g. noun). Tagmemes are also sensitive to 'roles', such as the distinction between actor versus experiencer subjects, and to 'cohesion' features such as agreement (Pike 1982: 75–79). Pike developed a notational system to capture language-specific details in the distribution of tagmemes – which may be optional or obligatory, fixed or moveable – as they combine into constructions, or 'syntagmemes'. Waterhouse (1974: 11) provides the example of the English sentence *The boy has the book* represented as three tagmemes: '+S:NP +TPred:TVP +O:NP', or 'obligatory subject slot filled by noun phrase, followed by obligatory transitive predicate slot filled by transitive verb phrase, followed by obligatory object slot filled by noun phrase'.

These characteristics place Pike's tagmemics at home in the context of mid-twentieth-century American structuralism, the context in which Sapir, Bloomfield, Fries and **Charles Hockett** worked, and from which generative grammar later emerged. Some versions of tagmemics acknowledge the utility of systematically relating certain constructions to other constructions, in ways reminiscent of (and evidently inspired by) early generative grammar's concept of transformational rules. Pike's grammatical writings also include several innovations. One has been extended to disciplines as far from linguistics as nursing, music and organizational studies (Headland *et al.* 1990). That innovation is Pike's coinage of the terms 'etic' and 'emic' to name two contrasting approaches to the analysis of language (and hence to cultural phenomena in general). An 'etic' standpoint is external and typological; it looks at phenomena 'based on prior sampling ... before one begins the analysis' (Pike 1954–60/1967: 37). An 'emic' standpoint is system-internal. It is discovered rather than imposed, because it represents 'the view of one familiar with the system and who knows how to function within it' (*ibid.*: 38). Tagmemics values both etic and emic perspectives, while accepting that the former yields to the latter as an analyst achieves familiarity with the language being studied.

It is characteristic of Pike's approach that he examined not only components of language (sounds, tones, words, grammar, gestures) from etic and emic points of view, but other aspects of human behaviour as well. Pike gives the example of the behaviour (including speech) of a family at the breakfast table (*ibid.*: 120–28). A similar synthetic vision informs another Pikean innovation, the claim that language, like structured phenomena in general, can be conceived in three ways, either statically (as particles), dynamically (as waves), or functionally (as a patterned system or field). In writing about language, Pike (1982: 19–39) characteristically shifted his orientation iteratively from particles (phonemes; words) to waves (coarticulation; text written longhand) to fields (pitch and intonation systems; inflectional paradigms). Of course, many linguists, including those who do not employ the metaphors of particle, wave and field, analyse multiple facets of language. But what appeared to be at stake in Pike's use of these terms was an assertion of the non-autonomy of language from other human phenomena, in opposition to formalist linguistics. Pike seemed to link this stance to a larger point in insisting that tagmemics grants '*person* ... theoretical priority above formalism, ... above idealized abstractions' (*ibid.*: xi).

Pike's two other contributions to twentieth-century linguistics are related. As a field worker, his publications on Mixtec are still sometimes cited, as are his analyses of other languages, especially those of the Andes and Amazon areas. The recent worldwide acceleration of language loss has increased the value of the descriptive field studies that Pike and others carried out through living with native speakers of indigenous languages. Such work is now conducted by linguists with a variety of goals and theoretical orientations (see **Kenneth Hale**). SIL International, depicted in its early days in Brend and Pike (1977), has flourished and outlived Pike. Retaining a focus on little-studied 'minority' languages worldwide, SIL linguists have now worked with 2500 such languages, potentially affecting 1.7 billion speakers. In 2010, the organization reported 5500 active personnel from sixty countries carrying out SIL-supported language- and literacy-related projects (www.sil.org). Academic and literacy-related publications by SIL workers now number 24,500. Some build on Pike's tagmemics, while others adopt different theoretical frameworks. All are freely accessible over the internet. A representative sample of 2010 publications includes 'A survey of the languages of the Javari River Valley, Brazil'; 'Lika phonology'; 'Language maintenance among the Parya of Tajikistan'; 'Foreground and background in Mbyá Guaraní clause chaining'; 'A sociolinguistic study of Setaman'; and '1-handed PERSONs and ASL morphology'. Moreover, SIL's website hosts a searchable electronic catalogue of the world's living languages, *Ethnologue*, which provides summaries of each language's geographical distribution, number of speakers, and genetic relations (www.ethnologue.org).

Thus the scale of this work has grown enormously since the summer of 1935 in Arkansas, when Pike was one of five who responded to Townsend's call to prepare missionaries for linguistic field work. SIL International now supports a large academic sub-culture, sponsoring varied linguistic and anthropological research. It remains, however, only partially integrated into the international discipline of linguistics, because some consider its commitment to religious evangelism to be a source of cultural and perhaps linguistic bias. Stoll (1982) reviewed substantial controversy over SIL International's political and sociological roles, and questioned whether the organization has been disingenuous in selectively presenting its concerns as linguistic versus religious as circumstances warrant. Pennycook and Makoni (2005) evince scepticism of the integrity of missionary linguistics in general, in contexts where indigenous peoples confront explicit or subtle pressure to abandon some of their values and practices – pressure that can be applied even by outsiders avowedly committed to helping preserve indigenous cultures and languages. Dobrin (2009) introduces a series of papers that present several sides to this important debate.

Pike's theoretical work has also not escaped critique. His writing sometimes veers into folksy references and illustrations that diffuse a

reader's attention; such passages can appear alongside dense expositions and off-putting notation that Pike developed but did not
himself always exploit. Pike's insistence on the importance of con-
textualizing linguistic facts, and on integrating language with culture
and behaviour, sometimes disregards the natural limits to these appeal-
ing and plausible principles. More pointedly, linguists such as Postal
(1966) have criticized tagmemics for ignoring the distinction between
the surface and underlying structures of utterances. Postal cites the
classic generative analysis of English imperatives, wherein a deep-
structure second-person subject surfaces in reflexive objects or tag
questions (e.g. *Help yourself, won't you?*). Presumably tagmemics would
have to account for the exclusive presence of second person pronouns
in these contexts by special stipulation. Longacre (1967) replies.

Whatever the limits of tagmemics, or of the politics of SIL
International, a photograph reprinted in Wise *et al.*'s (2003: 14) memorial volume captures something of what makes Pike's contributions
memorable. Over the caption 'Collecting language data from an
Aguaruna man in the Peruvian Amazon in 1956', the picture shows
Pike and his informant seated facing each other, in front of a tropical
river landscape. Each is dressed according to his own culture: Pike
in shirt sleeves and khakis, his partner in feathered head-dress and
face paint. Arms akimbo, Pike's posture spontaneously mirrors that of
the other man as he leans forward, listening intently; the two men's
eyes are locked on each other's faces. Pike's left hand casually
holds a sheaf of papers, probably field notes, but his attention is not
on them. Rather, in this portrait of cross-cultural receptivity, Pike
seems unconsciously to illustrate what he meant by insisting that
'*person* [be granted] priority above formalism, ... above idealized
abstractions'.

Pike's major writings

Phonetics, 1943, University of Michigan Press, Ann Arbor, MI (reprinted
1976).
Phonemics, 1947, University of Michigan Press, Ann Arbor, MI (reprinted
1961).
Language in Relation to a Unified Theory of the Structure of Human Behavior, 1967
(2nd revised edn), Mouton, The Hague (1st edn 1954–60, Summer
Institute of Linguistics, Glendale, CA).
*Kenneth Pike: Selected Writings to Commemorate the 60th Birthday of Kenneth Lee
Pike*, 1972 (R. M. Brend, ed.), Mouton, The Hague.
Linguistic Concepts: An Introduction to Tagmemics, 1982, University of Nebraska
Press, Lincoln, NE.

'A linguistic pilgrimage', 1998, in E. F. K. Koerner (ed.), *First Person Singular III: Autobiographies by North American Scholars in the Language Sciences*, John Benjamins, Amsterdam and Philadelphia.

Further reading

Bloomfield, L. (1933) *Language*, New York: Henry Holt.
Brend, R. M. and Pike, K. L. (eds) (1977) *The Summer Institute of Linguistics: Its Works and Contributions*, The Hague: Mouton.
Dobrin, L. (2009) 'SIL International and the disciplinary culture of linguistics', *Language*, 85, 618–19.
Headland, T. N., Pike, K. L. and Harris, M. (eds) (1990) *Emics and Etics: The Insider/Outsider Debate*, Newbury Park, CA: Sage.
Longacre, R. E. (1967) 'Reply to Postal's review of *Grammar Discovery Procedures*', *International Journal of American Linguistics*, 33, 323–28.
Pennycook, A., and Makoni, S. (2005) 'The modern mission: The language effects of Christianity', *Journal of Language, Identity, and Education*, 4, 137–55.
Postal, P. (1966) 'Review of *Grammar Discovery Procedures* by R. E. Longacre', *International Journal of American Linguistics*, 32, 93–98.
Stoll, D. (1982) *Fishers of Men or Founders of Empire? The Wycliffe Bible Translators in Latin America*, London: Zed Press.
Wise, M. R., Headland, T. and Brend, R. M. (eds) (2003) *Language and Life: Essays in Memory of Kenneth L. Pike*, SIL International and the University of Texas at Arlington Publications in Linguistics.
Waterhouse, V. G. (1974) *The History and Development of Tagmemics*, The Hague: Mouton.

H. PAUL GRICE (1913–88)

As in the case of 'Grimm's Law' and 'Broca's aphasia', coinage of the term 'Grice's maxims' established public recognition of an important language scholar, albeit by singling out only one of his contributions. Grice was a British philosopher of language associated with Oxford and, in the last twenty years of his life, the University of California at Berkeley. His central concern was the nature of meaning: what words and sentences mean, what speakers mean, and how listeners determine a speaker's intended meaning. He distilled his ideas about the cooperative basis of communication into a set of maxims that articulate the tacit assumptions governing conversational exchange. Grice's innovative work in semantics and pragmatics, including his analysis of how speakers and listeners employ Gricean maxims in conversation, has been seminal in modern linguistics.

Grice depicted his intellectual stance as 'dissenting rationalism' (Grice 1986: 46). He was raised in the industrial midlands town of

Birmingham, and educated on scholarship at Clifton College in south-western England, then at Corpus Christi College, Oxford where he studied Classics. Grice taught school for a year and then returned to Oxford, working his way up to the position of fellow in philosophy. He interrupted his career to serve in the British Navy between 1940 and 1945. After the war, he returned to Oxford, now as a married man, and resumed his position in an atmosphere invigorated by the debate between logical positivism and ordinary language philosophy (see **Ludwig Wittgenstein**; **J. L. Austin**). In 1967, Grice was invited to Harvard to present the William James lectures. Later that year he left Oxford for Berkeley, where he taught until his death (Chapman 2005).

Grice apparently guarded his privacy closely. Nevertheless, several biographical sketches advert to his attachment to playing cricket, piano (where in both cases his verve exceeded his finesse), bridge and chess, and to his tolerance for disorder. Two colleagues marvelled at the condition of Grice's office, 'a dreadful litter of ashtrays, old clothes, scattered books and papers, cricket balls and bats, and (always unanswered, often unopened) correspondence', adding that 'He was a man of formidable intellectual gifts, enormous energy, brooding temperament, and fiercely competitive spirit' (Stroud and Warnock 2004).

During Grice's student days, he studied with J. L. Austin and participated in Austin's famous Saturday morning meetings. Ever the dissenting rationalist, Grice took exception to certain practices and assumptions of Austin, and of Oxford philosophers in general (Grice 1986: 46–61). Neale (1992: 512) characterized him as 'at once an accomplished practitioner and the most resourceful critic' of ordinary language philosophy. Grice was unconvinced that philosophical dilemmas could be resolved by more perspicuous use of words. He also freely employed logical notation as a tool for capturing the meaning of natural language, and evinced scepticism that ordinary language philosophy had successfully evaded technical terminology. On the other hand, Grice accepted what he viewed as Austin's working assumption, that the properties of ordinary language are finely honed to meet communicative purposes, and that in this sense close examination of words could yield insight into the nature of philosophical problems, if not solve them outright.

Grice wrote a lot, lectured and taught a lot, and talked even more. But he published little, since he considered publication worthy only of completed projects. In the last years of his life, however, he did edit and assemble his most important works in *Studies in the Way of Words* (Grice 1989). One persistent theme was the problem of defining the meaning of utterances (defined broadly to include non-verbal communication). Wittgenstein had exhaustively identified the meaning of an utterance with its use. Grice's ideas evolved throughout his career, but he distinguished several dimensions of meaning, among them what a particular sentence means; what a speaker said by uttering the sentence; and what the speaker intended to mean by uttering it. These aspects of meaning are sometimes hard to differentiate, but emerge robustly in the interpretation of, for example, the false-jovial morning greeting 'Well, it's another day in paradise!' when spoken by one prison inmate to another. For Grice, part of the meaning of an utterance resides in the hearer's recognition of the speaker's intention. Speakers rely on their audience to work out rationally the specific intentions they harbour when they speak a particular utterance.

In developing his notions of meaning, Grice drew boundaries between semantics and pragmatics. That is, he had to articulate which parts of meaning derive from the properties of words and sentences, and which parts from the way words and sentences are used in social interaction. Grice's William James lectures (revised and published in 1989: 1–143) address the relationship of semantics to pragmatics, associating it with the relationship of meaning to implicature. His most famous essay from the lecture series, 'Logic and conversation', led the way by introducing Grice's two signature proposals: the Cooperative Principle and Gricean conversational maxims.

Grice first distinguished conventional from conversational implicature. About conventional implicature, he discussed the example 'He is an Englishman; he is, therefore, brave.' According to Grice (1989: 25–26), the speaker states outright that the man's bravery follows from his being English, but *not* that the source of the man's bravery is his Englishness. That latter aspect of meaning derives instead from a reasonable conventional implication of the sentence. Conversational implicature, in contrast, derives from 'certain general features of discourse'. Chief among them is that 'talk exchanges do not normally consist of a succession of disconnected remarks, and would not be rational if they did. [Rather, they are] cooperative efforts; and each participant recognizes in them [...] a common purpose or set of purposes' (*ibid.*: 26).

In other words, interlocutors generally observe a Cooperative Principle, stated as 'Make your conversational contribution such as is required, at the stage at which it occurs, by the accepted purpose or direction of the talk exchange in which you are engaged' (*ibid.*: 26). Conversation works as well as it does because speakers rely on each other to cooperate in these terms. In specifying what counts as a cooperative conversational move, Grice articulated his famous maxims under four categories.

> Category of Quantity
> (1) Make your contribution as informative as is required (for the current purposes of the exchange); (2) Do not make your contribution more informative than is required
> Category of Quality: Try to make your contribution one that is true
> (1) Do not say what you believe to be false; (2) Do not say that for which you lack adequate evidence
> Category of Relation
> (1) Be relevant
> Category of Manner: Be perspicuous
> (1) Avoid obscurity of expression; (2) Avoid ambiguity; (3) Be brief (avoid unnecessary prolixity); (4) Be orderly.
> (*ibid.*: 26–27)

The linguistic-theoretical and psychological status of Grice's maxims is not made explicit. In fact, Grice once wrote informally that the maxims may simply be 'special cases of what a decent chap should do' (Chapman 2005: 102). Nevertheless, the maxims are basic to his notion of conversational implicature. If an utterance seems, at face value, to flout one of the maxims (or, less conspicuously, violate it; opt out of it; or initiate a clash between opposing demands of different maxims; Grice 1989: 30), a hearer will search for ways to construe the utterance as still compliant with the Cooperative Principle. That is, hearers exploit their knowledge of the context of an utterance and of the interlocutors, drawing on plausible conversational implications that would rescue the utterance – rendering it informative, relevant, true, unambiguous, concise, etc., and thus conversationally cooperative. For example, imagine that a prison inmate says 'I'm bored', and his or her cellmate responds 'It's Thursday'. At face value, the response seems uncooperative because it apparently flouts Grice's maxim of relevance. Therefore listeners will look for reasons to reinterpret 'It's Thursday' as carrying some context-specific implication that on Thursday an event occurs that abates, exacerbates, or otherwise is pertinent to the prisoners' boredom. Insofar as some such implication is identified, the cellmate's response reminds the first speaker about the existence of the relevant Thursday event, and he or she will perceive the response as cooperative. It is important to Grice that conversational implications do not derive from the utterance itself, but from the external social-interactional context and speakers' expectations that conversation observes the Cooperative Principle. In this way, Grice distinguishes semantics from pragmatics.

Grice's impact has been felt widely in many fields (Lindblom 2001). Among scholars who have adapted or applied Grice's proposals are philosophers of language. Searle (1969: 42–50), who like Grice had studied with Austin, accepted Grice's investment of meaning in hearers' recognition of speakers' intentions. But Searle objected that Grice did not sufficiently bind meaning to the rule-governed nitty-gritty of words and sentences, and moreover failed to exploit the Austinian distinction between illocutionary and perlocutionary acts. In another influential work, Searle (1975) incorporated Grice's Cooperative Principle in his analysis of indirect speech acts. Speakers can perform the illocutionary act of requesting indirectly, Searle claimed, by questioning the felicity conditions associated with requesting. 'Could you drop me at the station?' therefore indirectly accomplishes the speech act of requesting, but only because hearers, holding fast to Grice's Cooperative Principle, construe the relevance of questioning the hearer's ability ('*Could* you ... ') to carry out the request.

Grice's authority has extended far into semantics and pragmatics, and adjacent fields. Anthropologists Brown and Levinson's (1978) influential analysis of linguistic politeness phenomena took Grice's maxims and his theory of conversational implicature as foundational. Brown and Levinson explored, cross-linguistically, speech that is perceived as 'polite', assuming with Grice that speakers and hearers expect conversation to be informative, relevant, true, unambiguous, etc., and therefore that deviations from those expectations may implicate attempts to communicate politeness. For instance, the utterance 'Your hat is ugly' may perfectly satisfy Grice's maxims. But because (in ways that Brown and Levinson analysed) it may not be interpreted as polite, the message is likely to be communicated in a more elaborated, less perspicuous, potentially ambiguous utterance such as 'Well, you seem to be wearing quite an unusual hat.'

Sperber and Wilson's (1986/1995) text *Relevance* is critical of Grice, but nonetheless constructs a theory of human communication directly on the platform of his work. They assert that the single essential organizing factor in communication is relevance – that is, the extent to which incoming information can be richly and readily integrated into existing information. Relevance in this sense does not simply subsume all Grice's maxims under the Category of Relation, but

Sperber and Wilson's exposition engages throughout in lively give-and-take with Gricean pragmatics. In a different approach, Ochs Keenan (1976), among others, questioned the cross-cultural validity of Grice's proposals. Ochs Keenan's classic fieldwork in Madagascar brought to light conversational norms that apparently eschew maxims like 'Be informative'. Speakers of Malagasy do not expect their conversational partners to satisfy their informational needs; to do so is relatively unusual behaviour.

In what may constitute the highest acknowledgement of Grice's influence, a heterogeneous subdiscipline labelled 'neo-Gricean pragmatics' began to emerge from the 1970s, often centring on critique of Grice's concept of implicature. Neo-Griceans have been succeeded by 'post-Griceans' (Davis 1998; Cosenza 2001; Atlas 2005: 80–148), signalling that Grice's reputation continues to evolve.

Grice's major works

Studies in the Way of Words, 1989, Harvard University Press, Cambridge, MA.

Further reading

Atlas, J. D. (2005) *Logic, Meaning, and Conversation*, Oxford: Oxford University Press.

Brown, P. and Levinson, S. C. (1978) *Politeness: Some Universals in Language Usage*, Cambridge: Cambridge University Press.

Chapman, S. (2005) *Paul Grice, Philosopher and Linguist*, Basingstoke: Palgrave Macmillan.

Cosenza, G. (ed.) (2001) *Paul Grice's Heritage*, Turnhout, Belgium: Brepols.

Davis, W. A. (1998) *Implicature: Intention, Convention, and Principle in the Failure of Gricean Theory*, Cambridge: Cambridge University Press.

Grandy, R. E. and Warner, R. (eds) (1986) *Philosophical Grounds of Rationality: Intentions, Categories, Ends*, Oxford: Oxford University Press.

Grice, H. P. (1986) 'Reply to Richards', in R. E. Grandy and R. Warner (eds), *Philosophical Grounds of Rationality: Intentions, Categories, Ends*, Oxford: Oxford University Press.

Lindblom, K. (2001) 'Cooperating with Grice: a cross-disciplinary meta-perspective on uses of Grice's cooperative principle,' *Journal of Pragmatics*, 33, 1601–23.

Neale, S. (1992) 'Paul Grice and the philosophy of language', *Linguistics and Philosophy*, 15, 509–59.

Ochs Keenan, E. (1976) 'The universality of conversational postulates', *Language in Society*, 5, 67–80.

Searle, J. R. (1969) *Speech Acts*, Cambridge: Cambridge University Press.

——(1975) 'Indirect speech acts', in P. Cole and J. Morgan (eds), *Syntax and Semantics: Vol. 3*, New York: Academic Press.

Sperber, D. and Wilson, D. (1995) *Relevance: Communication and Cognition* (2nd edn), Oxford: Blackwell (1st edn 1986).
Stroud, B. and Warnock, G. J. (2004) 'Grice, (Herbert) Paul (1913–88), rev.', *Oxford Dictionary of National Biography*, Oxford: Oxford University Press (www.oxforddnb.com/view/article/40655).

JOSEPH H. GREENBERG (1915–2001)

Joseph Greenberg was a controversial, highly original anthropological linguist regarded as one of the foremost scholars of the late twentieth century in the fields of typology, language universals, and the genetic relationships among languages.

As Greenberg (1986) himself tells the story, he started learning languages as a hobby in adolescence. Before he finished high school in Brooklyn, New York, he had studied German, Latin and Hebrew, picked up a little Yiddish at home, and taught himself some Classical Greek and Arabic. As an undergraduate at Columbia University, Greenberg took as many language courses as he could. In his last two undergraduate years, he discovered comparative linguistics and anthropology. A class with Franz Boas (1858–1942) introduced him to Native American languages. He also developed an interest in African studies. Greenberg entered a PhD programme in anthropology at Northwestern but also spent a year at Yale, where he was disappointed not to meet **Edward Sapir** but did study with **Leonard Bloomfield**. He conducted fieldwork in Nigeria for a dissertation on the influence of Islam on African religions. While he was there, he learned Hausa and puzzled over its genetic relation to other African languages.

After receiving his doctorate in 1940, Greenberg spent five years in the Army, then resumed his academic career with a teaching job at the University of Minnesota. In 1947, he accepted a position at Columbia, staying there until 1962 when he moved to Stanford. He retired in 1986 but continued his research at Stanford until his death.

Thus, in the course of his early career, Greenberg was exposed to a range of languages and to seminal figures in anthropology, American structuralist linguistics and Prague School linguistics – which he encountered through **Roman Jakobson**, whom he met at Columbia in the late 1940s (*ibid.*: 11). All of these influences contributed to Greenberg's distinctive approach to typology, universals and the genetic classification of languages.

Greenberg's lifework may have first come to him in his early exposure to languages. As a self-taught adolescent learner of Arabic, he marvelled at its similarity to Hebrew, although 'the reason for this similarity, of course, eluded me' (ibid.: 2). Much of his career was devoted to defining the nature and limits of cross-linguistic similarities, and to addressing the reasons behind them. Bloomfield and the mid-century American structuralists who trained Greenberg downplayed comparative and historical study of languages in the pursuit of 'scientific' description, building up from the smallest material units of a language, phonemes, to larger ones (see **Charles Hockett**). But Greenberg was not wholly at ease in this style of linguistics. In particular, he felt reluctant to abandon his commitment to comparison, or his curiosity about historical relationships. He found Prague School contrastive studies attractive, as well as Jakobson's notions of markedness and of implicational relationships holding across the features of languages. On the other hand, along with some post-Bloomfieldians, he questioned the rigour of European structuralist linguistics.

A breakthrough occurred for Greenberg in 1953 at a Linguistic Society of America summer Linguistic Institute seminar, where, disguising his own ambivalence, he presented to an audience of scholars from diverse disciplines the then-current descriptivist procedures for analysing languages. After Greenberg's talk, the psychologist Charles E. Osgood (1916–91) responded mildly that although those procedures all seemed admirable, a more impressive goal for linguistics would be to discover 'something that was true about all languages'. To Greenberg, the comment 'was to haunt me thenceforth and helped determine the direction of much of my future work' (ibid.: 13). Until then, typology had meant nineteenth-century wholistic classification of languages as isolating, agglutinative or inflecting in the styles of **Wilhelm** and **Friedrich von Schlegel**, **Wilhelm von Humboldt** or **Friedrich Max Müller**. Greenberg began to rethink typology using the tools of American and Prague School structuralists. Teaming up with Osgood and another psychologist, James J. Jenkins (b. 1923), Greenberg published a 'Memorandum concerning language universals', which sketched out plausible kinds of universals. The memorandum helped launch a meeting at Dobbs Ferry, just north of New York City, in April 1961, co-hosted by Greenberg. Linguists, psychologists, anthropologists and other scholars came together to propose varied universals of language and to discuss their relevance to different disciplines.

The conference proceedings, published as Greenberg (1963), include the memorandum and Greenberg's often-reprinted paper 'Some universals of grammar with particular reference to the order of meaningful elements'. This text set the tone for what is now recognized as Greenbergian typological studies. Greenberg surveyed a convenience sample of thirty languages, conceding its obvious biases due to over-representation of Indo-European and under-representation of Native American and Indo-Pacific languages. In his cautious, judicious, authorial voice, Greenberg distilled from this database forty-five generalizations about 'basic word order' properties, morphological categories, and the syntax of questions and subordination (*ibid*.: 58–90).

Some of Greenberg's universals are implicational: 'If a language has dominant SOV order and the genitive follows the governing noun, then the adjective likewise follows the noun.' Some are statistical: 'With overwhelmingly more than chance frequency, languages with dominant order VSO have the adjective after the noun.' Some are absolute: 'A language never has more gender categories in non-singular numbers than in the singular.' On the basis of forty-five such statements, Greenberg concluded the article by generalizing about how these facts pattern together to create coherent types of languages, and suggested a few overarching principles relating typological properties. But the heart of the article is the numbered list of universals loosely arrayed by topic. In this pioneering essay, Greenberg minimized whatever difficulties he encountered in classifying the properties of languages, implying that it is easy to decide whether a given language is predominantly prefixing or suffixing, or whether nouns precede or follow adjectives. Moreover, he did not justify his universals with respect to external generalities, nor try to explain why these forty-five universals obtain and not others.

Greenberg's article did model techniques for step-by-step induction of what human languages share, presented in accessible, easily recognizable terms. His work gave impetus to the Stanford Project on Languages, which continued from 1967 to 1976 under Greenberg's co-direction. The goal of this large, collaborative project was to amass a body of empirical generalizations about the structures of human languages. It produced a four-volume collection, Greenberg (1978), covering phonological, morphological, lexical, syntactic and semantic universals. Varied as the papers in the collection are, Greenberg's influence is evident throughout, in the priority authors give to empirical accuracy over theoretical cogency, or even over perspicuity of generalization; in their concern for wide cross-linguistic representation; in their depiction of language differences as a web of hierarchical relationships; and even in the convention of presenting universals in numbered lists.

This style of 'data-driven' Greenbergian research opened the way for modern linguistic typology, which has since developed richly in the work of scholars such as Bernard Comrie (b. 1947), Matthew Dryer (b. 1950), Martin Haspelmath (b. 1963), John A. Hawkins (b. 1947) and Hansjakob Seiler (b. 1920). It has had a cool reception from another contemporary research programme into language universals, that associated with 'theory-driven' generative grammar (e.g. Coopmans 1984). Generativists look deeply into small numbers of languages, or even a single language – deeply enough to locate properties instantiated in native speakers' knowledge of grammar, but which are incompletely displayed in the surface facts of everyday language. To generativists, mass cross-linguistic comparisons are unlikely to locate the subtle properties that define language differences. Not one to retreat from controversy, Greenberg (1983/1991) responded to this critique by insisting that the two approaches are complementary and, moreover, that explanations in linguistics necessarily incorporate comparative and diachronic facts.

Greenberg's argument did not win over all critics, but neither style of cross-linguistic inquiry has supplanted the other. Since the early 2000s, a new initiative in language-typological research has been to assemble large numbers of descriptive studies of single languages or specific language features into massive, electronically searchable, databases such as the World Atlas of Language Structures (http://wals. info), supported by the Max Planck Institute for Evolutionary Anthropology. (For a review of WALS, see the journal *Linguistic Typology* 13.1, 2009.) The theoretical heterodoxy of this project, the range of data it encompasses, and their ease of access and manipulation, are novel. But the conception behind WALS, and much of its content, owe a debt to Greenberg's Stanford Project on Languages.

Greenberg's other major contribution, his research on the genetic classification of languages, is likewise both original and controversial. For Greenberg, the two branches of his work cohere: typological discoveries inform genetic classification and *vice versa*. Greenberg brought his familiar low-tech, data-intensive working style to bear on the classification of languages. Despite sometimes harsh criticism, he developed and persisted in a technique of multilateral comparison, looking for individual morphosyntactic and lexical sound/meaning correspondences across many languages. Greenberg painstakingly filled notebook after notebook, always in pencil, lining up words or grammatical features in one direction, then filling in cognates from diverse languages in the other direction (Croft 2001). Through this technique, he compiled evidence that (for example) many indigenous languages in the Americas, from modern Chile to Oregon, use *n* in first person pronouns or inflections, and *m* in second person

(Greenberg 1987a: 49–55). That a handful of languages might converge on these same pairings of sound and meaning might be due to borrowing or coincidence. But when Greenberg found many such sound/meaning matches across many languages, those facts counted for him as evidence for genetic relatedness.

Applying this technique (and excluding non-linguistic and typological evidence), Greenberg (1966) arrived at the conclusion that the languages of Africa comprised four families: Afroasiatic, Khoisan, Niger-Kordofanian and Nilo-Saharan. His claim first scandalized Africanists, but gradually achieved acceptance as correct. Greenberg subsequently investigated the languages of Oceania, Australia, and then Native America (Greenberg 1987a). His repeated syntheses of large numbers of languages into small sets of families met with increasing scepticism. Some scholars objected that Greenberg's criteria for similarity were obscure or unprincipled, and that he ignored the gold standard of genetic proof, comparative reconstruction of a proto-language. Others complained about factual errors in his data (Chafe 1987; Goddard 1987; Campbell 1988). Undaunted, Greenberg replied that his work was a necessary preliminary to reconstruction, since it reveals which languages would repay closer comparison. Moreover, he insisted that his search for sound/meaning pairs recapitulated work nineteenth-century historical linguists had carried out, if less self-consciously, in the groundbreaking analyses that led to the reconstruction of Indo-European (Greenberg 1987b).

Greenberg's final work, published posthumously, advanced his method to postulate a single, breathtakingly comprehensive, 'Eurasiatic' family comprising Indo-European, Uralic-Yukaghir, Altaic, Korean-Japanese-Ainu, Gilyak, Chukotian and Eskimo-Aleut. It would be of interest to a psychobiographer to note that on his deathbed, Greenberg regretted having not worked on Southeast Asian languages. They alone remain outside his synthetic vision of the relatedness of human languages.

Greenberg's major works

Universals of Language, 1963, MIT Press, Cambridge, MA.
The Languages of Africa, 1966, Indiana University Press, Bloomington, IN.
Language, Culture, and Communication: Essays by Joseph H. Greenberg, 1971 (A. S. Dil, ed.), Stanford University Press, Stanford, CA.
Universals of Human Language: Vols 1–4, 1978 (J. H. Greenberg, ed.), Stanford University Press, Stanford, CA.
'On being a linguistic anthropologist', *Annual Review of Anthropology* 15, 1986, 1–24.

Language in the Americas, 1987a, Stanford University Press, Stanford, CA.
Language in the Americas: Author's précis and reply to book review, *Current Anthropology* 28, 1987b, 647–52; 664–66.
On Language: Selected Writings of Joseph H. Greenberg, 1990 (K. Denning and S. Kemmer, eds), Stanford University Press, Stanford, CA.
'Two approaches to language universals', 1991, in L. R. Waugh and S. Rudy (eds), *New Vistas in Grammar: Invariance and Variation*, John Benjamins, Amsterdam and Philadelphia, PA (paper originally presented in 1983).
Indo-European and Its Closest Relatives: The Eurasiatic Language Family, 2001–02, 2 vols, Stanford University Press, Stanford, CA.

Further reading

Campbell, L. (1988) 'Review of *Language in the Americas* by J. H. Greenberg', *Language*, 64, 591–615.
Chafe, W. (1987) 'Review of *Language in the Americas* by J. H. Greenberg', *Current Anthropology*, 28, 652–53.
Coopmans, P. (1984) 'Surface word-order typology and universal grammar', *Language*, 60, 55–69.
Croft, W. (2001) 'Joseph Harold Greenberg', *Language*, 77, 815–30.
Goddard, I. (1987) 'Review of *Language in the Americas* by J. H. Greenberg', *Current Anthropology*, 28, 656–57.
Greenberg, J. H, Croft, W., Denning, K. M. and Kemmer, S. (eds) (1990) *Studies in Typology and Diachrony: Papers Presented to Joseph H. Greenberg on his 75th Birthday*, Amsterdam and Philadelphia, PA: John Benjamins.

CHARLES F. HOCKETT (1916–2000)

The American linguist Charles Hockett was a prominent post-Bloomfieldian, a scholar of the generation that variously developed language research inspired by **Leonard Bloomfield**. As one of the younger post-Bloomfieldians, Hockett also played a role in the sometimes constructive, sometimes bitter debates that accompanied the emergence of generative grammar as a competitor to post-Bloomfieldian linguistics. It is probably too early to assess objectively the extent to which generative grammar represents intellectual rupture versus continuity with its immediate disciplinary predecessors. But Hockett's writings will be important to that assessment. His other accomplishments are equally important: his fieldwork on Algonquian languages; his contributions to linguistic theory; his commentary on American descriptivism/structuralism as he and his peers (Bernard Bloch [1907–65], Zellig Harris [1909–92], George Trager [1909–92] and others) developed it in the 1940s and 1950s; his analysis of human language as a communicative system; his influential 1958 textbook.

Hockett first encountered linguistics, as an undergraduate and son of a faculty member at the Ohio State University, in the pages of Bloomfield's *Language* immediately after it was published in 1933. He was then studying Greek and ancient history. In graduate school at Yale, where he worked with, among others, **Edward Sapir** and **Benjamin Lee Whorf**, Hockett developed an interest in Native American languages and an abiding linguistic-anthropological mind-set. He conducted dissertation fieldwork in northern Wisconsin on Potawatomi, a Central Algonquian language now spoken by fewer than 1300 people, mostly residing in southern Ontario. Later, he worked on other Central Algonquian languages, Kickapoo and Eastern Ojibwa, with additional fieldwork in Mexico. At the 1938 and 1939 Linguistic Society of America summer Linguistic Institutes, he met Bloomfield and other luminaries. When he graduated with a doctorate in Anthropology in 1939, they helped him continue his studies at the universities of Chicago and Michigan during the pre-war dearth of academic jobs (Hockett 1980).

In 1942, Hockett was drafted into the Army. As Cowan (1991: 75) told it, he became a key player in the American Council of Learned Societies-sponsored Intensive Language Program (ILP), through which, under Cowan's oversight, linguists with training in fieldwork tried to meet the wartime need for foreign language materials and expertise. Cowan recalled Hockett's involvement as the ILP's 'best success story, the Chinese Episode'. In the autumn of 1943, the US military announced that it urgently required 205 officers to learn to speak and understand Chinese. Private First Class Hockett, with no knowledge of Chinese, was retrieved from his duties raking leaves at a military base in Virginia and sent to Yale for a quick orientation to ILP materials and methods. Six native speakers of Mandarin Chinese were recruited in New York and San Francisco as informants. Hockett, the informants, and the cohort of military officers assigned to learn Chinese boarded a slow boat across the Pacific. As the boat travelled west, the informants modelled the spoken language while the officers studied feverishly under Hockett's direction. By the time they arrived in China, they were reported to be in control of a 'respectable amount of colloquial Mandarin', sufficient to carry out their mission. Hockett himself learned enough to produce learners' texts and a dictionary. After the war, he published journal articles on Chinese phonology and morphophonemics (reprinted in Joos 1957/1966). When Cornell University hired Cowan to readapt the ILP to college-level foreign language instruction, Cowan in turn hired Hockett who taught (first) Chinese and (later) linguistics and anthropology. He remained at Cornell until his retirement thirty-six years later, publishing steadily through the 1950s and 1960s, into the 1970s. In 1964, Hockett served a term as President of the Linguistic Society of America.

A 1954 paper (reprinted in Joos 1957/1966) illustrates Hockett's contributions to the development of post-Bloomfieldian linguistics. He discussed what he called 'two models of grammatical description'. An 'item-and-process' model describes linguistic differences as resulting from the application of processes such as affixation or vowel harmony. In contrast, an 'item-and-arrangement' model avoids the implied prioritization entailed in deriving one form from a basic, underlying form; instead, it describes linguistic differences as patterned differences in the distribution of morphemes relative to each other. For example, in place of describing a particular word as generated by a process of reduplication of a root with voicing, a description in the spirit of item-and-arrangement might depict that word as consisting of two near-identical morphs, the second exhibiting a predictably different representation (i.e. voicing). Hockett conceded weaknesses to item-and-arrangement, but asserted that contemporary linguistic practice was prejudiced in its favour because it had been more thoroughly formalized (and he presupposed the advantages of formalization). The article points out analogies with mathematics that help clarify differences between the two models, then offers a skeleton formalization of the item-and-process model. Hockett ended with a list of criteria for evaluating models: ideally, they are valid cross-linguistically; specific; inclusive of all observed data; productive; and probably – Hockett hesitated here – efficient (Hockett [1954] 1957/1966: 398). Throughout the article, he contrasted how the two models variously succeed at reconciling problematic data.

Thus Hockett ([1954]1957/1966) illustrated the post-Bloomfieldian drive to develop an explicit, formal science of language founded on observation of language facts. In this, the paper corrects a common complaint that post-Bloomfieldian linguistics was essentially taxonomic, in the sense that it aimed only to label and classify language data, a misconception that Hymes and Fought (1975: 165–74) counter at length. Hockett and his peers were certainly concerned with describing, labelling and classifying language data, as preliminary steps in linguistic analysis. Some, in fact, preferred to call themselves 'descriptivists' rather than 'structuralists' (Joos 1957/1966: 96). But they developed elaborate, sometimes competing proposals about what the distribution of linguistic elements indicated about those elements' categorial memberships, and about their relationships to each other.

Many post-Bloomfieldians avoided relying on meaning to determine, say, what counts as an adjective. Some went so far as to treat meaning as scientifically intractable, trying to 'determine the forms of language, and all the patterns by which they combine into larger forms, without any reference to meaning at all' (Hockett 1968: 24). In the place of meaning, they relied on the distribution of words. A trademark procedure was Immediate Constituent Analysis (ICA), which recorded in diagram form the internal organization of a sentence (or phrase, or word) as a series of hierarchically arrayed, usually dichotomous subunits. An ICA of *She bought the new hat* is represented as a rectangular box divided into multiple strata, stacked up on top of each other in horizontal layers. Reading from the bottom up, the lowest stratum separates the words *She bought the new hat* from a marker of declarative intonation, set off by a vertical cut on the right side of the box; this indicates that a particular intonational pattern is separable from, but related to, the sentence as a whole. The next higher stratum isolates *She* from *bought a new hat* by a vertical cut, to represent the subject–predicate relationship. One stratum up, a vertical cut segments *bought* from *a new hat*, and so forth (*ibid.*: 158). In this way, ICA specifies the relevant hierarchically organized units and subunits and their relationships of constituency. Hockett's (1955: 150–54) *A Manual of Phonology* applied the technique to segment 'macrosegments' such as the sentence *I don't want to* into intonational units. Likewise, 'microsegments' such as the word *believer* can be segmented into variously stressed syllables; and syllables can be segmented into onsets, peaks and codas; etc. ICA was used widely as a tool for recording the patterned distribution of forms. Of course, the technique leaves open myriad questions about how to determine segmental boundaries non-arbitrarily. **Noam Chomsky** (1957), for one, argued that ICA subverts the assumptions of post-Bloomfieldian linguistics, in that it covertly relies on meaning to judge that *a new hat* coheres as a unit separable from *bought*.

A great deal of attention went to proposing, evaluating and modifying successive ideas about how to analyse and classify units of language. But at least in Hockett's writings, questions of distribution and classification are integral to theory construction. For instance, at each step of a critique of a proposed phonemic analysis, Hockett (1947, reprinted in Joos 1957/1966) reflects on the consequences of (e.g.) certain definitions of 'morph' *vis-à-vis* 'morpheme', or of accepting minus features or zero features as varieties of non-overt morphs.

Alongside this stream of work, Hockett also produced an influential essay on a topic that at first glance seems discontinuous with post-Bloomfieldian linguistic theory. Hockett (1960, reprinted in Hockett 1977) argued that language is qualitatively distinct from animal communication on the grounds that every attested human language displays twelve specific 'design features'. No animal communication system possesses all twelve, although birdsong and the behaviour of bees, gibbons and stickleback fish meet certain of the criteria. Hockett's features include some that seem incidental to the typical medium and context of use of human language rather than intrinsic to the definition of 'language': employment of a vocal-auditory channel (Hockett does not discuss the status of sign languages); broadcast transmission; rapid fading; the interchangeability of the roles of speaker and hearer; the fact that speakers can hear themselves speak while speaking. Others of Hockett's design features seem intrinsic to anything one might identify as a language: communicative gestures are specialized to accomplish particular goals, rather than being incidental to other states or processes; language has semantic content; signal/meaning relationships are arbitrary; linguistic units are discrete. Finally, human language is a productive, unbounded system; it is comprised of links between minimal meaningless, differentiating elements and minimal units of meaning; it is culturally transmitted.

The identity of, and the distribution of attention to, specific design features in Hockett's essay provides insight into his overall conception of language. It also instantiates his anthropological orientation, and the extent to which language was for him a key to 'Man's Place in Nature' – the title of one of his last books, and of the last section of Hockett (1958).

Post-Bloomfieldian linguistics was lively and productive in the 1940s and 1950s, but lost momentum in the face of the great vitality of generative grammar starting in the mid-1950s. The transition was sociologically tumultuous: the older generation resented being the object of what they experienced as brash, sometimes flippant critique; the younger generation resented what they perceived as wilfully uncomprehending obstruction of their powerful and comprehensive new linguistic model. The intellectual status of generative grammar relative to post-Bloomfieldian American descriptive/structuralist linguistics is still debated. Hockett, for one, at first cautiously welcomed Chomsky's contributions but, on further exposure, expressed strong reservations. In 1968, he presented a nineteen-point summary of Chomsky's views as of 1965, views Hockett rejected wholesale (although he found the exercise still fruitful in that it strengthened his confidence in 'our heritage of scientific linguistics as largely channeled to us through Bloomfield' [Hockett 1968: 88]). Hockett's assault on generativism met with little rejoinder.

A few years later, Voegelin and Voegelin (1971: 12) famously lamented what they called generativists' 'eclipsing stance', which discounted out of hand the work of earlier scholars and discouraged students entering the field from acquiring historical expertise. Doubtless Hockett found generativists' 'eclipsing stance' grating (although Voegelin and Voegelin suggested that **Roman Jakobson** and Bloomfield had each in their day adopted similar postures). However, this often-cited expression fails to recognize that eclipses are temporary, regularly occurring events: one object becomes aligned between the viewer and another, more distant object, occluding the latter. However, the viewer as well as both the closer and distant objects continue, unscathed, on their trajectories. Eventually, the closer object moves to disclose the distant object, still intact. Eclipses are spectacular – but they are transient, even predictable events in the complex ecology of time and space.

Hockett's major works

'Problems of morphemic analysis', *Language*, 23, 1947, 321–43 (reprinted in Joos, M., *Readings in Linguistics I: The Development of Descriptive Linguistics in America, 1925–56*, (4th edn), 1966, University of Chicago Press; 1st edn 1957).
'Two models of grammatical description', *Word*, 10, 1954, 210–34 (reprinted in Joos 1957/1966).
A Manual of Phonology, 1955, Waverly Press, Baltimore, MD.
A Course in Modern Linguistics, 1958, Macmillan, New York.
'Logical considerations in the study of animal communication', in W. E. Lanyon and W. N. Tavolga (eds), 1960, *Animal Sounds and Communication*, American Institute of Biological Sciences, Washington, DC.
The State of the Art, 1968, Mouton, The Hague.
The View from Language: Selected Essays 1948–1974, 1977, University of Georgia Press, Athens, GA.

Further reading

Chomsky, N. (1957) 'Review of *A Manual of Phonology*, by C. F. Hockett', *International Journal of American Linguistics*, 23, 223–34.
Cowan, J M. (1991) 'American linguistics in peace and at war', in K. Koerner (ed.), *First Person Singular II*, Amsterdam and Philadelphia, PA: John Benjamins.
Hockett, C. F. (1980) 'Preserving the heritage', in B. H. Davis and R. K. O'Cain (eds), *First Person Singular: Papers from the Conference on an Oral*

Archive for the History of American Linguistics (Charlotte, NC, 9–10 March 1979), Amsterdam and Philadelphia, PA: John Benjamins.

Hymes, D. and Fought, J. (1975) *American Structuralism*, The Hague: Mouton.

Joos, M. (1966) *Readings in Linguistics I: The Development of Descriptive Linguistics in America, 1925–56* (4th edn), Chicago, IL: University of Chicago Press (1st edn 1957).

Voegelin, C. F. and Voegelin, F. M. (1963) 'On the history of structuralizing in 20th century America', *Anthropological Linguistics*, 5, 12–37.

ROGER WILLIAM BROWN (1925–97)

Roger Brown was an American social psychologist whose pioneering data and distinctive research style have had lasting impact on the study of how children learn language. Through his publications, and through a forty-year-long teaching career at Harvard University and, briefly, the Massachusetts Institute of Technology (MIT), Brown's personal influence on a generation of young scholars shaped the late-twentieth-century culture of psycholinguistics, especially the subfield of child language development.

Brown identified himself as a psychologist interested in language, rather than a linguist. Consistent with that identity, he left several insightful reflections (e.g. Brown 1989) on why and how his career took shape. He was raised in Detroit, Michigan, in a large working-class family of boys that experienced financial hardship during the Depression. Brown's interests in literature, philosophy and opera would probably never have developed without the GI Bill, which supported his undergraduate education after a World War II tour of duty in the US Navy. His wartime service seemed memorable to him mostly for the hours he spent on board ships crossing the Pacific reading classical Greek drama and B. F. Skinner's book *Behaviorism*. The latter inspired him to major in psychology at the University of Michigan, continuing on to receive Master's and doctoral degrees. But his PhD dissertation on authoritarianism (a popular topic in post-World War II psychology) seems to have represented the endpoint of his commitment to the 'ancient and difficult problems' of his chosen field (Brown, in Kessel 1988: 396). During a disaffected post-doctoral year at Michigan, a lecture by the American descriptivist linguist Charles C. Fries (1887–1967) on the phoneme convinced Brown in one stroke that his future lay in the psychology of language.

In 1952, Brown accepted a junior faculty position at Harvard. He developed his gift for teaching by conducting courses on the

psychology of language, without having ever formally studied linguistics. In this he was hardly alone, since in his account (Brown
1958: x) the field of psycholinguistics had only been founded in the
summer of 1951 at Cornell in an effort to enrich psychological study
of language with the conceptual repertoire of American descriptivist
linguistics. But when Brown joined other scholars at Harvard, including
psychologists John B. Carroll (1916–2003), Jerome Bruner (b. 1915)
and George A. Miller (b. 1920), and linguist **Noam Chomsky** (all of
whom in different ways challenged the anti-mentalism of the day), he
found a different model emerging, of language as rule-governed,
creative behaviour. Out of his early experiences in this heady milieu,
Brown wrote *Words and Things* (1958), a captivating, unconventional
textbook that ranges over (among other topics) acoustics, techniques
for teaching reading, phonetic symbolism, talking animals, Whorfian
linguistic relativity, aphasia, and the language of propaganda. What
holds the book together is Brown's engaging, playful, but never self-
indulgent authorial voice, and his ever-ready susceptibility to the
prodigious wonders of language. Brown went on to write other
textbooks in psychology and social psychology. Some followed *Words
and Things* to become best sellers, while others proved too quirky or
too sophisticated for wide adoption (e.g. Brown 1965).

Words and Things undoubtedly attracted students to the field of
psycholinguistics, but it didn't quite persuade Harvard to offer Brown
a permanent position. He spent the years between 1958 and 1962
teaching at nearby MIT before being recruited again by Harvard
(retiring in 1994 as the John Lindsley Professor of Psychology in the
Memory of William James). Brown's return to Harvard marked a
new phase in his research. With the support of a five-year grant from
the National Institute of Mental Health, he initiated an ambitious,
imaginative project that produced his signature contribution to psycholinguistics. Brown conceived of a plan to record weekly or bi-weekly
samples of the spontaneous speech of preschool-aged children
growing up in monolingual English-speaking homes, for an interval
extending over several years. Kagan (1999: 8) depicted Brown's plan
as 'Baconian in the extreme' in that it deduced principles directly and
strictly from observation. The goal was to document the course of
normal language development, the study of which was emerging
from the tradition of casual and spotty parental diary studies, whose
generality and freedom from bias were open to question. Capitalizing
on the recent invention of the portable tape recorder, Brown or his
graduate students visited the homes of three children living in the
vicinity of Cambridge, Massachusetts, whom Brown named 'Adam',

'Eve' and 'Sarah'. They played with the children and observed their interactions with family members, recording at least two hours a month of natural language use per child.

Brown collected data in this way from Eve for ten months, and from Adam and Sarah for four years (Brown 1973a: 53). The recordings were then transcribed and meticulously analysed in a weekly graduate seminar that proved to be a hothouse for the next generation of psycholinguists. Brown and his students developed the technique of calculating a child's 'mean length of utterance' (MLU), measured in morphemes. The MLUs of Adam, Eve and Sarah turned out to advance at different paces, but Brown and his students used MLU as a basis for calibrating the three children's emerging grammars. They then mapped learners' linguistic achievements onto a staged developmental path. Having done so, Brown (*ibid.*) identified commonalities in how children at Stage I (including Adam, Eve, Sarah, and other children whose transcripts he analysed) expressed semantic relations. At Stage I, a child's MLU is approximately 1.75; Brown tentatively articulated eleven semantic relationships that children at this stage encode in (mostly) two-word utterances. For example, Sarah's utterance 'Sun gone' exemplifies the operation of reference 'Nonexistence'; 'Adam go' exemplifies the semantic function 'Agent + action.' Brown also noted (*ibid.*: 179) semantic relations that were rare at Stage I, such as 'Instrumental' utterances ('Sweep broom') or 'Classificatory' utterances ('Mommy lady'). A second focus of Brown's analysis was the acquisition of functional morphemes, which begin to emerge in Stage II (MLU *c.* 2.25). Working with data from various child learners of English, he found the order of acquisition of fourteen morphemes (such as progressive *–ing*, locative *in* and *on*, nominal plural *–s*) surprisingly invariant (*ibid.*: 271).

Thus, using MLU and a gridwork of staged developmental landmarks as tools, and buoyed by a sense of adventure, Brown and his students enthusiastically and meticulously explored diverse aspects of child language. Not all of the group's hunches or innovations panned out, and some of their discoveries now seem somewhat hollowly descriptive. Moreover, eventually the group conceded that the complexity of child language exceeded the analytical instruments then available. Nevertheless, Brown's students went on to lead the field of developmental psycholinguistics, and to transmit to their own students the intellectual excitement that marked their painstaking, collaborative analysis of the language of Adam, Eve and Sarah. Thus, aside from its scientific outcome, Brown's seminar cemented his reputation as an extraordinarily effective teacher. He trained a cohort of students who have had distinguished careers in diverse subfields of linguistics and psycholinguistics. Kessel's (1988) festschrift provides a list of the stellar students Brown mentored, and showcases their writings.

Another contribution Brown made is related. Not all of Brown's students inherited his distinctive working style, but it set a particular tone to the emerging discipline of psycholinguistics. Brown depicted his approach as 'a laborious, low-tech, minimally mathematical research style' which 'has always started out with some phenomenon and only later became theoretical' (Brown 1989: 49–50). Brown wrote that early in graduate school:

> I discovered a way of working that fully engrossed me and caused the hours to fly, and it has been a principal pleasure ever since. I have an almost Talmudic taste for poring over data, for hands-on solitary contact unmediated by machine, involving no human interaction, uncommitted to particular statistical analyses – involving nothing but the free exercise of the principles of induction.
>
> (*ibid*.: 49)

Although Brown adopted generative linguistics' mentalism and its commitment to the rule-governed nature of linguistic knowledge, his predisposition for 'informal but exhaustive induction' (*ibid*.: 51) was at odds with the theory-driven linguistics that was rapidly gaining momentum. Chomsky (1964: 39), for example, dismissed the collection and analysis of masses of data as largely futile; at best, it was a distraction from the more pressing task of discerning children's underlying competence. He suggested that psycholinguists abandon recording spontaneous data in favour of 'indirect and ingenious' experimental methods. In a characteristically mild response, Brown (1973b: 99) conceded certain flaws to his methods, but remarked that, although one cannot learn everything about children's linguistic knowledge through analysis of their performance, one can still learn something.

After Brown completed the first volume of a projected two-volume analysis of the data from Adam, Eve and Sarah (Brown 1973a), however, he reluctantly abandoned work on the later transcripts. He found that the sharp increase in grammatical complexity and evident greater individual variation as the children reached three or four years of age rendered generalizations much less secure. But that decision did not close the book on Brown's data. Since the outset of the project, Brown had freely shared his transcripts in mimeograph form with all interested parties. In 1981, Carnegie Mellon University psychologist Brian MacWhinney (b. 1945), along with some of Brown's colleagues and students at Harvard, conceived of an electronic archive of child language data, transcribed and uniformly coded so that users could search it for a wide range of language phenomena. The project since developed into the massive Child Language Data Exchange System ('CHILDES'; http://childes. psy.cmu.edu), subsuming more than 130 learner corpora (some accessible in audio and video) in more than twenty languages, alongside tools for transcribing and coding data, and an array of computer programs for conducting customized searches of the database (MacWhinney 2000). From 1999, CHILDES became a component within TalkBank (http://talkbank.org), an even larger online research database in linguistics and communication.

Despite Brown's own preference to work directly with real, unmediated language, he was pleased to see his data disseminated in electronic guise to others who found it useful. The Adam, Eve and Sarah transcripts are neither the earliest nor the most sophisticated among those archived in CHILDES, but they are still held up as prototypical. An electronic search reveals a sharp increase in the rate of citation of the Brown corpora since 1990, so that linguists and psychologists are still avidly dissecting utterances these three preschoolers made in the 1960s.

Brown's famous study achieved such prominence that it is surprising he published nothing on child language after the midpoint of his career. He did produce diverse and innovative short works (some collected in Brown 1970) on linguistic relativity, music and language, tip-of-the-tongue phenomena, and the sociolinguistics of politeness and pronouns. Brown was elected to the American Academy of Arts and Sciences and the National Academy of Sciences; awarded honorary degrees from York, Bucknell and Northwestern Universities; and honoured with the American Psychological Association's Distinguished Scientific Achievement Award.

Brown also deliberately left behind a gruelling psychosexual memoir of his last years (Brown 1997), a book that meditates with painful self-awareness on the afflicted private life of a man celebrated as much for his generosity and genial mentorship as for his professional success.

Brown's major works

Words and Things, 1958, The Free Press, Glencoe, IL.
Social Psychology, 1965, The Free Press, New York (2nd edn 1984).

Psycholinguistics: Selected Papers (with A. Gilman), 1970, The Free Press, New York.
A First Language: The Early Stages, 1973a, Harvard University Press, Cambridge, MA.
'Development of the first language in the human species', *American Psychologist*, 28, 1973b, 97–106.
'Roger Brown', in *A History of Psychology in Autobiography, Vol. VIII* (G. Lindzey, ed.), 1989, Stanford University Press, Stanford, CA.
Against My Better Judgment: An Intimate Memoir of an Eminent Gay Psychologist, 1997, Haworth Press, Binghamton, NY.

Further reading

Chomsky, N. (1964) 'Formal discussion', in U. Bellugi and R. Brown (eds), *The Acquisition of Language: Report of the Fourth Conference Sponsored by the Committee on Intellective Processes Research of the Social Science Research Council*, The Society for Research on Child Development.
Kagan, J. (1999) 'Roger William Brown 1925–97,' *National Academy of Science Biographical Memoirs*, Vol. 77. www.nasonline.org/site/PageServer?pagename=MEMOIRS_A
Kessel, F. S. (1988) *The Development of Language and Language Researchers: Essays in Honor of Roger Brown*, Hillsdale, NJ: Lawrence Erlbaum.
MacWhinney, B. (2000) *The CHILDES project: Tools for Analyzing Talk: Vols 1–2* (3rd edn), Hillsdale, NJ: Lawrence Erlbaum.
Pinker, S. (1998) Obituary: Roger Brown. *Cognition*, 66: 199–213.

M. A. K. HALLIDAY (b. 1925)

Michael Alexander Kirkwood Halliday, born in Leeds, England, and now affiliated with the University of Sydney, developed a distinctive and wide-ranging approach to language that has come to be labelled 'systemic functional linguistics' (SFL). SFL prioritizes meaning in the study of language, and is attentive to the social and textual context in which language is used. Halliday's ideas have been applied in particular to language education, stylistics, and the study of child language development. His influence remains strongest in the UK, Australia, Canada, and East and Southeast Asia, extending recently to Latin America. In the United States, Halliday is probably best known among educators and teacher-educators who find SFL's emphasis on what an utterance means in its context of use more attractive than generative linguistics' practice of studying idealized speech viewed as a product of an autonomous formal grammar faculty.

Halliday's career has been unusually protean. In 1942, at age seventeen, he volunteered to study foreign languages for the British armed forces, and was assigned to Chinese. Within three years, he was teaching that same course (Halliday 2002). When World War II ended, he went to China to continue his studies. There he worked with Chinese scholars, including Luo Changpei (1899–1958) and Wang Li (1901–86), whose insights deeply impressed him as he reflected on the nature of Chinese, and on the nature of language in general. Returning to England in 1950 to enter a doctoral programme, he ended up writing a dissertation on fourteenth-century Chinese under **J. R. Firth**. Some assign Halliday to a 'neo-Firthian' school, or view Halliday as having applied and elaborated Firth's innovations. Halliday has not adopted those self-representations, although he certainly acknowledges his teacher's influence on his own thinking, alongside that of the writings of **Benjamin Lee Whorf** and, through Firth, the Polish anthropologist Bronisław Malinowski (1884–1942).

During Halliday's graduate studies and as a young PhD, he explored a wide range of theoretical stances. He participated in working groups of linguists, ranging from the venerable Philological Society, to the linguistics group of the British Communist Party, to a Cambridge University research unit on machine translation, and to an informal precursor of what later became the Linguistic Association of Great Britain. By 1954, Halliday was a full-time instructor in Chinese at Cambridge while he finished his dissertation. Four years later he moved to the University of Edinburgh, where he first began teaching linguistics and exploring its relevance to education. In 1963, when he returned to London, to University College, Halliday continued collaborating with teachers and writing about language and grammar both for and with educators.

Rather than settling in London, however, Halliday moved repeatedly over the next decade, accepting short appointments at the Center for Advanced Study in the Behavioral Sciences at Stanford, at Brown University, and at the Universities of Nairobi, Illinois and Essex. In 1976, Halliday immigrated to Australia to join the faculty of the University of Sydney. Since being appointed Emeritus Professor in 1988, he has been honoured as a visiting scholar in Singapore, Japan, Greece, Canada and China. Halliday has co-authored many of his major works with collaborators from around the world, so that the international scope of his career has no doubt shaped the development of SFL. His travels have also effectively spread his ideas: an International Systemic Functional Congress has convened annually since 1974, rotating among venues in the UK, Australia, Asia and Canada, often hosted by local national associations that bring together scholars who work with SFL.

The spread of SFL is also a product of Halliday's extraordinary scholarly productivity and catholicity. Drawing data mostly from English and Chinese, he has authored or co-authored more than twenty books and 100 other publications, ranging over computational linguistics, language pedagogy, literacy, sociolinguistics (especially language and social class), intonation, stylistics and literary analysis, speech versus writing, child language development, corpus linguistics, the language of science, and many aspects of descriptive linguistics (including transitivity, semantics, word order, prosody, lexis).

Unifying these diverse topics is Halliday's distinctive outlook. SFL takes a functionalist, social-semiotic approach, that is, it assumes that language is what it is because of its role as a tool of social communication. Texts, both written and spoken, communicate meaning through the choices writers and speakers make within specific social contexts; those choices reflect subtly different communicative purposes. Hallidayan theory characteristically deals in triads. For example, Halliday (1994) posits three 'meta-functional constructs' of language, or three 'kinds of meaning'. These are (1) ideational: the capacity of language to inform, associated especially with clausal transitivity (i.e. the presence of an object with a verb like *slap*, versus absence of an object with *disappear*); (2) interpersonal: the linguistic expression of social-relational meaning, associated with modality (i.e. constructions that communicate permission, obligation, possibility, necessity, etc.); and (3) textual: whereby the relevance and local utility of a text is established, such as through devices that enhance textual coherence, or that identify thematic (given) versus rhematic (new) information. Halliday aligns each of the three meta-functional constructs to one of three features of the 'context of situation' of a text (a term borrowed from Malinowski, and also central to Firth's writing; Halliday 1989: 5–7). The ideational meta-function he aligns with the 'field of discourse' of a text, essentially what a text is about, in the sense of being recognized as (say) a letter of apology or a congratulatory toast. The interpersonal meta-function Halliday aligns with the 'tenor of discourse', by which he refers to the participants in a communicative act and their roles and relationships. The textual meta-function he aligns with the 'mode of discourse', under which rubric he discusses matters such as the organization of a text, its status as written or spoken language, or its identification with a specific rhetorical mode such as persuasion or exposition (*ibid.*: 12–14).

The double threefold distinctions between meta-functional constructs and the field, tenor, and mode of the context of situation are one of SFL's best known analytical tools. Halliday has also created an intricate taxonomic metalanguage that extends from the scrutiny of individual words and sounds to the analysis of large-scale linguistic phenomena in fields such as sociolinguistics, literary studies and historical linguistics. Much of Halliday's work is highly original, or at least can surprise a reader narrowly trained in twenty-first-century formal linguistics. As examples of his intellectual independence, consider Halliday's self-confident embrace of the virtues of descriptive linguistics; his exposition of the grammar of English by beginning with the clause, then proceeding to address levels 'below' the clause (phrases), 'above' the clause (subordination), 'beside' the clause (intonation), 'around' the clause (ellipsis), and 'beyond' the clause (metaphor) (Halliday 1994: v–viii); his detailed discussion of the special features of what he calls 'little texts', including product labels ('Quality Tomatoes'), instructions ('Take key from lock'), or headlines ('Market Buoyant') (*ibid*.: 392–97); and his robust appreciation (*Collected Works*, Vol. 3: 258–61) of the British sociologist Basil Bernstein (1924–2000), whose contrast between the 'restricted code' of working-class speech and the 'elaborated code' of middle-class speech has been criticized as elitist.

A provocative 1990 paper illustrates both the unconventionality and the scope of Halliday's work. 'New ways of meaning: the challenge to applied linguistics' was originally presented in Thessaloniki, Greece, as a plenary address to the Ninth World Congress of Applied Linguists (*Collected Works*, Vol. 3: 139–74). Halliday begins by observing that language-planning initiatives by applied linguists commonly address the lexical resources of a language but rarely its grammar, aside from efforts to correct perceived errors. Grammar is less amenable to language planning because – adopting a position he attributes to Whorf – Halliday claims that lexicogrammar ('grammar plus vocabulary', *ibid*.: 145) shapes human experience, providing speakers with a theory by which they construe the material world. At the same time, changing material circumstances influence language, so that lexicogrammar 'construes reality according to the prevailing means and relation of production'. Thus language evolves slowly over the course of human history, and in doing so provides new metaphors by which speakers understand the world (*ibid*.: 145–46).

Halliday claims that upheavals in human history have co-occurred with linguistic upheavals, 'change[s] in ways of meaning' (*ibid*.: 147). He identifies three such events: (1) the shift from hunting to agriculture gave birth to writing and a lexicogrammar that attends to things over processes, and that counts, lists and classifies nominals; (2) the Eurasian iron age extended that trend, objectifying experience in complex nominalizations and technical language; and (3) the Renaissance and industrial revolution gave rise to even more abstract, 'learned, bureaucratic, and technocratic' (ibid.: 149) language. Although Halliday asserts that lexicogrammar reflects a society's technological basis, he does not expect 'semohistory' to account for every detail of language. Moreover, because linguistic phenomena may mix layers of the semiotic residue of different historical experiences, he allows that within the same speech community, subgroups (for example, different social classes) may differentially draw on those residues to create speech styles that vary in their propensity for abstraction and objectification.

With this introduction, Halliday then looks more closely at the history of English. He sees evidence for a realignment of the language's metafunctional priorities from the ideational to the textual in the sense that modern spoken English takes less and less for granted about the listener. For example, increased use of passive voice and phrasal verbs shift new information into sentence-final position, explicitly marking what counts as rheme (novel or unpredictable information) rather than theme (already established, predictable information). This apparent drive to accommodate listeners whose orientation the speaker cannot anticipate tacitly undermines the assumption of shared experience between speaker and hearer. Meanwhile, in scientific discourse, the information age has produced – and has been construed through – increasingly complex and metaphorical nominalizations in which 'the world of things [is] symbolically fixed so that they can be observed and measured, reasoned about, and brought into order' (ibid.: 159) in the service of an unquestioned commitment that 'growth is good' (ibid.: 162). Together, these trends define a stance that relentlessly objectifies other people as distinct from the self and treats the material world as the natural target of exploitation.

The prestige of this register (where 'the ways of meaning of the listener are precisely not taken for granted'; ibid.: 156) is not limited to English, but affects other languages as well. But taking English as an example, Halliday analyses four instances of how the inner properties of lexicogrammar, as a 'theory of experience', impose what he views as dysfunctional ways of construing the world: (1) the mass/count noun distinction treats natural phenomena such as air, water, soil, oil or coal as inherently unlimited; (2) among gradeable nouns, value predictably correlates with quantity: 'the grammar of "big" is the grammar of "good"' (ibid.: 165); (3) humans are the most likely agents of transitive verbs, except for the semantic class of verbs of destruction or damage; (4) the grammar of pronouns, inter alia, sharply distinguishes conscious versus non-conscious entities, setting human beings (using the terms *I*, *she*, *us*, *them*) apart from all other 'living' or 'non-living' forms (*it*).

To redress rampant 'growthism', Halliday does not recommend that language planners manipulate English lexicogrammar. He advocates, rather, that speakers rethink some of the choices they make, perhaps replacing the discourse of war with that of peace; commercialism and credit with saving; and building with keeping under repair.

Halliday's presentation to the Ninth World Congress of Applied Linguists has been identified as an early contribution to an emerging subfield of 'ecolinguistics'. Although Halliday is too dynamic and ambitious a thinker to produce a 'typical' text, this essay demonstrates the breadth of systemic functional linguistics' analysis of language within its social and textual context.

Halliday's major works

Language, Context, and Text: Aspects of Language in a Social-Semiotic Perspective (with R. Hasan), 1989, Oxford University Press, Oxford.
An Introduction to Functional Grammar (2nd edn), 1994, Edward Arnold, London.
Collected Works of M. A. K. Halliday: Vols 1–10, 2002–07, (J. Webster, ed.), Continuum, London and New York.

Further reading

Butt, D. G. (2001) 'Firth, Halliday and the development of systemic functional theory', in S. Auroux, E. F. K. Koerner, H.-J. Niederehe and K. Versteegh (eds), *History of the Language Sciences: Vol. 2*, Berlin and New York: Walter de Gruyter.
Halliday, M. A. K. (2002) 'M. A. K. Halliday' in K. Brown and V. Law (eds), *Linguistics in Britain: Personal Histories*, Oxford: Blackwell.
Halliday, M. A. K. and Fawcett, R. P. (eds) (1987) *New Developments in Systemic Linguistics: Vol. 1: Theory and Description*, London: Pinter.
Fawcett, R. P. and Young, D. (eds) (1988) *New Developments in Systemic Linguistics: Vol. 2: Theory and Application*, London: Pinter.

WILLIAM LABOV (b. 1927)

William Labov is one of the most influential American linguists of his generation. He has made significant contributions to scholarship on language variation and language change (especially sound change), and established a recognizable style of research on regional, ethnic and social class-based dialects that attends to how 'native speakers communicat[e] with each other in everyday life' (Labov 1972a: 184). In addition, because Labov has characteristically worked at the interface of academic linguistics and public policy, his ideas have had an impact on educational practice in the United States, and on debate about the status of non-standard dialects.

Labov came to linguistics late. He grew up in New Jersey, then studied English and philosophy at Harvard, where he 'spent most of [his] time talking' (Labov 2001: 457). From 1949 to 1960, Labov was employed as an industrial chemist, making printing ink for a firm in Ridgefield, New Jersey. Later, he credited that experience as having developed in him an abiding regard for the linguistic skills of working-class people, and (after he left the printing industry to go into linguistics) a commitment to study authentic language as it occurs in actual, concrete conversations.

Abandoning his first career, Labov entered Columbia University to study under Uriel Weinreich (1926–67), whose research in bilingualism, dialectology and, especially, language change connected Weinreich to the work of his teacher, French functionalist André Martinet (1908–99). Koerner (2002) proposed an intellectual genealogy connecting Labov through Weinreich to Martinet, and hence to Antoine Meillet (1866–1936); then from Meillet through **Ferdinand de Saussure** to **William Dwight Whitney**. Labov's 1963 Master's thesis (reprinted in Labov 1972a) remains one of his most frequently cited works. This study analysed language change on the island of Martha's Vineyard, off the coast of Massachusetts. Labov found that young people who identified with the local community were reintroducing a centralized vowel in the place of the diphthongs in words such as *right* and *house* by way of covertly distinguishing their own indigenous Vineyard speech from the speech of summer visitors to the island and people recently arrived from the mainland. This study of Martha's Vineyard vowels anticipated much of Labov's later work, in two ways. First, it presupposed the salience of social context in language change, a consistent theme throughout his career. Second, it sought ways to work around the 'Observer's Paradox' (*ibid.*: 209), that is, the problem of collecting valid data despite the distortions imposed by speakers' self-consciousness of having their speech observed.

Labov went on to write a dissertation at Columbia that analysed social class-based linguistic variation in New York City. Published as Labov (1966/2006), the thesis subsumes another influential study, an analysis of post-vocalic *r* that pioneered ingenious techniques of 'rapid and anonymous' (Labov 1972a: 210) data collection. Labov set out to discover whether the frequency of r in New Yorkers' spontaneous speech correlated with social status and with self-consciousness of pronunciation. He gathered data from 264 employees at three department stores, by approaching each one to pose a question strategically designed to elicit the r-containing response 'Fourth floor' (e.g. he might ask 'Where are the women's shoes?'). To elicit a more self-conscious pronunciation of the same phrase, Labov feigned incomprehension by saying 'Excuse me?' He then tabulated the presence versus absence of word-medial r in 'fourth' and word-final r in 'floor' as a function of casual versus careful pronunciation, and also of the employee's sex, estimated age and occupational role (clerk, cashier, stockboy, etc.). Labov incorporated social class as an additional variable by collecting data in three Manhattan stores that cater to high-, middle- or working-class clienteles – Saks Fifth Avenue, Macy's, S. Klein – under the assumption that employees 'tend to borrow prestige from their customers' (Labov 1966/2006: 41), shaping their linguistic behaviour accordingly.

Labov's results showed sharp stratification, with employees at Saks displaying r at an overall rate of 62 per cent; at Macy's 51 per cent; and at S. Klein 20 per cent (ibid.: 47). In all three stores, employees used more r in careful than casual speech. Moreover, by comparing rates of r use among speakers of different ages within different (presumed) social class identity groups, Labov discovered a complex pattern of ongoing change within the total speech community.

After completing his doctorate in 1964, Labov joined the faculty of Columbia, where he continued developing fieldwork techniques and ways of quantifying empirical data so as to reveal the underlying orderliness of natural, unguarded speech. He worked increasingly on the language of inner-city African-Americans, especially adolescents. Labov's 1969 paper 'The logic of non-standard English' (reprinted in 1972b) champions the validity and systematicity of African-American vernacular English. Through multiple reprintings, this paper has played a key role in raising awareness of the features of 'black English' among linguists and educators, as well as in the popular press. Since the 1970s, Labov has contributed to legal disputes regarding language, including court cases that protested educational inequities originating in covert language prejudice. He has also brought public attention to linguistic issues at the root of schools' frequent lack of success in teaching reading, especially to African-American children.

In 1971, Labov moved to the University of Pennsylvania, where he began studying the evolution of white versus black speech in

Philadelphia. His research showed that the two dialects were growing further apart, a claim that contributed to a sociolinguistic debate known as the divergence controversy (Fasold *et al.* 1987; Bailey and Maynor 1989). In 1992, Labov and his colleagues launched a survey of contemporary dialectal variation that sampled, by telephone, the speech of about 800 English speakers across the United States and southern Canada. Data from Labov's 'Telsur' study have been ana-lysed acoustically and made available both in *The Atlas of North American English* with its accompanying CD-ROM, and on a website where the recorded voices of a selection of survey participants are accessible, organized by region. Results support Labov's long-standing claim that language change is increasing the diversity of American English, contrary to the common assumption that exposure to national mass media erodes variation. In particular, Labov cites an ongoing 'Northern Cities Vowel Shift' centred in urban areas between Syracuse, New York and Madison, Wisconsin, wherein the low vowels ɔ, *a*, and æ are rotating forward and upward in their places of articulation, while the front short vowels ɛ and ɪ are shifting back-ward. For these speakers, the first vowel in *coffee* approaches that in *father*, *lock* sounds like *lack*, and the vowel in *bet* is shifted backward toward that in *but*. A different but similarly complex chain shift, the 'Southern Vowel Shift', is under way in rural parts of the South, roughly from Virginia to western Texas. In these areas, Labov found evidence that front short vowels are being raised and tensed, while front long vowels are moving downward, and back long vowels for-ward. A third sound change has its locus in two areas, eastern New England and western Pennsylvania, spreading out from the latter region to influence speech across the western states. This change is the 'Low Back Merger', which neutralizes differences in the vowels of *cot* versus *caught*.

Labov asserts that such large-scale sound changes together have the effect of increasing dialectal differences in modern American English, especially since not all ethnic groups participate evenly. His work shows that the speech of African Americans living in inland northern cities shows little evidence of the Northern Cities Vowel Shift. Rather, their speech shares traits with that of urban African-Americans across the country. These data bolster the argument that white and black vernaculars are diverging.

Labov eschews the term 'sociolinguistics' on the grounds that it artificially segregates social factors from linguistics at large. Nevertheless, arguing as he has since the 1960s for an empirically based linguistics that is necessarily social, Labov continues to be a creative force of the first order in the field of sociolinguistics. He has been honoured by the Linguistic Society of America, serving a term as President in 1979; he is a member of the National Academy of Sciences and the National Academy of Arts and Sciences; he has been awarded various honorary degrees and, twice, Guggenheim Fellowships.

Labov's high profile does not, of course, exempt him from controversy. A theme in his work, that non-standard dialects are in every way as intricate and rule-governed as high-prestige standard dialects, has attracted popular and scholarly attention. But public consciousness has not accepted the idea, as revealed in 1996 when the Oakland, California School Board ignited the national 'Ebonics' controversy (Baugh 2004) by recognizing the legitimacy of African-American vernacular English. Moreover, Labov's 'socially realistic linguistics' (Labov 1972a: xiii) has not deflected generative grammarians from developing linguistic theory under what he considers the artificial, laboratory-like assumptions of an ideal speaker–hearer in a homogeneous speech community. There are also other critics: Vaughn-Cooke (1987) disputed Labov's evidence for the divergence of black and white English on the grounds that it indicates only differences, not change over time; Cameron and Coates (1985) argued that Labov's assumptions about the roles of women versus men in language change need refinement; Figueroa (1994: 69–110) reviewed objections that scholars have raised against his methodology, definition of a speech community, and employment of Saussure's *langue/ parole* distinction.

Labov's most controversial idea is the 'variable rule', proposed in the context of early generative grammar, which classified rules as either obligatory (applying whenever their input conditions are met) or optional (applying freely and unpredictably). In a classic article (revised as Labov 1972b: 65–129), Labov used variable rules to quantify the differential incidence of the copula in African-American vernacular, in which a speaker may say *But next thing I knew, he was on the ground* right alongside *He fast in everything he do*. Labov worked out the probabilities of deletion versus retention of the copula in specific phonetic and syntactic environments, associating each environment with a quantity between 0 (always absent) and 1 (always present). Cedergren and Sankoff (1974) developed Labov's idea, proposing in addition that such rules might be extended to specify variation associated with social class, age or gender.

A range of scholars, including Romaine (1981) and Newmeyer (1983: 77–80), have criticized Labovian variable rules. A common complaint is that they seem to entail that individual speakers keep track of, and adjust, their output so as to approximate group norms of variability. Bickerton (1971: 461) parodied this problem, imagining a variable rule for contraction migrating out of the predicted range of probability for speech community members A and B, causing B to '[say] to himself things like: "Good Lord! A's percentage of contractions ... has fallen to 77! I'll have to step up mine to ... what? About 86%?"' Another, related, critique is the unclarity of the status of variable rules with regard to the distinction between competence and performance: do they quantify what people know about language, or how they behave? That this issue would emerge makes sense within the overall context of Labov's work, granted that his abiding commitment to understanding real people's actual speech contrasts with the abstraction and idealization of language common in the linguistics of his time.

Labov's major writings

The Social Stratification of English in New York City (2nd edn), 2006, Cambridge University Press, Cambridge (1st edn 1966, Center for Applied Linguistics).

Sociolinguistic Patterns, 1972a, University of Pennsylvania Press, Philadelphia, PA.

Language in the Inner City, 1972b, University of Pennsylvania Press, Philadelphia, PA.

Principles of Linguistic Change, Vol. I: Internal Factors, 1994, Blackwell, Oxford; *Vol. II: Social Factors*, 2000; *Vol. III: Cognitive Factors*, 2008.

'How I got into linguistics, and what I got out of it', *Historiographia Linguistica*, 28, 2001, 455–66.

The Telsur Project (with S. Ash, M. Baranowski, J. Barrow and C. Boberg), http://ling.upenn.edu/phono_atlas/home.html

The Atlas of North American English: Phonetics, Phonology, and Sound Change. A Multimedia Reference Tool, 2005 (with S. Ash and C. Boberg), Mouton de Gruyter, Berlin.

Further reading

Bailey, G. and Maynor, N. (1989) 'The divergence controversy', *American Speech*, 64, 12–39.

Baugh, J. (2004) 'Ebonics and its controversy', in E. Finegan and J. R. Rickford (eds), *Language in the USA*, Cambridge: Cambridge University Press.

Bickerton, D. (1971) 'Inherent variability and variable rules', *Foundations of Language*, 7, 457–92.

Cameron, D. and Coates, J. (1985) 'Some problems in the sociolinguistic explanation of sex differences', *Language and Communication*, 5, 143–51.

Cedergren, H. J. and Sankoff, D. (1974) 'Variable rules: performance as a statistical reflection of competence', *Language*, 50, 333–55.

Fasold, R.W., Labov, W., Vaughn-Cooke, F. B., Bailey, G., Wolfram, W., Spears, A. K. and Rickford, J. (1987) 'Are black and white vernaculars diverging? Papers from the NWAVE XIV Panel Discussion', *American Speech*, 62 (Special Issue), 3–80.

Figueroa, E. (1994) *Sociolinguistic Metatheory*, Oxford: Pergamon.

Koerner, E. F. K. (2002) 'William Labov and the origins of sociolinguistics in America', in *Toward a History of American Linguistics*, London: Routledge.

Newmeyer, F. J. (1983) *Grammatical Theory: Its Limits and Its Possibilities*, Chicago, IL: University of Chicago Press.

Romaine, S. (1981) 'The status of variable rules in sociolinguistic theory', *Journal of Linguistics*, 17, 93–119.

Vaughn-Cooke, F. B. (1987) Commentary in 'Are black and white vernaculars diverging?' *American Speech*, 62, 12–32.

NOAM CHOMSKY (b. 1928)

It is commonplace to identify Noam Chomsky as the most frequently cited living social scientist, and as a scholar whose work (spanning linguistics and sociopolitical commentary) is referenced on the order of Freud or Hegel (Barsky 1997: 3; www.chomsky.info). In linguistics, Chomsky is arguably the single most influential contemporary figure, a thinker whose ideas other linguists take into account in defining their own positions, whether they agree with him or not. Nevertheless, Chomsky himself characteristically adopts the stance of an outsider, insisting that his views hold little weight with the majority of other linguists, and that he works on the edge of the discipline (Chomsky 1982/2004: 67–70). The paradox of a self-perceived outsider's apparent centrality to the field can be resolved, however, by recognizing that Chomsky's work pursues a very specific goal, namely that of explaining – not describing – the nature and acquisition of language as an instrument for probing the human mind. By insisting on his marginality, Chomsky communicates the value he ascribes, quite narrowly, to this goal. Claiming for himself a position outside the mainstream of linguistics is also consistent with his public stance within his other vocation, as a political activist and commentator on current events and the media from a libertarian-socialist standpoint. In this field as well, Chomsky has achieved international stature (if not acceptance) for his fierce and tireless criticism of every sort of institutionalized abuse of power, especially that by governments, corporations and academics.

Chomsky grew up in lower-middle-class Philadelphia. Both his immigrant parents were professionally involved in Jewish education. His father was a scholar of Hebrew of some renown. Chomsky was raised in an atmosphere of intense engagement with Jewish cultural and intellectual issues. In adolescence, he explored left-wing politics, avidly reading about and debating anarchism, Marxism, fascism, the Spanish Civil War, and the possibility of Arab–Jewish cooperation in Palestine. Chomsky entered the University of Pennsylvania at age sixteen, but found college student life so alienating that by his second year he considered dropping out. Then, in 1947, he met faculty member Zellig Harris (1909–92), a major structuralist linguist influenced by **Edward Sapir**, who was sympathetic to Chomsky's political and intellectual commitments (Barsky 1997: 47–52). Harris's interests were in mathematical models of language, methodology of linguistics and discourse analysis. At Harris's suggestion, Chomsky enrolled in courses in philosophy, mathematics and linguistics. He wrote an honours thesis on Modern Hebrew morphophonemics, which he expanded into a Master's thesis submitted in 1951.

Chomsky then left for Cambridge, Massachusetts, where he had been named a Junior Fellow of the Harvard Society of Fellows. This position supported him during four heady years of independent study and informal interaction with both young and established psychologists, philosophers, computer scientists and linguists, some of whom were instrumental in the emergence of cognitive science. Chomsky had little sympathy for humanistic study of language, and also viewed sceptically the extension of behaviourist psychology to linguistics, then in vogue at Harvard. Nevertheless, he found the atmosphere highly stimulating. While simultaneously keeping up his political activities, he produced a long, unwieldy manuscript in which he tried to formalize an innovative linguistic theory that challenged American structuralism. Chomsky submitted a chapter to Harris in 1955 in lieu of a doctoral dissertation, and was granted a PhD from the University of Pennsylvania.

Chomsky then got a job at Massachusetts Institute of Technology (MIT). At first he held a vaguely defined position within a machine translation laboratory, an experience that hardened his critique of the structuralist and behaviourist assumptions underlying that branch of research (*ibid.*: 86–87). Eventually, Chomsky began teaching undergraduates his novel approach to linguistics. With the publication of materials he created for this course as the book *Syntactic Structures* (Chomsky 1957), and of his detailed and negative review of B. F. Skinner's 1957 book applying behaviourism to language (Chomsky

1959), he quickly achieved notoriety as a critic of the disciplinary *status quo*. Some were put off by Chomsky's point-blank rejection of established assumptions and methods in linguistics, as well as by his personal brashness. Others were intrigued. A critical mass of scholars and students gathered at MIT to work through these new ideas, originally labelled 'transformational generative grammar', later 'generative theory'. A graduate programme developed, with Chomsky appointed professor of linguistics in 1961. He remained at MIT, and continues to write prolifically about both linguistics and politics and to lecture worldwide.

In Chomsky's work in linguistics, certain interlocking themes have persisted from the late 1950s, sustained alongside distinct stages in the development of generative theory. One such theme is the creativity of language, cited throughout Chomsky's writings. He points out that ordinary speakers routinely generate novel utterances, rather than imitate fixed configurations of words from a finite repertoire. On the basis of this observation, Chomsky (1959) asserted the fundamental inadequacy of any linguistic theory that reduces language to an accretion of stimulus and response contingencies. To Chomsky, grammar is not a set of habits or memorized patterns, but rather a system of abstract, formal rules (or – in later versions of generative theory – principles), the operation of which produces an infinite output.

Another consistent theme in generative theory is related. Contradicting what he viewed as the rigid empiricism and anti-mentalism of post-Bloomfieldian structuralism, Chomsky affirmed that the object of scientific linguistic scrutiny must necessarily be the tacit, internal knowledge that speakers possess, rather than the external evidence of how speakers use language. In his terms, linguistic theory should account for competence, not performance. By shifting the focus of inquiry from observable behaviour to the mind, Chomsky (1965: 3–9; 1966/2009) self-consciously allied generative theory with what he perceives as a rationalist tradition, in which such earlier language scholars as **Wilhelm von Humboldt** and the Port Royal grammarians **Claude Lancelot** and **Antoine Arnauld** also participated. Despite questions historians of linguistics have raised about Chomsky's juxtaposition of rationalism and empiricism (Thomas 2004: 109–19), he maintains that generative theory is a modern outcropping of a long-standing intellectual tradition that American descriptivism/structuralism had submerged.

A third theme is also related to Chomsky's assertions about the creativity of language and its basis in the mind. Chomsky rejects data-driven research that starts with collection and comparison of linguistic facts in the style of **Joseph Greenberg** or **Leonard Bloomfield**. Instead, his approach is informed by demonstrations of 'the poverty of the stimulus', that is, evidence that children have limited and haphazard exposure to the structure of language, yet exhibit strikingly complex and convergent grammatical knowledge. On these grounds, Chomsky argues that the rules or principles that govern language constitute part of a biologically based human language faculty. The environment provides learners with information about the sounds and forms of individual words. But learners do not construct their complex structural knowledge via induction from the environment: the poverty of the stimulus requires that that knowledge be given to them by nature (Chomsky 1980: 33–35).

These observations led Chomsky to reject post-Bloomfieldian linguistics, which in his view simply amassed and organized surface facts. Instead, generative theory aims to understand *why* language is what it is, and *why* languages both differ from and resemble each other. It looks deeply into small numbers of languages (or even a single language) – deeply enough to articulate the complex structural knowledge that constrains human grammars, but which may be only partially displayed in attested speech. Speakers' judgments of (un)grammaticality and of whether two utterances have the same versus different meanings are a key methodological tool. For example, in English as in other languages, an innate constraint may rule out the reflexive *herself* in its configurational position in *★We noticed that herself left early*. (The exact profile of this constraint varies cross-linguistically, and is the object of ongoing research; Chomsky 1984: 210–22; 1995: 92–110 illustrate successive stages in that research.) But, granted the robust linguistic creativity of children, the mere absence of such sentences in the environment does not suffice to inform children that reflexives are disallowed in that position. The goal of generative theory in this context would be to develop a model of speakers' competence that predicts their judgements about the distribution of reflexives, allowing *She considers herself resourceful* but ruling out *★We noticed that herself left early*.

Such an approach recognizes the creativity inherent in ordinary language use; it presupposes the poverty of the stimulus; and it ascribes knowledge of language to an internal, biologically given language faculty. Adopting these assumptions (more or less explicitly) from the start of his research career, Chomsky has consistently pursued the goal of explaining why human grammars assume the shape that they do, as an aspect of human cognition.

Over the course of fifty years, however, Chomsky has proposed
and then abandoned a succession of frameworks for carrying out this
research programme. At least three major stages in Chomsky's development of generative theory can be described, although a closer look
at his voluminous bibliography reveals far more complexity.
Chomsky (1957, 1965) represents his first approximations of a grammatical theory aimed at displacing American structuralism. This 'classic' model employed phrase structure rules (which define the order of
units of language: for English, subjects precede verbs, and verbs precede objects) to create abstract 'deep' structures. Transformational
rules (which depict how units can be moved, copied or deleted) act
on deep structures to produce the surface structures of everyday
speech. Chomsky (1957: 60–84) demonstrated how this version of
generative theory succinctly accounts for the complex distribution of
English auxiliaries in declaratives, questions, passives and negative
statements.

Chomsky's subsequent 'principles and parameters' model (Chomsky
1984, 1986) evolved to better address cross-linguistic variation.
Disposing with phrase structure rules and transformations, Chomsky
re-envisioned a language faculty composed of universal principles that
specify features necessarily present in all languages, and a set of parameters that constrain the application of those principles in cases where
they are instantiated differently in different languages. For example,
Japanese verbs follow direct objects, whereas English verbs precede.
Chomsky's 1980s grammatical model conceptualized this difference as
due to a switch-like parameter with two settings (Japanese: 'Object +
Verb'; English: 'Verb + Object') embedded in a principle governing
word order in general. Each of these two options presumably correlates with other grammatical properties, so that one challenge to
1980s generative theory was to discover the range of consequences of
each parameter setting.

Relative to earlier versions of generative theory, the principles and
parameters model more closely satisfied the criterion of explanation
over description. Chomsky (1995, 2002) advanced generative theory
further in that same direction by proposing a 'minimalist programme'.
In this framework, Chomsky reconceived and radically economized
the apparatus of generative theory by admitting only extremely general constraints. These constraints interact with the abstract features
that comprise words to eliminate unattested structures, obviating
specific principles such as those that govern reflexives. The minimalist
programme also aspires to better accommodate the biological basis of
language, granted that Chomsky has long insisted that the language

faculty be accorded the same status in the mind/brain as functions such as respiration or vision.

Chomsky's work has attracted abundant praise and abundant criticism. He has engaged in many controversies about the history, form and content of generative theory, with scholars who identify themselves as generativists and those who do not. Linguists worldwide participate in the development of Chomsky's specific theoretical proposals, explaining or building them up (Boeckx 2006) and dismantling them (Seuren 2004). There is also ongoing critique of Chomsky's background assumptions, such as the notion of the poverty of the stimulus (Ritter 2002). **William Labov** and **M. A. K. Halliday**, among others, object to analysis of language independent of its social and communicative context. Chomsky's contributions, nevertheless, remain vital.

Chomsky's major works

Syntactic Structures, 1957, Mouton, The Hague.
Review of *Verbal Behavior* by B. F. Skinner, *Language*, 35, 1959, 26–57.
Aspects of the Theory of Language, 1965, MIT Press, Cambridge, MA.
Cartesian Linguistics, 1966, Harper & Row, New York (3rd edn Cambridge University Press, 2009).
Rules and Representations, 1980, Columbia University Press, New York.
Lectures on Government and Binding, 1984, Foris, Dordrecht.
Knowledge of Language: Its Nature, Origin, and Use, 1986, Praeger, New York.
The Minimalist Program, 1995, MIT Press, Cambridge, MA.
On Nature and Language, 2002 (A. Belletti and L. Rizzi, eds), Cambridge University Press, Cambridge.

Further reading

Antony, L. M. and Hornstein, N. (2003) *Chomsky and his Critics*, Oxford: Blackwell.
Barsky, R. F. (1997) *Chomsky: A Life of Dissent*, Cambridge, MA: MIT Press.
Boeckx, C. (2006) *Linguistic Minimalism*, Oxford: Oxford University Press.
Chomsky, N. (1987) *The Chomsky Reader* (J. Peck, ed.), New York: Pantheon.
——(2004) *The Generative Enterprise Revisited*, Berlin and New York: Mouton de Gruyter (revised edition of interview first published in 1982).
Otero, C. P. (ed.) (1994) *Chomsky: Critical Assessments: Vols I and II*, London: Routledge.
Ritter, N. (ed.) (2002) 'The poverty of the stimulus', Special Issue of *The Linguistic Review*, 19.
Seuren, P. A. M. (2004) *Chomsky's Minimalism*, Oxford: Oxford University Press.

Thomas, M. (2004) *Universal Grammar in Second Language Acquisition: A History*, London: Routledge.
The Noam Chomsky Website: www.chomsky.info

KENNETH L. HALE (1934–2001)

Ken Hale was a legendary polyglot, a theoretical linguist, and an educator who worked to raise popular and scholarly awareness of endangered languages. He was affiliated with the Massachusetts Institute of Technology (MIT) in Cambridge, Massachusetts for most of his career. Although Hale's extraordinary linguistic expertise spanned languages of six continents, the bulk of his research was on the indigenous languages of Australia and the southwestern United States.

When he was six years old, Hale's family moved from Chicago to a ranch in Canelo, Arizona, in the mountains south of Tucson less than twenty miles from the border with Mexico. His linguistic talents emerged early, so that he picked up the Native American languages Hopi, Jemez, Navajo, O'odam and Pachuco (as well as Polish) before graduating from high school. Hale went on to major in anthropology at the University of Arizona. On the side, he participated in rodeos. He took first place in a bull-riding event as a college senior; a belt buckle he won as a prize he wore proudly for the rest of his life (Kenstowicz 2001: 411).

Hale enrolled in a graduate programme in linguistics at the University of Indiana, where he completed an MA thesis on Navajo and a doctoral dissertation on Papago (now called Tohono O'odam). Graduating in 1959, he spent two years in Australia documenting indigenous languages under a grant from the National Science Foundation. The initial goal was to determine the historical relations among Australian languages, although Hale also collected descriptive and typological data. He travelled around the western and north-eastern coasts of the continent, but settled with his wife and toddler son in the central Australian town of Alice Springs, to focus on members of the Arandic language family. Over the course of six subsequent visits to the country, Hale invigorated Australian linguistics by collecting and analysing data from speakers of dozens of languages, often in collaboration with other linguists (Simpson *et al.* 2001).

In his work overall, Hale set a famously high standard as a fieldworker. He had a knack for establishing easy, unassuming rapport with language informants of many walks of life, and then absorbing their languages with astonishing speed and accuracy. Hale's field notes and recordings, now archived at the Australian Institute of Aboriginal and Torres Strait Islander Studies, increase in value every year as the cohort of native speakers of languages he worked with dwindles.

After Hale's first trip to Australia, he returned to teach at the University of Illinois. He moved to the University of Arizona in 1964. His first publications, on Australian languages and languages of the American southwest, addressed anthropologists or comparative-historical linguists. But during the early 1960s, Hale discovered **Noam Chomsky**'s emerging work on generative grammar. He found it very congenial, and quickly adopted its terminology and conceptual apparatus. Hale (1965), for example, argued that grammatical transformations provide a succinct account of passive and nominalized structures in Lardil, spoken on Mornington Island off the coast of North Queensland. Far from being 'primitive' or 'archaic', Lardil is cut from the same cloth as familiar Indo-European languages, sharing the same fundamental properties as articulated by generative grammar.

In 1966, Hale moved to Chomsky's home department at MIT. Although he published occasional work in an anthropological vein throughout his career, after arriving at MIT his orientation shifted away from the description of languages towards specification of a human language faculty understood to be responsible for the range of cross-linguistic variation. He continued to study and document Australian and Native American languages, but also researched Irish, Basque, Igbo and Dagur (*inter alia*), and carried out extensive field-work on two indigenous languages spoken in Nicaragua, Miskitu and Ulwa.

Hale applied his formidable linguistic knowledge to the development of generative theory in at least two major initiatives still associated with his name. First, in 1983, Hale proposed the existence of a 'non-configurationality parameter' to account for certain properties of Warlpiri. Warlpiri is a Pama-Nyungan language – a family Hale had identified on the basis of his fieldwork – spoken near Alice Springs. It has features that make it intractable within then-existing generative theory. For example, Warlpiri word order is very flexible if not wholly free. The only apparent constraint is that an auxiliary-like element must appear as the second constituent in a Warlpiri sentence; nominal and verbal elements appear in any order relative to each other and to the auxiliary. Warlpiri also exhibits discontinuous constituents in the sense that apparent modifiers of the head of a phrase may be separated from it. For example, in a sentence meaning 'The two small children are chasing the dog', the word for 'small' may appear before or after 'children', with either or both (or neither) of the words for 'dog' and 'chase' intervening (Hale 1981: 1–2); the demonstrative 'that' in 'I will spear that kangaroo' may be separated from the noun 'kangaroo' by any number of other sentence constituents (Hale 1983: 6). A third salient feature of Warlpiri is extensive null arguments, in that subjects and objects of apparently transitive verbs may or may not be overt. Hale cites the fully independent utterance glossed 'spear-NONPAST AUX' as covering the range of meanings of 'He/she is spearing him/her/it', with context providing disambiguation as needed (Hale 1983: 7).

Hale viewed Warlpiri's flexible word order, discontinuous constituents and null elements as evidence that the relationship holding between the argument structures of words and their expression in the syntax differed fundamentally for Warlpiri compared with that relationship in, say, English. To label that difference, he built on a pre-existing but under-articulated contrast between 'non-configurational' and 'configurational' languages. In configurational languages like English or Chinese, a transitive verb imposes the requirement that its subject and direct object positions be filled in syntax (although in precisely-defined contexts, those positions may be phonetically null). In non-configurational languages like Warlpiri, however, arguments of a verb need not be linked to specific syntactic elements. Furthermore, a 'flat' syntactic structure prevails, rather than one in which subject versus object constituents bear predictable hierarchical relations with respect to each other.

In addition to Warlpiri, Hale questioned whether Navajo (Hale 1981: 36–42) and Japanese (Hale 1983: 44–45) were also non-configurational. He proposed that languages vary in their expression of non-configurationality, since independent grammatical principles may interact to block flexible word order, discontinuous constituents or null elements. For Warlpiri, however, Hale deduced additional consequences of non-configurationality, namely lack of evidence in the language that transformational rules move noun phrases; absence of expletives such as English pleonastic 'there' or 'it'; and lack of correlation between case assignment and sentence position.

Hale developed his concept of Warlpiri non-configurationality to account for a range of properties that challenged 1980s generative theory. His graduate student Julie Ann Legate conducted new fieldwork on Warlpiri by the light of 1990s generative theory. She found that its word order was more constrained than was previously believed, that 'flat' non-configurational syntactic structure was untenable, and that other facets of Warlpiri turned out to be theoretically tractable (Legate 2002). Hale did not live to see configurationality abandoned as a macroscopic syntactic parameter. But Legate's resolution of the apparent exceptionality of Warlpiri is very much in the spirit of Hale's 1965 work on Lardil.

A second major contribution that Hale made was through his long-sustained collaboration with MIT colleague Samuel Jay Keyser (b. 1935) on argument structure (Hale and Keyser 1986, 2002). This research addressed a broad swath of issues in the relationships between the meanings of words and their syntactic representations. In particular, Hale and Keyser probed contrasts between two types of verbs: strict intransitives like *laugh*, and verbs like *break*, which exist both as intransitives ('The glass broke') and as transitives ('She broke the glass'). The contrast surfaces in other languages, albeit variously exhibited. Hale and Keyser derived verbs like *laugh* from underlyingly transitive constructions. That is, in English 'He laughed', *laugh* is initially an object that moves to supplant the head of a semantically 'light' verb phrase, roughly parallel to 'He did a laugh'. The other kind of apparently intransitive verb, *break* in 'The glass broke', is also underlyingly transitive. *The glass* is initially in object position of *break*, but moves to fill the verb's empty subject position, albeit while remaining a non-agentive subject. By construing all verbs as various kinds of transitives, Hale and Keyser made sense of a range of morphosyntactic phenomena in (among other languages) English, Hopi, Miskitu, Navajo, O'odam, Ulwa and Basque.

Hale's research on transitivity aimed at specifying the nature of universal grammar in the generative sense. For him, the point of studying linguistic diversity was to distil out of it what is inherent in human knowledge of language, and therefore to deduce how languages are learned. In the case at hand, Hale worked to show that because there is a limited set of argument structure options wherein all verbs have underlying objects, learners can conceivably identify the syntactic structure of a verb on the basis of its meaning.

Hale's work on configurationality and on argument structure are two of his best recognized contributions. A powerful common denominator in all of Hale's linguistic research was his awareness of its cultural and sociopolitical context. Early training in anthropology had probably alerted him to the fact that a tide of extinction was already sweeping across Native American, as well as Australian, languages. From the middle of his career, Hale devoted considerable attention to programmes for language preservation and revitalization. He taught at a Navajo/English bilingual summer programme; developed curricula for language preservation initiatives; mentored graduate students in linguistics who were native speakers of endangered languages; and co-edited a handbook (Hinton and Hale 2001) on language revitalization for teachers, policy-makers and academics. The book presents practical, how-to advice for language preservation through education, advocacy, political action and the strategic application of modern media and technology, highlighting programmes that have been successful across the globe. Hale also organized a symposium on endangered languages at the annual meeting of the Linguistic Society of America (LSA) in 1991 (appearing in print as Hale *et al.* 1992), and made the topic a theme of his 1994 term as President of the LSA.

Hale represented language endangerment as a threat to linguistic scholarship and to human understanding of the diversity of language and culture. He also recognized it as a complex sociopolitical and human rights issue. Hale's long-abiding and culturally sensitive commitment to speakers of languages outside the mainstream and to their speech communities, in addition to his academic stature, placed him in a strong position to call attention to language endangerment. What many now view as the ongoing worldwide catastrophe of language death began before Hale's birth, and has outlived him. But because of his efforts, more people – native speakers of endangered languages as well as scholars and policy-makers – are engaged in the debate about its consequences.

Hale's major works

'Australian languages and transformational grammar', *Linguistics*, 16, 1965, 32–41.

'On the position of Warlbiri in a typology of the base', 1981, manuscript distributed by the Indiana University Linguistics Club.

'Warlpiri and the grammar of non-configurational languages', *Natural Language and Linguistic Theory*, 1, 1983, 5–47.

'Some transitivity alternations in English' (with S. J. Keyser), *Lexicon Project Working Papers No. 7*, and in *Anuario del Seminario de Filología Vasca Julio de Urquijo/International Journal of Basque Linguistics and Philology*, 20, 1986, 605–38.

'Endangered languages' (with M. Krauss, L. Watahomigie, A. Yamamoto, C. Craig, L. Masayesva Jeanne and N. England), *Language*, 68, 1992, 1–43.

An Elementary Warlpiri Dictionary, 1995 (revised edn), IAD Press, Alice Springs (originally work from 1974).

The Green Book of Language Revitalization in Practice, 2001 (ed. with L. Hinton), Academic Press, San Diego, CA.

Prolegomenon to a Theory of Argument Structure, 2002 (with S. J. Keyser), MIT Press, Cambridge, MA.

Further reading

Halle, M. and Richards, N. (2007) 'Kenneth Locke Hale 1934–2001'. National Academy of Science Biographical Memoir.

Kenstowicz, M. (ed.) (2001) *Ken Hale: A Life in Language*, Cambridge, MA: MIT Press.

Keyser, S. J. (2003) 'Kenneth Locke Hale', *Language*, 79, 411–22.

Legate, J. A. (2002) *Warlpiri: Theoretical Implications*. PhD thesis, MIT, www.ai.mit.edu/projects/dm/theses/legate02.pdf

Simpson, J., Nash, D., Laughren, M., Austin, P. and Alpher, B. (eds) (2001) *Forty Years On: Ken Hale and Australian Languages*, Canberra: The Australian National University.

JAMES D. MCCAWLEY (1938–99)

Jim McCawley first emerged as a leader within a cohort of upstart ex-students and colleagues of **Noam Chomsky** who challenged the tenets of early generative theory under the rubric of 'generative semantics'. Generative semantics caused a major rupture in linguistics in the USA from the mid-1960s into the early 1970s. Eventually, the critiques and counter-proposals that McCawley and others raised against generative grammar were either rejected, retracted, revised, ignored, or – in some cases and in some accounts – dismissed only to reappear later in altered guise within the next wave of generative grammatical orthodoxy. Unrepentant, McCawley went on to flourish as an independent-minded and versatile linguist, following his own intellectual muse with characteristic verve and remaining a principled conscientious objector to selected facets of generative grammar. His publications spanned the syntax and semantics of English, Japanese and Chinese; language and logic; phonology; the history of linguistics; **Otto Jespersen**; orthographical systems; lexicography; and pragmatics. He also commented on language issues in the popular press. Although McCawley became a prominent figure in American linguistics, his intellectual contribution worldwide is not of the same order as that of key thinkers such as, say, **Pāṇini** or **Ferdinand de Saussure**. Still, McCawley's work is important because it illustrates the heterogeneity of late-twentieth-century linguistics; and, granted the international scope of American linguistics PhD programmes, the tone he helped set for the study of language in the USA has also influenced linguistics in other countries.

McCawley was born in Glasgow, Scotland, to a surgeon mother and journalist/businessman father. In 1944, his family immigrated to the United States. They settled in Chicago. McCawley excelled in school, entering the University of Chicago at age 16 to study mathematics. He also enrolled in a few linguistics courses. After McCawley graduated in 1958, he got a scholarship to study mathematics in Germany at the University of Münster, but ended up spending most of the year taking language classes. (He eventually learned, among others, Japanese, Chinese, Russian, German, Dutch and Yiddish.) Back in the USA, he attended the 1961 Linguistic Society of America (LSA) summer Linguistic Institute, then entered the inaugural class of Massachusetts Institute of Technology (MIT)'s doctoral programme in linguistics. He studied with Chomsky, **Roman Jakobson**, Paul Postal (b. 1936), Edward Klima (b. 1931) and others. Chomsky directed his 1965 dissertation, 'The accentual system of modern standard Japanese' (Lawler 2003).

McCawley was hired by the University of Chicago directly out of MIT. He spent the whole of his career affiliated there, although he travelled widely as a guest lecturer and visiting professor. He frequently taught at the LSA summer Linguistic Institutes, and served as President of the LSA in 1996.

McCawley's first publications were in phonology. Faced with teaching courses in English syntax as a junior faculty member, he sought help from his friends and former teachers, principally Postal, John Robert ('Haj') Ross (b. 1938), a former classmate newly appointed to the MIT faculty, and George P. Lakoff (b. 1941), who had an undergraduate degree from MIT and was back in Cambridge while finishing his doctorate at Indiana University. Until McCawley moved to Chicago, all four were part of a lively and contentious linguistics counter-culture centred in Cambridge, within which Chomsky's ideas held unique prestige even among those who disagreed with him. McCawley, Postal, Ross and Lakoff debated Chomsky and others about the features of then-current grammatical model, later labelled the 'standard theory' (e.g. Chomsky 1965). In the course of many late-night telephone calls between Chicago and Cambridge, McCawley and his collaborators shifted from probing underdeveloped aspects of the standard theory, to questioning its adequacy, to a full-scale challenge. Other linguists took sides, supporting either generative semantics (GS) or Chomskyan standard theory (some aspects of it called 'interpretive semantics', in contrast to GS). McCawley, Postal, Ross and Lakoff shared responsibility for the initial agenda of GS and its iconoclastic tenor.

McCawley repeatedly (e.g. McCawley 1982: 1) pointed out the infelicity of the name 'generative semantics' insofar as it misleadingly

JAMES D. MCCAWLEY (1938–99)

suggested that the representation of semantics or the identity of what is 'generative' in a grammar exhaustively defined differences between the two camps. GS did, indeed, propose major reforms in the treatment of semantics, but that amounted to only a single target. Among the interconnected counter-establishment initiatives that comprised GS are the following, drawn mostly from McCawley's publications from the 1960s and 1970s (which I cite as they appear in three collections of reprints: McCawley 1976a, 1979, 1982):

(1) The centre of attention in Chomsky's standard theory was the syntactic component of grammar, which specified the operation of transformational rules that moved (and in some versions, inserted or deleted) lexical items to generate, for example, English questions with 'who' or 'what' in sentence-initial position. Standard theory left the semantic component of grammar underspecified. GS brought semantics into centre stage, and argued for its greater articulation, proposing in particular that: (i) semantic structures can be represented by formal and logical features, parallel to the morphological features used to represent syntactic structures (McCawley 1976a: 106–14); and (ii) grammar can dispense with standard theory's level of 'deep structure', the input to transformational rules, as separate from the representation of semantic structures (*ibid.*: 155–66). In other words, GS wanted to replace the derivation of 'Lee tore the paper' from the deep structure 'Lee tear+PAST the paper' (which in turn derived from underspecified semantic entities corresponding to the relevant lexical items), in favour of a semantic structure constructed largely of abstract semantic and logical units, such as '[Lee DO SOMETHINGX (X CAUSE (BECOME (NOT (BE WHOLE paper))))]'.

(2) In GS, unordered transformations constrained the combination of semantic units, creating more complex units, with lexical insertion taking place freely in the course of a derivation, whereas in standard theory transformations apply only after lexical insertion is complete (*ibid.*: 155–66; 343–56). Therefore, in opposition to the received understanding that transformations operate exclusively on deep structures to generate surface structures, McCawley and his colleagues reconceived of transformations as applicable (at least) globally, pre-lexically and post-cyclically.

(3) McCawley retained then-current notions of constituency and of cyclic application of transformational rules, that is, the

262

understanding that transformations apply first to the most deeply embedded clause, then stepwise to each more super-ordinate clause (*ibid.*: 290–93). But GS challenged what McCawley and others viewed as standard theory's self-imposed artificial separation of syntax from semantics (*ibid.*: 114–17). The goal was to develop a grammatical model that embraced the complexities of dealing with meaning. As GS gathered steam, what counted as 'meaning' incorporated more and more, extending to what was traditionally labelled pragmatics, and to **J. L. Austin**'s speech act theory (*ibid.*: 84–89 summarizes Ross's proposals). Thus the declarative 'Lee tore the paper' derived from a superstructure constituting a superordinate perfor-mative like 'I say to you that [Lee tore the paper]' (represented, of course, in abstract semantico-logical terms). In short, GS low-ered the boundaries across semantics (subsuming logic), syntax and pragmatics, challenging their compartmentalization in standard theory. McCawley (1976b: 10) raised 'a question that would have been outlandish in 1965, namely the question of whether anything was to be gained by distinguishing between syntax and semantics'.

(4) GS dismissed standard theory's carefully defined taxonomy of syntactic categories. McCawley (1979: 96–100) argued that English modals like *can* and *must* share the features of verbs, and should be classified as verbs, not as a special (sub-)syntactic category of auxiliaries. McCawley (1976a: 257–72) further argued that tense markers (treated as features like '[+PAST]' in standard theory) are underlyingly verbs as well. Some generative semanti-cists proposed that it was possible to reduce the number of syntactic categories to as few as three (S, V, NP; or proposition, predicate, argument); others that the boundaries between cate-gories was necessarily imprecise, or 'squishy' (McCawley 1982: 176–203). Moreover, if *can* and '[+PAST]' are verbs, not aux-iliaries, this posed a threat to Chomsky's (1957: 60–84) famous analysis of the English auxiliary system.

(5) GS rejected standard theory's assumption that sentences could be readily labelled as '(un)grammatical' independent of context. Rather, McCawley (1980: 915) argued that 'sentences are well-formed ... only relative to classes of meanings and contexts' in the way that 'a particular menu is not in itself a well-formed example of Japanese cuisine but is well-formed as a winter-time breakfast, ill-formed as a wedding banquet, etc.' This stance threatened a basic premise, Chomsky's often-repeated (e.g.

Chomsky 1965: 3–9) definition of a grammar as a system that generates an infinite set of well-formed sentences.

(6) GS, unlike standard theory, was unconcerned with developing a precise and constraining notational system, and did not look to mathematics and other sciences for models of how to classify, label or evaluate linguistic phenomena.

Less theoretically salient, but still a fieldmark of GS, was its showy anti-authoritarianism and deliberate flouting of cultural and professional norms, which stand out even amidst the taboo-breaking socio-political context of late-1960s America. McCawley gleefully participated in this aspect of GS rhetorical style. In hindsight, some readers find it refreshing; others, puerile.

Generative semanticists' in-your-face iconoclasm doubtless contributed to the rawness, even outright rancour, that came to permeate both sides of their debates with Chomsky and Chomsky's supporters. Numerous publications, written from diverse perspectives, have dissected the efflorescence and subsequent abandonment of GS (e.g. Newmeyer 1980; McCawley 1980; Lakoff 1989; Harris 1993; Huck and Goldsmith 1995). The collapse of GS has variously been attributed to its overambition in trying to incorporate too wide a range of grammatical phenomena (Harris 1993: 230 cites the popular belief that GS 'tried to swallow the whole world, and choked on it'); its adherents' failure to establish an academic power base; the fast pace with which generative semanticists modified or abandoned their positions; the near-unassailable prestige that orthodox generative theory had acquired by the 1970s, even though it too had started out as a rebellion, against post-Bloomfieldian descriptivism/structuralism; and Chomsky's own very heavy polemical footsteps.

Focusing on the specific role that McCawley played, it is apparent that he valued being right more than being consistent. Like his colleagues, he openly disavowed certain views he had advocated during the height of GS when he perceived an error. For example, in his post-GS career, McCawley retreated from the claim that the inventory of syntactic categories is extremely limited (McCawley 1980; 1988: 182–206). He also revisited a proposal that had achieved the status of a kind of parade case for GS, namely an argument he made in 1970 that English is underlyingly a VSO language (or, expressed in the idiom of GS, that it is a predicate-initial language; McCawley 1976a: 211–28). As McCawley (1982: 7) later recognized, a grammar based on semantic structure renders differences of word order immaterial. Therefore, whether English is VSO or SVO is essentially moot with respect to GS.

Whatever generative semantics may look like in retrospect, McCawley's leadership role in it remains conspicuous. After the 1970s, he kept on writing and teaching about language in a vein that was consistent with the insights of GS, if not an explicit continuation of it. He produced a well received textbook on logic for students of linguistics (McCawley 1981/1993), and a two-volume survey of English grammar (McCawley 1988) that revisits the highlights of early generative grammar such as tests for constituency; cyclical application and interactions of transformational rules; anaphoric domains; island constraints; negative polarity; ellipsis; quantifiers and scope. McCawley's approach manages to be both quirky and classic.

Accounts of his life always mention that McCawley was a charismatic teacher, an accomplished classical musician, and a superb international cook. Famously, he combined his avocations with his vocation by enthusiastically organizing parties for his graduate students and colleagues, using as excuses for conviviality such events as Bastille Day, Hangeul Day (see **King Sejong**) and St Cecilia's Day.

McCawley's major works

Grammar and Meaning, 1976a, Academic Press, New York.
Adverbs, Vowels, and Other Objects of Wonder, 1979, University of Chicago Press, Chicago, IL.
Everything that Linguists have Always Wanted to Know about Logic – But were Ashamed to Ask, 1981, University of Chicago Press, Chicago, IL (2nd edn 1993).
Thirty Million Theories of Grammar, 1982, University of Chicago Press, Chicago, IL.
The Syntactic Phenomena of English: Vols 1 and 2, 1988, University of Chicago Press, Chicago, IL (2nd edn 1998, published as one volume).

Further reading

Chomsky, N. (1957) *Syntactic Structures*, The Hague: Mouton.
Chomsky, N. (1965) *Aspects of the Theory of Syntax*, Cambridge, MA: MIT Press.
Harris, R. A. (1993) *The Linguistics Wars*, Oxford: Oxford University Press.
Huck, G. J. and Goldsmith, J. A. (1995) *Ideology and Linguistic Theory*, London and New York: Routledge.
Lakoff, R. (1989) 'The way we were; or; the real actual truth about generative semantics', *Journal of Pragmatics*, 13, 939–88.
Lawler, J. (2003) 'James D. McCawley', *Language*, 79, 614–25.
McCawley, J. D. (1976b) 'Introduction', in *Syntax and Semantics: Vol. 7, Notes from the Linguistic Underground* (J. D. McCawley, ed.), New York: Academic Press.

——(1980) 'Review of *Linguistic Theory in America*, by F. J. Newmeyer', *Linguistics*, 18, 911–30.
Newmeyer, F. J. (1980) *Linguistic Theory in America*, New York: Academic Press (2nd edn 1986).

DEBORAH CAMERON (b. 1958)

Deborah Cameron is a British language scholar and feminist, much of whose work is in the fields of sociolinguistics and linguistic anthropology. She is probably best known for her writings on language, gender and sexuality, but has also published widely on the topics of communication, discourse analysis, language in public life and in the media, language ideology, language and globalization, and the methodology of sociolinguistics. Most of Cameron's writings address academic readers, especially linguists and specialists in Women's Studies. But, on principle, she also produces books and articles for the popular press since she accepts a dual responsibility, namely to 'be responsive to the needs and concerns of women outside academic life; and ... [to] challenge the practices and values that keep women outside' (Cameron 1985: vii).

Cameron was born in Glasgow, but spent her early life in the north of England. After her mother died, she left school at seventeen to take jobs at a laundry and a bank, while also caring for two younger siblings at home. This experience proved transformative, as it opened her eyes to gender discrimination in the working world and convinced her of the value of higher education. Cameron returned to school, studying first English and later, at Oxford, linguistics, where she worked under the supervision of iconoclast philosopher of linguistics Roy Harris (b. 1931). While still a graduate student, Cameron published her first book, *Feminism and Linguistic Theory* (1985). It has since appeared in two editions, a dozen reprints, and translations into Japanese and Finnish. Cameron taught at Roehampton Institute (now, University) in London; Strathclyde University in Glasgow; and the Institute of Education at the University of London, interspersed with guest professorships in the USA, Sweden and Germany. In 2004, she was appointed the Rupert Murdoch Professor of Language and Communication at the University of Oxford.

Feminism and Linguistic Theory surveys then-current work on differences between how women versus men use language, and on the nature and effects of sexism in language. Cameron summarized and evaluated feminist interpretations of this research. She concluded that by reflecting on, and changing, one's habits of language use, one can resist the assumptions on which gender-based inequality is based – but that direct restructuring of social institutions that support those assumptions is primary. In her words, 'we must acknowledge the limitation of theories of oppression that do not go beyond the linguistic' (Cameron 1985: 171).

Since the publication of *Feminism and Linguistic Theory*, research on both the language that women use (or are purported to use), and language that bears on the status or representation of women, has multiplied. Cameron contributed a study that she often cites (e.g. Cameron 1997; 2006: 64–68, 173–74; 2007: 74–77; Cameron and Kulick 2003: 65–69), which analyses the causal gossip of American male college students. Her data show males participating in exchanges stereotypically attributed to females: talk that 'affirm[s] the solidarity of an in-group by constructing absent others as an out-group, whose behavior is minutely examined and found wanting' (Cameron 1997: 54).

Cameron's major contributions to the study of language and gender, however, have been less through original empirical research than through reflection on existing research. Going as far back as *Feminism and Linguistic Theory*, she has developed influential running critiques of several landmark texts. For example, she expressed reservations about Australian feminist Dale Spender's (b. 1943) *Man Made Language* (1980). Spender argued that language pervasively reflects the experiences and opinions of men. She wrote, for example, that 'Males made up the rules of prescriptive grammar and males are still in the main the custodians of those rules' (Spender 1980: 160). This disadvantages women, who are excluded from controlling meaning and disabled in their linguistic self-expression. While treating Spender's groundbreaking book respectfully, Cameron (1985, 2006) rejected its assumption that the meanings of words and structures are, or even can be, fixed. Rather, Cameron views language as indeterminate and contextually defined, since '[a]ll language users construct their own meanings and are endlessly creative in their interpretations of what others say' (Cameron 2006: 16).

Cameron also takes exception to another early classic, Robin Lakoff's (b. 1942) *Language and Women's Place* (1975). Lakoff characterized women's speech as riddled with features that communicate social subordination: approval-seeking tag questions ('That's enough, *isn't it?*'); the imposition of rising intonation on the ends of statements, which makes declaratives like 'I'm leaving at 6:00' sound like questions; hedges and indirection; and exaggerated language that seems to valorize frivolous concerns ('I'll just die if you won't give me the recipe'; 'What a divine sweater!'). Many have pointed out that Lakoff's pioneering work blithely assumes the generality of data based on her own introspection or on anecdotal observations of an educated, white, upper middle-class speech community. Subsequent attempts to establish empirically whether women do, indeed, routinely use these speech features to the exclusion of men, or at least more commonly than men, have challenged many of Lakoff's claims, as have arguments that what some of these features mark is not femaleness *per se*, but lack of social authority. To take one example, several studies have pointed out that tag questions play multiple roles in discourse: tag questions do sometimes signal indecision or powerlessness; but in other contexts, they communicate presumption, or even aggression. Speakers also sometimes use tag questions as a 'facilitative' device, to encourage the participation of their conversational partners. Building on this last observation, Cameron et al. (2006: 45–60) added to debate over what has come to be labelled Lakoff's 'deficit' model of women's language. She proposed that some tag questions (or other purportedly gender-linked phenomena) may not – as Lakoff assumes – signal women's subordination, but rather their resistance to subordination. Women may employ facilitative tag questions in the role of conversational manager, a role that subverts the presumption of female powerlessness.

Cameron sometimes conflates (but sometimes distinguishes) her critique of Lakoff's deficit model and her critique of a 'dominance' model of women's language. The dominance model is exemplified by Zimmerman and West's (1975) seminal study, which showed that in male–female conversation, males interrupted females far more frequently than *vice versa*, and males more frequently controlled discourse topics. For Cameron, the issue is, again, that of interpretation: merely counting the incidence of simultaneous or overlapping speech doesn't distinguish among of kinds of 'interruptions'. Some simultaneous speech does in fact instantiate a struggle for dominance, with an interrupter attempting to wrest away the role of speaker. However, other simultaneous speech may be collaborative, that is, it may constitute an 'interrupter's' attempt to support or augment the speaker's conversational turn.

In addition to her analyses of the 'deficit' and 'dominance' models of women's language, Cameron has most fully developed her critique of a third stance, the 'difference' model. Associated with Deborah Tannen (b. 1945) (1990) and John Gray (1992), among others, this model characterizes men's versus women's language as due to the two sexes' contrasting discourse styles and goals. According to Tannen, women are socialized to value cooperation and to use conversation to connect with other people, while men use conversation to solve problems and enhance their social status. Cross-gender talk misfires when the two parties fail to accommodate each other's differing conversational styles. Cameron (2006, 2007) has analysed both popular and academic writings that conceptualize women's versus men's language as a kind of quasi-dialectal difference. Although some of these works achieved tremendous public acclaim, Cameron finds them unsatisfactory on several grounds. One problem is that, despite conceiving cross-gender miscommunication as the fault of neither party, the 'difference' model is framed for, and apparently received by, a (virtually) exclusively female audience. Women – not men and women together – take away from this literature the burden of learning to accommodate gender-based communicative differences.

Another feature of the 'difference' model that troubles Cameron is that it takes male/female language differences for granted, instead of inquiring into why girls and boys are socialized differently, and what consequences ensue. For instance, Cameron cites Tannen's advice to teachers that women may learn better through small-group discussion rather than teaching practices based on adversarial debate. Without rejecting the value of either pedagogy, Cameron notes that:

> Debate and argument are the 'languages of power' in our culture. If, as Tannen claims, women experience them in classrooms as 'public humiliation', this is surely bound up with the conflicting pressure women face in that setting: for women, intellectual autonomy and academic success conflict with social and sexual acceptability [...] A feminist solution to this very real problem involves not removing women from the context that causes discomfort, but going to the roots of their positioning as 'outsiders' to powerful language and trying to change the conditions (including male behaviour) that keep them outside.
>
> (Cameron 1995a: 42)

A third reservation Cameron expressed is that the difference model adopts too simple a concept of 'male' versus 'female', as if people can be exhaustively classified under two non-intersecting rubrics. Cameron and Kulick (2003) explored what a more complex, realistic, non-'heteronormative' understanding of sex means for the study of language and gender.

Cameron's feminist perspective and her commitment to both popular and academic interest in language extends to topics outside language and gender. In *Verbal Hygiene* (Cameron 1995b), she analysed widespread instantiations in the Anglophone world of metalinguistic commentary and prescriptivism. Cameron's case studies include editors' usage guidelines and their histories; Britain's national controversy about grammar in the school curriculum; the convoluted debate surrounding 'politically correct' speech; and language self-help initiatives directed at women, including assertiveness training programmes and advice about how to sound 'professional'. Cameron documented how deeply invested the general public is in matters of verbal hygiene, probably because 'one common function of arguments about language is to stand in for arguments on subjects people are reluctant to broach more directly' (*ibid.*: 217). Many verbal-hygienic initiatives attribute to language a power over cognition that Cameron finds irrational. However, she accepts that some kinds of norms for language are desirable, and encourages readers to challenge authoritarianism or mystification in any proposal for what counts as 'appropriate' language.

Similar themes emerge in Cameron (2000), a critique of specific verbal-hygienic practices aimed at ameliorating 'poor communication' or generating self-consciousness about what counts as successful (conceptualized as correct, powerful, aesthetically pleasing or moral) verbal communication. She examined contemporary publications that instruct readers in how to improve their communication skills, and then dissected programmes and materials that corporations use to train employees in how to interact with the public, including specific customer-service scripts that personnel are required to memorize. The experiences of workers at call centres, where businesses interact with their clients or customers solely by telephone, is of particular interest to Cameron. Employees of call centres ('communication factories'; *ibid.*: 93) are taught specific verbal routines that 'style' their speech for maximum efficiency. Education about communication in schools, and coaching about 'communication skills' in psychotherapeutic contexts, are also addressed. Cameron evinces scepticism of many such efforts to improve verbal communication on the grounds that they control people, rather than empower them to make autonomous decisions, and that the underlying model of the range of verbal communication is impoverished.

Much of the originality of Cameron's work resides in her thoughtful and discerning analyses of other scholars' research. Her appearance in *Fifty Key Thinkers on Language and Linguistics* thus represents the accomplishments of more than a single person. It seems apt, then, that as the sole female in this group, the specific tenor of

Cameron's work calls attention to issues that have, historically, limited the contributions of women in the language sciences, as in other academic fields.

Cameron's major works

Feminism and Linguistic Theory, 1985, Macmillan, London.
'Rethinking language and gender studies: some issues for the 1990s', 1995a, in S. Mills (ed.), *Language and Gender: Interdisciplinary Perspectives*, Longman, London.
Verbal Hygiene, 1995b, Routledge, London and New York.
'Performing gender identity: young men's talk and the construction of heterosexual masculinity', 1997, in S. Johnson and U. H. Meinhof (eds), *Language and Masculinity*, Blackwell, Oxford.
Good to Talk? Living and Working in a Communication Culture, 2000, Sage, London.
Language and Sexuality, 2003 (with D. Kulick), Cambridge University Press, Cambridge.
On Language and Sexual Politics, 2006, Routledge, London.
The Myth of Mars and Venus, 2007, Cambridge University Press, Cambridge.

Further reading

Cameron, D., McAlinden, F. and O'Leary, K. (2006) 'Lakoff in context: the form and function of tag questions', in D. Cameron, *On Language and Sexual Politics*, London: Routledge, 45–60.
Gray, J. (1992) *Men are from Mars, Women are from Venus*, London and New York: HarperCollins.
Lakoff, R. (1975) *Language and Woman's Place*, New York: Harper & Row (revised and expanded edn 2004, Oxford University Press).
Spender, D. (1980) *Man Made Language*, London: Routledge & Kegan Paul.
Tannen, D. (1990) *You Just Don't Understand*, New York: Morrow.
Zimmerman, D. H. and West, C. (1975) 'Sex roles, interruptions and silences in conversation', in B. Thorne and N. Henley (eds), *Language and Sex: Difference and Dominance*, Rowley, MA: Newbury House.

GLOSSARY

ablative   In languages with case marking, a noun may be marked with ablative case to identify it as a location away from which movement takes place. In the sentence *She got out of the car*, a language that employed ablative might mark *car* with ablative case. Ablative case is also sometimes used to mark nouns with other semantic roles, such as the instrumental noun *screwdriver* in *I opened it with a screwdriver*.

ablaut   A process of marking the inflection of a root by altering the quality of an internal vowel, as in the English verb *drive* (present), *drove* (past), *driven* (past participle).

accusative   In languages with case marking, a noun may be marked with accusative case to identify it as the direct object of a transitive verb. In the sentence *Our waiter spilled the soup*, languages that employ accusative case would mark *soup* as accusative.

affix   A morpheme that cannot stand alone as an independent form, but rather attaches to a root or to a stem. For example, prefixes such as *un–* in *unnecessary*, and the plural suffix *–s* in *nightmares*, are affixes.

affixation   One of the principal processes by which words are built up, namely by attaching affixes to roots and to stems to form more morphologically complex words. Some languages employ affixation profusely, some not at all.

agent   The semantic role attributed to the noun that is the 'doer' or instigator of the action of a transitive verb. A typical agent is an animate noun subject, such as *Tracy* in *Tracy fixed the window*.

agglutinative   A typological characterization of languages that commonly employ multiple segmentable affixes to form complex words. The affixes are little modified by the process of affixation, and so retain consistent shapes and meanings. The English phrase *uncharacteristically demanding and impatient* exhibits agglutination, since *un–*, *–istic*, *–ally*, *–ing* and *im–* are easily segmentable from *character*, *demand* and *patient*. Moreover, the affixes *un–*, *–istic*,

–ally, –ing, and *im–* freely attach to other roots or stems to form other words: *unwholistically; rewarding; imprecise.* Agglutinative languages contrast with isolating and fusional languages.

agreement   The grammatical phenomenon by which two or more linguistic units are marked to indicate that they share some feature, such as number, gender or person: English *A weed is growing in the yard* indicates the singularity on the subject by the absence of plural marking; singular *weed* agrees with the singular verb *is.* In *Some weeds are growing in the yard,* plural *weeds* agrees with plural *are.* In this sense, agreement indicates the cohesion of units that 'go together'.

allophone   Predictable variants of the same phoneme; different realizations of the same abstract minimal sound-unit when it appears in different phonetic environments. For example, two allophones of the English 'l' phoneme appear in the words *leave* (so-called 'clear l') versus *milk* ('dark l'). In British Received Pronunciation, 'clear l' appears in syllable onsets (at the beginning of syllables) whereas 'dark l' appears in syllable rhymes (from the vowel centre of a syllable to its end).

analogy   A term that labels the tendency of speakers to extend an existing grammatical pattern to new material, or to replace exceptions 'by analogy' to a regular pattern. Analogical levelling can lead over time to the reduction of exceptions.

antecedent   The antecedent of a pronoun is a noun that identifies the reference of the pronoun; in *Alice said that she felt ill,* Alice is a plausible antecedent to the pronoun *she.*

aorist   A verb form marked for past tense, and which may also (in the grammars of certain languages) be marked for perfective aspect (i.e. marked to indicate that the action was completed).

aphasia   Disorder or loss of the ability to produce or comprehend language, or both, due to trauma or disease affecting the brain.

apical   Speech sound made with the tip of the tongue, usually in contact with the roof of the mouth or the front teeth.

argument   A nominal that is required to co-occur with a certain verb or other governing element. For example, a transitive verb has two arguments: subject and object, while an intransitive verb has a single argument: the subject. In a slightly different sense, an argument complements a predicate: the sentence *The sky clouded over at dusk* can be divided into a predicate *clouded over at dusk,* and its argument, *the sky.*

argument structure   The inventory of arguments that co-occur with a specific verb. For example, the argument structure of the verb *disappear* requires a single nominal, the subject (*The cat disappeared*), whereas the argument structure of *give* requires three nominals, a subject, indirect object and direct object (*We gave the Boy Scouts the cookies*).

aspect   Along with tense and mood, one of the prime grammatical categories typically marked on verbs, or communicated inherently by verbs. Aspect is a cover term for various dimensions of the meanings of verbs, including whether the state or action of the verb has been completed; is ongoing; is habitual; is repeated over time; is approaching a goal, etc. Languages vary in the inventory of aspects they mark on verbs, and verbs vary in their susceptibility to aspectual marking.

aspiration   Some consonants, usually stops, are articulated with a puff of breath following the release of the consonant. The classic example is English *pin*, where the initial voiceless *p* is aspirated, in contrast with *bin*, where the initial voiced *b* is not aspirated. Aspiration may be allophonic: in English, *p* is aspirated in initial position or at the beginning of a stressed syllable, but unaspirated elsewhere, such as following *s* in *spin*. Aspiration may also be phonemic, as it is in Thai, in which aspirated and unaspirated voiceless stops constitute separate phonemes.

autosegmental phonology   A school of phonology that conceptualizes the sound features of words as distributed across several layers, or tiers, with linkages established from tier to tier. For example, a segmental tier includes information about the order and identity of sound units, whereas (in the case of a tone language) a tonal tier indicates the distribution of high and low tones linked to specific segments on the segmental tier.

auxiliary language   A language constructed artificially for the purpose of serving as a means of communication across speakers of diverse native languages. Esperanto is probably the best known example.

bound morpheme   A minimal meaningful unit that cannot function independently. Affixes such as *–ed*, *–ation* or *pre–* are all bound morphemes, which must combine with free morphemes such as *jump, consider, modern*, etc. to form independent words.

case   A system for marking the roles that nouns play with respect to verbs, prepositions or other governing elements. Not all languages mark nouns for case, but among those that do, a common strategy is to attach an affix, the case marker, to the base form of the noun to indicate its case in a given sentence. Alternatively, case may be marked by internal modification of the noun.

Typical cases include nominative (indicates the subject), accusative (direct object), dative (indirect object), genitive (indicates a possessor), and vocative (indicates a person to whom speech is addressed). The term 'objective' case is used where a language does not distinguish accusative from dative case.

coarticulation   The process in which the articulation of one sound affects the articulation of adjacent sounds. For example, the effect of the *n* in *finish* may spread backward onto the pronunciation of the first *i*, producing a nasal vowel by coarticulation.

cognate   A word or feature in one language which is historically related to a word of feature in another language, because both are derived from the same source. For example, the words for 'school' in English, French (*école*) and Spanish (*escuela*) are cognates, having all descended from Latin *schola*.

comparative-historical linguistics   The study of how and why languages change over time, through comparison of forms in two or more languages to determine whether or not they are related. The outcome of this study is to determine subgroups of languages and their relationships to each other, to reconstruct common ancestral languages, and to define changes that have taken place in the descent of daughter languages.

complementizer   A grammatical class of words that mark clause boundaries, such as English *that* in *He knows that you admire him* or *if* in *He asked if you admire him*. Some traditional grammars subsume complementizers under the class of conjunctions.

compound word   A word formed by joining two independent words – two free morphemes – to form a new word (as opposed to joining a stem to a bound morpheme). For example, joining the free morpheme *white* to the free morpheme *wash* yields the compound word *whitewash*. (*Whitewash* may then participate in normal processes of affixation to create *whitewashed* or *whitewashing*.) Some compounds are endocentric, that is, like English *record player*, the head of the compound (*player*) is one of the units that makes up the compound. Others are exocentric, such as Spanish *tocadiscos* ('record player', lit. *toca* 'play' + *discos* 'records'), where neither compounded element counts as the head, since *toca* is a finite verb, as opposed to the English *player*.

conjugation   In Latin traditional grammar, verbs can be classified into four subgroups or conjugations, defined according to the patterns generated when the verb is attached to inflectional markers (for person, number, tense, mood, voice). The term 'conjugation' is also used to refer to the array of inflected forms that a given verb can assume; extended to English, the conjugation of the verb *eat* includes *eat, ate, eaten, eats, eating*.

constituent A grammatical subunit of language that has internal coherence, such as a noun phrase, or preposition or verb phrase. Constituents may be nested within each other: the noun phrase *a long-lost friend of mine from high school* forms a constituent, the subject, within the sentence *A long-lost friend of mine from high school appeared at the door*. At the same time, the noun phrase subsumes a smaller constituent, the prepositional phrase *from high school*, which in turn subsumes an even smaller constituent, the noun phrase *high school*.

copula A verb that links a subject to a predicate without con- tributing substantial meaning, for example by merely asserting a relationship of identity. In English, certain uses of the verb *be* and, arguably, other verbs have the role of copula: *She is a civil engineer; He seemed discouraged*.

dative In languages that mark nouns for case, dative marking may appear on a noun that is an indirect object, that is, the semantic beneficiary or recipient of the action of the verb, such as *the kids* in *I gave the kids lemonade*.

declension In Latin traditional grammar, nouns can be classified into five subgroups or declensions, according to the patterns generated when the noun is attached to a case marker. In some patterns, the noun is simply affixed by the case marker; in others, a specific vowel is inserted between the noun and the case marker; in other patterns, a vowel in the noun is replaced by a different vowel, etc.

deep structure Early generative grammar proposed that abstract deep structures underlie the concrete surface structures of lan- guage. Deep structures record basic relationships among the sen- tence constituents, so that comparison of deep structures can reveal differences between superficially similar pairs of surface structures. For example, *John is easy to please* resembles *John is eager to please* in surface structure, but the deep structure of the former indicates that *John* is associated with the null direct object of *please*, whereas the deep structure of the latter indicates that *John* is associated with the null subject of *eager*.

dental A place of articulation, or speech sound produced at that place of articulation, which involves contact between the tip of the tongue and the inside of the upper, and sometimes lower, teeth.

derivation (1) The word-formation process of attaching an affix that induces significant semantic change in the base, and may also change the grammatical category of the affixed word. Derivation contrasts with inflection, which does not alter the grammatical category of the affixed word, and little affects its basic semantics. Derivational processes in English include nominalizing suffixes like *–ity* as in the contrast between *fragile* [adjective] and *fragility* [noun], or prefixation with *counter–*, which inverts the meaning of the base to which it is attached (e.g. *counter-revolutionary*).

(2) The grammatical process of development of a linguistic unit from an abstract underlying form to its surface form, during which it may undergo processes such as deletion or movement.

descriptive A descriptive grammar indicates how a particular speech community actually uses language, without reference to standards of correctness. Descriptive grammars contrast with prescriptive grammars, which aim to reform popular usage.

diachronic Characterized by the study of language as it changes over time, in opposition to 'synchronic'.

direct object The nominal that is directly affected by the action of a transitive verb. For example, *the floor* is the direct object of the verb *scrub* in *They scrubbed the floor vigorously*.

ellipsis A common process of deletion of part or parts of a sentence, the identity of which can be reconstructed from context. In the sentence *I arrived late, but they didn't*, part of the verb phrase in the second conjunct has been subjected to ellipsis, namely *arrive late* (*I arrived late, but they didn't* arrive late).

empiricism The proposition that the only source of valid knowledge is direct experience through the senses. Empiricists typically reject or downplay claims that instinctive or inborn knowledge exists, or that human intellect, logic or rational powers contribute to knowledge.

etymology Study of the origins and history of words. Early study of language often assumed that etymology provided special insight into the 'real' or authentic meanings of words.

formalism, formal linguistics A linguistic theory that defines the features and roles of linguistic processes and elements without relying on the functions that those processes or elements play in human communication. In this sense, 'formal' linguistics contrasts with 'functional' linguistics. Formal linguistics typically emphasizes the systematicity of language structure and freely admits abstractions; it aims to account, explicitly and comprehensively, for how the parts of a language work without referring to social context or communication.

free morpheme A minimal meaningful unit that can function independently, without being attached to another morpheme. Free morphemes (e.g. *dull, swallow, patient*) necessarily constitute words, but not all words are constituted of free morphemes, since many can be resolved into smaller units that cannot stand independently: *comprehen+sive, out+sid(e)+er, enjoy+ed*.

fricative A manner of articulation, or speech sound so produced, involving narrowing the vocal tract without fully obstructing the flow of air. Fricative consonants all produce perceptible friction, such as in the initial and final fricatives in the English word *fizz*.

fronting (of vowel) Alteration of the conventional place of articulation of a particular vowel, so that it is pronounced somewhat more toward the front of the mouth, sometimes due to the proximity of a consonant with that place of articulation. Vowels may likewise shift from their usual place of articulation by processes of backing, centralization, lowering or raising.

functional categories Grammatical classes, or parts of speech – such as articles, complementizers, prepositions, conjunctions – whose roles are essentially grammatical or structural, rather than lexical. Functional categories indicate the formal architecture of a sentence, as opposed to lexical categories (nouns, verbs, adjectives), which are rich in meaning.

functional morphemes A term that subsumes functional categories, and expands to include not only independent words (free morphemes) such as *an, of* and *to*, but also bound morphemes that bear functional rather than lexical roles: *–ed* in *proved*; *'s* in *brother's*.

functionalism, functional linguistics A linguistic theory or proposal that prioritizes the role of human communication in defining the features and roles of linguistic processes and elements. 'Functional' linguistics contrasts with 'formal' linguistics in that it accepts that how people use language to communicate meanings effects language structure, and can help explain language structure.

fusional A typological characterization of languages in which inflections of a root are not readily segmentable into separate morphemes. The English third person masculine singular pronouns are *he, him* and *his* in the nominative, objective and genitive cases, respectively; the corresponding feminine forms are *she, her* and *her*. There are no obvious separate markers for person, gender, number or case that can be segmented away from these six forms. Rather, each form fuses its features for person, gender, number and case into a unique lexical item.

gender   (1) In grammar and morphology, gender refers to a system present in some languages wherein the nouns are assigned to subgroups, sometimes labelled 'masculine' and 'feminine' (also 'neuter'). For the most part, nouns grouped under these labels have no meaningful relationship to masculinity or femininity *per se*. Rather, the marking of a noun for gender serves as a cohesion device insofar as the gender marking on the noun is copied onto modifiers of that noun. (2) In sociolinguistics, the gender of speakers and listeners – generally conceived of as male or female – is an important variable relevant to language use and conversational practice.

genitive   In languages that mark case, a noun that is the possessor of another noun may be marked with genitive case to indicate its role as a possessor. English marks genitive case in the phrase *my brother's bicycle* by affixing *'s* to *brother*.

glide   A phonetic segment that has the properties of a vowel but is distributed like a consonant; *y* and *w* are often classified as glides. Sometimes called 'semivowels'.

glottogenesis   The origin of the first human language.

government   A syntactic relationship in which one word imposes a specific form or status, often expressed as a morphophonemic alteration, on another word which it is said to govern. The same expression is used to described the relationship between the dominating word and the specific morphophonemic alteration it imposes. Thus the English preposition *for* in *I made it for him* is said to govern its object *him* and, moreover, *for* governs the dative case, so that the third person singular masculine pronoun appears as *him*, not as *he* or *his*.

grapheme   Minimal significant unit of writing: a letter or intact symbol that functions independently in an orthographic system. The letter 'j' is a grapheme of English, but the dot placed at the top of the downstroke is not an independent unit and therefore not a grapheme.

head   The most essential and defining member of a constituent. For example, in the English expression *a ripe peach*, the noun *peach* is the head of the noun phrase.

historical linguistics   Study of language change over time; also called 'diachronic linguistics'.

iconicity   The linguistic property of representing meaning non-arbitrarily, where the form of a word or construction bears some resemblance to its meaning. Most words are not iconic, but arbitrary; onomatopoeia is an obvious exception. Some linguists argue that iconicity plays a larger role in words and structures than usually acknowledged. For example, in some languages, reduplication is used to signal repetition or intensification of an action.

imperfect   A verbal form that views the time structure of an action or event in the past as if from inside, without implying that the action or event was completed. English past progressive is imperfect in *She was washing her hair*, where *be V-ing* highlights the washing not as a closed event, but as an ongoing past action. Different languages attribute different subtle semantics to imperfect verb forms.

infixation   A morphological process wherein an affix is inserted inside a root, rather than affixed to the beginning or end of the root.

inflection   The morphological process of attaching to a word an affix that adds grammatical meaning to the affixed item, but does not induce significant semantic change. Inflection contrasts with derivation, which may alter the meaning or grammatical category of the affixed form. Common inflectional processes in English include suffixation of *−s* on nouns (which marks the noun as plural), and *−ing* and *−ed* on verbs (which alter the tense and aspectual features of the verb).

interlocutor   A person with whom a speaker converses; a conversational partner.

internal reconstruction   A technique used in comparative-historical linguistics to infer the properties of a language at an earlier, unattested stage of its history. Internal reconstruction examines evidence such as allophonic variation and irregularities in a later version of a language as clues to the sounds, words and grammatical patterns of the parent language.

International Phonetic Alphabet   (IPA) A system of symbols, created in the late 1800s, to represent unambiguously the sounds of human speech. IPA provides symbols for the transcription of every phoneme in every language, and a set of diacritics for modifying them so as to capture the speech sounds of every language as closely as possible.

intonation   The melody or pitch contour of a sentence; an aspect of prosody.

intransitivity   The intrinsic property of some verbs that they do not appear with a direct object. English *go* is intransitive: *I am going the library* is ungrammatical without the presence of *to*, which marks *the library* as the complement of the preposition (*I am going to the* *library*). Verbs that require the presence of a direct object are called 'transitive'.

isolating   Languages vary in the extent to which they employ affixation and compounding. In some languages, words are invariant, rarely or never participating in morphological processes such as compounding, prefixation, infixation or suffixation. Such languages are characterized as isolating languages, in opposition to fusional or agglutinative languages.

labial   A place of articulation, or speech sound produced with that place of articulation, that involves either full or partial closure of the lips, such as in English *b* or *m*. 'Bilabial' sounds involve both lips.

laryngeal   A place of articulation, or speech sound produced with that place of articulation, involving the larynx or voice box.

lax   A quality of vowels characterized by relatively short duration, with reduced movement and muscular effort, as opposed to tense vowels.

length   Certain vowels or consonants may be intrinsically long or short. Their durations may also be lengthened or shortened as a result of their participation in a morphophonemic process, or as a result of juxtaposition with, or loss of, adjacent speech sounds.

lexical categories   Categories of words, or parts of speech – such as nouns, verbs, adjectives, adverbs – whose roles are to add meaning. Lexical categories are semantically rich, whereas functional categories provide the structural architecture of a sentence.

lexical item   An entry in the lexicon, which, arguably, includes both free morphemes (independent words) and bound morphemes (affixes that cannot stand alone: *–ness, –tude, re–*).

lexicography   The creation of dictionaries.

lexicon   The mental dictionary of a speaker of a language, listing both words and affixes, with their meanings and their syntactic and phonological properties, as recognized by the speaker.

lexis   The vocabulary of a specific language.

linguistic relativity   The controversial hypothesis that the particular features of a language affect the cognition and perception of speakers of that language, and that therefore speakers of different languages will think and perceive reality differently.

manner of articulation   One of three major axes for classifying consonants according to articulatory processes, the others being place of articulation and voicing. Manner of articulation refers to the manner and extent to which the articulators restrict the flow of breath through the vocal tract. Complete closure of the vocal tract results in stops or plosives; partial closure results in fricatives; release of breath through the nasal cavity results in nasals; minimal closure results in glides (or vowels).

markedness; marked/unmarked   Terms used to label the status of one member of a pair of linguistic forms relative to the other member, where the 'unmarked' form is conceived of as a default relative to the 'marked' form. The basis for that judgement varies: unmarked forms may be more commonly used, more widespread across languages, simpler morphologically, less syntactically elaborate, or more neutral and more general in meaning. Oral vowels are unmarked relative to nasal vowels; *widow* is unmarked relative to *widower*, *I like bagels* is unmarked relative to *Bagels, I like*.

metalanguage   Language that is used to talk about language. The vocabulary of linguistics (such as the entries in this glossary) forms a metalanguage that can be employed to analyse parts of a language.

minimal pair   A pair of words which are identical except for a single feature that distinguishes them. English *sing* and *zing* form a minimal pair, with the contrast resting entirely on the difference in voicing between *s* and *z*. The fact that speakers treat *sing* and *zing* as distinctive words indicates that voicing is a criterion of difference between *s* and *z*. Likewise, *pet* and *pit* form a minimal pair.

modifier   A linguistic unit that adds additional meaning to the head of a constituent. Adjectives and relative clauses modify nouns; an adverb modifies a verb.

mood   Along with tense and aspect, mood is an important grammatical category that comments on the reality of a proposition. Mood may be marked on verbs, or communicated by independent words or particles.

morpheme   A minimal grammatical unit, that is, the smallest part of a word that carries independent meaning. The English word *each* forms a single morpheme. The word *transportation* arguably is comprised of three morphemes: the affixes *trans–* and *–ation*, and the root – *port* –. Morphemes are classified according to whether they can exist independently (*each* is a free morpheme, *trans–* is a bound morpheme), and whether they contribute lexical or grammatical meaning (*each* is a lexical morpheme; *–ation* is a grammatical morpheme because by affixation to *transport* it changes the grammatical class of the word from verb to noun).

morphology   The study of the internal structure of words. The term also labels the structural properties of words themselves, including compounding and affixation (both inflectional and derivational), as in the statement 'Russian has complex morphology'.

morphophonemics Analysis and classification of phonological alterations of morphemes and the factors that bear on their alterations. For example, a typical morphophonemic change occurs when the vowel in the word *sign* shifts on being suffixed with −*al* to yield the word *signal*. In Europe, a more common term is 'morphophonology'.

morphosyntax Grammatical items or processes that affect both syntax and morphology. For example, affixation of an English verb with −*ing* is a morphological process with syntactic consequences, since V+*ing* co-occurs with a form of the verb *be* to indicate progressive aspect: *He plays the piano*; *He is playing the piano*.

nasal A place of articulation, or speech sound produced with that place of articulation, which involves release of breath through the nasal cavity, such as English *m* or *n*.

neuter A gender class. Along with masculine and feminine, neuter gender may or may not be assigned to nouns that have intrinsic semantics associating them with masculinity, femininity or neutrality with respect to sex.

nominal A noun or noun phrase. 'Nominal' may also refer to a group of words that take the place of a noun, such as the expression *The wealthy* in the sentence *The wealthy control the government*.

nominalize A process by which a word is modified to turn it into a noun. For example, the complex stem *nationalize*, a verb, can be nominalized by affixation with the nominalizing suffix −*ation*, to yield the noun *nationalization*.

nominative In languages that mark case, nouns in subject position are marked with nominative case. Nominative-marked nouns are often the agents of active transitive verbs, such as *Lee* in *Lee ate the sandwich*. Subjects of intransitive verbs may also be marked with nominative case.

null element An argument or other linguistic element that does not appear phonetically, but is posited to exist on theoretical grounds. Spanish allows null subjects in sentences such as *Tengo hambre* (lit. 'have+1st person+present hunger'), 'I'm hungry', where, arguably, the explicit first person singular pronoun *Yo*, 'I', has been deleted. English *I know she left early* may instantiate a null complementizer (cf. *I know that she left early*).

objective   In a language that marks nouns for case but does not distinguish between accusative and dative case (or sometimes, between accusative, dative, and nouns in other non-subject case positions), the term 'objective' is used as a cover term for non-nominative case. Nouns that are direct objects, indirect objects, and sometimes objects of prepositions are assigned objective case in these languages.

orthography   The writing system of a language.

particle   A term used to label various classes of uninflected words that do not obviously fit the traditional system of parts of speech.

parts of speech   Grammatical classes of words. Traditionally, the parts of speech include noun, pronoun, verb, adverb, participle, conjunction, preposition and interjection; adjective and article are sometimes either added to the list, or supplant participle and/or interjection.

patient   The semantic role attributed to the noun that is affected by, or undergoes the action specified by, a transitive verb. In the sentence *Tracy fixed the window*, the direct object *the window* bears a patient semantic role.

philology   The study of older languages, or the study of a language through the evidence of older written records. Sometimes used as a synonym for historical or diachronic linguistics, the study of language changes over time.

phoneme   The minimal unit in the sound system of a language. A given phoneme may have more than one realization (i.e. more than one allophone) in actual speech, depending on its phonetic context. But all the allophones that speakers perceive as variants of the same minimal sound unit count as a single phoneme. Phonemes are therefore abstractions, realized differently according to context. Some languages have as few as fifteen phonemes, some as many as seventy or eighty.

phonetics   The study of human speech sounds, from the perspectives of articulation (how speech sounds are made), acoustics (the physical properties of speech sounds), and audition (how speech sounds are perceived aurally).

phonology   The study of the sound system of a language, and the patterns that the sounds of a language participate in, including the individual segments, along with intonation, tone, pitch, stress, etc.

phrase   A syntactic unit or constituent that is smaller than a clause, and which typically consists of a head, any modifiers and, optionally, a specifier. The phrase is named for the lexical category of the head, so that *a long, crooked fence* is a noun phrase or

NP; *buying groceries* is a verb phrase or VP; *on the shelf* is a propositional phrase or PP.

pitch The rate of vibration of the vocal chords in producing speech. In general, a faster rate of vibration is perceived as higher pitch, a slower rate as lower pitch, although other factors are also relevant to perception of pitch. Modulation of pitch contributes to intonation and tone.

pitch-accent language A language in which words are assigned inherent pitch patterns. One syllable is marked by higher pitch, rather than marked by greater volume, longer duration or a change in pitch level. Pitch-accent languages therefore employ pitch differently than do stress and intonation or tone languages

place of articulation Along with manner of articulation and voicing, one of three major axes for classifying consonants according to articulatory processes. Place of articulation refers to the location in the vocal tract where the sound is articulated, or the important articulatory gestures involved. Key places of articulation include labial, dental, alveolar (on the hard ridge behind the inside of the front teeth), palatal, velar, uvular, pharyngeal and glottal. Lateral and retroflex consonants fill out the inventory, along with intermediate places of articulation such as labio-dental or alveo-palatal.

pragmatics The study of the meaning of language in its communicative context, especially its meaning as a social tool. Subsumed under pragmatics is the study of politeness phenomena, conversational implicature, how language is employed to carry out specific communicative acts, etc.

predicate All the constituents of a sentence, viewed together, but excluding the subject. Typically, this means the verb and its modifiers and dependent elements. In the sentence *The clouds slowly dissipated on the horizon*, the constituent *slowly dissipated on the horizon* serves as the predicate.

preglottalized A sound that is preceded by full closure of the flow of air in the vocal chords, then release of the closure, before articulating the sound.

prescriptive A prescriptive grammar aims to define the standards for what counts as appropriate or correct usage. In contrast, a 'descriptive' grammar depicts how a particular speech community actually uses language, without reference to standards of correctness.

proposition The core meaning content of a sentence. The proposition of a sentence may be expressed in diverse forms, so that all of the following have the same propositional content: *Kim gave me a basketball; Kim gave a basketball to me; I was given a basketball by Kim; A basketball was given to me by Kim.* Questions such as *Did Kim give me a basketball?* likewise share the same proposition as the declarative versions of the sentence, with that proposition embedded in a question, which can be paraphrased as 'Is the proposition *Kim gave me a basketball* true?'

prosody   Study of the sound properties of the language, but excluding the sequence of phonemes that make up words. Prosody subsumes stress, intonation, pitch and rhythm.

psycholinguistics   Study of the relation of language and the mind. This subfield covers language perception, processing and production, language acquisition, language and memory, language and the brain, etc.

raising (of vowel)   Certain vowels may (on the influence of surrounding sounds, or due to allophonic variation) be pronounced in a way that shifts their acoustic properties to the point where they take a different position in vowel space. A raised vowel has at least some of the acoustic features of a vowel in the inventory of the language to which a 'higher' location is attributed, whether or not the height of the tongue is actually raised in the process of articulation.

rationalism   The proposition that valid knowledge is not necessarily derived only through sensory experience, but may derive from deduction or intellectual reasoning. Rationalists are open to claims that instinctive or inborn knowledge exists and can be accessed.

reduplication   A word-formation process in which a morpheme is affixed to a copy of itself: either an identical copy (English *bye-bye*), or a partial copy (*wing-ding*).

referent   The conceptual or real-world entity that, in one sense, is the meaning of a word. The referent of the noun phrase *the current mayor of Boston* is, therefore, a specific living person.

reflexive   A type of pronoun that refers back to another noun in the sentence, with the noun and reflexive sharing the same referent. In the sentence *Steven understands himself quite well*, the noun *Steven* and the reflexive *himself* pick out the same referent, the man who is identified as Steven.

root   The smallest residual unit that remains after removing all the affixes from a morphologically complex word: *friend* is the root underlying the complex word *unfriendliness*, to which the affixes *–li*, *–ness*, and *un–* have been added.

rules: ordered; context-sensitive   Many grammatical theories aim to articulate general patterns in the distribution of linguistic forms and in the relationship of forms to meanings. Those patterns may be stated as grammatical rules. In some linguistic theories, it is argued that those rules are ordered, so that rule A necessarily applies before, and not after, rule B. Some theories also posit context-sensitive rules, that is, rules whose application is triggered only in a particular context, and cannot apply where that context does not prevail.

semantic roles   The various meaningful roles that nouns fulfil with respect to verbs. An inventory of semantic roles includes agent (typically assigned to the noun in subject position of an active transitive verb), patient (typically a direct object), benefactive (indirect object), instrument, location, goal, experiencer.

semantics   Study of the meanings of words and sentences.

semiotics   The study of signs and symbols, and their relationships to meanings, often with emphasis on the social dimension of signs and symbols as used in human communication. Some scholars place linguistics under the purview of semiotics.

sociolinguistics   The study of the role of language in society, and the relationships of language to social issues. Subfields include language planning and standardization, language attitudes, language variation, dialectology, multilingualism, discourse analysis, language and gender, etc.

specifier   A grammatical subclass that includes determiners (articles), demonstratives (*this, these*) and, arguably, other members of phrases that are neither heads nor modifiers, such as intensifiers like *very* in the adjective phrase *very self-satisfied (with his accomplishments)*.

stative   A subclass of verbs like *be, own, know, concern* or *seem* that cannot appear in progressive aspect (i.e. are ungrammatical in context, like *★I am owning a car; ★That was seeming strange*), or in imperatives (*★Know the answer!*). Semantically, stative verbs depict states or instantaneous cognitive processes, not events or actions. Non-stative verbs are called 'dynamic' verbs.

stem   A morphological unit that may consist of a bare root, or a root to which derivational morphology has been attached. Inflectional morphemes then attach, in a new layer, to the stem. For example, to the root *nation–* the derivational morphemes *–al* and *–ity* can be affixed, in that order, to create the stem *nation-ality*. The plural inflectional morpheme *–s* can then be affixed to the stem to create the word *nationalities*.

stop   A manner of articulation, or speech sound so produced, involving complete obstruction of the flow of air through the vocal tract. Stops, or 'plosive' consonants, are illustrated in the initial and final sounds in the English word *drop*.

stylistics   The study of literature from a linguistic perspective, often involving analysis of literary works, using terms and concepts from linguistics.

subject   A prominent sentence constituent, often definable as the agent, actor or experiencer of the verb; the sentence constituent excluded from the predicate. Individual languages mark subjects in diverse ways, for example through word order, or marking with nominative case, or by agreement with the verb.

subordination   A process of embedding one constituent, typically a clause, inside the structure of another so that the subordinate clause forms a constituent inside the embedding (or matrix) clause.

substantive   A noun or constituent that is distributed like a noun, such as pronouns and headless nominals such as *the young* and *the reckless*.

suprasegmental phenomena   Sound properties of speech that can spread across more than single sound segments (conceptualized as the realization of individual phonemes), such as stress, intonation, rhythm, pitch.

suppletion   An exceptional process whereby two etymologically unrelated words come to be treated as morphologically related. For example, in English the first person singular present tense of the verb *be* is *am*. Historically, *be* and *am* are unrelated. Rather, they belong to two separate verb roots. By suppletion, however, *am* serves as an inflected version of *be*.

surface structure   In grammatical theories that posit underlying, abstract forms, surface structures are the fully developed outcome of morphological and syntactic processes. Surface structures are therefore input into a phonological component of the grammar, and hence determine the basis for spoken language.

SVO/VSO/SOV   Three of the most common basic word orders across the world's languages, characterized according to the relative position of the S (subject), V (verb) and O (object) in unmarked, active, declarative sentences.

syllabary   An orthographic system in which the minimal unit of writing is the syllable, not the letter or word. A typical grapheme in a syllabary represents a consonant plus vowel unit, or a single vowel.

synchronic   Characterized by the study of language as a coherent state at any single point in time, abstracting away from its history, in opposition to 'diachronic'.

syntax   The grammar of a language, including word order and the patterns governing structural deletion, copying or movement of words.

tense   (1) Tense indicates the time-reference of the action or state of the verb. Past, present and future are typical verb tenses, although many languages develop diverse finer distinctions. Moreover, tense marking on verbs may be extended to signal distinctions not related to time, suchas a speaker's attitude toward the plausibility of the action of the verb. (2) In phonology, a quality of vowels produced with either heightened pressure and movement of the articulators, or longer duration (or both) relative to lax vowels.

tone language   A language that assigns specific tones, or pitch contours, to individual words or morphemes. In a tone language, two words comprised of the same phonemes in the same order, but which are assigned different tones, may differ in meaning and constitute a minimal pair.

transitivity   The property of some verbs that requires them to appear with a direct object. English *destroy* and *construct* are transitive verbs. In contrast, *disappear* and *digress* are intransitive verbs and do not appear with direct objects.

typology   Classification of languages into types, based not on their historical relationships, but on their structural properties. Language typology may be carried out on various bases, for example, according to morphological propensities (agglutinating versus fusional versus isolating languages); word-order facts (SVO/VSO/SOV); tone versus not tone languages, etc.

umlaut   A process of marking the inflection of a root by altering the quality of a vowel in the root to assimilate with a feature of the vowel in the affix, such as frontness. Umlaut is prominent in the history of the Germanic language family.

underlying form   A linguistic form which, in grammatical analyses that tolerate abstractness, may diverge from its realization as a surface, phonetic form. Generative grammar's 'deep structure' is a notion of underlying form, but the concept of underlying form is not restricted to generative grammar.

universal grammar   As developed by American linguist Noam Chomsky, a theory of the necessary formal constraints on human grammars, imposed by the structure of the language faculty. The contents of universal grammar are abstract and theory-internal. According to Chomsky, universal grammar can best be defined not by searching for the shared properties of languages, but by determining what knowledge of language children exhibit in the absence of means by which they could have acquired that knowledge from the environment.

velar   A place of articulation, or speech sound produced with that place of articulation, involving the velum, at the back of the oral cavity, often in contact with the back of the tongue.

vocative   In languages that mark nouns for case, vocative case indicates the noun is used in direct address to the interlocutor, such as *Henry* in *Henry, where are you going?*

voice, grammatical   Voice is a major verbal category, principally subsuming passive versus active voice in transitive sentences. In active voice, the semantic actor or agent is assigned the role of subject, and the patient the role of object. Voice is marked differently in different languages, but in the active English sentence *We ate all the snacks*, *we* is the agent associated with the verb *ate*, and the subject of the sentence (hence it appears before the verb, and is marked for nominative case). *All the snacks* is the patient of *ate* and appears post-verbally in direct object position. In the passive sentence *All the snacks were eaten by us*, *we* is moved out of subject position (and loses nominative case). *All the snacks* is now in subject position, and causes plural agreement to appear on *be*. (Also note that the form of the verb changes between active and passive variants of the sentence.) Despite movement of both noun phrases, their semantic roles with respect to the verb remain constant across the difference in grammatical voice.

voiced/voiceless   One of three major axes for classifying consonants according to articulatory processes, the others being place and manner of articulation. Voiced speech sounds are produced by impeding the flow of breath through the vocal chords, producing vibration during the articulation of a consonant, as in the *d* in English *door*. Voiceless (or unvoiced) speech sounds are produced by allowing the breath to pass unimpeded through the vocal chords so that vibration is suppressed, as in the *f* in *face*. Vowels are usually voiced, although some languages include devoiced vowels, where vibration is suppressed, or nearly suppressed, in the articulation of a vowel.

vowel harmony   A phonological rule which requires that all the vowels in an affix attached to a root share some salient properties of the root, which could be height, backness, roundedness, etc. In inflected languages with vowel harmony, the qualities of vowels in affixes therefore vary to reflect the qualities of vowels in the word to which they are attached.

zero form   A linguistic form that lacks a phonetic realization, but is posited to exist as an abstraction, so as to preserve the generality of a theoretical claim. For example, English count nouns are marked for plurality. However, the count nouns *sheep*, *deer* and *fish* appear with plural meaning and induce plural verb agreement without plural marking: *Sheep/deer/efish are plentiful in this land.* Therefore some linguists claim that plurality is marked on *sheep*, *deer* and *fish* with a zero affix: *sheep+0*, *deer+0*, *fish+0*, thereby preserving the generality of the English plural formation rule. Controversially, there may also exist zero complementizers, zero verbs, zero articles, etc.

INDEX

Aarsleff, H. 70, 71, 78, 81, 93, 97
ablaut 102, 146, 272; in Arabic 37
abstractness in grammatical
  description: and Arnauld and
  Lancelot 59; and Baudouin 139,
  160; and Chomsky 251, 253; and
  First Grammarian 43; and Firth
  182; and Hjelmslev 201–2, 204–5;
  and Jesperson 153; and Jones 157;
  and Labov 248; and McCawley
  262–63; and Pāṇini 4, 6; and Pike
  213, 215; and Sībawayhi 36, 37;
  and Varro 23
Académie Française 77
affixation 106, 149, 272; in Arabic
  37; in Latin 21; in Sanskrit 4
Africa, languages of 158, 226
African-American English 245–46; see
  also Ebonics controversy
agglutinating languages 51, 95, 105,
  111, 223, 272–73
Aguaruna 215
Alexander the Great 14
Algeria 29
Algonquian languages 6, 168–69,
  170–71, 227, 228
allophone 42, 273
alphabet 52, 54, 57
Altaic 51, 111, 226
American Anthropological
  Association 163
American Council of Learned
  Societies 171
American Oriental Society 120
American Philological Society 120
American structuralism 167–72, 227,
  229–30; and Chomsky 250; and
  Greenberg 222–23; and Hjelmslev

201; neglect of meaning in favor of
  distributionalism 229–30;
  'mechanistic' linguistics 170; and
  Pike 212–13; and Sapir 165; see also
  structuralism
analogy 135, 143–44, 273; in Arabic
  37, 38
Anatolian 38
Anglo-Saxon 125, 129
animal communication 18, 79, 84–85,
  111, 231, 234
animals vs. humans 78, 84, 120–21,
  187
anthropology: and Austin 210; and
  Broca 115; and Condillac 81; and
  Firth 180–81; and Greenberg
  222–23; and Grice 220; and Hale
  255–56; and Halliday 239; and
  Hockett 228, 231; and Jakobson
  193–94; and Sapir 162–64; and
  Pike 212; and Saussure 150
anti-Semitism 175, 185; see also Nazi
aphasia 115–18, 193, 234, 273
Arabic 14, 45, 28, 222–23; grammar
  of 34–39; study of 94
Arandic 255
arbitrariness in language 10–11, 22,
  149, 150, 191, 231
argument structure 257, 258, 273–74
argument, grammatical 257, 263,
  273; null 257
Aristotle 13–18, 20, 54; Aristotelian
  logic 47, 48, 63; and Austin 206;
  and Donatus and Priscian 33, 'four
  causes' 47; and Speculative
  Grammarians 45, 47; and Sweet
  130; 'ten categories' 17, 47, 63
Armenian 90